MW00806211

Best regards,

Kyle Keiderling

2-1-10

Heart Of A Lion

THE LIFE, DEATH AND LEGACY OF HANK GATHERS

Kyle Keiderling

Foreword by Bo Kimble

Morning Star Books
Morning Star Communications • New York

Published in the United States of America by Morning Star
Communications, LLC, New York, New York.

Requests to the publisher for permission to reproduce selections from
this book should be addressed to the Permissions Department,
Morning Star Communications, LLC, 231 Lenox Avenue, New York,
NY 10027, (212) 865-7170, fax (212) 208-4570, or online at HYPER-
LINK "http://www.ljlagency@aol.com"www.ljlagency@aol.com.

Jacket design: Gilbert Fletcher
Front Cover Photograph: Courtesy LMU
Interior design by GF Graphics
Production coordinator: Oh Snap! Design

All photographs courtesy LMU

ISBN: 978-0-9778-9968-5 (hardcover)
Library of Congress Cataloging-in-Publication Data:
Keiderling, Kyle.
Heart of a Lion: The Life, Death and Legacy of Hank Gathers.
p. cm.
Includes bibliographical references.
1. Gathers, Hank. 2. Basketball players—United States—Biography.
I. Title.
Printed in the United States of America

For Ky
And for all those who, like Hank, dare to dream.

To live in hearts we leave behind, is not to die.

—Thomas Campbell

CONTENTS

FOREWORD

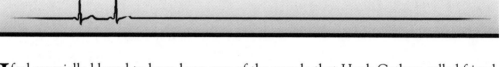

I feel especially blessed to have been one of the people that Hank Gathers called friend. Hank was an extraordinary human being. He was one of the most competitive people I have ever met. At the same time he was the funniest person I have ever been around. Hank had a special way about him. He took particular delight in making people laugh. It was that rare combination of being a comedian off the court and a tough competitor on the court that made Hank unique.

When he and I first met on the playgrounds of north Philadelphia, we shared a passion for basketball. We both recognized that our only chance to escape the poverty that surrounded us each day was to be as good at basketball as we could possibly be. We were both fierce competitors. Even in those early days, when my skills were further advanced than Hank's, he never stopped trying to get the better of me. It was Hank's incredible determination to get better than me that made him a great basketball player.

We were both fortunate that, in the tough neighborhood where we grew up, we had the unselfish and caring mentoring that we needed to get us out of there.

Father David Hagan took us under his protective and nourishing wing and made certain we stayed on the course we both had set our sights on. He never doubted us, and his guidance and counsel enabled us to succeed where so many others—some with far more talent—had failed. We were both blessed by his guidance and owe him more than we could ever say, much less repay.

Our high school coach, Richard Yankowitz, kept us on the straight and narrow in school—even though our frequent squabbles must have given him headaches. Yank, as we called him, drove home the point that basketball could lead to a scholarship to college, which was the only way we could ever go to college. He made sure that our classwork came first, even though neither of us was that thrilled about it at the time.

When David Spencer came along and started to recruit us, we found yet another mentor who wanted nothing but the best for us. He was a father figure to us while on the West Coast, and through him we eventually landed at Loyola Marymount University (LMU).

It hardly seems possible that twenty years have come and gone since our last season with coach Paul Westhead and our team at LMU. We were the highest-scoring team in college basketball. As much fun as it was for fans to watch us, it was even more fun to be a part of a team that took a hundred shots a game. That would not have been possible anywhere else, and both Hank and I profited from Westhead's "system."

Those years we spent at LMU were special years. Hank loved LMU and everyone at LMU loved him back.

We matured as players and as human beings there. The education we got there prepared me for life after basketball. Our success there brought national attention to the university and to us. We took turns leading the country in scoring. We won three conference titles, and we went to three straight NCAA tournaments.

Not bad for two kids from the streets of north Philly.

When Hank died during our final season at LMU, I felt like a part of me died, too. We had been together so long and done so much together, I didn't know how I could go on without him. After a talk with Father Dave I decided to pay tribute to Hank by playing as hard as I could in the NCAA Tournament. Hank, I realized, would always be a part of me.

Father Dave and I decided that I would pay tribute to Hank by taking my first free throw left-handed to honor Hank's memory. It never occurred to me that it would have such a huge impact on people. Yet in all the years since, whenever I am around other people, not a day has gone by when someone invariably mentions that shot.

The impact of Hank Gathers on our team was apparent in that tournament. We exceeded everyone's expectations and went to the very doorstep of the Final Four, and we did it without Hank's dominating inside presence. I am still convinced that, had Hank lived, we would have become national champions. Our Elite Eight appearance may have been our greatest achievement, our own national title in honor of Hank.

Hank and I will be forever joined together. I am honored that my name and his are mentioned together. Our jerseys hang together above the court at LMU, where we hung together so many times during our four years there.

While playing in a game a few years ago in a YMCA league in Camden, New Jersey, a young man named Robert Smith fell to the floor in cardiac arrest. I watched with others as the young man's life ebbed away. For me, it was like watching Hank die all over again. I decided that I had to do something to ensure that Hank's death was not in vain and that other Robert Smiths would be saved.

With Dr. Tamara L. Goode, whose father died of heart disease when he was only forty-four, I cofounded the Forty-four for Life Foundation. Our motto is "Saving lives one beat at a time." It is a nonprofit organization dedicated to educating people about heart disease, CPR training, the use of automatic external defibrillators (AEDs), and providing ready access to them. I testified before Congress on behalf of legislation to ensure that all federal buildings and parks and recreation centers have AEDs on the premises. The bill became law, a first step toward our goal. I can think of no better way to pay tribute to my friend than to prevent the death of others.

Heart of a Lion is the story of Hank Gathers's life—an extraordinary life by any measure—and one I am honored and proud to have been a part of.

I loved and respected Hank Gathers and will continue to demonstrate that in my own way through the foundation. If we save just one life, our effort will have been worthwhile.

When we were just kids, Hank and I shared a dream together, and though Hank may be gone, the dream is alive.

Bo Kimble

PREFACE

In March 1990, Philly native Hank Gathers, a senior at Loyola Marymount University in Los Angeles, was the leading candidate for college basketball's player of the year. As a junior, he had led the nation in both scoring and rebounding. He was a certain NBA first-round lottery pick in the draft just a few months hence. Since the age of twelve his goal had been to reach the NBA and release his mother and brothers from the grip of poverty in one of the worst slums in America.

His dream became a nightmare during a West Coast Conference Tournament game on March 4 that was watched by his family and thousands of fans at courtside and later on national television. Hank threw down one of his trademark tomahawk dunks and was headed back up court to the cheers of his fans. He slapped his teammate's hand, then slowly fell to the court. Within minutes Hank Gathers, who had proudly boasted of being the strongest man alive, was dead.

I never met Hank Gathers while he walked this earth, but I wish I had. In researching and writing this book I got to meet him through the eyes and words of those who played with and against him, coached him, counseled him, and loved him. No one who met him ever forgot him. Yet today, if you mention his name to anyone old enough to remember what happened, the invariable response is, "Oh, yeah, the guy who died on the court."

That Hank Gathers should be recalled solely for his passing is as tragic as his demise. The ghastly images of this death ignore the complexity of his life, the nobility of its purpose, and his lasting legacy.

The ancient Greeks used the word *hero* to describe a "warrior-chieftain of special strength, courage, or ability."[1] Those who knew him would agree that Hank Gathers qualifies on all counts.

Hank was a role model for all young people who aspire to achieve a goal that seems beyond their grasp. He dared to dream in a place where dreams die aborning and where the evidence of failed dreams surrounded him every day. Yet Hank would not be denied. He eschewed drugs and alcohol, honored his family, stayed in school, and learned to excel academically as well as on the basketball court.

He led his team to national prominence and to heights the other players had never dreamed possible. Hank never doubted for a moment that national acclaim and perhaps even a championship could be theirs if everyone worked as hard as he did. His teammates responded to his urging and example, and Hank's inspirational leadership took them within a game of the Final Four. They loved him for it.

"We went to him for points. We went to him for rebounds. He was the very essence of our being," said his coach, Paul Westhead.

Everyone who knew him says that Hank Gathers was special.

"Hank was the most unique personality I ever coached," Westhead said. "He dominated every moment on our team. He was such a strong-willed young man. He had incredible exuberance in his words, his expressions, and humor. He had the team in the palm of his hands."[2]

His impact on his teammates was so strong, so personal, so overwhelmingly powerful that when I interviewed them nearly twenty years later, they were still overcome by memories of his death.

Hank's ferocity and competitiveness earned the respect of his opponents and the accolades of the press, yet he never lost his innocent enjoyment of life and all it offered. His passion and his bliss were written on his smiling countenance off the court, and none could miss it. He was a gentle giant adored by the children who worshipped him. There was no evidence of the "privileged jock" mentality in his demeanor or interactions with other students. The kid from the ghetto was just another kid, even if he was on the cover of national magazines.

No one has ever played the game of basketball harder than Hank, and few have played with more at risk than he.

"If someone told me I had a fifty-fifty chance of dying if I ever played basketball again, I wouldn't play. Hank would," said his friend Bo Kimble.

Despite the billions of dollars it generates and the madness it creates each March, college basketball is, after all, just a game. And games by definition are frivolous pursuits. But sometimes games can promote meaningful change. Such a game took place on March 4, 1990.

The death of Hank Gathers triggered sweeping and dramatic changes in the way sports medicine practitioners view physical examinations and medical surveillance of all college athletes who have taken the field since. The defibrillators now at the ready in all major arenas have saved the lives of athletes and spectators alike and are part of the legacy of Hank Gathers.

Heart of a Lion is Hank's *life* story. I believe that the title is one he would have chosen because it captures the way he lived, the way he played, and the way he died.

Hank Gathers walked this earth for only twenty-three short years, but he left us with his dream—that anything is possible.

Hank may be gone, but his dream is alive.

Kyle Keiderling

CHAPTER

1

BROTHERLY LOVE

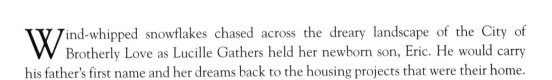

Wind-whipped snowflakes chased across the dreary landscape of the City of Brotherly Love as Lucille Gathers held her newborn son, Eric. He would carry his father's first name and her dreams back to the housing projects that were their home. It was February 11, 1967, and a freak atmospheric condition had sent disquieting thunder rolling across the city in the depths of a winter storm.

Lucille and her two boys—Christopher had been born in 1963—faced a world as turbulent as the angry skies overhead. The country was in the throes of an ideological struggle over the conduct of the ever-escalating war in far-off Vietnam. Soon the dissension that divided the nation would force Lyndon Johnson from office and help elect a former Vice President, Richard Nixon, who promised that he had a plan for ending the war.

When Eric was little more than a year old, the mass exodus of white Americans from the cities suddenly accelerated. It had begun after World War II and continued into the 50's, but after Martin Luther King Jr. and Robert Kennedy were assassinated in the spring and early summer of 1968, urban blacks took to the streets in anger and frustration. Frightened by the riots and the black power movement's mantra of "burn, baby, burn," the last white holdouts fled. The 1968 presidential election saw Nixon and George Wallace blatantly pandering to the fears of white middle-class America, which easily recognized such campaign slogans as "Law and Order" as race-related code words. The dual candidacies of Nixon and Wallace, and the tarnish from having served as LBJ's Vice President, combined to thwart any chance that the liberal Democrat Hubert H. Humphrey might have had to address the cities' problems.

The remaining residents of major U.S. cities were left to cope as best they could. The Nixon administration regarded city dwellers as hostile, while trotting out lofty-sounding programs supposedly designed to address their problems. "Urban Development Block Grants" were administered by cynical local governments that used loopholes in the legislation to give the money to their police departments instead of aiding city residents. The block grants were an abject failure. The poverty of the inner cities only worsened, and cities found themselves encircled by impenetrable rings of white middle-class suburbs, home to the people Nixon would claim as his own "silent majority." Those who still commuted to jobs in the cities fled at 5 p.m. each evening. Soon, even their employers, recognizing the difficulty of attracting a viable workforce to a dangerous and decaying inner-city site, had relocated to the sprawling new suburban office parks. The people who remained behind, like the Gathers family, had no other choice.

As peace marches and draft card-burning antiwar protesters continued to dominate newspaper headlines and television screens in the early 1970's, the actions of the paranoid Nixon threw the country into a political crisis that threatened the very fabric of democracy. America survived Watergate, although Nixon's presidency did not. But with Congress so distracted for so long by the constitutional crisis, in its aftermath, the people in the housing projects of north Philadelphia found themselves worse off than ever—trying to survive in living conditions that most Americans would find deplorable, dangerous, and uninhabitable.

The family of little Eric Gathers—soon nicknamed "Hank" by his father and "Hankie" by Lucille—was typical of families then living in the Philly projects. In most of these homes, only one parent was present, and the mother or grandmother would raise the children with little or no support from their absentee father.

Although Hank's parents were married, his father was soon to become a nonfactor in his son's life. The senior Eric Gathers had a small haberdashery on Columbia Avenue where he sold and cleaned hats. Like so many others in the projects, though, he soon disappeared into alcoholism, and he became a shadowy presence in the family, vanishing entirely after Lucille divorced him when Hank was 10.[1]

"In all the years Hank played for me, I only remember seeing his father once or twice," said Rich Yankowitz, who coached Hank in high school. "He was never around."[2]

Before Lucille banished her husband, she became pregnant twice more. Derrick was born a scant 11months after Eric, and Charles was born in 1970.

Lucille Gathers was the rock of the family. Employed as a hospital orderly, she was a determined and stubborn parent who was committed to doing whatever it took to give her four boys a chance to escape the economic circumstances in which she was forced to raise them. In 1967, with a low-paying job, two boys younger than five, and a husband who was becoming increasingly unreliable even then, her housing choices were limited to what was available through the Philadelphia Public Housing Authority, not a choice one would make unless absolutely necessary. The apartment to which Lucille and her infant son returned from the hospital was in the Raymond Rosen Homes at 23rd and Diamond.

The Raymond Rosen Homes opened in 1954, eight 13-story, brick-faced monuments to insensitivity. They rose, like a stand of phalluses, above a neighborhood where the economic, social, and political impotence of the residents was obvious to the most casual observer. The projects also included a number of two-story row houses. When, in 1983, resident Gloria Singleton was at last allowed to relocate to a row house from the high-rise she had occupied for years, she described it as one of the happiest days of her life. Leaving the trash-strewn hallways where a stray bullet had once pierced her door, and where her five-year-old had slipped and fallen to her death through a broken window, was "like moving to the suburbs," she said.[3]

Not quite.

In describing the Raymond Rosen Homes, Father David Hagan once wrote that they were, by the late 1960's, "truly a catastrophic place to live . . . the atmosphere was rife with drugs, crime, and violence. I always suspected that the odds of any young person making it out of that kind of environment were rather nil."[4]

David Culbreth, a Philadelphia police officer for 30 years, described a "proliferation of gang activity added to what was already a great deal of violence—we routinely responded to rape, robbery, and assault calls, and gunshots were commonplace. . . . If you didn't live there, you didn't go there. No one should have had to grow up there."[5]

Many simply had no choice, and the consequences were often dire. "When I was a little over 12 years old," Carol Pierce related, "I was raped in the high-rise of the Rosen projects. I was baby-sitting. . . . My girlfriend's brother, who was a drug addict, burst into the apartment and raped me. He tried to push me out the window and I fought him off until a maintenance worker heard the ruckus and saved me from being thrown out a window of one of the highest floors." Reflecting just how low expectations were for those trapped in the projects, she added, "When I told my mother what had happened right afterwards, she said that that was my problem and that I shouldn't have been there."[6]

If the pious Quaker brethren who first populated the area could have seen it 300 years later, they would have had ample cause to doubt their faith.

How bad was it? Another veteran of the Philadelphia police force, someone well familiar with the Rosen Homes when Hank Gathers was growing up there, confided that, when police received a report of gunfire in the neighborhood, they would wait half an hour to respond, so fearful were they that they'd be caught in the cross fire.

Indeed, years later, when a teammate showed Hank around Watts in an attempt to impress upon him how bad conditions were in that infamous Los Angeles neighborhood,

Hank said, "Compared to where I grew up, this is like the suburbs."

He wasn't exaggerating. His neighborhood was one that few Americans, black or white, are capable of imagining. Once you have seen it, you never forget it. It was, in the words of a priest who spent three decades there, a "place of desolate normalcy."[7]

Residents referred to their neighborhood as "The Jungle." Survival was the best that they could hope for. The jungle they inhabited encroached steadily, inch by inch, day by day, concealing and nearly obliterating hope. No chilling jungle scream or crashing sound could induce any more terror than the gunshots that echoed through the streets every night. No exotic fungus or tropical fever could ravage the mind any more than the desolation and despair that these Philly residents faced every sunrise amid the rubble and ruin. The neglect and defeatism of the city's bureaucrats had long since consigned this poverty-stricken patch to the dung heap, although they paid it just enough attention to give the area a depressingly accurate nickname: The Ruins.

To be born there, as Hank Gathers was, is to be born poor. And, with few exceptions, those born there die poor.

"It's not as if we didn't have our basic needs met," said Dawn Staley, a former resident who is now a coach at Temple. "We had a roof over our heads, food, and clothing. What was lacking there was any real opportunity."[8]

Lucille Gathers was determined to get her family out someday, somehow. She didn't know quite how she would do it, but she was steadfast in her resolve. It was, truly, a place that hope had abandoned. But Lucille would never stop hoping.

A large woman whose weight increased with the years and each pregnancy, Lucille Gathers presented an imposing figure when she felt she or her boys was being mistreated. You would not want to argue with her if you could avoid it. She knew that to have any chance to escape the projects, her boys first had to learn how to survive there.

"I was on the playground court near the Rosen projects one day when I saw Hank, around 10 or 11years old at the time, and his brother Derrick being beaten by two older neighborhood kids," recalled Darrell "Heat" Gates, who grew up in that neighborhood and played basketball with Hank in high school.

"Hank had lost a chain from around his neck in the scuffle and ran home, crying, to his place on the ground floor at the Rosen projects. A few minutes later, out came the boys, with Lucille leading the way. She marched them right back onto the court and made them fight those two kids until they ran off. It was the only way you could survive there. Lucille, by making them fight back, made sure that they would."[9]

Another childhood friend, Doug Overton, recalled, "The neighborhood where Hank lived was bad. You had to fight your way in and fight your way out."[10] Under Lucille's tutelage, the Gathers boys managed to do so successfully during their formative years.

Just as Lucille recognized the value of a good right cross, she appreciated the value of a good education. She knew that the educational opportunities afforded by the public school system in that neighborhood were few. Armed guards stood outside the schools and patrolled inside. Even so, fights and gang-related struggles dominated the halls and classrooms. Learning was secondary to surviving—for both students and teachers.

The alternative was parochial school, even for a Baptist family like the Gatherses. The Catholic Church, and its priests and nuns, filled the needs of their mostly non-Catholic students by providing a decent education in a relatively safe and secure environment. These dedicated servants of the church received little or no support from their archdiocese, which had difficulty recognizing the benefits of providing mostly black Baptists with a solid education.

As difficult as her economic circumstances were, Lucille would manage to squeeze from her modest earnings enough tuition money to permit Hank and Derrick (who were so close in age that they were in the same grade) to attend nearby St. Elizabeth's Parochial School. The investment was critical to her plan to get the boys out of The Ruins, and it would pay huge dividends.

They arrived in the form of a large, gruff, chain-smoking, somewhat curmudgeonly priest named David Hagan. Father Dave, as he preferred to be addressed, had a fondness for Black Russian cocktails, which he enjoyed at a convivial neighborhood tavern named Rembrandt's. He also had a passion for basketball and, as a result, became the father figure that Hank Gathers needed.

Hagan had grown up in an affluent area of Philly called Mt. Airy, between the Germantown and Chestnut Hill sections, still in the city but a world apart from the Raymond Rosen Homes. He attended Holy Cross, a Catholic parochial school in Mt. Airy, and went on to North East High School in the Juniata section. North East was one of two Catholic high schools (the other was Father Judge) that were run by the Order of St. Francis de Sales, a small teaching order founded by Louis Brisson. Although Dave Hagan's mother described him as "the least Catholic of my children," he entered the Order of St. Francis de Sales in Childs, Md., after his high school graduation.[11]

The priests and brothers sent him to Niagara University, where the oblates of the order did undergraduate work, and then to the Catholic University of America in Washington, D.C., for his master's in theology. He then taught at several Catholic high schools, notably, Bishop Ireton in Arlington, Virginia, a Washington suburb.[12]

"While there, he became convinced, as many of us of that generation were, of the immorality, if you will, of the Vietnam War," related Hagan's long-time friend Father John McNamee. "He began speaking out against the Vietnam War in his Sunday ministry in various parishes around the Arlington area."[13] Considering that the Arlington area was home to many government employees, Father Dave's parishioners, especially those employed at the nearby Pentagon, were less than thrilled with his outspoken opposition to U.S. policy and conduct of the war. Ultimately, one or more suggested that sitting in the rectory and criticizing the country was easy—he didn't have to worry about being drafted or that his children would be drafted.

"He thought maybe he should put his body where his mouth was," McNamee said.[14]

The man who counted among his idols the antiwar activist Daniel Berrigan and the farm labor organizer Cesar Chavez, as well as Dorothy Day, founder of the Catholic Worker House (pictures of all three adorned the walls of his home), decided to spread his version of the Gospel among the poorest of the poor. Institutional neglect of the poor would become his issue.[15] Father Dave was, without question, a Christian soldier, but all his life he marched to the beat of a different drummer.

His first intention was to leave Arlington and live among the poor in Washington, D.C. He quickly found out that he couldn't afford to purchase a home in The District, and that brought him back to Philadelphia and a church called St. Elizabeth's at 23rd and Berks. His parents had been married there almost 50 years before. Hagan first lived with another oblate there who operated a group home for "fellows who by law or need required some kind of care," McNamee said. Eventually, Father Dave bought a house in the neighborhood. It was a ramshackle old dwelling of 15 rooms that he was able to buy for $2,800 because the neighborhood was so awful. A few years later, the city's appraisers set its value at $650.[16]

Father Dave had been trained as a math teacher. In that neat, strictly structured, and orderly world every problem he diagrammed on the blackboard had only one correct answer. In the world in which he now lived, no such absolutes existed. There he found only a staggering, ever-changing multiplicity of problems for which there were no easy answers.

Father Dave's house soon became the favorite neighborhood hang-out for young people looking for a "place to go and. . .hang out. . .without the cops chasing them," McNamee said. The television was on 24 hours a day, always tuned to basketball on the cable networks during the season. Everyone was welcome and almost everyone came. Hank and his brother Derrick, then in about the fifth grade, became frequent visitors. Eventually, Father Dave would come to refer to his home as "Inner City House" in his fund-raising appeals to former parishioners and students back in the affluent Virginia suburbs that he had abandoned.[17]

Devoted to his mission to aid the residents of The Ruins, Father Dave, at 6 feet 3 inches and 270 pounds, nevertheless was a victim of his surroundings on numerous occasions. He was robbed at least three times—once at knifepoint—and his home was broken into frequently. Yet he stubbornly stayed the course he had chosen, convinced that it was what he was destined to do.[18]

Unburdened by mundane parish duties, Hagan could freely pursue his goal of improving the lives of young people in the bleak neighborhoods around his home. One way to do that, he decided, was through basketball. He became the coach of the St. Elizabeth's elementary school team and attracted kids from the surrounding neighborhoods to his gym. He offered refuge and recreation.[19]

Hank and Derrick became regulars in Father Dave's informal basketball game, and Lucille regarded the refuge as a blessing, because the only change in the neighborhood's fortunes since Hank's birth had been downward. Outside the thin metal door to the Gathers' family's ground-floor apartment was a bustling world of gang activity, wandering drunks, and drug dealers working the street. Stray gunshots from dealers defending their turf would ricochet off the exterior walls and doors.

But at least the family didn't have to use the elevator. "It was pitch black in there. The lights and fans were broken. You couldn't see anything and it smelled real bad," Darrell Gates recalled. (Still, the elevator was better than the stairway, where drug deals were transacted and down-on-their-luck, strung-out prostitutes serviced their clients.)[20]

Inside the Gathers apartment, Lucille ran a tight ship. "You walked in, and there was a place to hang your coat, a living room, kitchen area, and two bedrooms. That was it. But it was always neat and clean in there," Gates said.[21]

Eventually, alerted to a vacancy by Phyllis Crump, a neighbor, Lucille would relocate her brood to a row house. It was two stories and had a small dirt yard surrounded by chain-link fencing. Modest as it was, in return for 30 percent of Lucille's income, it offered a vast improvement over the tower where they had started.[22]

When she visited the area on assignment years later, Maryann Hudson, a writer for the *Los Angeles Times*, would muse, "The name of this place sounds planned, but one has to wonder how any place like this could be built on purpose."[23]

Hank and Derrick had long been regular participants in the pick-up games on the cement basketball court near their home. Basketball required only a ball and a basket and was the most affordable and popular form of recreation in the inner-city neighborhood. All the players aspired to play in the NBA. Certainly the landscape of burned-out houses and the rusty, stripped auto carcasses that framed the courts offered incentive to play their best.

But the perimeter offered Hank and the others perhaps the starkest reminder of the consequences of failure. Like the buildings behind them, the older men loitering on the sidelines were gutted. Once they, too, had been eager young basketball players with promise. But that promise had evaporated with the missed classes, wine bottles in paper sacks, and easy drugs that led inevitably to the petty crimes that supported their habit. They were there, watching with dull eyes, as Hank threw his body into the game with wild abandon.

As bleak as their neighborhood was, the young players on that hard concrete court were not without hope. Temple University was located nearby, and Philadelphia was blessed with fine basketball teams—Villanova, LaSalle, and Penn, as well as St. Joseph's University. The neighborhood closely followed the success of the Big Five teams, as they were known. Once school let out in June, summer leagues were everywhere and offered opportunities for instruction and competition at all grade levels.

Darrell Gates had told his friends the Gathers brothers about the basketball program at St. Elizabeth's, where Lucille had already enrolled them. Heat, as he was known (derived from his ability to "burn" opponents with his speed and flashy dribbling on the playground courts, as well as from his grandmother's pet name for him, "Heaky"), had made the team there as a fifth grader, and was an extraordinary ball handler. Even in the sixth and seventh grades he was considered the best player on the team. Derrick Gathers showed a natural talent for the game and displayed the promise of becoming an accomplished performer. Hank loved the game, but he was so inept that no one ever figured he'd have a future on the basketball court.

"Hank was the worst player I ever saw," Heat recalled. "He couldn't pass, dribble, or shoot. He couldn't even make a lay-up. He was horrible. He had one shot. It was a hook shot he attempted from around the free-throw line and hardly ever made. He was just big, that's all."[24]

In the seventh grade Hank was 6 feet 2 inches, a towering, if unimpressive, presence. What he lacked in natural ability he more than compensated for in desire. "He was determined to learn," Heat said.

While Hank may have lacked any discernible ability on the court, he was not lacking in powers of observation. Once he recognized that Heat was the team leader and possessed the best skills on the floor, he became Heat's shadow. "I couldn't get rid of him," Heat said. For the next several years, it seemed like Hank "was at my house every day. He wanted to learn how to dribble and handle the ball. We played in the streets and I showed him what I knew, and he soaked it up like a sponge. He couldn't get enough. Later we would attract crowds of onlookers from the neighborhood that watched us dribbling in the street."

Heat took Hank with him to the summer league games and playground courts, where Hank became his "big man." They played nonstop year-round, and Hank gradually improved. By the time they graduated from high school, Heat would acknowledge that the once-horrible Hank "could dribble the ball as well as me—maybe better."[25]

The drive and determination to learn were not lost on Father Dave, who was watching the gradual transformation of the gangly Gathers kid. It was not an overnight transformation, by any means. Hank still saw little playing time in real games and was often on the brink of losing a spot on the team. Like Heat, Hagan was impressed with Hank's determination to improve, and in his own gruff manner, Father Dave encouraged Hank to continue to work hard.[26]

For Hank, and Heat, and many others who encountered Dave Hagan in those years, he was more than just a coach or an eccentric white priest adrift in a black ghetto. In addition to teaching lessons of life and basketball that he hoped the kids would use to escape the ghetto, he served as their role model.

"Father Dave was my dad," Heat explained. "When I needed something to eat, I got it from him. When I needed a haircut and had no way to pay for one, he made sure I got one. I had no clothes that were appropriate for school. He made sure I had clothes. He kept me straight. I would never have gotten through high school without him."

Heat, like Hank, lacked a male presence in his life, and both received from Father Dave the support and firm hand of guidance that they desperately needed. "He raised us all. I loved him, and he loved me and showed me in so many ways," Heat said. "God put him here for a reason."[27]

The profound effect that Father Dave had on the lives of the inner-city kids he coached was magnified in the case of Hank Gathers. Lucille had divorced Eric after years of struggling to maintain her marriage to a man who was losing his battle with the bottle. Hank's older brother, Chris, had already begun to drift toward the seductive siren song of the streets, and it ultimately claimed him.

Hank assumed the role of man of the house and arbiter of his mother's behavior. Cleo Jackson, a neighbor in the Rosen projects, recalled how Hank "reformed" his mom. "Hank didn't smoke, didn't drink, he didn't do drugs," Jackson declared. "His mother used to smoke cigarettes. Hank got on her about it until she stopped. If he saw her drinking a beer, he'd have a fit. So she stopped altogether. Lucille used to say, 'That Hank, he thinks he's my father.' And you know what we'd all say? 'We all want to be Hank's mother.' Every woman in these projects. They all wanted to be Hank's mother. You don't meet kids like Hank Gathers [here] too often."[28]

CHAPTER

2

A Foot In The Door

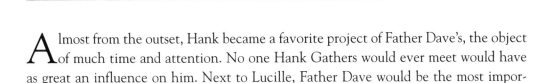

Almost from the outset, Hank became a favorite project of Father Dave's, the object of much time and attention. No one Hank Gathers would ever meet would have as great an influence on him. Next to Lucille, Father Dave would be the most important person in Hank's life.

After Derrick, Hank, and Heat graduated from the eighth grade at St. Elizabeth's, they were headed for a public high school whose name, Strawberry Mansion, belied its rough reputation. Father Dave had other plans. First, he tried to get them admitted to Roman Catholic High School, a perennial hoops power. But when they failed to pass the entrance exam, he had to look elsewhere.

He had taught for a time at Murrell Dobbins Vocational and Technical High School, until a teachers' strike there forced him to leave in sympathy with the unionized teachers. He was familiar with the school and its reputation for outstanding basketball and interceded with the principal, Ed Magliocco, on the boys' behalf. "He told the principal that if he took these kids in, Dobbins would win the public school basketball championship," said the coach, Rich Yankowitz.[1]

Father Dave's blustery salesmanship carried the day. Hank, Derrick, and Heat enrolled at Dobbins. The school, at 22nd and Lehigh, was a few blocks from the Rosen projects and across the street from the former site of Connie Mack Stadium. It was a tough area, but the school had a reputation for producing outstanding basketball players (Horace "Pappy" Owens went to Rhode Island and on to the NBA; Linda Page, an All-American at North Carolina State, had once scored 100 points in a game for Dobbins, smashing Wilt Chamberlain's high school scoring mark). Several Dobbins players had used its team as a springboard to college, even though the school's curriculum was decidedly not college prep (although it did provide a basic academic curriculum, in addition to its vocational-technical program). When Hank entered Dobbins, 73 percent of the students enrolled there were found to be below the 50th percentile in academic achievement as measured by the California Achievement Test.[2]

What the school lacked in academic excellence, it more than made up for with its prowess on the hardwood. "Yank," as the basketball coach was universally known, was a strict disciplinarian who emphasized fundamentals and team play in a city where individual displays of playground-style moves ("ballin' it") were the norm. With the exceptions of nearby Temple, which would not sign John Chaney to coach basketball till 1982, and Penn, which was notable for its lack of talent, the other city colleges had made fast-paced "Philly-style" ball as famous as the city's cheese steaks.

The principal proponent of the fast and furious pace of Philly basketball was the former coach at LaSalle, Paul Westhead. During his tenure at the school, from 1970 to 1979, Westhead, a Philly native and St. Joe's graduate, had conducted summer basketball camps in Canadensis, in the nearby Pocono Mountains. The fortunate campers would escape the stifling summer heat and humidity of the city while learning the torrid style that Westhead espoused.

Father Dave knew Westhead through a neighborhood social worker named Mary Ellen Sheridan, and prevailed upon the coach's wife, Cassie, to secure a scholarship to the camp for Heat. Upon his return, Heat shared with Hank his favorable impression of the running style taught by Westhead.[3] Heat's high praise no doubt made an impression on Hank, but it would be years before it meant anything.

Yank was not a Westhead disciple, although he was an admirer of the success that LaSalle enjoyed while Westhead was its basketball coach. Yank's style was much more structured and disciplined, and he coached a team that competed in the tough Philadelphia Public School League in which every game was a war.[4]

In the fall of 1981, when the players began shooting around in the tiny gymnasium at Dobbins, Yank was an interested observer. Among the players who stood out in the crowd of eager participants that afternoon was Gregory Kimble, "Bo," as he was known to all. Yank also saw "Heat and Derrick and this tall, skinny kid, and I remember thinking to myself, 'Please don't let them be freshmen.'"[5] Of course, they were, and Yank would have to wait a year for them to be eligible to compete at the varsity level for the Dobbins Mustangs.

Bo Kimble grew up about a 15-minute walk from Hank Gathers's apartment. Even so, Kimble's neighborhood was, as he said, "a world apart from the neighborhood Hank came from."[6]

It was a tough, working-class neighborhood, and it wasn't without its share of inner-city dangers. As a youngster, Bo had found himself in the crosshairs of a rifle-wielding stranger, and bullets had whizzed past his head as he fled to the safety of his parents' apartment. He, too, learned to negotiate streets where gang members hung out. When it became apparent to others, though, that young Bo was a gifted athlete, he enjoyed a certain advantage. "The gang members and others in that neighborhood had a respect for talent," Bo recalled. "Often, when some serious gang activity was about to go down, they would tell me, 'Young buck, go home. You don't want to be here when the trouble starts.'"[7]

Bo Kimble was raised in a church-going family. His grandfather was a Baptist preacher at the Second Unity Baptist Church, and his mother, Hilda, made certain her son attended services every Sunday and Wednesday. Despite his forced participation, Bo displayed a flair for preaching that led many in the congregation to believe he'd follow a path to the pulpit. But he had another, stronger calling, to the decidedly less divine world of playground basketball. The concrete courts would become his sanctuary from the violent world around him.[8]

"Basketball saved me," he said, recalling the events of his early years. "It gave me purpose. I loved basketball from the start, and the streets of my neighborhood toughened us to believe we were invincible."[9]

The court closest to Bo's home at 26th and Clearfield was the one at Whittier Playground. That was where he spent his free time. His dedication to the game was characterized by the shovel he carried with him in winter so he could clear the court of snow and continue to work on his ever-improving game.[10]

Blessed with a natural ability that hard work and practice sharpened and honed to a fine edge, Bo drew admiring reviews in the neighborhood for his basketball skills. By the time he was in the eighth grade, he was dunking the ball, even though he was only about 6 feet tall. He already had a following, and his competitive nature soon took him to other city courts, where he tested himself in tough Philly competition. One of those courts was located outside the Moylan Recreation Center (now renamed the Eric Hank Gathers Recreation Center and Youth Access Center, in his honor), at 25th and Diamond.

"I was there one day in the summer before my freshman year at Dobbins with my cousin, and I was dunking the ball and just fooling around," Bo recalled. "Also at the court was a kid down at the other end, who was watching us. He eventually came over and asked, without any preliminaries, 'Where you play at?'"[11]

The way the fellow posed the question, it was more like a challenge. It was how Hank Gathers both introduced himself and sized up the competition, and it remains vivid in Bo's mind to this day. Bo took it all in stride, replying calmly that he usually played at Whittier.

"What grade you in, man?" Hank asked. When Bo said he was in the eighth grade, Hank responded, "You in the eighth grade and you dunkin'?"

Bo smoothly and assuredly replied that he was "just doing my thing."[12]

The confrontation ended, Hank and Bo made some more small talk, and went their separate ways. Within months they met again at Murrell Dobbins Vocational and Technical School as eager aspirants for a spot on Yank's team, the junior varsity, because they were only freshmen. Had they been eligible, Bo and Heat certainly could have made the varsity squad, but Hank Gathers displayed no such promise.

"He was skinny and tall," Heat said, "and that's about all there was to him."[13]

While Heat and Bo—and Derrick, to a lesser degree—showed considerable ability, Hank's long suits were determination and bravado, which failed to conceal his obvious on-court shortcomings. Although he was fleet of foot, could elevate, and would not be out-hustled by anyone, he couldn't shoot and he was "skinny as a pole," Yank recalled. "He looked like a Scripto pencil without the lead."[14] Still, Hank's determination and drive got the 130-pounder off the bench, even if it was mainly in practices and brief minutes on the court in games that were long since decided.

The junior varsity squad enjoyed a successful season and finished second in its division, primarily through the efforts of Heat and Bo, who were the obvious team leaders. Hank saw only spot action, yet remained convinced he was their equal; all he needed was a chance to prove it on the floor. "He didn't play much that year at all," Heat said. Yet Hank never stopped working to improve his game. "He had exceptional drive to succeed," Yank said. "He had to work for everything, because nothing came easy for him. For Bo, it was all natural and smooth. With Hank, it was a constant struggle, and it took tremendous effort. Yet he was willing to do whatever it took to get better. He was willing to pay the price."[15]

While Bo was "real easy going and ultra-athletic," Hank was "a fighter and he had to fight for everything he got," Yank would say of them.[16] Hank's fighting often involved the two teammates, and Yank would have to pull them apart during intense scrimmages. Their disagreements rarely were more than heated shouting matches, and strongly worded challenges from Hank that Bo usually ignored, but they were an early sign of the competitiveness between them.

At Dobbins, Hank was an average student, but his struggle with reading placed him in a remedial class. He majored in heating and air conditioning, as did his friend Heat. "I couldn't even get rid of him in school," Heat laughed. "He followed me everywhere."[17]

The small classes at Dobbins enabled Hank to get individual instruction, and his teachers monitored his progress. Although he did not display any unusual skill level in his chosen vocation, he was advancing in his avocation under the tutelage of Yank and Heat. He spent the summer before his sophomore year in the city leagues and on the playgrounds with Heat.

Tryouts for the varsity were intense and highly competitive. Only 12 players were selected, and during the preseason tryout periods, Yank would post the names of those who had made the cut on the wall outside his tiny cubicle above the gymnasium. "Bo, Mark Stevenson, and me were ballin'," Heat said. "The returning seniors attempted to tell us that Yank only played upper classmen. They hoped we'd get discouraged and quit. We just ignored their trash and kept tearing them up in the scrimmages."[18]

Hank was not so impressive. "Each day he'd race up to that office to see if his name was still on the list," Heat said. Impressed more with the tall lanky kid's desire and determination than anything else, Yank kept Hank's name on the list, and eventually a much-relieved Gathers made the final roster for the upcoming season.[19]

Making the team was only the beginning for Hank. He was convinced, even if no one else was, that he would become a dominant force on it, if given a chance. He apparently decided that one way to get that chance was to learn to keep up with Bo. "Scoring came easy for me," Bo said, "and Hank wanted to keep up with me."[20] They would play one on one all the time, at Hank's insistence. "We played it for defense, because if we played it for offense, we argued too much," Bo said. The intense competitiveness "made us each better." The laid-back Bo found the intensity level difficult to take and complained. Hank would ignore the complaints or throw them back at Bo as a sign of weakness. Hank wanted to be as good as Bo, no matter how long it took or how hard it was going to be. He would not, could not, accept that Bo was obviously better.[21]

With Bo and the 6-foot-5 Mark Stevenson leading the way, Dobbins managed to go 12-9 with three, and sometimes four, sophomores getting significant playing time. Hank was not one of them, although he gained minutes as the season progressed. When Dobbins upset Frankford and then lost in the play-offs to Overbrook, everyone got a glimpse of the future.

"At the end of the game, Hank got in and started scoring and rebounding," Heat recalled. "I said to myself, 'What the heck is going on here?'"[22]

"Hank had managed to become one of the best players in his neighborhood with the body he had," Yank said. "But when he saw the caliber of players on the team ahead of him, he knew he needed to work on his physical conditioning to get stronger or he would never be able to compete."[23]

Hank quietly vowed to achieve the skill level and athleticism of Bo, Mark Stevenson, and others who played ahead of him. During the summer between his sophomore and junior seasons, he immersed himself in a physical conditioning regimen that passed the border between hard work and obsessiveness, and kept on going. Driving him day after day was the combative, competitive nature that Lucille had bestowed on him.

"He lifted weights in the recreation center and at St. Elizabeth's. He even had a rusty old set of weights at his house. He worked out every day and made me go along with him," Heat said. Hank's work ethic also impressed Doug Overton, who would become a teammate that fall: "I watched him in his apartment working out. . . . He had a crude weight bench in there also. He did push-ups. A lot of push-ups."[24]

As Hank, and Heat, and Bo competed in the summer league and on the playgrounds, the "new" Hank started to emerge. "We played against kids from Franklin and Overbrook, and Hank was holding his own," Heat said.[25]

In the Sonny Hill League—a Philadelphia summer league organized by a former small college player and labor organizer whose image adorns the league's literature as a logo—Hank and his Dobbins teammates developed their game together against top-flight competition.

For Hank, the intense weight program and training regimen—which had worn Heat out when he tried to keep pace—achieved the desired results. "When he came back to school for his junior year, he was a different person," Yank said of Hank. "He was a man among boys. He was scoring, rebounding, and blocking shots with a body that was simply intimidating. Hank was determined to become the 'strongest man in the world.' After seeing the transformation he'd made, I had no reason to doubt him. Hank wanted perfection, and he was willing to pay whatever price it took to achieve it. He wouldn't take no for an answer."[26]

That drive to excel made Hank a potent force on the court. No one would outwork, out-hustle, or outplay him again. He was not going to allow a lack of natural ability to stop him. In fact, once he recognized what it would take—hard work—he never looked back.

Hank was now more than 6-feet-5-inches and had topped 200 pounds.[27] He would be an important component of the Dobbins Tech Mustangs for the next two seasons.

Off the court, he remained a fun-loving jokester. "He was a comedian," Bo recalled.[28] Hank's drive and determination were not the only traits Hank had inherited from his mother. He also had her sharp wit and a mocking sense of humor that had people in stitches whenever he displayed it.

"No one was spared," said Yank, whose wardrobe was often fodder for Hank's biting critiques. "He was hilarious." He was expert in the sort of broad satirical put-down typical of "playing the dozens," verbal sparring with a long tradition in the black community, except that he was in competition with no one but himself when he would start a humorous riff at someone else's expense. "If Hank perceived a weakness in you or your character, it was all over," Heat said. "He would [playfully] use it against you unmercifully."[29]

In his memoir, Bo fondly recalled Hank's humor: "Like his mom, he was a great mimic, and he would do impressions of you and others that were dead-on perfect. He had Father Dave down so well that once, when a call came in to Father Dave's house, Hank answered it, pretending to be the priest. When the caller asked for a handout, Hank replied, 'Sure, come on over and I'll give it to you.' When the guy showed up promptly and sought out

Father Dave for the promised largesse, Hank burst out laughing while Father Dave stood in the doorway sputtering in confusion over the demand for the 'promised money.'"[30]

In using his ability to make others laugh—at themselves and their bleak surroundings—Hank helped them escape the bleak reality around them, if only for the moment. "Hank loved life more than any person I ever knew, and if you were around him a lot, as I was, you had to enjoy it too," Bo said. "You would be drawn into his zany, crazy world with him, and you had to become his friend. Everyone did."[31]

As fun- loving and joyful as Hank was off the court, on the floor he was an intense force of pent-up energy and determination. His play was serious and his goal was in sight. "He always wanted to be in the NBA," Yank said.[32] Like so many other youngsters in the projects, Hank saw his way out—his opportunity—in basketball. It was his burning desire and he was not going to be denied. It wasn't just for himself. Hank wanted desperately to get Lucille and his brothers out of the projects, and he confidently, proudly told his mother—and everyone else—that he would do so.

He soon had yet another reason to reach for an NBA career: a son. Aaron Crump, named after Hank Aaron, one of Hank Gathers's heroes, was born when his father was a junior in high school. Hank Gathers was at the side of Marva Crump, his quiet, pretty neighbor, when their son was born.

Marva was a bit older than Hank when they met in the Rosen projects. He was 13 and she was 15 when their relationship began. "He was always a comedian, such a delight," Marva said. "He was always tall, so he was a basketball player. And he always said he was going to play basketball. I never doubted that he would."[33]

Though Marva and Hank's romantic relationship ended soon after their child was born, Aaron became yet another person for whom Hank felt responsible—and another reason why he couldn't, and wouldn't, allow himself to fail. He never stopped being a father to his son, and even years later, Marva would still say of Hank, "He was a great guy."[34]

CHAPTER

3

AMERICA'S MOST WANTED

Philadelphia's high school basketball program was in the top ranks nationally. The Philly teams' fall schedules would test them against teams all across America, and the local boys were seldom found wanting. They regularly faced DeMatha of Hyattsville, Maryland, and Dunbar in Baltimore, while making frequent forays across the Delaware to take on top New Jersey programs in Camden, Atlantic City, and Trenton. In addition to their summertime travels on the Sonny Hill League squads, Philly's best high school players would enjoy trips to places as far away as Kentucky, Las Vegas, and even Hawaii for the Christmas time Holiday Tournament. If you could compete at the top level in this type of competition, you could compete anywhere. And no one understood this better than the college coaches who combed the country for recruits who could take them to the top of the collegiate basketball world.

Those college coaches had already noticed the play of Bo Kimble as a sophomore standout. They were about to discover another prospect or two on the Dobbins Mustangs' roster for 1983-84, but Mark Stevenson was not one of them; over the summer the sharp-shooting forward had transferred to Roman Catholic.

"There weren't enough balls to go around," Heat said by way of explaining Stevenson's departure.[1] Mark would go on to enjoy an outstanding career at Roman Catholic and later at Notre Dame University, but in the coming season, Dobbins would need to make up for his offensive production.

The answer came quickly: the new Hank Gathers. Nearing 6 feet 6 inches and heavily muscled from the intense weight-lifting regimen he would never abandon, Hank would provide the offensive punch inside that Dobbins needed.

The Mustangs were a force to reckon with in a tough league: Bo and his potent scoring from outside (he had averaged more than 15 points a game as a sophomore); Derrick, now healed from an ankle injury and returning as forward; Heat, who could distribute the ball with speed and precision seldom seen on high school courts; and the lone returning senior, Darryl Dirickson, back at the other guard spot.

But Yank was not convinced that his Mustangs were invincible. He was such a consummate worrier and frenetic presence on the sidelines that Ted Silary, basketball writer for the *Philadelphia Daily News*, likened the coach to a Mexican jumping bean, and Ray Parrillo of *The Inquirer* called Yank "a hyperactive gerbil."[2] Yank wasn't at all sure how far Dobbins could go with four juniors starting and Mark Stevenson missing.

The previous season, Yank had lived up to his nicknames, often replacing young players who were making the sophomore mistakes that drove him to distraction. This season he would be less likely to yank his starters, but no less committed to the heavily structured offensive style of play favored by John Chaney, who was now coaching at nearby Temple. Discipline was the key to Yank's offense, and he was constantly reminding his team: "Don't shoot too often, and give it a whole lot of thought before you do so."[3]

It was Yank's 13th season at the helm, and he had twice led his team to the semifinal round of the citywide play-offs, first in 1976 and again in 1979. Maybe 13th would be lucky—but he wouldn't allow himself to even think about it.

Dobbins proved to be a powerful team capable of besting any team in the area, winning 10 games and losing only one before play began in the Public League portion (the public school division) of the Mustangs' schedule in January. They had impressed area sportswriters enough to rate a second-place ranking in Southeastern Pennsylvania as the new year began.[4]

The Public League opener was a winning one as Dobbins demolished Simon Gratz, a team that was considered one of the city's powerhouses, with a score of 82-62. Hank had 28 points, 8 rebounds, and 3 blocked shots, while Bo accounted for 20 points and added 5 blocks of his own. Together, they contributed 54 points to the offense.[5] But together may not be the right word.

"It was also hard not to notice that a wide-open Kimble was upset when Gathers neglected to pass him the ball on several occasions," Silary observed in his *Philadelphia Daily News* account of the Simon Gratz game. When the reporter mentioned Hank's lapses to Yank, the coach replied, "Eric got a little carried away. He was trying to do too much. Greg got mad and we took care of it."[6]

Hardly John Wooden but nonetheless effective, Yank would continue to try to assuage the egos of his two stars without upsetting the tempo they had managed to convert into an auspicious start. But Silary's story did nothing to make that part of Yank's job easier, mentioning that sportswriters were now debating "which player is better," Bo or Hank. The writer concluded that "the answer is no clearer now than it was [in the fall] season, though it was Kimble who started and Gathers who had to settle for making significant contributions off the bench." Silary conceded that Bo was "the smoother of the two" because his driving ability led to quick bank shots. He added, though, that Hank Gathers, "in the opinion of most, will do nothing but get better and better."[7] Though Yank would never say it, the Mustangs, as a team, were getting better and better, too. What they had was pretty darn good—and apparent even to their coach. Yank, who had unleashed his imitation of a wild man during the contest, said he wouldn't change his demeanor. "It makes me sweat and keeps the weight off. Plus, I have the kind of team that responds to an emotional coach." If he was right, they would have little trouble the rest of the way. "We were all kind of looking forward to next year," Bo told Parrillo, "but it's starting to look like we can do it this year if we play the way we're supposed to."[8]

Dobbins, with Bo and Hank leading the way, continued to improve with each game. One reason was Doug Overton, who complemented Heat at the other guard spot and provided even more offense to an already-potent scoring machine. He was a freshman, but the rules for freshman eligibility had just been changed, so he was able to join the varsity immediately.

A product of the Germantown section in Northwestern Philadelphia, Doug and his sister were raised by their mother, who had divorced their father when Doug was about nine. He attended public school and also frequented the area playgrounds with his cousin James Smith, a student at Dobbins. James told Doug to check out the Dobbins team, which was pretty good. "I was already a pretty good player in grade school, and he [James] knew it would be a better situation for me [than the high school in Germantown]," Doug said. "It would get me out [of] my neighborhood, and I would be with James, so it seemed like a good fit for me."[9]

Doug was not unaware of the Dobbins players. "I knew Hank and Bo and Heat from watching them play in the Sonny Hill League that summer. I didn't know them personally but I knew who they were."[10] And Doug Overton knew talent when he saw it. So he took the entrance exam and was admitted to Dobbins.

Doug, whose neighborhood in Germantown was serene compared to that around the Raymond Rosen projects, became a witness to the determination and resolve of the young Hank Gathers. "It was like Beirut or Baghdad there," he recalled.[11]

As Bo Kimble had noted earlier, the code of the streets, unwritten but clearly understood by all, was that if you were an athlete and showed promise of becoming an outstanding performer, you were given a "pass" through the area.

"Basketball is a street game," Doug explained years later. "For those who were into the drugs and gang life of the streets, there was an unspoken but unmistakable desire to see you get out, if you could develop the talent and ability to do so," Doug explained. "If they saw you were trying, they pretty much left you alone. Hank was very well respected in his neighborhood. And he didn't take any stuff from anybody there, anyway. He demanded respect."[12] The neighborhood watched. And hoped. And its shattered dreams lived again, vicariously, through the players on the court.

Hank and his Dobbins teammates were also gaining increasing respect from the sportswriters as the Mustangs rolled through the season under Yank's tutelage. By early February, with a 17-1 record, the Dobbins team had risen to fifth in the *Inquirer's* weekly rankings for Southeastern Pennsylvania.

College coaches were also noticing how well Bo and Hank were playing. They were sending them recruiting letters in which they extolled the virtues of their school and complimented a young player's performance on court. The letters arrived in a trickle in January and February; by spring they would flow steadily.

By early February, even Yank was confident that his Mustangs could beat the top-ranked team in the city, Franklin High's squad, which was led by Jerome Richardson (since childhood known to everyone as "Pooh," because his grandmother thought he looked like Winnie-the-Pooh).

The game was played in the Dobbins gym, where "the acoustics. . . made the 500 that crammed their way in sound like 5 million" to the *Inquirer's* Parrillo. Franklin and Dobbins were tied for first in their division, and the February 7 game lived up to the hoopla that preceded it. Riding the boisterous wave of enthusiasm of their home-court fans, the Mustangs raced to an 11-4 lead before the Franklin Electrons scored 12 straight unanswered points. Led by Brian Smith with 26 points and Richardson with 20, Franklin beat back numerous Dobbins runs to win, 74-67. Hank had 24 points and Bo chipped in with 17, but it was not enough to hold off a Franklin squad that also boasted a University of Hawaii-bound Will Bolds.[13]

In the *Inquirer*, Parrillo credited Richardson's "tenacious defense" for holding down Hank and preventing him from dominating play in the second half, "the way he often does." The 6-foot-2 Richardson told the reporter, "Let me tell you, Eric Gathers is one of the toughest dudes in the league. I tried to get him mad to make him lose his concentration. But that didn't work, so I just tried to stay in front of him all the time."[14] Key to Franklin's game plan was double- and sometimes triple-teaming Hank, who was listed as 6 feet 5 in the program. Franklin's strategy prevented Heat's entry passes from reaching the ever-eager Gathers. But, just as important, it freed Bo up to score more easily from outside. That was what Richardson meant when he referred to trying to make Hank angry—part of Franklin's strategy was built on knowledge of the fierce Kimble-Gathers rivalry, so Franklin was trying to frustrate Hank by having him see Bo do well.[15]

Both the Electrons and the Mustangs coasted through the rest of the season, bound for another showdown in the play-offs. Along the way, Hank continued his dominating play beneath the basket, while Bo maintained his pace from outside with his smooth, long-range jumpers. Somehow the rivalry worked to Dobbins's benefit. For example, in the first round of the play-offs, Bo was saddled with early foul trouble against Edward Bok Tech, limiting him to only 11 points. Hank eagerly picked up the slack, pouring in 27 to go with his 18 rebounds. The Mustangs beat Edward Bok, then rolled over Washington before facing another technical high school, Jules Mastbaum, in the semifinals.

The semifinals proved tougher than Dobbins had reckoned, with the Mustangs finally eking out a 45-40 win. In describing how his team managed to prevail, Yank told Silary, "I'd say it was our tough defense and rebounding," adding grimly, "it certainly wasn't our shooting. This was the first time we played like we had four juniors in the lineup. . . .I had to use two time-outs in the first period, alone, just to calm them down. I had to ask them, 'Why are we not thinking?'"

Fortunately, at least one Mustang was thinking. The lone senior starter, Darryl Dirickson, who usually didn't get much ink, had been impressive, drawing raves for his defensive play. "Around school, they call me the Secretary of Defense," he told Silary.

"Darryl fits right in with the rest of us." He's a hard worker and he wants to win, Hank said, citing traits in Dirickson that he admired above all else.

Despite the Mustangs' poor shooting, Yank's charges had reached the Public League Championship game for the first time. The Mustangs would be facing Franklin for the crown, but they'd be the underdog: Franklin had been 3-0 against Dobbins in the Greater Philadelphia summer league and had beaten Dobbins again in February. Yank downplayed the record, telling Silary, "Last summer, last month, last year. They mean nothing. Sunday's the only game that means anything. And we'll be ready."[16]

A crowd estimated at 3,000 filled Temple University's McGonagle Hall as Franklin and Dobbins faced off for the Public League Championship on March 11, 1984. In a wild, controversy-filled game that featured a technical foul against Franklin's coach, Ken Hamilton, for tossing a chair—a foul that, improbably, was later reversed—the Electrons prevailed 53-49. "It was one of those rare gems when the play exceeded the high expectations," Ray Parrillo told his readers.[17]

Led by the stalwart performance of 6-foot-7 Will Bolds, who took control in the final quarter, Franklin held Dobbins off, despite a sensational performance by Bo, who account-ed for 26 points and 20 rebounds. Hank grabbed 12 rebounds, but Franklin's smothering defense limited him to only 7 points.

Dobbins fought to the end, drawing to within one point with 18 seconds to play, thanks to a hectic 3-point play from Bo. When Pooh Richardson made the front end of a one-and-one and then missed the second, Dobbins raced up court with a chance to at least tie. Hank, never an outside threat, made an uncharacteristic attempt at a 17-footer. It fell harmlessly short, and Franklin's Rodney Miller grabbed the rebound and was fouled. Miller converted his one-and-one with two seconds left, sealing the Mustangs' fate.

"That wasn't the shot I would have wanted Hank to take," Yank told Silary. "A couple guys were open underneath, including his brother, Derrick. There was a lot of congestion. Guess he couldn't see him."[18] It was a lame excuse for Hank's failed attempt at game-ending heroics.

That Hank would take the shot at all was typical of his attitude. He knew he wasn't a good outside shooter, yet he felt challenged to do what others thought him incapable of. He may have failed to convert, but he gave it his all. And from that moment on, he was resolute in his determination not to fail again.

"That's all he talked about that next summer," Heat remembered. "We were going to win the championship. Simple as that. He said it over and over, and pretty soon, we all started to believe it, too."[19]

Dobbins may have lost the championship, but the 1983-84 season was not without its accolades. Yank was accorded Coach of the Year honors by the *Philadelphia Inquirer*, a tribute to his ability to take a young squad to the finals. The *Inquirer* also cited both Bo and Hank among the best juniors in the city, and in his season recap, Ray Parrillo predicted that the "team to watch" in 1984-85 would be Dobbins.[20]

Although the season was over, one game remained to be played at Dobbins. It was the Flame and Steel game, a traditional event that took its name from the school colors and was held at season's end, when all the returning players from the varsity and junior varsity formed mixed squads and faced off, coached by the graduating seniors.

"Bo and Hank were on opposite teams for the game. It was a battle. And the game wound up with Bo's team winning by 2 points or so," Yank said. "They shook hands after the game but then went down to the locker room and started fighting. I had to break them up. It was mostly mouthing off and shoving, but it was intense and heated, and I had to step in and stop it.

"Hank wanted that game real bad. He knew it was the last time he'd be in the Flame and Steel game, and it meant a lot to him. Bo was an ultra-athletic guy that everything came easy to, and his personality was also easy-going. Hank was a fighter and had to fight for everything he got. Nothing came easy to him. He wanted to win that game so bad, and he was deeply hurt and frustrated [when his team lost]. And [to make matters worse] Bo won, and Hank's emotions just took over then."[21]

After that chaotic scene in the locker room Hank became obsessive about winning the Public League Championship the following season. It was in the forefront of his mind and colored every conversation. He was convinced the Mustangs would win it all—and that his resolute determination would convince the rest of the players too, whether they liked it or not.

For Doug Overton, the memory is still vivid. "He would be at my house by seven in the morning every day. 'Let's go. We're gonna play some guys from Southern over in their park.' Or he'd arranged for us to play a bunch of guys from Franklin at his court. He wouldn't take no for an answer. He was there, in my room, and I had to get up and go with him. He wanted us to be better than everyone else, and nothing was going to stop him."[22]

On the asphalt courts of Philadelphia, throughout the spring and summer of 1984, Hank and his Dobbins teammates prepared for their next season. They were so mesmerized by the intensity that burned so brightly in Hank's eyes that they followed his vision obediently, if not always willingly. Among the many watching as both Hank and Bo continued to improve their game was a slender, young, sandy-haired assistant coach from the University of Southern California. His name was David Spencer—known to all as "Spence." "He was always around. I saw him all the time at our games and practices," Doug said.[23] One of the places where he showed up that summer was Princeton University, for the annual summer ritual sponsored by Nike and known as the ABCD Camp. It featured the top players in the nation, and Hank and Bo were both there. They performed well against the nation's elite players, and before long, the tiny mail slot for the Gathers home in the Rosen projects was crammed with letters from college recruiters. The coaches often sent decals along with their brochures, and Lucille proudly pasted the school logos on the front door. With each expression of interest that Hank received, her dream was closer to becoming reality—her escape from Rosen a serious possibility.

The weight training and push-ups continued at a feverish pace at the Gathers home and nearby Moylen Recreation Center. A fiercely determined Hank was constantly rousting Heat and Doug from their beds in the early morning hours to "go ballin'." "Hank would ride his bike over and get me up, and we'd play outside my house," Heat recalled. "Right there, out in the street, dribbling one-on-one. People would come out of their homes to watch us. Here was this 6-foot-7 guy dribbling like [Globetrotter legend] Curley Neal. I'm a guard and I can't get the ball away from him."[24]

"He dribbled better for a man that size than anybody I ever saw," said Doug, who played for a dozen years in the NBA. "People knew he wasn't from our neighborhood and they'd ask me, 'Who is this guy?' Just being around Hank helped my confidence. I saw how hard he worked and how determined he was, and it inspired me to get better."[25] Hank's insatiable appetite for competition once caused Doug to barely escape the wrath of his family. "I was supposed to be in a wedding, and Hank had me out on the court at Moylen. I told him I had to go to the wedding. He thought I was just looking for an excuse to stop playing, and he wouldn't believe me. Finally, I begged him to let me go and he relented. I changed into my tux on the fly and just made it in time." Doug, who would go on to LaSalle University before his career in the NBA acknowledged that it was "Hank Gathers's example that made me the player that I was."[26] The obsessiveness that had driven Hank in the summer between his sophomore and junior years now went into overdrive, and he was becoming known, not just to Doug's neighbors but throughout the city and beyond, as a force to be reckoned with. "He was like a man possessed," said Yank of Hank's determination to improve and to make his teammates improve. "Hank had an obsession to become the strongest [player]. The best scorer. The best rebounder. He wanted perfection and he was willing to pay the price."[27]

Given the schedule that Yank had prepared for his Mustangs, they would have to improve if they wanted to succeed. The stellar performance of Dobbins in the 1983-84 season had brought invitations, seldom extended in the past, to play in several prestigious tournaments. Yank happily accepted, eager for the opportunity to showcase his talented squad in the rarefied atmosphere of tournament play. Dobbins would participate in the National Bank of Washington Classic at George Washington University in Washington, D.C., early in the season and then in the Johnstown Tournament in Pennsylvania just before the New Year's break. In between they would travel to the prestigious King of the Bluegrass Tournament in Louisville, Kentucky. A 16-team field of top basketball powers would compete in the basketball Mecca for four days.

At each and every stop scores of college recruiters would be appraising the top talent in the land, and Hank and Bo were right at the top of their lists. Still paying the most attention was Dave Spencer of USC. He had grown up in nearby Wilmington, Delaware, and he made frequent trips to Philadelphia to check on the development of Hank, Bo, and other Dobbins players. Spence would fly in for all the key Dobbins contests and stay with his parents, then return to the West Coast.

Yank and Father Dave noted Spence's presence and obvious interest in Hank, especially, early on. That Spence represented a school in far-off California didn't faze the two older men, but the distance did seem a bit off-putting to Hank.[28]

The top Eeastern programs, as well as Sonny Hill himself (and others), were pressing Hank to choose a school near home. Over the summer Hill had impressed on Hank the importance of "giving back to the community" by staying in Philly at one of the Big Five schools. Bo, who was seriously considering Temple, recalled that Hill, who was close to Chaney, touted Temple's Owls to Hank. But Hank was more interested in Providence, where Rick Pitino was then the coach, and a few other Eastern schools. Chaney, himself, was not pursuing Hank with much enthusiasm, and Chaney's structured style was not well suited to Hank's talent.[29]

Besides, that summer Hank and Bo had seen a side of the self-promoting Hill that made his advice suspect. "We had played in the high school division that summer and done real well," Bo said. "At the end of the season, we played a team that was sponsored by comedian and former Philly resident Bill Cosby and was named after his wife. We had won the game and the championship—at least we thought so—but Sonny made a ruling that took the title from us and awarded it to Cosby's team. Both Hank and I protested the injustice, and finally Sonny admitted to us that it was about the money. Cosby was a financial backer of the league, and Sonny wanted to repay his largesse with the title to keep the spigot open. In the end, he gave both teams trophies, but we lost a lot of respect for him after that."[30]

Hill also used his leverage as the league's organizer to keep the top Philly players from attending the numerous summer camps around the country that were inviting them. "If you go," he'd threaten, "you're banned from the Sonny Hill League." That power play kept the top seniors—Pooh Richardson, Hank and Bo, Lionel Simmons, Rodney Shorter, and others—at home, and allowed Sonny to crow about their "development" in his league when they later achieved success at the college level.[31]

Hank's progress on the court continued to impress his teammates and everyone who watched him play. "We traveled down to Baltimore as a junior team representing the Sonny Hill League that summer," Heat said. "Hank scored 30 points on a high school All-American, and we knew then and there he was ready."[32]

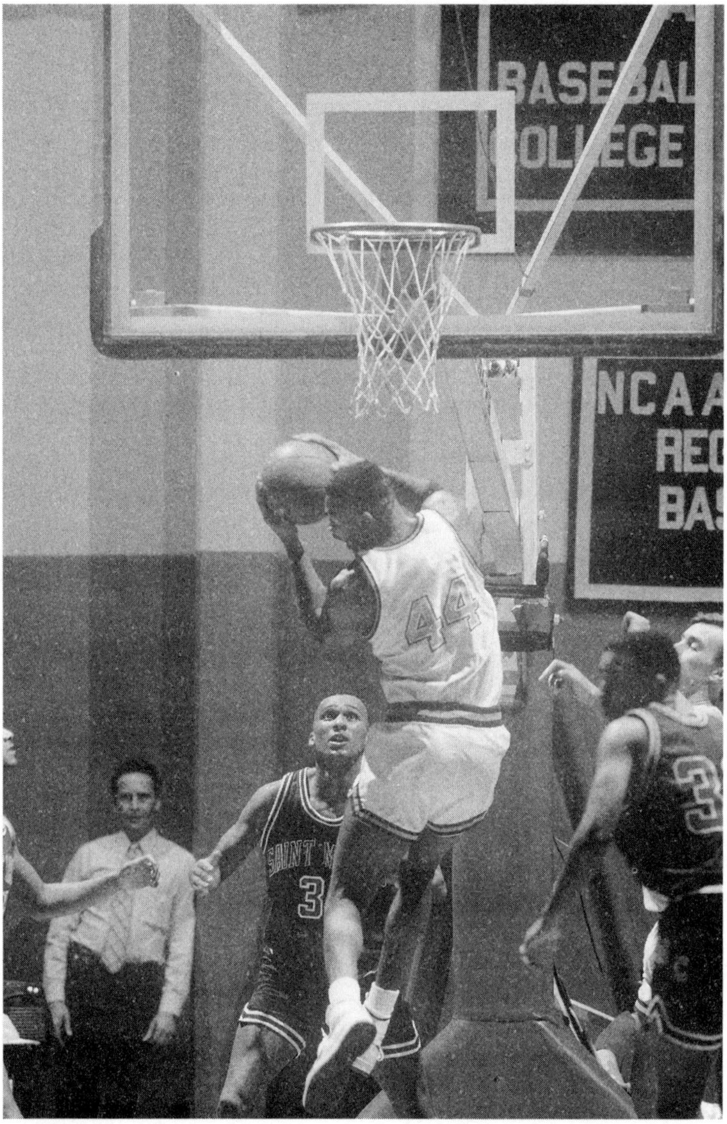

BASEBAL
COLLEGE
NCAA
REG
BAS
44

MAKING THE GRADE

Father Dave continued to offer advice to Hank, who discussed with the priest the pros and cons of the various programs. Hank and his teammates had devoted months and months of intense practice to improving their basketball skills, but they had spent considerably less time on academics. That neglect would now become a serious issue, because the colleges and universities that were courting them also had minimum requirements for admission and eligibility. Although Dobbins was quite proficient at preparing its students for careers in refrigeration and air-conditioning repair, and in Bo's case in arc welding, it was of no help in preparing them to gain admission to a four-year college that demanded proficiency in core academic subjects, which were a struggle for both Hank and Bo.[1]

Father Dave took the academic preparation of the Mustangs in hand. The former math teacher and his brother, Jack, who was an attorney, acted as tutors for various members of the Dobbins team, including Hank and Bo. The intense sessions were often conducted in the relative peace and quiet of Father John McNamee's rectory at St. Malachy's. Although Hank and Bo both had struggled to maintain minimum grade-point averages for eligibility at Dobbins, they now responded eagerly to the one-on-one tutoring. In those days, it was not possible to jump from high school directly to the professional ranks. If they wanted to get to the NBA, they had to go to college first.[2]

Hank's senior year at Dobbins would be his springboard to college, and that would lead him inevitably to the NBA. "He always talked about making it to the NBA and getting his mom and family out [of the projects]," Yank said.[3]

Hank and Bo's final season at Dobbins began with sportswriters debating which Philadelphia school would field the better team, Franklin or Dobbins. At Franklin, the team was led by Pooh Richardson, the talented six-one guard who had averaged 17 points per game while the Electrons racked up a 46-3 record the previous two seasons. Pooh had already committed to basketball powerhouse UCLA. Making the Electrons even stronger for the 1984-85 season was Paul Graham, a 6-foot-6 forward who had transferred from Olney, where he had averaged 28 points per contest.[4]

One coach was only half-joking when he offered Ray Parrillo his opinion of Philly's best team. "How about Franklin or the '76ers?" he quipped.[5] But Dobbins wasn't going to get any sympathy cards from the other coaches. Bo had averaged 26.5 points and nearly 11 rebounds, and Hank had averaged nearly 23 points and 10 boards the year before. Heat had averaged 9 assists and more than 11 points, and both Derrick Gathers and Doug Overton were both returning to the team.

"Strength and experience are in our favor," Yank said. "But we're questionable on defense." But Yank's moans failed to convince Parrillo, who predicted in November that if the juniors of 1983-84 progressed normally, "Dobbins could be a truly great team."[6]

A week later, Parrillo previewed the season and listed for his *Inquirer* readers "the Top 20 Players to Watch." Both Hank and Bo were on the list. The article also revealed the appraisal of the players by a scouting service, the High School Basketball Index, which was put together and circulated by Tom Konchalski. Rating the players on a scale of 1 to 5, Konchalski gave Bo a 5—and accorded Hank a 4. Parrillo noted that Richardson had also received the highest rating possible and that while he was headed to UCLA, both Hank and Bo were unsigned, with Bo leaning toward Nebraska and Connecticut, and Hank favoring Virginia Commonwealth, USC, Eastern Kentucky, Iowa, and Connecticut. Parrillo included his opinion that Hank and Bo would give Dobbins the "best 1-2 punch" and noted that Hank "was fearless around the boards."[7]

Now all Bo and Hank needed to do was live up to the high expectations.

Hank's final season at Dobbins would mark the first time that a Yankowitz-coached squad would stay overnight in a hotel. It would also be the first time that any of the players had ever stayed in one. "All through the spring and summer, the kids talked about going away on these trips," Yank said. "We even got new 'away' uniforms."[8]

Now the Dobbins Mustangs would have an opportunity to see some of the country outside their dreary, depressing environs. But first, Dobbins had to figure out how to pay for these road trips. In all, Dobbins would appear in four tournaments. The school rallied around the team, raising money by selling candy, pretzels, and soft drinks. The Dobbins Gospel Choir held concerts, giving the proceeds to the team, and some alumni dug into their pockets. During football games a hat was passed through the stands. The National Bank of Washington Tournament, the Mustangs' first test, would guarantee the team $1,000 and would pay for food, transportation, and lodging. With all the fund-raising, plus the bank's sponsorship, Yank figured the school wouldn't lose any money.[9]

In devising the schedule, Yank was mindful of the attention that the tournaments would focus on his team and players. While Hank and Bo were well known to the college recruiters, Yank figured that other players would catch the recruiters' eyes. To Yank, the expense was well worth it if it resulted in a scholarship offer to a less- well-known player.[10]

In Washington, D.C., the Mustangs made it to the finals before losing to perennial national power DeMatha of Maryland. When they got back to Philly, Yank found offers for Derrick awaiting him at Dobbins. His play had attracted attention from four Division II schools. Although Yank was still upset with the officiating in the tourney final, he was pleased that the appearance had yielded scholarship offers. The DeMatha game, which Dobbins lost, 75-60, had been an eye- opener for Yank and the team. DeMatha was a team that played a solid schedule each year against the best teams in the country, yet Dobbins had held its own for most of the contest.

Continuing what Ray Parrillo would term a "grueling tournament schedule," the Dobbins players piled into two cramped vans for the 16-hour trip to Kentucky, made only just bearable by Hank's nonstop patter, and gentle jibes at Yank's attire, and Hank's sarcastic comments about his teammates. They would be appearing in the King of the Bluegrass Holiday Classic at Fairdale High School, just outside Louisville. Held December 17-22, the prestigious event was a 16-team affair that included three of the nation's top 20 teams: the host, Seneca, which was rated 2nd; Dobbins, which was ranked 6th; and 16th place Northeast Jones of Laurel, Mississippi. The tournament was a double-elimination event that ran five days and put some of the top teams and players in the country up against the local quintets from basketball-crazy Kentucky. It was a pre-holiday feast for fans who loved their hoops as much as their deep-fried Christmas turkeys.

Among the featured players in the tournament were the 6-foot-8 All-American Kenny Payne of Northeast Jones, in Laurel, Miss.; 6-foot-9 David Robinson of Eastside High School, in Gainesville, Fla.; 6-foot-11 Mike Scott of Greenup County High School in Greenup, Ky.; and 6-foot-5 Gary Massey of St. Raymond High School in the Bronx, NY. The stars included host Seneca's highly regarded Tony Kimbro, who was 6-foot-8 and the player generally considered to be the top junior in Kentucky; Rex Chapman of Owensboro-Apollo, who averaged 31 points per game; and Felton Spencer of Eastside High, who was 7-foot-1 and a member of Florida's top-ranked team, whose five starters all averaged in double figures. Yank's charges would face Eastside High in the opening round on Wednesday, December 17, at 6:30 p.m.[11]

In the stands as play began were dozens of college coaches. Hank Gathers hadn't traveled all the way to Ky. to be overlooked. So as Dobbins turned back Eastside 85-59, he put on a show for the recruiters. Gathers dominated the heralded Eastside center, David Robinson, who was bound for the University of Louisville. Hank poured in 14 of 16 field goal attempts and grabbed a game-high 11 rebounds from the taller Robinson. Hank clearly enjoyed the ability to dominate inside and brought the crowd to its feet in the final quarter with a thundering dunk over Robinson that drew a technical foul when he hung from the rim a bit too long for officials to ignore. Immediately after the free throws, Hank followed up with another thundering dunk off an alley-oop pass from Heat that hit Hank as he streaked in from the baseline. As the knowledgeable Kentucky fans roared in appreciation, there was no way any scout in the audience could ignore his dominating play. Hank tallied 31 points, Bo added 28, and Heat dished up 15 assists to go with his 13 points— as Dobbins ran the Florida team off the court.[12]

Hank had held Robinson, who was 6 feet 9, to 4 of 7 from the floor and just 6 rebounds, proving to any lingering doubters that Hank could dominate a taller player. "This is the best team I've seen all year," an impressed Robinson offered. "We got hurt by their rebounding and they took us out of our game."[13]

"It was," Mark Shallcross told his *Louisville Times* readers, "an impressive performance."[14]

Proving that the Mustangs' first-round win was no fluke, they continued their torrid shooting (61 percent) and handed St. Raymond's of the Bronx its first loss in 10 games by destroying the New Yorkers, 89-63. Hank had a game-high 16 rebounds, along with 20 points, as he battled with Villanova-bound senior Gary Massey. Bo added 32 points as the two Dobbins stars combined to make a phenomenal 49 of 67 field goal attempts in the first two games, a 73 percent average against top-flight competition. Dobbins dominated throughout and led by as much as 30 points in the final quarter.[15]

"This was the best game we have played this year consistently over four quarters," Yank told Mark Shallcross. "Where we come from, the name of the game is defense. We probably only run our set offense 15 times a game. Most of our points get set up off our press defense."[16]

While the Mustangs were romping along, Rick Cushing, a reporter for the (Louisville, Ky.) *Courier-Journal*, had watched Yank as the ever-animated, increasingly hoarse coach urged his charges to "work, work, work." Cushing explained to his readers that Yank demanded hard work from his players and got it. "I drive myself nuts and I expect the same from them," Yank said, oblivious to his malapropism. "I give everything I've got. They know it, and they know I expect them to give their all. I go berserk when they don't."[17]

For Hank Gathers, Richard Yankowitz was the perfect coach at the perfect time. A graduate of Philly's Overbrook High, which had given the world Wilt Chamberlain a short time before, Yank played basketball there from 1959-1961 with Walt Hazzard, Wayne Hightower, and Walli Jones, all of whom went on to the NBA. After graduating from West Chester State Teachers College, Yank arrived at Dobbins. Now he was hopeful that this, his 14th season as head coach, would see his team capture the Public League title that his Mustangs had narrowly missed the year before. In the tough 28-team league, Dobbins would have to fight its way to the top. Hard work was Yank's strategy, and in Hank Gathers, he had a disciple who was not only a true believer but spread his coach's message relentlessly among his teammates. They were a perfectly matched pair, and Hank thrived under Yank's tutelage. He would be Yank's most rewarding project during his tenure as head of the Dobbins Mustangs.

But before the regular season quest could begin, the Mustangs had unfinished business in Kentucky. Next up for Dobbins was a semifinal game against Valley High of Kentucky. In a tight game, Dobbins broke out in the second quarter, then turned back the Vikings, 80-66. The headline in *The Courier-Journal* the next morning read "PHILADELPHIA SCHOOL NO CREAM CHEESE." An impressed Valley coach, Fred Copass, said afterward, "Those two Dobbins kids [Bo and Hank] are major college prospects. We were definitely outmanned." Hank and Bo had combined for 57 points and 25 rebounds.[18]

Now Dobbins would face hometown favorite Seneca High in the final round, and the organizers of the King of the Bluegrass Tournament couldn't have scripted a better tournament final if they had tried. Obviously, a majority of the 2,000 fans were hoping the local quintet, not the invaders from Philly, would capture the crown. With scarcely a backward glance, though, Dobbins doused the high spirits of the partisan crowd.

Dobbins started strong and continued its torrid shooting pace. In the first half, the Mustangs shot 71 percent from the field and were as much as 15 points ahead on three occasions. But the local favorites refused to fold. Trailing by 44-29 at the half, Seneca mounted a furious charge to climb back into contention. With Kimbro leading the way, Seneca closed the score to 69-67 with only 2:34 left to play. The crowd was urging Seneca on, and the momentum seemed to have shifted in its favor.

Dobbins then fouled sophomore center Robert Peyton, who stepped to the line with a chance to tie the game. He made his first shot, which brought Seneca to within a point. The noise level in the steamy gymnasium rose to a new high. Then he missed the second shot, and Dobbins sped up court, clinging to the lead. Bo drove to the basket but was fouled about 16 feet out. But after the whistle, Bo continued on, slamming down a dunk and drawing a technical foul for doing so.

After Bo made his two free throws, giving Dobbins a 3-point cushion, Kimbro took his two free throws for the technical foul against Bo and missed. Seneca still had the ball out of bounds, but then Dobbins intercepted a long in-bounds pass. Bo was quickly fouled and converted his two free throws, opening a 5-point spread. The two teams traded free throws as the clock wound down. At the buzzer Dobbins prevailed, 75-70, putting a "bah humbug" damper on the mood of the partisan crowd.[19]

"I can imagine how stunned everyone was, but we've been getting off to a good start in every game," Hank told Bob White of the *The Courier-Journal*. "Then we started to rush things and we put Seneca back in the game. We had a nice lead and should have taken our time and taken only good shots."[20] Hank acknowledged the other reason that Seneca had managed to charge back into contention: the outstanding performance of Tony Kimbro, who had accounted for 38 points. "He's a helluva player," Hank said. "I've played against a lot of players similar to him, but he's the best outside shooter for a big man I've ever gone up against."[21]

The defeat of the top-ranked team was a huge victory for Yank's charges. After some doubt about accepting the invitation, their coach had decided to test them against the best in the land, and they had exceeded his expectations. It was a total team effort: Derrick Gathers's suffocating defensive effort held Seneca's Keith Williams to 6 points, although he had been averaging 17 points a game. Heat accounted for 17 points, and Hank added 16, as Bo led the team with 23. Kimbro was understandably upset at the loss but tried to find a bright side, saying, "Anytime you play a team like that, you can't do anything but gain from it."[22]

Hank, Bo, and Kimbro were named to the All-Tournament Team, along with Williams, Garry Massey, Kenny Payne, Barry Goheen, Felton Spencer, Rex Chapman, Maurice Jones, Mike Scott, and John Tisdale.[23]

The Mustangs showered and dressed after their victory, then headed out to a large banquet room to eat before piling into the vans for the long ride home. Yank noticed something had changed.

"Before the final game, we had passed a large reception area where they had balloons and bunting decorating the room and a lavish buffet spread of steaming hot food," Yank said. "After we had won, I went back with the team and there was nothing there. No decorations, no food, no nothing. When I asked someone where the food was, he told me if we wanted something to eat, he could offer us some leftover cold cuts. Obviously, we weren't expected to win and spoil their party."[24]

Shortly after the Christmas break, Yank had his Mustangs on the road again. This time, they would be appearing in Johnstown, Pennsylvania, in the 36th annual War Memorial Tournament.

Sam Ross Jr. of the (Johnstown, Pa.) *Tribune-Democrat* suggested that the Dobbins team motto should be: "Have basketball, will travel." In a preview of the tourney action, he recounted the travels of a team that had seen "more territory than the Harlem Globetrotters." Explaining why he'd set such a tough schedule, Yank said, "We're going out and playing the best we can. Everything is geared toward making us a better team when we begin play in the Philadelphia Public League."

Their shared obsession with winning that title drove Hank and his coach. While they thrived on the tournament play and the challenges it offered, they were of a single mind about their ultimate goal. Nothing was going to distract them from that, and Yank made that clear to the Johnstown reporter: "Coatesville [the Mustangs' first-round opponent] is a very good ball club, but our big thing is the Public League. We use every other game as a buildup to that."[25]

Coatesville was highly regarded, but the Mustangs trounced the suburban high school, 83-55, convincing Coatesville coach Ross Kershey that "Dobbins is the best team I've seen since the 1977 West Philadelphia team with Gene Banks." John James told his *Tribune-Democrat* readers that the Pennsylvania Interscholastic Athletic Association (PIAA), to which Coatesville—but not the Philadelphia teams—belonged, would need "a month to wipe the egg off its face" after the bruising loss.

Yank told James he'd thought all along that "Coatesville was using the game as a PIAA vs. Public League" match-up, and he'd told the Dobbins players that, as well, to motivate them. "I know it had an effect on them," he said. The most recent Dunkel Index ratings had also given the team incentive. "Two weeks ago," Yank pointed out, "Dobbins was ranked second and Coatesville fourth. Since then, we won five games and they won one. The latest ratings dropped us to fourth and Coatesville moved up to second."[26]

At the press conference after the game Kershey, the Coatesville coach, posed an interesting rhetorical question to the assembled reporters: "How many Coatesville players could play for Dobbins?" No one offered a response, so he answered his own question: "They had five men out there tonight and we had five boys. Their players looked like they could have been our players' fathers." Bo had accounted for 23 points and Hank had added 17. Heat had another outstanding game with 16, and Doug, who was improving with each outing, added 12.[27]

In the final, Dobbins continued its ungrateful habit of defeating the host team, stomping Johnstown, 70-44.

Despite the shellacking, Yank was not pleased with the Mustangs' play: "The first 10 minutes, I was unhappy with the tempo of the game. Doug (Overton) was a little tight and we weren't playing that well. We switched to a four-corner offense and tried to work the ball down low to Kimble." When the Johnstown Trojans went to a zone to prevent Bo from pounding the baseline, Dobbins had responded by feeding Hank, who made two thunderous dunks to punctuate a 23-point performance. Bo injured his ankle during the third period after missing a baseline jam attempt because he hung on to the rim, moving the portable backboard so far forward that it nearly tipped over. Trojans coach Paul Litwalk was incensed that the showboat move failed to garner a technical foul, but after the game, he marveled at the Dobbins performance: "They're without a doubt the best team we've played, and we've played some good ones the last couple of weeks."[28]

Hank earned MVP honors for the tournament after his dominating performance and joined Bo and Heat on the All-Tourney Team with Schenley High's Les Squair and Tim McNair of the Trojans.[29]

The ease with which Dobbins had handled Johnstown had everyone paying attention, especially the coaches of teams that the Mustangs were scheduled to play. *The Philadelphia Inquirer's* Basketball Top Ten had Dobbins in second place, right behind Ben Franklin and ahead of Roman Catholic in Southeastern Pennsylvania.

Nearby, though, was a team that was not easily impressed. Baltimore's Dunbar High was a national power with a high profile, and its front line was imposing: 6-foot-9 Terry Dozier and his twin brother, Perry, who was 6 feet 10 inches, and they were only the latest stars of a team with a storied history. Under Coach Bob Wade, Dunbar had compiled a dazzling record of 302-18 over 10 seasons and only two years before had claimed the coveted national championship after a perfect 32-0 campaign. Thirteen former Dunbar team members were playing for Division I programs, including David Wingate and Reggie Williams at Georgetown. In fact, since 1978, every one of Wade's senior players had gone on to college. So with Dunbar, which entered the season ranked second in the nation by the Blue Ribbon College Basketball Yearbook, Yank's Mustangs would be facing as stern a test as could be administered.[30] No one doubted that Dunbar was as good, if not better, than the DeMatha team that had dealt Dobbins its only defeat so far that season.

The Pepsi Challenge Tournament was to be played on Saturday and Sunday, January 5 and 6, 1985, at Temple's McGonagle Hall. Sam Carchidi told readers of the *Inquirer* that it was "arguably the East Coast's best high school tournament."[31] He was not exaggerating. All four teams entered—Camden, New Jersey, and Franklin (both the top-ranked teams in their respective states), Dobbins, and Dunbar—were ranked in *Street and Smith's High School Basketball Yearbook*. *USA Today* ranked Dunbar as the nation's top team, with Dobbins 13th and Franklin 18th.[32]

Ted Silary told his *Philadelphia Daily News* readers that the tournament "might be better termed the Pepsi Suicide Mission." The combined record of the four teams was 33-3. And, Silary asked, "When was the last time you saw a suicide mission that was uneventful?"[33]

Of course, the stands would be packed with scouts from major college programs. Silary said they'd be eyeing Heat as well as Hank and Bo, and Paul "Snoop" Graham and Will Bolds from Franklin.

Dobbins had to settle for a third-place finish, but Hank and Bo were named to the All-Tournament Team. Hank had accounted for 41 points in two games, as well as 27 rebounds and 6 blocked shots. Bo had scored 52 points, was credited with 18 rebounds, and made 16 of 19 free throws. He was a perfect 7-7 against Camden, but his miss with 17 seconds to play in the opening round game against Dunbar had ended the Mustangs' hopes for an upset win.

"It seemed like every 10 minutes," Bo told Silary, "there I was, thinking about it again. The missed foul shot was really bugging me, especially since I consider myself a good foul shooter." Silary summed up the weekend by offering that "no matter what happens the rest of the season, Dobbins's players probably won't quite be able to forget how they missed out on a chance to dump Dunbar."[34]

The Mustangs had little time to bemoan their fate in the tournament. Public League action was about to begin, and the goal Hank had set for them lay straight ahead. He wouldn't allow them to look back.

Yank's ambitious scheduling had set Dobbins against some of the top teams and players in the nation. His relatively unknown team from a vocational-technical school in inner-city Philly had more than met the challenge. He was aware of the denigrating comments, the snickering about his all-black team and its core curriculum of wood shop and welding. He'd heard the cruel whispers, that his players were not smart enough for a real school, one that taught "geometry and Latin" instead of "refrigeration and heating." Showing remarkable restraint, the combative coach allowed none of the disparaging talk to bother him. His players had passed the only test that mattered—his. Along the way they had also earned the grudging respect of their detractors. They had played several Top Ten teams and faced off against a half-dozen McDonald's All-American players and had held their own. Now they were ready to go after the trophy they really wanted.

Dobbins had suffered only two losses—to DeMatha and Dunbar, teams that year after year enjoyed well-deserved reputations as among the nation's finest. With the exception of the Virginia prep school Oak Hill Academy, DeMatha's and Dunbar's programs and their legendary coaches had produced more high school All-American players than any other.

Now the grueling tournament schedule that Yank had devised to prepare his team for Public League play began to pay off. Yank's starting lineup for the Public League schedule was Hank Gathers, Bo Kimble, Heat Gates, Doug Overton, and Derrick Gathers. Their coach believed in them and they knew it. And, just as important, they believed in each other—they wouldn't let him down. Dobbins slashed its way through the Public League schedule without a loss.

Hank and Bo were dominant, and both seemed to be maturing enough to realize that they needed each other to succeed. Hank, while never conceding that anyone would or could outwork him, was at least demonstrating a recognition that he didn't need to do it all. He was learning that encouraging Heat and Doug, instead of admonishing them, made the team better. Hank would not cut anyone any slack if he felt he was not putting forth a full effort, but Hank was less confrontational now when the guards fed Bo because he was in the better position.[35]

As play progressed and the victories mounted, the team became a cohesive unit. Fueled by Hank's burning desire, Bo's undeniable talent, the backcourt play of Heat and Doug, and Derrick's defense, they rolled over their opponents with relative ease.

The game they had all been waiting for was their midseason match-up with Franklin. Throughout the summer, as they pounded the concrete courts of the sweltering playgrounds, they had played the game in their minds a hundred times. They took that determination and drive indoors with them on February 14, 1985, and played the much-anticipated "regular season game of the decade."[36]

At game time, both teams were ranked in USA Today's Top 20 in the land–Dobbins was 13 and Franklin was 11. The crowd of 1,300 included about 30 college coaches. ESPN covered the game along with all three local network affiliates. It was a major event in a sports-minded city, generating attention rivaling that usually reserved for Big Five games.

Except for the usual chants of "Bullshit!" when fans thought the refs had missed a call, the crowd was well behaved, with none of the fights or riots that often marked Public League games.[37] All the action was confined to the court. And there was enough to satisfy everyone.

Hank, who had a strong motive to perform at his best, did so. He made 12 of 20 attempts from the field and finished with 26 points and 17 rebounds, erasing all memories of last year's dismal record of 1 shot in 6 and his scoring only 7 points in the championship game that Dobbins had lost. As the fourth quarter wound down, Hank, whose aggressive play Silary later credited with intimidating Franklin, went up strongly for an offensive rebound and put it in, tying the game at 61 as the horn sounded.

In overtime, the two exchanged leads. To no one's surprise, the player who delivered the fatal blow to Franklin's chances was named Gathers. But to almost everyone's amazement, it was Derrick, not Hank, who supplied the winning bucket. (As Silary wryly noted, Derrick was so overlooked on the talent-laden Dobbins team, "he didn't even have a nickname.")

With time running down and Franklin clinging to a one-point lead, Hank was screaming over the roaring crowd at Doug Overton to shoot the ball. "Heck, they were leaving him wide open," Hank said. Finally, Doug heeded Hank's instructions and reluctantly put up a leaning 12-footer. The shot fell off the rim to the left side.

"When I saw the ball coming my way," Derrick said, "I immediately went down low. I saw the ball and said, 'Get the rebound and go straight up with it.' That's what I did."

Game over: Dobbins 69-Franklin 68.

"My brother has a tendency to be in the right place at the right time," Hank said. "He's always been like that, even back in grade school. You know, I don't want to be greedy, but I think he was fouled, too." Then Hank added, "I'd like to see my brother get just as much publicity as me. He deserves it." With Hank and Bo lighting up the scoreboard each game, that wasn't likely and Derrick knew it. "My job on the team is to help if I can on offense; but really it's to play defense. The way I see it," Derrick explained, "if you ain't got no defense, you ain't got no team." Nevertheless, in the biggest game of the year for the Mustangs, it was Derrick who provided the offensive blow that avenged the previous year's stinging defeat.

"Coming out, I knew that Franklin was going to play me real tight," Hank said. "I also knew that wasn't going to stop me any. I told myself if I got the ball in the paint, where I can usually make 85 percent of my shots, I was going to put it up there, regardless of how many people were around me," he told Silary, who was the first of many to hear Hank Gathers matter-of-factly describe his approach to the game. That unfailing self-confidence came to be the constant that defined his game.

The nail-biting win took its toll on Yank. When Franklin's Snoop Graham scored with little more than a minute to go in regulation, "I was running low right then," Yank told Silary. After the final buzzer and ensuing celebration Yank's usually jangled nerves had calmed so much that he looked downright relaxed. "That was fun," Yank said. "I feel looser than I thought I'd be."

Franklin's Pooh Richardson, who had fouled out of the game against Dobbins, was generally conceded by the press to be the best player in the city. Doug Overton, still a sophomore, had drawn the unenviable assignment of trying to hold the Franklin star down. Doug did a remarkable job. Richardson managed to score 17 points, but Doug's defensive pressure resulted in a poor night for Pooh, who made only 8 shots in 19 attempts. Another Dobbins player impressed the college scouts and fans alike. Heat, often overlooked by reporters, who focused almost exclusively on Richardson, displayed his considerable skills under the sternest of circumstances. His superb generalship left many wondering whether Heat, not Pooh Richardson, wasn't the best point guard in the city.[38]

But as well as the Mustangs were doing on the court, they were not faring quite so well in the classroom, and that gave Yank cause for concern. Yes, he was their coach, but he was also a teacher. Yank knew that all their success on the court would be meaningless to his players if they couldn't convert it into an opportunity to get a college degree. Yank loved winning games, yet he never lost sight of the underlying goal.

Basketball success was the only way out of the harsh neighborhood and grim future that awaited those who remained there. It was his players' only hope.

Yank was a vigilant watchdog during the school day. He constantly monitored his players' classroom progress and grades. If they were failing, he was in their faces—and begging and pleading with their teachers. On the last day of the marking period, after he had been assured that all his players were in good shape, he just happened to pass Bo's math teacher in the hallway. "She said Bo had a B average but that she would give him an F unless he turned in five tardy homework assignments," Yank said. "I was frantic. I went looking for Bo, and when I found him and told him what the teacher said, he told me, 'Oh, yeah, I've got those, right here in my book bag.' So he takes them up to the teacher, and in five minutes he went from an F to a B. I'm convinced a lot of failures occur in this system not because the kids are stupid but because they're forgetful, and they tend to slip every so often unless you really stay on top of them.

"I know some coaches don't do a blessed thing in this [academic] area. [They feel] that it's up to the kids. . . . If you make a kid like Hank or Bo ineligible now, he may spend the rest of his life on the streets," Yank said. "I'm not sure that I like the idea that an E instead of a D in something like music or health could make the difference between success or failure for a kid."[39]

Richard Yankowitz may have been a self-proclaimed nut case on the court, but he was a sane, rational realist off it. He was a dedicated, caring teacher, and his concerted and unselfish effort to give his players every possible chance to make it in the world after Dobbins would change many of their lives. They gave him their all on the hardwood, and he returned the favor a hundred times over.

By the beginning of February 1985, Hank and Bo had received piles of scholarship offers that would be worthless if they couldn't maintain the 2.0 grade-point average required by the NCAA for eligibility to play for a Division I school in their first year of college. Despite the tutoring sessions at St. Malachy's, "most everyone on the team was in some kind of trouble, in danger of failing one or two courses," Hank had told Silary in late January. "Myself, I was sweating it out in algebra and biology. I know the work, but I've got bad study habits. In a course like algebra, once you fall behind in the basic principles, it takes a while to catch up."[40]

Yank constantly drummed into Hank and Bo the consequences of failure: no Division I scholarship. They'd have to go the junior college route or try a smaller school without a scholarship. Neither alternative was acceptable to Yank or to them.

"Everyday, when I wake up, I say the same thing: 'Get to school and get that 2.0,'" Hank said. "It's constantly on my mind. The first two report periods, everybody on the team was worrying about what kind of grades they'd accumulate. I'll tell you, that's some kind of pressure. For the most part, I agree with what they (the NCAA) are doing. If that's the way they have to go to make sure athletes get some kind of education, it's real good."[41]

The list of those willing to provide Hank with that education for free was growing with each passing week. He knew that the offers, so graciously proffered, would be just as abruptly pulled should he fail to qualify. Yank and Father Dave continued to hammer that point home. Without the grades, you can't get out, and if you can't get out, you can't help your mom, your family, or your son, they told him emphatically. So did his mother, Lucille.

The hourglass was running out. Hank needed to get his grades up, keep them up, and then decide where he would take his considerable talent. "Going away wouldn't bother me, but I can also see the advantages to staying in Philly. I just want to be able to go somewhere," said Hank,[42] giving voice to his anxiety and no doubt seeing in his mind's eye the stars of yesteryear huddled around the crumbling asphalt courts in his devastated neighborhood. They once had all the promise he had, and they hadn't gone anywhere but down. He wouldn't allow himself to fail.

Like all the other challenges he faced, Hank took on the academic requirements with a vengeance. It wasn't easy, and it never would be for Hank. But when the SAT's came around, both he and Bo scored high enough to qualify for admission to most of the schools that were pursuing them and for NCAA eligibility to play basketball. They also managed to get the grade-point average they needed for Division I play.[43]

CHAPTER 5

UNFINISHED BUSINESS

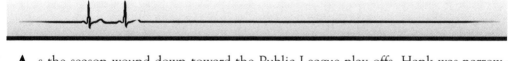

A s the season wound down toward the Public League play-offs, Hank was narrowing his college choices. But first, he and the Dobbins Vo-Tech Mustangs had some unfinished business. The Mustangs had exceeded even Yank's wildest expectations for them and had sailed through the regular season undefeated. The Franklin game was the only real scare, and all the players were eager for the next square-off, which they were certain would come in the citywide finals.

The entire city was waiting eagerly for the game—and the entire city was to be disappointed. While Dobbins, led by Hank and Bo, steamrolled its way through the play-offs, with wins over Central, Overbrook, and Jules Mastbaum Tech, Franklin lost in the quarter finals and was eliminated.[1] The much-anticipated rematch was not to be.

Instead, Dobbins met Southern High, whose team featured Lionel Simmons, who would carry the nickname "the Train" or "L-Train" with him to greatness at LaSalle University, where sportswriters would name him collegiate Player of the Year four years hence. But if the Mustangs were impressed by Simmons, their game sure didn't show it.

Fulfilling Hank's goal for them, the Mustangs were unstoppable. Hank and Bo lit up the scoreboard with 27 points apiece in their 86-62 pummeling of Southern in the final. Played at Temple's McGonagle Hall in front of an overflow crowd of 5,000, televised by ESPN and all three local network affiliates, it was the culmination of a dream season for Dobbins. "There were so many people trying to see the game that many who were denied entrance stood outside peering through the windows. And it was a bitter cold night," Yank recalled.[2]

It may not have been the rematch with Franklin that everyone had sought, but the victory was no less sweet, and the Mustangs' redemption was complete. Soon they'd have to decide which college they'd be playing for next season.

Recruited heavily by John Chaney, Bo was definitely leaning toward nearby Temple University. "He [Chaney] was at all our games and [a] lot of our practices," Heat said.[3]

The school that was wooing Hank the strongest continued to be the University of Southern California, whose assistant coach, David "Spence" Spencer, continued to pop up wherever the Mustangs were playing.

In order to impress a wary Hank, who was a bit reluctant to travel so far from home, especially when top schools in the East were calling, too, Spencer devised a plan that he executed more than once. "I would go to one of his games in the afternoon, and let him know I was there and then catch a flight to Los Angeles," he explained. "When I landed, I'd go immediately to the pay phone and call Hank at home. I'd say something like, 'Well, Hank it's about 78 degrees and sunny here now, and the palms are blowing in the breeze.'"

"'Bullshit!' Hank would say. 'You aren't there. You can't be there already!'

"'Well, I am and the weather is just fine. If you don't believe me, call me back at this number, collect, and you'll see,'" Spence would reply.

"When he'd call back to an L.A. area code, I'd answer, and he knew by the 213 area code that I was in L.A.," the creative assistant coach recalled.

"During the process [of recruitment], he'd often complain about the distance from home to USC, and I'd show him a map of the U.S. and measure the distance in inches with my fingers, between Philly and L.A., and say, 'See, it's really not that far away. Only a few inches, Hank, only a few inches.'" Hank would just smile at Spence's little spin.

Spencer hoped to land not just Hank, but Bo, as well, noting that he'd been following both since the ABCD Camp at Princeton. "Neither one of them was a really good student," Spence said, "but I hoped that they would be eligible to play for us."

During the courtship of Hank and Bo, Spencer learned that Bo had some requirements. "Bo told me that wherever he went to school, he wanted his girlfriend to be there with him," Spencer said. "Since neither one [Hank or Bo] was too strong academically, I went back and said to [Head Coach] Stan [Morrison], 'Look, I don't think we can afford to be getting into this. It's gonna be too messy. He's not going to make it academically, and if we have to worry about helping his girlfriend get to L.A. somehow, finding her a job, and so forth….So we decided just to recruit Gathers.'"

During Hank and Bo's senior year at Dobbins, Spence said, "I think I made about 17 trips back there. But I was really only recruiting Hank, then. But Gathers was certainly worth recruiting, and [U]SC had an unlimited recruiting budget, and for me it was like going home."

His vigilance paid off one day. "Towards the end of their senior year I was sitting in the gym before one of their games, and they were both already out on the court," Spence recalled. "Bo came by and I said, 'Hi, Bo. How's your girlfriend?' He said, 'Oh, we broke up.'

"What did you say?"

"We broke up."

"I said, 'Obviously, then, you're not going to be bringing her wherever you go to school, are you?'

"And Bo said, 'No, we broke up.' "

Spence jumped on this new reality, asking Bo, "Would you still be interested in coming to [U]SC?"

"Well, yeah, Coach. I really never quite understood why you quit calling me," Bo told Spence, who had never explained why he'd cooled on Bo.

"OK, I'll call you when I get back to L.A. and we'll talk then," Spence told him, mindful of NCAA regulations.

"I called later that night and started talking to him, and after that talk, I started recruiting him, as well."[4]

Eventually, Spence got his boss, Morrison, to Philadelphia, and he visited with Hank and Lucille at their home in the Rosen projects. "She told me to call ahead when I got off the plane and that she would arrange to meet me outside the apartment," Morrison said. "That way, she told me, no one would give me any trouble about being in the neighborhood." Morrison, who is a towering presence, hardly looked like someone who would need any protection. But in that neighborhood he would, and he knew Lucille was right the minute he set foot in it.

"The neighborhood was awful," Morrison said. "But once you entered the apartment, everything was neat and clean and orderly inside. Lucille was a gracious and warm hostess, and we were made to feel very comfortable in her presence."[5] Now Morrison invited Hank and Bo to visit the campus.

"Hank came out first and he committed [verbally]," Spence said. "But he didn't want us to tell anybody that he'd made up his mind." After some time went by, "one day he called me in my office and asked me what I was doing for the next couple of days. I said, 'Nothing really important, why?'

"'Well, if you bring your ass back here, I'm ready to sign,'" he said, referring to the National Letter of Intent, which represents a formal commitment.

"It was pretty funny to me. Here I am, a college coach, and Hank's a high school kid telling me what to do," Spence laughed. Spence hopped a red-eye that night, eager to sign his prize recruit before he changed his mind. "Hank still didn't want anyone to know about it. He was still dealing with the pressure of staying in Philly," Spence said. "He was also very interested in Providence, and he hadn't figured out a way to tell [Rick] Pitino he wasn't coming."

Later, Spence convinced Bo, who was still unaware of Hank's decision, to visit the campus. "I had this kid named Clayton Oliviet, a 6-foot-10, red-headed kid, who'd been a high school All-American, and he was assigned to accompany Bo on his visit. We had a policy that the coach who was responsible for recruiting the visiting player would stay in the same hotel as they did during their visit so there was some security. I said to Bo, 'When you get back in tonight, come on down and knock on my door so I know you're back.' It got to be around 1 or 2 [a.m.]and still no knock on my door. I wasn't too worried, though, knowing kids, and finally went off to sleep. About 5 in the morning came a loud banging on my door. I jumped up and asked, 'Who is it?'

"'Coach, it's Bo.'

"Oh, my God, I thought, something's happened for sure.

"'Bo, what's the matter? What happened?'

"'Nothin', Coach. You told me to knock when I got back in, and I'm back in, so I'm knocking.'

"I thought right then, 'Hmm, 5 a.m., huh? I've got him,'" Spence said.

Still, Bo struggled with the decision, so Spence finally told Hank he had to tell his teammate he was going to USC. Then Spence told Bo he had to ask Hank to tell him what Spence couldn't tell him.

"'What are you talking about?' Bo asked.

"'You've just gotta get him to open up,' I told him."[6]

Bo, too, was under intense pressure from Sonny Hill to stay at home and attend Temple. "He let me know it would be like a betrayal if I left Philly to play," Bo said of Hill. "Sonny was already extremely upset with Pooh Richardson, who had decided to go to UCLA, and he [Sonny] let us all know that. When I decided to leave, he was as mad as all get out.

"I liked Spence. I respected him and liked him," Bo said. "But by the time we were through our senior year, the last place in the world I wanted to be for another four years was wherever Hank Gathers was going to be."[7] Bo, who had endured Hank's prodding, goading, and verbal battering for four years, had had quite enough of Hank Gathers.

Despite his strong misgivings about playing with Hank for another four years, and what he'd have to deal with as a result, Bo recognized that the two could coexist, if need be, and even complement each other, as they had in their final season at Dobbins. The championship season had proved that the two stars could play on the same team and even flourish.

"Both of us realized at the beginning of the season that you can't do it alone," Hank told Silary in March, after the writer remarked on their frequent flare-ups in the past. "We knew if we stayed together and played as a team, not too many teams were capable of beating us. We talked a lot of times. I'd tell Bo, 'You look for me and I'll look for you.' When you face junk defenses like we did all year, you have to work together to be effective."[8]

Bo appreciated what the two players had in common: "We were both gym rats. We were always the first in the gym and the last to leave, and that is what I respected most about Hank. We both just really enjoyed being on the court more than anything else. That set the tone for all the other players on all the teams we played on together."[9]

"They made each other better," Yank said. "After we won that title, they changed." Only a year earlier he'd had to pull the two stars apart. Recalling the scene, Yank shook his head and wondered aloud: "From fists to hugs in 12 months. When I see something like that, it makes me believe they'll spend the next four years together with no problem."[10]

But while Hank could see the possibilities in their playing together again, Bo continued to wrestle with the decision. Finally, he decided that the benefits of playing with Hank in a major college program in a top conference outweighed the numerous nagging minuses. Bo agreed to attend USC as well.

On April 24, the two Dobbins stars told the world of their intentions. At a press conference attended by both Philadelphia dailies and all three local television stations, they announced that they would be going to USC together. Also participating in the press conference were Yank; Ed Magliocco, the principal at Dobbins; and Sandy Beach, the Dobbins athletic director, as well as the Kimble and Gathers families.[11]

The reporters all knew of Bo and Hank's run-ins in the past, so Bo addressed their history head-on, saying, "We had said that if a school recruited us both, we'd only go together if it would benefit our interests as individuals When I got back [from visiting the USC campus], I looked at my priorities and then I talked to Hank. We thought alike. You could say he had a good impact on my decision. When you go that far away, it helps to have a friend to lean on."

Bo went on about how impressed he'd been with the campus, until Hank broke in, saying, "You ask me about talking him into it. After he got back, he wouldn't shut up about the place."

Yank acknowledged that he had "had no idea Bo was going anywhere but Temple. But he did such a good job of selling me, I'm sure he made the right decision. As far as Hank is concerned, I'm convinced he was determined to go there even before the season started. If they both feel strongly about the place I'm behind them 100 percent."

Another person who attended the press conference was forced to disguise his true feelings. Sonny Hill had expected to deliver Bo to Chaney at Temple and was not happy about the turn of events. Recognizing that if the pair did manage to achieve success at USC, it would reflect well on his summer league, Hill managed to put a positive spin on things. He even managed to compliment the two on how well they handled themselves at the press conference. "But the job is not done. You cannot sit back, take a deep breath, and say it's over. When you take a deep breath, somebody may be gaining on you," warned Hill, shamelessly stealing Satchel Paige's famous line.

In a reflective moment several weeks earlier, Yank had suddenly realized that he would be losing Bo and Hank to another coach. "I can't believe I'm no longer going to be coaching Hank and Bo and Derrick and Heat," he told Silary. "These three years seem like they've lasted my whole coaching career. It seems like they've been my sons forever. . . .

"It's something to think about," he whispered, looking at the floor.[12]

He'd not only brought them athletically to the place where they would always be remembered as champions; he had nurtured them academically so they could have a chance at a decent life. The rest, he knew, was up to them. Now all he could do was watch—and wait—and hope, with all his heart, that they would make it.

While Hank and Bo were on their way to USC with full scholarships, Father Dave was pondering the future of Derrick and Heat. Father Dave had unabashedly used the considerable leverage he wielded with Hank Gathers to help two players who otherwise would have been left behind. The NCAA be damned. Two of his flock were in need, and if Father Dave didn't help them, who would?

"He insisted that if [U]SC wanted Hank, they had to take Derrick and Heat as well," McNamee said.[13] Heat confirmed the story, saying, "Father Dave talked to Spence about me, and he arranged for Spence to take me out to California along with Derrick."

But Derrick and Heat had not scored well enough on the SAT's, and their grades were below the minimum acceptable to the NCAA. They couldn't qualify for admission to USC. "Spence took us out and placed us in a junior college, Taft College, up near Bakersfield," Heat said.[14]

"The plan was to have them play a year or so at JC [junior college] and to get their grades up enough to play for us at SC," Spence said. Although his classroom performance was subpar, Heat's performance on the court was Phi Beta Kappa. Those who saw him play in high school and junior college attest to his prowess without reservation. "Heat was as good as any point guard I ever saw," Bo said.[15]

Derrick, while not as flashy as Hank or Bo, was a talented player who excelled at defense while playing on a team with offense to spare. In fact, Spence was now pursuing Doug Overton, planning to reunite the Mustangs. "If it worked out, I'd have the entire Dobbins championship team with us out at [U]SC," he said.[16]

The four Philly kids left for the West Coast in the late summer of 1985. It had been a particularly traumatic summer for the city, marked by the fire bombing in May of a tenement house. Led by an ex-con, a defiant group of armed black activists calling themselves MOVE had erected a bunker on the rooftop of a house they had occupied illegally for more than four years. Responding to neighbors' complaints, the city decided the squatters had to go. The city's black mayor, Wilson Goode, decided to try negotiation first, but then police spotted a hooded man on the roof, and he taunted the police through a bullhorn and displayed firearms.

As a force of 15 police vehicles, 2 armored cars, and fire trucks assembled in front of the house, the streets were barricaded. The whirring blades of a helicopter broke an eerie silence. After lengthy negotiations with the MOVE members failed (they refused to leave until members of the group were released from prison), Goode and his advisers decided to try to force the occupants outside. A state police helicopter dropped a satchel of concussion grenades onto the second-floor rooftop bunker, and one of the grenades ignited a fire. The resulting conflagration at 6221 Osage Avenue was accompanied by gunfire coming from within. The 250 police officers at the scene used more than 7,000 rounds of ammunition as they exchanged fire with the occupants and fleeing MOVE members. When the flames were finally extinguished, 11 people were dead, including children of MOVE members, and 7 row houses had burned to the ground.[17]

These memories of their city were fresh in the minds of Hank and Bo as they boarded their plane for California. As the pilot banked the Eastern Airlines Silverliner gently to the west, they could see the Delaware River and the skyline of Philadelphia below them. They spotted the naval shipyard and Center City skyscrapers, even Billy Penn's statue. Down there too, they knew, were their families and friends in the squalid projects and all the despair and danger they represented. Ahead lay the bright sunshine and promising future of a new start in Southern California.

Hank Gathers was 18. He carried a single duffel bag, his portable radio, and the hopes and dreams of Lucille and his brothers. It was a heavy burden, but he was certain he could handle it.

CHAPTER
6

PROMISED LAND

For Hank and Bo, arriving in sunny southern California was "like landing on Mars," and the two transplants from the inner city of Philadelphia felt out of place for a while.[1]

After the obligatory visit to Disneyland and other tourist attractions, they made their way to nearby Venice Beach. There they found acres and acres of beautiful, tanned southern California girls who had the youngsters' heads swiveling—and a basketball game that was the "in thing" on the beach. If they felt a little out of place on an almost all-white California beach, they soon made themselves right at home on the court. Hank and Bo took the measure of the locals who played there and had heads swiveling in their direction when they left.[2]

At USC, among the benefits of being a highly recruited athlete was that you did not have to endure endless lines to register for classes the way all the other students did. "We were ushered through the lines and had our schedules with all the courses we wanted in about 5 minutes," Tom Lewis remembers.[3]

Hank and Bo signed up for the full academic load: philosophy, history, and even Russian were on their class schedules. As poorly prepared as the two vo-tech kids were, they needed help, and USC saw that they got it. Stan Morrison was a stickler for athletes' maintaining their academic status, and had all the players in a mandatory study hall, where they got any help they needed.[4]

Hank and Bo were warned about the neighborhood adjoining the USC campus, as it had been deteriorating for years. "We just laughed when they said that," Bo recalled. "Compared to where we came from, it looked like the suburbs."[5]

Although the two transplanted Philly kids were joined at the hip as they explored the sights in this new lily-white world, their closeness did not extend to living arrangements. At Pardee Towers, the dormitory where athletes lived, Bo made certain that he did not share a room with Hank. Hank wanted to room with Bo, but Bo could take only so much of Hank, because Hank always wanted things his way.[6]

But soon the lush, warm climate and laid-back southern California lifestyle had won two converts. Hank and Bo loved USC and everything about southern California. Still, there is a down side to everything, and, like any good salesman, Spence had accentuated the positive aspects of the USC experience. Of necessity, he had omitted the negatives, and there were two big ones: USC's basketball program was always overshadowed by UCLA's, and the arena where USC played its home games was just plain awful.

In Los Angeles, beginning in the mid-1960's, college basketball was defined by the phenomenal success of the nearby UCLA Bruins and their professorial coach, John Wooden. From 1963- to 1975, Wooden's teams captured the NCAA championship 10 times, including a streak of 7 straight—from 1966-1973.

This disciple of the game's earliest coaching legends, James Naismith and Phog Allen, owned the Los Angeles market for talent. The Wizard of Westwood's team totally dominated local press coverage in LA, eclipsing the amount of space devoted to all the other teams combined. Every school in Los Angeles that competed in Division I, no matter how much success it attained, played a distant second to Wooden's teams in terms of coverage and fan interest. The University of Southern California, best known for its hugely successful gridiron teams, which regularly turned out Heisman Trophy winners, was a victim of these circumstances.

Bob Boyd, who coached basketball at USC during that era and achieved a record that would be the envy of any other school in the nation (216 wins from 1967-1979), had resigned after waging a losing battle with the cross-town campus for talent. Although his teams occasionally beat the Bruins and secured a lofty national ranking, USC was shut out of the NCAA Tournament because only the conference champion was eligible. To win the conference championship, a team had to beat UCLA and everyone else. As talented as he was, Boyd never managed to top the Bruins and every other team in the conference, in the same year. He left after the 1979 season and was replaced by his assistant coach, Stan Morrison.

Morrison had been a member of Pete Newell's California Golden Bears squad that had won the NCAA title in 1959 and finished in second place the next year. Morrison, was a center, and he thrived under the tutelage of Newell, who would become the acknowledged expert on the play of "big men." (Newell's camps, devoted exclusively to big men, would become a requirement on the resume of any aspiring post player, and few greats would miss the opportunity to learn his secrets of the game.)

Morrison took over the Trojan program and diligently worked to overcome the disadvantages of competing with UCLA for talent on its home turf. That was a lost cause: all the decent high school players in southern California wanted to play for UCLA. The key to Morrison's success was luring top players to his program from around the country. Gradually, Morrison had USC positioned to compete in the very tough Pac-10 Conference and even displayed an ability to pry a California product or two away from his bitter foes at UCLA.

The 1984-85 season had marked the culmination of Morrison's efforts. His Trojans had captured a piece of the coveted Pac-10 crown and an NCAA bid. He then built on that success by luring one of the top recruiting classes in the country to his urban campus. Along with Bo and Hank, USC had landed Tommy Lewis from nearby Mater Dei High School in the Orange County community of Santa Ana. Lewis was a McDonald's and Parade Magazine All-American, regarded by most services as one of the top prospects in the nation. The 6-foot-6 shooting guard had been pursued by almost every major college coach in the land—Lute Olsen, Walt Hazzard, Jerry Tarkanian (an especially ardent suitor), Joe B. Hall, Billy Tubbs, Jim Boeheim, Ralph Miller, and Denny Crum, among others.[7]

After narrowing his choices to the University of Nevada–Las Vegas, Arizona, UCLA, and Southern Cal, Tommy chose Morrison's program. "Southern Cal had no negatives for me except their facility," he said. "Everything else was three times better. I never even took an official visit. I liked Morrison, who recruited me personally. He was always there, it seemed. Even at the McDonald's All-America game at SMU in Dallas, he was there to support me.

"Eventually, I decided on USC because it offered me the best opportunity to make an immediate impact. While Stan never promised me that, I saw that I'd have the opportunity there, more so than at the other, better-known programs. After I had finally committed, they told me that they had two blue-chip guys from Philly and a kid named Rich Grande on the way."[8] Grande, a California All-State performer, had led Glendale High School to a perfect 28-0 mark and was Player of the Year in his division. The Trojans also landed Jeffty Connelly, another highly sought California schoolboy (whom Morrison ultimately decided to redshirt).

The class that Spence and Morrison assembled for the Trojans was outstanding by any measure. Hank and Bo were both blue-chip prospects, but they were not nearly as well known or as highly coveted as Tommy Lewis. Lewis was the top high school star in California, and landing him was Morrison's crowning achievement. With a team built around Lewis, Kimble, and Gathers, Morrison felt certain he was poised to beat the Bruins and rival the Trojan football team in prominence. Simply put, Lewis was the kind of player who could make an average program great.

The growth in popularity of college basketball can be traced to 1979 and the classic confrontation between Larry Bird of Indiana State University and Earvin "Magic" Johnson of Michigan State. That the game's two biggest stars would go head to head in the NCAA championship game was sheer luck, considering that the tournament began with 64 seeded teams. Fans and NBC executives, alike, considered it a dream game, and the meeting of Magic and Bird bestowed upon NBC a vast audience, the second largest (after the Super Bowl) for any program aired that year. To this day, it remains the most-watched contest of any Final Four game.

The ratings bonanza instigated a bidding war for the right to air NCAA championship games. NBC had paid the NCAA $5 million for rights to televise the tournament for five years. When its agreement expired in 1982, CBS won the contract and has held it ever since, paying nearly $54 million to renew in 1988, $975.6 million for the 1991-97 contract, and $1.75 billion for the contract that ended in 2002. The current contract, which runs until 2013, gives the NCAA $6.2 billion for television and ancillary rights.[9] When all sources of revenue are counted, the Division I men's basketball tournament accounts for 90 percent of the NCAA's operating budget. Only 2 percent of that budget is spent on enforcement of NCAA rules.[10]

Network hype, alone, does not explain the growth in popularity of college basketball. While CBS was handing over increasingly enormous fees to the NCAA, cable television was bringing basketball into the nation's living rooms almost every night for five months. Only three years before Lewis, Gathers, and Kimble landed at USC, ESPN had made its bones by airing all the early games of the championship tournament. ESPN's success was followed by the decision of several regional cable sports networks to televise games of local interest. As their teams' television exposure increased, so did the pressure on college coaches to win in front of this growing audience.

Indeed, television changed the stakes for college basketball coaches, once beholden largely to their school's alumni. Now fans were everywhere, scrutinizing college programs and the coaches' decisions. Television also changed the game because of the money involved. Under the NCAA's formula for distributing to the schools the revenue it receives under its latest television contract, each tournament win is worth $780,000 to the victors' college or university.[11]

Nor are CBS's dollars the only ones raining on college basketball. Sneaker companies reward loyal coaches with lucrative "consulting" fees for insisting that their players become walking unpaid endorsers for the company's products. Appearances on television and radio shows add to the coaches' income, as do numerous local endorsement deals for car dealerships, restaurants, and the like. Colleges and universities extend extremely favorable terms to their basketball coaches if they use the campus for summer camps, and many write bonuses pegged to high attendance and winning teams into their coaches' contracts. Thus the income from outside sources and bonuses for a major college coach can, and often does, exceed his base salary.

Although all this was in its infancy in 1984-85, whether the coaches won or lost did matter, and in substantive ways. Winning had always been important, but now it had become profitable, as well. Fortunately, in college basketball, unlike football, it's not necessary to recruit 20 or more top prospects each year— for a winning team, you need only one or two. As the late Al Maguire, the former Marquette coach whose team won the NCAA Championship in 1977, once said of a team with an 8-19 record, "With one aircraft carrier you could have flip-flopped that record around."[12] The colorful analyst was making the point that just one special player could change a team's fortunes dramatically.

The coaches competed hard for Tommy Lewis's nod because he was the aircraft carrier in Maguire's prescription. And as Alexander Woolf and Armand Keteyian detail in *Raw Recruits*, it was common knowledge among the coaches that a key consideration in Lewis's decision was going to be "special benefits."

Pat Barrett, with whom Lewis lived, was both his coach and surrogate father. Barrett also dealt with the recruiters on Tommy's behalf. He acknowledged to Woolf and Keteyian that his thoughts began to stray toward self-enrichment. "I was 27, and everyone was so interested in doing things for me to get the kid. Hell, it was going to be easy," Barrett told the authors. "A college goes, 'We want the kid to come here, what do we have to do?' It's a broad question and the mind wanders. It could mean anything."[13]

How, then, did Lewis decide on USC? Barrett explained it this way: "USC was the compromise choice. We decided on the last day. Morrison did a great job. All the support systems were there."[14]

As Woolf and Keteyian reported and my own interviews confirmed, such support could mean anything from a cushy summer job to the free use of a new car. Whether Barrett, himself, profited is unknown. He had no official position on the staff but was a ubiquitous presence at USC practices and games while Tommy was there. After Lewis left the Trojans, Barrett landed at Pepperdine University with Jim Harrick, who years later would fall in a cheating probe at the University of Georgia. While he was at Pepperdine, Lewis lived in a comfortable beachfront apartment in Malibu (minimum rental rates for a tiny apartment at the time were $1,500 a month, and Tommy's digs weren't tiny), and Barrett was hired to coach the son of a prominent Pepperdine booster, according to Woolf and Keteyian.[15]

According to Jerry Tarkanian, the legendary coach at the University of Nevada at Las Vegas, Barrett wanted an assistant coaching job at UNLV in exchange for delivering Lewis. "I told him he could come in as a manager and sit in on all the practices, if he really wanted to get into coaching like he said. But to tell the truth, I'm glad we lost Tommy. I didn't want a son of a bitch like Pat Barrett around here for four years," Tarkanian told Woolf and

Keteyian, adding flatly, "Stan Morrison is a good guy, an honorable guy, but USC bought Tom Lewis."[16]

Despite repeated attempts, I was unable to get Barrett's response.[17] Morrison told the authors that USC "did nothing improper to sign Lewis," and Morrison told me that it was his constant attention to Lewis that sealed the deal, which Lewis confirmed.[18] Whatever the circumstances, Lewis, Gathers, and Kimble, along with Jeffty Connelly and Rich Grande, were in Morrison's fold and the all-embracing arms of the USC "support system."

CHAPTER 7

HELPING HANDS

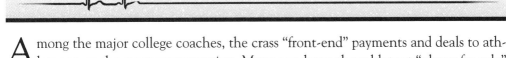

A mong the major college coaches, the crass "front-end" payments and deals to athletes cause the most consternation. Many condemn those blatant "player-for-sale"
auctions, while looking the other way at the "back-end" benefits provided by boosters
after players decide on a school.

Hank, Bo, and Tommy were in the latter group. They were accustomed to special
treatment because of their athletic abilities, and so the eager sponsors who came forward
to help them adjust to college were just another group of adults intent on rewarding the
trio's basketball prowess. They had been the beneficiaries of similar largesse for years.
Beginning in the late 1970's and early 1980's, sneaker companies would pick up the tab
to send young players far from their homes to play in tournaments on elite "travel
squads" of Amateur Athletic Union (AAU) teams. The companies showered the players with logo-laden clothes and gym bags, making the youngsters walking billboards. To
a 13-year-old, especially a 13-year-old whose parents couldn't afford fancy athletic
apparel, an expensive pair of Reeboks or Nikes was like gold. And so when recruiters
came calling during their high school years, no one was surprised when young players
took special treatment in stride.[1]

As the 2001 report by the Knight Commission on Intercollegiate Athletics noted,
"The influence of sneaker companies is now pervasive. . . . These companies have become
a part of the college recruiting process in many instances, and contribute to the special
treatment of athletes from a young age. This special treatment raises players' expectations,
shields them from the consequences of their own actions, and teaches them that the rules
applied to everyone else don't necessarily apply to them."[2]

The commission, originally formed in 1989 while Tommy, Bo, and Hank were still
in college, cited in its first report in 1991 numerous instances of college recruiters and
universities that were operating outside the bounds of legality. Shortly before the commission was formed, *Time* magazine had described the problem of corruption in college

sports as stemming from "an obsession with winning and moneymaking that is pervading the noblest ideas of both sports and education in America."[3] The commission reported that the NCAA censured, sanctioned, or put on probation 109 colleges and universities during the 1980's. Of that number, more than half were Division I schools, of which there are approximately 300.[4]

Numerous academic studies, most of which received little public attention, have produced a variety of explanations for student-athletes' willingness to break NCAA rules regarding recruitment and to commit other infractions after they enroll in college. Francis T. Cullen and Edward J. Latessa dismiss as causes "an impoverished background and. . . a lack of money while in college," adding their suspicion that "selective perceptions—focusing on certain cases but ignoring others—give life to the image of student-athletes taking payoffs to stave off economic deprivation."[5]

Indeed, Cullen and Latessa found that a "relatively small" percentage of students in their sample were involved in "any given infraction," which tended to involve amounts of money less than $20, and that "infractions involving larger sums . . . were relatively rare" (fewer than 2 percent of their respondents). However, "respondents who were highly recruited had more recruiting infractions. . . . [and] those who transferred from other colleges also had more infractions."

Further, Cullen and Latessa found that "highly recruited student-athletes appear to be more likely to commit infractions not only before, but after, entering college," perhaps because "they receive tangible benefits and suffer no consequences." The authors conclude: "It may be that these student-athletes are induced into infractions during their initial recruitment, which in essence teaches them that rule breaking is acceptable and thus places them at-risk for violations during their college careers."[6]

For the college coaches, landing a prized recruit was a high-wire act. A muddled network of advisers and friends, AAU coaches with ties to sneaker companies, and shadowy street agents would spell out a coveted player's terms and conditions for his signature on a letter of intent. Gaining that signature while staying within the letter of NCAA regulations kept the coaches nimble and wary. Success was only a player away, but disaster and disgrace were just as close if the player's recruitment, eligibility, or receipt of "improper benefits" became the subject of an NCAA investigation.

Commenting on the cars that boosters provided to his players, Tates Locke, a coach at West Point, Miami of Ohio, and Clemson in the 1960's, noted, "I stayed out of what was given. But I knew that these kids weren't buying the cars on their own."[7] The coaching fraternity had learned that to compete, you had to bend the rules a little or soon found yourself looking for another job.

Looking the other way is the coaches' preferred method of dealing with the special benefits that accrue to their players. Locke, who as far as I know is the only Division I coach to openly admit to rule breaking, reports, "It is one of the cute ways a college coach learns to stay clean. The smart ones stay away from those kind[s] of illegal transactions."[8]

 Locke's soul-baring account, *Caught in the Net* (1982), is a slim volume that exposes the inner workings of the recruitment of elite athletes at a Division I school, but it is heavy with lessons for all who coach. Locke, who was caught violating NCAA rules while at Clemson, knows precisely how the process works. "It is," he writes, "difficult to say which schools and coaches are not cheating. I am sure there are some who are not, but you start discussing the illegal recruitment of a collegiate athlete and you are talking about the degree of cheating, not the actual act of cheating."[9]

In *Caught in the Net*, Tree Rollins, a 7-foot-1 center for Locke, discusses his "deal" at Clemson, estimating that he got from his sponsor, an alumnus, "about $60,000 . . . including cars, clothing, gas money and pocket money." The talented Rollins reports that before he decided on Clemson, Florida State, Kentucky, Georgia, and Auburn all offered deals. One recruiter told him that "whatever I wanted or needed, I would get. Those were their exact words," he said.[10]

Before his retirement in 2008, Bob Knight, the winningest college basketball coach ever, the engineer of 902 victories at West Point, Indiana, and Texas Tech, said plainly, "In college basketball, if you get caught cheating, they should shoot you, because you are too dumb to be alive."[11]

How USC managed to land one of the top recruiting classes of the year remains unknown, but it did so in a hotly competitive atmosphere, and Lewis and Bo both have acknowledged that they received offers from other suitors that clearly were in violation of NCAA rules.

Los Angeles Times reporter Alan Drooz was among those who were impressed by the talented players that Morrison had signed. "There was no doubt that Morrison had managed to pull off a great coup with those kids," Drooz said.[12] Indeed, for USC basketball, the future promised a hoops version of the university's gridiron glory.

Morrison had just one problem to overcome for the 1985-86 campaign, and that was a lack of experience. The team that had captured a share of the Pac 10 title had been decimated by the graduation of four starters. Only two players were returning, forward Derrick Dowell and guard Larry Friend. Morrison hoped that the two veterans could provide the leadership and stability he needed while the newcomers adjusted to the demands of major college basketball.[13]

Meanwhile, his young players were becoming acquainted. Tommy Lewis's introduction to the two Philly kids was emblematic of the approach that Hank Gathers took to basketball and to life. "The first time I met them was a day or two before school started. Hank had an old army duffel bag and a huge radio or eight-track player under his arm. Bo had a small duffel and that was it. They had just gotten off the plane," Tom said. "After we were introduced to each other, Hank said, 'Let's go play some ball.' He wanted to prove something to me, I think."[14] More likely, Hank was testing himself, yet again. Proving himself, yet again. Of one thing Lewis was certain: "Hank wanted you to earn his respect."

After some discussion about where they could play, Grande, who was also present, suggested that they go to Glendale, his old high school, where he knew they would find an open gym. So that's where they went.

"We went at it for about two and a half hours," Tom remembers. "I suspect it was Hank's way of learning if we had the 'character'. . . to play with him. Would I play hard enough to satisfy his demands? If they [Hank and Bo] felt you hadn't earned respect, they would rip your heart out, chew it up, and spit it out at your feet."[15] Lewis passed the Hank Test with flying colors (to be precise, they were lurid purple bruises from the contact).[16]

In October, Morrison's team began preparing for the coming season in spirited practices that more often than not included fights on the practice court. "Hank loved it," Tom said. "For him it was a normal day. If there wasn't a fight, he thought it was a bad practice."[17]

Apparent to everyone on the team was the lack of a legitimate big man, and the entire team was enlisted to try to persuade Chris Monk, a high school star in the Bay Area of San Francisco, to come to USC the following year. "We all got involved in recruiting him," Tom said. "We felt with a dominant big man, and a point guard like Heat, [whom] Hank and Bo bragged about nonstop, we'd be one of the top teams in the country."

Ready or not, the Trojans soon had to play someone other than each other. After a public scrimmage at nearby Chapman College's Hutton Sports Center, the team met the Australian national team in a preseason exhibition on November 19 at the Trojans' "home court," the Los Angeles Sports Arena. The site was the other major negative about playing for USC (besides lack of local press coverage), and, indeed, a more inhospitable home would be difficult to imagine.

First, it was not on the USC campus, so few students bothered to make the trek to the games, denying the team the spirited encouragement of home court advantage that most teams enjoy. Second, the arena was a cavernous, lifeless venue where the sparse attendance caused a disquieting echo to accompany announcements and even play itself. The place was designed to hold 16,161, and the optimistic architects had built into the turnstiles an electronic counter that displayed the number of attendees to the assembled crowd. The display provided only a slow-motion accounting of the few fans who found their way into the arena, seldom more than 3,000 or 4,000.

Because so few people attended games at the arena, people in the stands could clearly hear the plays that the guards called out. Dribbling caused echoes to carom off the high ceiling and 12,000 empty seats. Instead of providing the Trojans with an enthusiastic and inspiring crowd of fellow students, the arena was a cold, sterile place with no redeeming qualities—and no home court advantage whatsoever.

UCLA's Bruins, on the other hand, enjoyed the decidedly friendly confines of Pauley Pavilion on their Westwood campus. The place was decorated in the Bruins' bright blue and gold, and draped in their numerous conference and national championship banners. (People not addicted to college sports know it as the Olympic venue where Mary Lou Retton won her All-Around Gold Medal in women's gymnastics during the 1984 Olympic Summer Games.) The student section was always full of boisterous youngsters attired in a sea of blue. A pep band blared the Bruins' fight song as pert and pretty cheerleaders whipped up the crowd.

The rabid support of the partisan crowd had more than once determined a close call, and the raucous atmosphere often unnerved visiting teams. By then in retirement, Wooden often attended Bruins' games, his trademark rolled-up program lending an almost regal air to his section of the stands.

Hank and Bo and other out-of-area recruits were oblivious to this decided disadvantage and were, of course, dismayed to find the interest in USC basketball to be less than they had expected.[18] But at the beginning of the season, the more pressing issue for Hank and Bo was not how many—or how few—fans they were playing in front of but how much playing time they were getting.

As the talented Trojans began the season, they had not yet coalesced into a true team. Morrison was struggling to balance the playing time of his freshmen with that of the veterans, and he was hoping that the younger players would learn the system and play their way into a starting role. It was a familiar scenario for teams in a "rebuilding year," which was the case with USC in 1985-86. Even so, knowledgeable observers like veteran *Los Angeles Times* writer Mal Florence agreed that USC was "enjoying a renaissance."[19] The program that had always been stuck in the middle of the pack was one player and a year, perhaps two, away from greatness.

And they were going to be great. No one doubted that Morrison had put together the makings of a Final Four team. It would just take a little time. Spence knew it, Stan knew it, the team knew it, and everyone in the Los Angeles press knew it.[20]

The Trojans began their preseason schedule on November 19 with an unsettling loss to the Australians before 3,466. The team made a number of youthful errors that Morrison, beginning his seventh season, bemoaned.[21] Lewis, the highly touted local star, had endured a nervous 1-8 night against the Aussies, and his stats typified the team's combined 37 percent shooting. Morrison used all four talented frosh, giving them a chance in a game that didn't count. Hank and Bo were in foul trouble immediately, and Rich Grande and Tommy struggled so much that Morrison observed, "We went blank out there."[22]

As the Trojans began to defend their Pac 10 co-championship, Morrison still had not figured out how to whip them into a winning team. All he knew for sure was that they were eager, feisty, and very, very young.

Baptist College was first up for the Trojans, and the team from South Carolina was thought to be an ideal opening opponent. The Charleston, South Carolina, school of 1,800 was expected to serve as cannon fodder for the Trojans, as they eased into their season three days after the debacle against the Australians. Baptist was competing in a "money game" (the college had accepted a large guarantee to make the trip) and would stop off in Austin on its way home for yet another payday against Texas.[23]

The Baptist coach, Tommy Gaither, had written a book, *Basketball: Mediocrity to Superiority in One Year*, prompting Larry Stewart of the *Los Angeles Times* to quip that Gaither probably hadn't intended it "to be a fairy tale," but that Baptist's recent performance on the court (13-15 the previous season) sure made it seem like one.[24]

Before a sparse crowd of 3,448, the visitors refused to roll over. The Buccaneers led by as many as 12 points in the first half before bowing, 81-71. What Morrison had intended as a confidence booster by serving up the Carolina cupcake very nearly became a messy embarrassment. The narrow win wasn't pretty, but it did allow Tommy and Hank to recover from their woeful start against the Australians. Lewis hit for 19 points, and Hank, who had shot a pathetic 2-9 against the visitors from Down Under, snapped back with a 5-6 performance, 11 points, and 6 rebounds.

Derrick Dowell, the veteran forward, had provided a soulful rendition of the Star-Spangled Banner to begin the night. His version lasted so long that, Morrison claimed, "He must have set an NCAA record for longest anthem."[25] Then Dowell, a native of Evansville, Indiana, promptly suspended himself for arriving late at practice the day before (Morrison had overlooked his tardiness). But Dowell had overslept and felt he should be disciplined. He spent two and a half minutes sitting on the bench. When he finally ended his self-imposed suspension, he accounted for 28 points, a career high.[26]

The small USC student rooting section, which grandiosely dubbed itself Morrison's Monsters, had tossed wadded-up newspaper on the court during Baptist's first possession. The Monsters' efforts at intimidation were noble, but they were so few in number that their effort drew attention to the thinness of their ranks—and a technical foul.[27]

Next up was Virginia Tech. The visitors arrived with a Playboy preseason All-America selection, Del Curry. A 6-foot-5 shooting guard, Curry was considered one of the four or five best guards in the nation. Because he played in the Metro Conference, he had attracted little attention in the major media markets, but he could play. He was averaging a gaudy 32.5 points thus far, and posed a significant threat to the Trojans' chances of winning their next game. So did the rest of the team: the Hokies had finished 20-9 the previous season against the likes of Louisville and Memphis State.

Living up to his reputation, Curry lit up the Trojans for 27 points—21 in the first half—as the Hokies raced to a 50-40 half-time lead and never looked back.[28] In the second half, Southern Cal concentrated on holding Curry down, so his teammates picked up the scoring slack. Forwards Bobby Beecher and Keith Colbert took over, providing the Hokies with the scoring they needed to beat the Trojans, 90-81.

On the bright side, USC had drawn to within one point of Virginia Tech in the second half, thanks to Tommy, who wound up with 19 points to accompany Derrick's 20 points, but it wasn't enough to overtake the more experienced visitors. The effort left Morrison scraping for something to say. "I'm very disappointed that we didn't win that game," he told the Los Angeles Times. "Virginia Tech played like the legitimate Top 20 team that it is."[29] Things wouldn't get any easier for Morrison. Ahead was a sea of orange at Syracuse University in the 33,000-seat Carrier Dome.

As their plane headed east for the match-up with the vaunted national powerhouse, Hank and Bo were more excited than most of their teammates because they'd be stopping in familiar territory after the game with Syracuse. USC was scheduled to meet Penn at the Palestra in Philadelphia. Hank and Bo would be coming home to play in front of their families and friends.

The duffels that they had lugged to California in September had contained barely enough clothes for a week. But a USC booster, Peter Priamos, soon took care of their sartorial needs. A childhood friend of Stan Morrison's, Priamos was a successful attorney and rabid USC basketball fan. He was among the many that the university had long used to "sponsor" its athletes, and he took seriously his role in helping the two inner-city kids from far-off Philly to adjust to their new environs.

"They didn't even have a change of underwear with them," Priamos recalled. "I took them to Miller's Outpost and bought them clothes for school."

The relationship between Priamos and the two Philly high school stars, which was established immediately upon their arrival in California, was one that would be examined closely in the years ahead. Priamos would explain matter-of-factly, with a straight face, that his relationship with the players evolved as a result of the friendship that Hank and Bo had struck up with his son Chris, who was then a junior at USC.

Priamos also noted the players' connection to his twin sons, Patrick and Peter Jr., who were teens when Hank and Bo arrived in Southern California. "They were friends with my twin boys and were always at the house playing ball with them," Peter Sr. explained.[30] Two towering black, inner-city, street-tough kids from Philly just naturally fell in with two shorter, younger, white, long-haired California rich kids. Improbable as it sounds, that was his story. And he was sticking to it—for good reason.

As an attorney, Priamos was well aware of the quirky regulations and gaping loopholes governing the conduct of boosters as outlined in the NCAA's voluminous rule book. Although they generally outlaw gifts to athletes—such as wardrobe items—they exempt such gifts when they are given to players who have a "pre-existing" relationship with the booster's family.[31] Indeed, according to the twins' older brother, Chris, Hank and Bo were friends of the Priamos family. But, Chris says Hank and Bo's relationship with the twins, then in their early teens, was his father's fiction and that the players were in fact closer to Chris, who was a junior at USC when they met.[32]

Whether Pete Priamos was acting within the rules in his relationship with Hank and Bo is of little import. Their relationship would be a lasting and important one in many ways—not the least of which was financial—throughout Hank and Bo's stay in southern California. Pete would be their friend, traveling companion, adviser, tutor, and confidant. He would provide assistance whenever they needed it, and he expected nothing in return but their company. Pete was a fan, and he became a friend to Hank and Bo. It was a genuine, caring friendship that evolved as he began to know the two kids who were clearly in over their heads. He would become as important to Hank Gathers as Father Dave had been. And, like Father Dave, Pete Priamos wanted only the best for Hank.

The Syracuse Orangemen would greet the visiting Trojans over the Thanksgiving holiday weekend. "I'm sure there will be 30,000 people there," Morrison said. "Our kids are tough. They won't let the crowd intimidate them."[33]

The crowd was the least of his worries. A team that Syracuse coach Jim Boeheim called "one of the best offensive groups I've ever had" did a job on Morrison's charges.[34] Led by Dwayne "Pearl" Washington, Rony Seikaly, Rafael Addison, and Wendell Alexis, the Orangemen trounced the Trojans, 102-68, on November 29. Syracuse took a 47-26 halftime lead and dominated the Trojans in every phase of the game. The 3-0 Orangemen were a team with national title aspirations and played like it. Bo did manage 12 points, most in garbage-time play, and displayed some of his playground moves against the Orange scrubs.

Still reeling from the pasting, Morrison confessed to Mal Florence of the *Los Angeles Times*, "It's the best team I've ever coached against." This from a coach who had faced the Bill Walton—led Bruins.[35]

Getting beaten by a talented team was still of little consolation. Southern Cal's record as the Trojans headed south to Philly was 1-2. When they got there, Tommy Lewis got Hank's personal tour of Philly.

"Hank took me with him to his home [in the Rosen projects] to meet Lucille and his brother Charles. It was an eye-opener for me," Tom said. "It was just an awful neighborhood. I'd never seen anything so bad. When we got there, Hank said to me, 'The only reason you're still alive is because you're with me. Otherwise you'd be dead by now.' I don't know if it was just another of Hank's jokes or if he was serious—but I believed him." The 6-foot-6 white California native was decidedly conspicuous in Hank's neighborhood.[36]

In the crowd for Hank and Bo's homecoming at the Palestra on December 2 were Yank, Doug Overton, Lucille, and Bo's mother, Hilda Moody. They were joined by plenty of fans from Dobbins and the neighborhood who wanted to see the two former high school stars in action.[37]

But most of action came from the Quakers of Penn and little from hometown heroes Hank and Bo. Down by 44-36 with a little more than 7 minutes remaining, the Quakers, led by 6-foot-5 guard Chris Elzey, outscored the Trojans, 27-10, down the stretch, to gain a 63-54 win. The Ivy Leaguers spoiled the homecoming by draining 16 of 17 free throws in the second half, as Southern Cal lost Derrick and Bo on fouls.[38]

Bo and Hank showed little of their former dominance as both were saddled with fouls throughout, rendering them ineffective and frustrated. "After the game, I threw a chair in the locker room and so did Hank," Tom recalled. "We were both frustrated by our poor performance."

Hank was even more upset when he found, on his return to Los Angeles, that his cherished stereo had been stolen. Hank and Bo's ground-floor apartment was near a bus stop, and someone had broken in while the team was on the road. Tom recalled that "Hank was beside himself. 'I've had it,' he screamed. I told him to go to see Morrison to complain of the loss and that I was sure he'd find a way to make up for it. Hank went over and complained to Stan about his loss of his stereo, his lack of playing time, and all the other frustrations that had been building up. A few days later, the stereo, his pride and joy that had been as big as a suitcase, was replaced by a small—about two-inch—transistor Morrison had brought from home. Hank was not happy. He told me, 'Your boy really took care of me.' But from then on Pete [Priamos] took care of it and replaced everything he'd lost."[39]

With the loss to Penn, the Trojans were 1-3. By now, Morrison was concerned that playing so many young players for so many minutes might be a mistake.[40] He decided that the experiment with his talented but youthful recruits was a failure, and the next game—against Texas at the Sports Arena on December 5—was only days away. He needed to regroup and rethink his strategy, and he had little time to do so before Pac 10 play would begin. "Stan knew it was going to take time, and he needed to see some indications that they would all be able to play together, and he wasn't seeing it at that point," Spence said of Morrison's delicate balancing act with so many huge egos.[41]

"We're in a very, very tough situation and it's not going to get any easier," Morrison told reporter Mal Florence. "Our confidence level is very low and we're up against three teams that are experienced and physical inside"—Texas, Colorado State, and Wyoming. Noting that Hank, Bo, and Tommy were among the top six in playing time, Morrison added, "We need to inject more experience in the lineup. We're going to play kids who know what to do and take the young people off the hook."

In a revealing moment of candor, Morrison said, "I've been somewhat blinded by our own recruiting success. Sometimes you think the talent is good enough and that it will find a way to get it done. That's not true at all." He announced he would be holding practices for three and a half hours on the day before each game. It would be a period of teaching, as well as coaching. "We need to back up a step to get five guys on the floor who know what they're doing and who will execute," he said.[42]

While he wasn't singling out any one of the touted newcomers by name, it was apparent to everyone that he would have to make changes. The two veteran players, Dowell and Friend, had not reacted well to the arrival of the heralded frosh. The chemistry essential to all winning teams was missing. Tom Lewis remembers "a lot of jealousy among the older guys."[43]

Morrison said that the intense physical style that Hank and the newcomers used at practice was intimidating to the older players, who were not accustomed to such an aggressive style of play.[44] But Tommy wasn't bothered by it at all.

"Hank would play so hard and come at you so hard. He would verbally tease you, and if you were weak and didn't make a stand on him, he'd just pulverize you, verbally and physically," he said. "The more respect he had for you, the more he'd want you to join his intense workouts with him. The less respect he had for you, the more he'd beat you up. He wanted you to make a stand on him, but most of the guys were too intimidated to make a stand on him. And they'd just take a pass on him. It was his way of getting the most out of them, and he respected you if you responded and tore you up if you didn't. He never stopped coming at you. It was Hank's crude way of making everyone better. But he was an intimidating force, and some of them [the veterans] couldn't handle the ferocity of his challenge."[45]

At the same time, Tom added, "Hank was also the funniest guy I'd ever been around in my life. He had a biting wit and used put-down humor and sarcasm to such effect you'd be rolling on the floor in stitches." Lewis clearly remembers Hank's library performance: "We had a study hall in Doheny Library, and [the heavily muscled] Hank would pump up his muscles and strut down the aisle in a skin-tight muscle shirt and shorts with biceps bulging. His massive thighs had veins popping out like cords. He'd stroll slowly down the aisle until every student in the room was watching him. We all thought it was hilarious to watch their reaction to this Superman act."[46]

Derrick Dowell remembers that the first time he met Hank, "I thought for sure he was high on something. Hank was always cracking jokes and bustin' on guys. I'd never been around anyone like him before. He was hilarious." Later, Dowell—or "D," as Hank always called him—would conclude, "What Hank was high on was life."[47]

No one was spared Hank's tart tongue. Not even the assistant coaches. "Hank brutalized Jerry Frietas. And the other assistant coach, grad assistant Jeff Jackson. He was always picking them apart," Tom laughed.[48]

But as much fun as he was having in college, Hank hadn't relinquished his role as head of the household, which he had taken on when his father had ceased to be a part of the Gathers' family life. From Los Angeles, he monitored Derrick's progress at Taft College, a community college near Bakersfield.[49] When Hank got some money from Pete, he would dutifully send it, by Western Union, to Lucille at home.[50] Hank "held the family together. He was the stabilizing force," Yank observed.[51]

Taking on the role of father so early gave Hank a maturity beyond his years. Yet, off the court and away from the pressures of holding the family together, he was just a big kid who loved to make people laugh.

After basketball, Hank's favorite thing was boxing. He idolized Muhammad Ali, and he was always slap-boxing with his teammates while doing his version of the Ali shuffle. As the phantom blows flew dangerously close to his startled friends' faces, Hank provided nonstop commentary in a remarkably accurate imitation of the nasal voice of Howard Cosell. "It was a riot to see and hear," Tom said. "He did it all the time and it was always funny."[52]

While Hank was creating comic relief, the Trojans had some serious matters at hand. The Longhorns of Texas rolled into Los Angeles on December 5.

When Morrison said he was going to ease the pressure on his young recruits, he hadn't been thinking of Tommy Lewis. The talented Lewis would start against Texas and lead the revamped USC lineup to an 84-62 romp over the Longhorns. Tommy accounted for 30 points while suffering from leg cramps that forced him to miss about six minutes in the second half.

But Hank and Bo saw little action as Morrison used veterans for most of the game. The coach rotated his players so that never more than two freshmen were on the court at the same time, and the Trojans held off the visitors despite John Brownlee's career-high 31 points. Most were scored in the paint, which only exacerbated Hank's frustration as he rode the bench and watched.[53]

"Stan was trying to find a mix [of players] that would work, and he didn't want to rush the kids in and have their confidence destroyed when they failed. It was tough to balance the mix of veterans and newcomers properly," Spence recalled. "I kept telling him that Hank could play. I told him, when given a chance, he'd show [Morrison] what he was made of." Meanwhile Spence was constantly reassuring Hank and Bo that they'd get their chance.[54]

That they had to be patient while the team struggled for wins did not please either one. Bo was seeing more action as the season progressed, but Hank was still playing a limited role, and he chafed at the bit. But while sitting on the bench was definitely not suited to Hank's fiery competitive nature, he was watching and learning. In that regard, he was fortunate to have come under the tutelage of Stan Morrison.

Morrison had an appreciation for Hank's raw talent and admired his burning desire. The coach also was able to show, by example, what Hank had to do to play effectively at the college level. Morrison, a big man himself, had a special understanding of the problems facing Hank, who at 6 feet 7 inches tall was short for a traditional post player and not gifted enough as an outside shooter to fill the power forward spot with any consistency. What Morrison did see in Hank, and what he would emphasize to him over and over again, was the need to use his dominating, intimidating style of play to control the boards and the area beneath the basket, in the paint.

"If I told him once, I told him a million times, 'Hank, when you go up with the ball, go up with it like it's the last thing you are ever going to do on this Earth,'" Morrison recalled years later. "I wanted to impress upon him the need to use his incredible intensity to control the game from underneath, as only a player with his fierce intensity and dominating style could." That style was Hank's greatest asset.[55]

The thundering dunks that became Hank Gathers's trademark—the intimidating hammer blows that he would rain down on defenders' heads for three seasons and more—were a product of Morrison's urging. He wanted Hank to just be Hank, and not try to be anything more. That, Morrison would tell him repeatedly, would be enough. Though it would take Hank a while to believe him, eventually he would accept, grudgingly, that he wasn't Bo or Tommy Lewis. Hank's game improved from then on.

"Hank was a great scorer. Not a great shooter but a great scorer," Morrison said. "He had more desire and determination than anyone I ever coached."[56]

The Southern California Trojans continued to play like a young team trying to find itself. They would turn back Colorado State decisively one night and lose to a young Wyoming team the next. No one, Morrison included, knew which version of the team would show up on a given night.

Derrick Dowell, the enigmatic veteran forward, would display flashes of brilliance and then disappear for long periods in a petulant funk. He could be extremely good, as he was against Colorado State on December 7, when he accounted for 13 points and 7 rebounds on the road, leading Morrison to crow, "Derrick gave us the leadership we expect from him."[57] Or he could be erratic, sulk, and get himself into early foul trouble when he thought Lewis was taking too many shots. With Derrick, like the rest of his team, Morrison just never knew what to expect.

What he got, though, was pretty much what everyone expected of this squad. Flashes of brilliance would emerge from time to time in an otherwise lackluster campaign. In those rare moments, though, observers would glimpse the future. From the outset, the play of Tommy and Bo made clear how much talent was on the team. As Hank's minutes on the floor increased and his confidence soared, even the most casual observers could see where the Trojans were headed. "Everyone recognized as the season wore on that they were going to become a good team," Alan Drooz said.[58]

In front of paltry crowds that seldom topped 4,000, the Trojans would turn back Loyola of Maryland behind a 24-point performance from Tommy and then trip and fall to Oregon State. With each game, though, the youngsters got better and mistakes became less frequent. While wins proved still elusive, they were showing signs—even in their losses—that they could compete against most teams in the conference. Blow-outs were infrequent. Nip-and-tuck battles to the buzzer were commonplace.

"I liked our tenacity," Morrison told Mal Florence after the Oregon State loss, by 4, at home, on December 22. "We played hard for 40 minutes but not with the level of maturity we will have by the end of the season." Still, he wryly noted, "It was a lousy way to start Christmas."[59]

As 1986 approached, Morrison was encouraged a bit by the team's more recent efforts, although its record stood at a ho-hum 5-5. "I saw some things to hang my hat on," he said. "We're doing some things right."[60]

On January 5 the Trojans entertained the Ducks of the University of Oregon at the Sports Forum before what Mal Florence would describe as "a cozy gathering of 2,512."

Before the game Bo, who was as impatient as Hank about his lack of playing time, had gone to the coach to ask how he could contribute more. "He said he wanted me to penetrate more, and that would open up the defenses more," Bo told Florence. Heeding his coach's advice, Bo scored a season-high 22 points and shut down Oregon's high-scoring guard Anthony Taylor, as the Trojans prevailed, 75-60. Hank had a good game too. "Hank Gathers," Florence noted, "tied a school record for field goal percentage in a game. His 7-7 from the floor equaled Jack Lovrich in 1956 and George Ratkovich in 1978."[61]

With the Trojans holding a slim 48-44 lead early in the second half, Morrison called a time-out and urged the team to get the ball inside to Hank. After play resumed, the Trojans put the Ducks away. Hank hit a short jumper, followed by a 3-point play by Derrick. Hank added two more lay-ups and then blocked an Oregon attempt at the other end. In between, he stole a pass and fired a bullet to a streaking Kimble that Bo converted. The Trojans had the game sewn up from that point on. Hank had made his statement. That only a few people saw it mattered little. He had opened the eyes of Morrison and his teammates. He may have been a bit late, but Hank Gathers had arrived.

"That game proved to Stan what I'd been telling him all along," Spence recalled. "After that he [Hank] was on his way. No one needed to be convinced Hank belonged on the floor in the Pac-10. He just got better and better."[62] Hank had held Oregon's Jerry Adams, the Pac-10's leading rebounder, to just a single carom in the second half and was an intimidator in the lane all night.

"We really opened the game up on defense and then our offense started to flow," Hank told Mal Florence after the game. In his postgame remarks Hank revealed that he had had to "perfect certain fundamentals this season, such as weak side help and boxing out on the boards."[63] Morrison's lessons were sinking in.

Hank also acknowledged the team's struggles publicly, candidly admitting that, as Florence reported, "it has taken time for the young players to blend in with the rest of the team."[64]

A loss to Washington State followed, but the Trojans played hard and took the Cougars down to the wire before losing to a team with two 7-footers, Todd Anderson and Kevin Mathia, who effectively bottled up the middle.

The always-quirky Derrick didn't start. This time, it was for superstitious reasons. After complaining of stomach flu, he had come off the bench against Oregon and accounted for 22 points. He figured, in some way only he could explain, that that was what he ought to do again for the game against Washington State. So he sat stoically on the pine for the first 3 minutes before informing Morrison it was "the right time" and racking up 18 points. Whatever works, Morrison thought, shaking his head.

After a transportation snafu that forced them to take a bus to Seattle, the Trojans took on the Huskies. The Californians lost 91-75, but Tommy told a reporter that the bus trip had nothing to do with the January 11 thumping.[65] Greg Hill of Washington simply "shot lights out," Morrison moaned about the 20-point performance of the Washington guard. The play of 7-footer Chris Welp complemented Hill's sharpshooting, and Washington was never really challenged.

Dowell was on the bench, involuntarily this time, with three fouls early in the first half, during which he managed just 2 points. Tommy, recovering from an ankle sprain, noted that the game had been very physical: "They probably thought because we were young that they could get physical and make us back off."[66] Fists and elbows flew, and technical fouls were assessed, but Hank and the other Trojans did not back off. They were beaten but would not be cowed. "I do like the way we battled," said Morrison of the otherwise unremarkable effort that left USC 6-7 for the year, to date.[67]

Spirit was never a problem for the Trojans, whose practices were often more rigorous than their games. Putting it all together on the court when it counted would be a more difficult task. But they were getting there.

Morrison, who had entered the season with the certain knowledge that it was going to be a difficult year, had to explain his team's struggles to the Los Angeles press on numerous occasions. At a loss to put his finger on what precisely was the problem, he resorted to a string of one-liners. Hoping it would satisfy the reporters, he tossed off sound bites that found their way into print and the evening news shows.

Mal Florence of the *Los Angeles Times* took note of Morrison's attempts at "gallows humor," listing his quips:

"We gave new meaning to the slogan, 'We give at the office.'"

"We put United Way out of business in the Northwest" (following the back-to-back losses to Washington State and the University of Washington).

"I was bragging recently that we were averaging only about seven turnovers a game. We made up for lost time." Morrison did remark on the progress of the three freshmen, who were getting plenty of playing time, even as he bemoaned their "degree of collective understanding."

"We talk a lot about cleverness in passing," he said. "We're about as clever as a rhinoceros dealing an ace off the bottom of a deck of cards. We might as well have had neon lights on our ears, saying, 'Here it comes.'"

Morrison's attempts at stand-up comedy ended when he revealed to Florence that he would be changing his starting lineup for the January 16 home game against the University of Arizona, which was 11-4 for the season thus far. He wouldn't tell Florence what the change was, saying only, "We have to be more productive."[68]

Morrison would turn to Hank for that increased productivity. At 1-3 in the Pac 10, there was little likelihood the Trojans could make a successful defense of their co-championship, so Morrison decided to go with the team that he would be leading the next year— and for the two seasons after that. The best use of the remaining games of the 1986 season would be to give the freshmen valuable experience. He was not unaware they might incur even more losses, but he was willing to bet the rest of the season on the future.

Hank's debut as a starter was less than spectacular. He replaced Rod Keller at center, quickly picked up two personal fouls, and found himself back on the bench. Morrison gave Rich Grande 21 key minutes at point guard, spelling senior starter Larry Friend. Dowell remained a force and had a steady 23-point game. The contest went down to the last seconds as USC displayed a ferocity and intensity that was exactly what Morrison had hoped to see. It also produced a narrow victory that no one had expected.[69]

The Sean Elliot–led Wildcats of Lute Olsen took command early and led the Trojans by as many as 13 points in the second half. But Derrick and Hank led the Trojans back into contention and took their first lead of the game at 59-57 at the 3:27 mark on a Dowell lay-up off a forced Arizona turnover. With only 26 seconds left, as USC clung to a slim 2-point lead, Elliot missed a driving lay-up that Hank altered in the lane. Anthony Cook put up a follow that spun out and was grabbed by Joe Turner of the Wildcats. He was fouled by Grande as time expired.

With no time on the game clock, the scoreboard showed USC 63-Arizona 61. With 4,587 screaming fans looking on, Turner, a 6-foot-9 sophomore from Bakersfield, stood at the free-throw line. Everything in his line of sight directly behind the basket was moving as spectators waved their shirts, their arms, and anything else they could think of.

Turner took his first shot. It banged hard off the backboard and banked in. As Mal Florence observed the next day, it was "hardly a clean shot." But it was good and narrowed the point spread to one. "After he made that first one, I became an atheist. There was no God," Morrison said.[70]

But Turner—a 75 percent free-throw shooter who was 15-20 for the season—had another chance. If he made it, they would go to overtime.

But the coach's prayers must have been heard. On the line, Turner was not exactly a picture of confidence. "I was nervous," he confessed later, "and when I banked that first free throw it didn't help me any." His second attempt clanged harmlessly off the iron.

Now Morrison was convinced that he was taking the right approach with his four highly regarded freshmen.[71] Their next game, against Arizona State at the arena two days later, confirmed his decision when the Trojans won by the more comfortable score of 81-72. Better yet, the frosh had accounted for 64 of the Trojans' points. The headline in the Los Angeles Times trumpeted the news: "FOUR FRESHMEN MAKE SWEET MUSIC IN USC VICTORY."[72]

Hank Gathers had been particularly effective in the closing minutes, as he grew more and more confident. Mal Florence told his readers, "He wound up with a career-high 20 points on 7-9 shooting and, remarkably, was 6-6 from the free-throw line, giving him a streak of 8 straight free throws. The word 'remarkably' isn't used loosely. Gathers, by his own admission, was simply an 'awful free throw shooter a few weeks ago.'"

Despite assiduous practice ("The first place Hank Gathers goes in practice is to the free throw line. I shoot about 150 a day," Hank told Florence.), he never did get to be a good free-throw shooter, although all the practice certainly improved his results. Still, his free-throw ability would become a nagging and constant frustration in a player who sought and demanded perfection in himself.

"He's like a kid with a new toy," Morrison said of Hank's efforts to improve. "But he's worked hard and he's a very coachable person."[73]

That was an understatement. Had he applied himself to Russian the way he applied himself to basketball, Hank Gathers would have been fluent by the end of his freshman year. He would never stop searching and learning to be better. He had to do it—it was the only way he knew to get where he wanted to be. And where Hank wanted to be was in the NBA. It was the ticket out of the projects for his mother and his brothers. If hard work was what it would take, then he would pay the price. Nothing was going to stop him.

Nothing.

"In two decades of coaching college basketball, I never saw a player who worked harder than Hank Gathers," Spence would say.[74]

Hank told Florence that while the win against Arizona State was satisfying, "we just became lackadaisical and stopped running. You can't do that against a team with all that quickness." Hank thought the Trojans' effort in the second half was less than stellar.[75]

As Florence noted, the win marked Morrison's 200th of his career and his 100th as the Trojans' head coach.[76] But Morrison wasn't looking back, only ahead.

However, Trojan fans got a dose of reality on January 22 with a 62-61 loss to the University of California in Berkeley. With just seconds to play in front of 6,600 in hot and hostile Harmon Gym on a Wednesday night, the Trojans worked the ball to set up a good shot. Bo, slightly off balance and under pressure from Jeff Huling, took the shot—and missed. A furious comeback effort from a 9-point deficit with less than 8 minutes remaining had fallen just short.[77]

Bo, who had harassed the Bears all night with a 9-12 game from the floor, explained the miss. "I probably should have taken it to the hole," he said. "I thought it was a last-second shot. I didn't know there were three or four seconds left." Morrison said, "I really thought we were going to win it. Even after Bo missed, I thought Hank or Derrick would grab the rebound. But it was just a hot potato."[78]

The loss dropped the Trojans to 8-8 and 3-4 in the Pac 10, despite the efforts of Derrick Dowell. The forward had contributed 17 points after being benched at the start for missing a practice. Still, it was the Trojans' third straight road loss in the conference, the tell-tale sign of a young team, but troubling nonetheless.

The see-saw fortunes of the Trojans continued as they traveled to Fayetteville, Arkansas, to meet the Razorbacks in a nonconference game that was aired on CBS. In a surprise to everyone, the Trojans handed the Razorbacks their first home loss in 11 years.

"Our team has taken on a personality that I find very, very positive. There is a tough-mindedness and greater attention to detail, and, foremost, there is a greater commitment to the team. That happens when your guys start to understand their roles, and even more importantly, how we want to play," Morrison said, as much for the benefit of the upper classmen, who were stewing over their reduced roles, as anyone else.

CHAPTER

8

TROUBLE IN PARADISE

Not everyone was as encouraged as Morrison was. The highly coveted Tommy Lewis, who before USC had played on teams that had compiled a record of 86-5, was having difficulty accepting the losses. "It's the most I've lost in four years," he said of the Trojans' 9-8 mark. "It has been hard. I guess some of the other players feel the same way."[1]

The *Orange County Register* in Santa Ana, Calif., had quoted Tommy as saying there was turmoil on the team and that some players were getting preferential treatment.[2] While he hadn't said so explicitly, it was understood that he was referring to how the coaches walked on eggshells around Derrick Dowell. (Years later, Tom revealed the real reason for his frustration: "Dowell hated me. He wouldn't pass me the ball. I would stand there wide open, waving my arms for everyone in the place to see, and he'd ignore me."[3])

Asked for his reaction to what Tommy had told the *Register*, Morrison replied, "If our team is in turmoil, given the way we've played over the last four games, I'll work very hard at substantiating turmoil."[4]

Bruised egos aside, the Trojans' wins were validating Morrison's decision. As he said, success was worth a little turmoil.

Lewis, who had enjoyed a particularly close relationship with his AAU and high school coach, Barrett, confessed years later that he was confused and angry when Morrison would "yank" him from a game. He wasn't accustomed to that kind of treatment and reacted reflexively against it.[5] But Tommy had also taken care to assure Mal Florence that he had no intention of leaving USC and that he was "going to take things as they come, one day at a time."[6]

The controversy ran its course, and the team went back to work against its cross-town rival, UCLA.

One man made, though, careful note of Lewis's remarks. He would hold on to them and use them for his own purposes. His view of the Trojans' future was decidedly different from Morrison's, and his view mattered a lot. He was the new athletic director at USC, Mike McGee.

McGee, a former Duke gridiron great who had won the coveted Outland Trophy, honoring the nation's best interior lineman, had been named to the job in July 1984. While coaching football at Duke, he had earned a reputation for no-nonsense conduct; his teams were respected for their toughness on the gridiron by the other coaches in the Atlantic Coast Conference.[7]

"When I got there [USC], the football program was on two years' probation. We were barred from television, and several assistant coaches had been dismissed," said McGee. The NCAA investigation of the football program and subsequent penalties were harsh reminders to the new AD that USC had been found in violation of recruiting policies in its pursuit of linebacker Dan Quinn. As a result, an assistant coach was fired immediately, and the NCAA and Pac-10 punished the Trojans' football program. By the beginning of the basketball year, McGee, in his short tenure at USC, had fired head football coach Ted Tollner in December and had forced the long-time baseball coach, Rod Dedeaux, into retirement. McGee was clearly charting a new course. As basketball season began, he had had a breakfast meeting with Morrison and advised him that his performance would be "under evaluation."[8]

When the Trojans headed into battle against UCLA at Pauley Pavilion on January 29, one of their Bruin foes was well known to Hank and Bo: Pooh Richardson. He and Reggie Miller led the Bruins, turning back the Trojans, 66-56.

The UCLA loss set off a string of defeats as the Trojans fell, in turn, to Washington State and the University of Washington at home. They lost to the Cougars of Washington State in overtime as the Trojans, battling a flu bug that had hit the team hard, shot a pathetic 36 percent, but still managed to extend the visitors to the limit. Gathers, who was getting more and more playing time, accounted for 14 points and 14 rebounds. Washington State coach Len Stevens singled Lewis out, saying, "Tom is going to be a great, great player. He's almost impossible to guard. He's just going to get better and better."[9]

Dowell was in another funk and had been limited to only 7 points by the Cougars, as USC fell to 3-6 in the conference. "There were tears of frustration in the locker room," Morrison reported. "I feel badly for the players."[10]

Dowell complained of the flu after that loss, but was feeling well enough to play the University of Washington two nights later, on February 8, and nearly came to blows in a heated exchange with the Huskies' Shag Williams.[11] Hank faced two future NBA stars, Detleff Schremph and Chris Welp, in that game. Both were nearly 7 feet tall, and

Hank responded to the challenge as only he could: he took them on and held his own. He was getting better and better.

Of course, Derrick Dowell had a perfectly plausible explanation for it all: "If the refs are going to just let that kind of stuff [rough interior play] go, they should forget about playing basketball and let people go out there and box." His sentiments probably resonated with Hank, who would have liked nothing better, but was smart enough to restrain himself on the court. Not Derrick. The hot-tempered Dowell was ejected, leaving the Trojans without his services. They could have used him; without him, they fell 70-64 to the Huskies. Still, Morrison could say, "I love the effort we have given the last two games. It's a winning effort, because they're winners."[12] Still, it was their third straight loss and came as they were about to go on the road to Arizona for two tough games.

Before the Washington State game, Mal Florence, who had covered USC for the *Los Angeles Times* for decades, had written of the Trojans' Philly connection. His February 6 story was accompanied by a picture of Hank and Bo, and recounted their intense recruiting by Spence. There may be even more Philly players on the way, Florence told his readers. Derrick Gathers and Darrell "Heat" Gates, who had formed the nucleus of Dobbins's city championship team the year before, were already on the West Coast, playing at Taft College, Florence reported.[13]

"It would be something if we could eventually wind up with all five starters from the Dobbins team," Spencer told Florence, sounding as if he'd only just had that thought. Florence reviewed the record that Hank and Bo had chalked up in their years at Dobbins, when they went 52-5 in their last two seasons under Yank. Contrasting that with their experience at USC thus far, Hank told Florence that their winning time would come, when they were more experienced.

And, Hank told Florence, if they add some more Philadelphia kids, so much the better. "You ought to see Darrell Gates," said Hank. "He is just as good as Pooh, or even better." To which Bo, standing nearby, added, "If he had the grades to come here, he might have been a starter."[14] *If* was the operative word, the one that would hang over Heat's career—the one that might have been—and the rest of his life.

Ever mindful that academics were important, Hank and Bo were working hard in the classroom, as well as on the court. They had to. Their eligibility depended on their grade-point average, not their scoring average.

"Hank and Bo and I all took Russian. It was great for Hank, because in Russian class, as opposed to history or English, where his poor academic preparation embarrassed him, he was on the same level as the rest of us," Tom Lewis recalled. "None of us had any experience with Russian, so we all started even, and Hank loved it."[15]

They weren't shy about using the aid that USC offered them, turning up daily at the learning center to work with the tutor, Jo Ann Gallagher. Both Hank and Bo profited from her dedication, well aware that her assistance probably meant they could achieve the academic success they needed to keep playing basketball. Hank, especially, worked hard and stayed eligible. It wasn't easy, but he did it, and he was proud of his accomplishment.

Up at Taft, Heat "just wasn't motivated then. I knew I should get up and go to class, but it was easier to sleep in. So, most of the time, I slept in," Heat said. "Nobody was really hassling me to go and making sure I did—my coach tried at first, but then even he gave up—so it was easy to just play ball and coast along out there. I was young and away from home, and studying didn't seem that important to me then. I wanted to play ball and party, and that's pretty much what I did." That was a decision he would later come to regret.[16]

Although Heat was playing with the flair and skill that drew oohs and aahs from all who saw him, he was tossing away his future in a way he'd never done with one of his no-look passes. The hope that Hank, Bo, Tommy, Spence, and Stan Morrison held— that Heat would be coming down to join them at USC—would evaporate when grades came out at the end of the semester.

The USC season was coming to an end. With only eight conference games remaining, the Trojans were only a half game out of the conference cellar.

The Pac-10 losing streak that began with the game against UCLA and continued in the contests against Washington State and the University of Washington, now included the two games against Arizona. The Trojans extended it to seven with a loss to Stanford and staggered back home to meet UCLA at the arena on February 22. They were just playing out the string. No NCAA or even National Invitation Tournament bid was waiting. There was nothing to play for now but pride. And they still had that pride.

Winless for nearly a month since they had topped Arkansas to give Morrison some false hope, the Trojans put it all together on February 22 against a season-high crowd of 9,000 that included many spectators wearing the blue and gold of UCLA. The Trojans, in control most of the way, turned back the Bruins, 79-64.

With 3:18 to play and UCLA within 7 points, Bo sank a 25-footer that was a dagger in the big bear's heart. "We had the shot clock down to a second and he just drained it," Walt Hazzard said of the pivotal bucket.[17]

Hank had an outstanding game, accounting for 18 points, while pulling down 9 rebounds. Derrick Dowell added 16 points, to break out of a slump that had lasted for five games. He didn't start, benched once more for tardiness. But Derrick, a former choirboy who harbored hopes of a singing career, had gotten the festivities underway by singing a soulful version of the national anthem. This time, he was accompanied by his sister, Cheryl, who played on the women's team for nearby Long Beach State.

When he did get into the game, he scored 16 points in 32 minutes. Not content to savor the victory, Derrick, still critical of the freshmen, said, "All year long, we've been a perimeter shooting team. Tonight we went inside and it opened things up."[18]

"We stuck to our game plan," Hank said. "In the past, we've played as individuals, if our guys had been throwing it in to the post earlier in the season, we would have been a much better team."[19] He agreed with Derrick, at least as far as the inside game was concerned. "UCLA was so conscious of our inside game today that it opened up our outside shooting," Hank said. Then he added, "A lot of tension was relieved today."[20]

As he walked off the court, Hank had pointed to his Philly friend and rival Pooh Richardson and said, "We're one up now, Pooh."[21] Actually, they were even at 1-1, but who was counting?

Two days later, the Golden Bears of Cal rolled into the arena and sucked all the joy out of the place. In yet another close game, they handed the Trojans a stunning 2-point loss, 65-63, on foul shots with no time remaining. In a draining game for USC, Derrick had picked up a third foul early in the first half and never came back into the game. Tommy had converted two free throws to tie the game with 5 seconds on the clock. Then Cal's Kevin Johnson weaved his way down court, put up a shot in the lane, and was fouled by Larry Friend. The clock read :00. Johnson had two shots. He made the first and added the second for good measure.[22] In their two meetings, no more than 3 points had separated the teams. The Bears had won both games.

Lewis with 20, Kimble with 16, and Hank with 13 had led the Trojans, as they had since Morrison decided to go with the youngsters. They'd been a factor in every game since, with one usually leading the team in scoring and another in rebounding.

At the media luncheon later that week, Morrison revealed that he'd suspended Dowell. The league's second-leading rebounder would not play again, he announced.[23] Before the Cal game, Dowell had made remarks to the press about the team's problems as he saw them and had heard from Pete Priamos after the comments appeared in print.

As Dowell recalled, "He said, 'Derrick, I need you to do something for me.'

"'What do you want me to do, Pete?' I asked him.

"'I want you to call the papers and ask them to print a retraction. Tell them you were misquoted or something. We don't need that kind of publicity,' he said.

"I told him, 'Well, Pete, it's all true. I don't know if I can do that.'

"He got pretty mad then, and I knew he was putting me in a bad place," Dowell said. "If I didn't do as he wanted, I'd be cut off. Finished. And that weekly meal card that I got [with his scholarship] wasn't enough to cut it. I knew if I didn't do what he wanted, I was in trouble. I told him I'd think about it.

"After I hung up, I called my mom back in Indiana and discussed it with her. She told me I should do whatever I felt was the right thing to do. I called Pete back and told him I wouldn't do it."

Priamos started yelling at Dowell, who finally told the booster that he had thought about retracting his remarks and "couldn't do it. It just wasn't right. That," Dowell said, "was the last I ever heard from Pete."[24]

As he had with Hank, Pete had entered Derrick Dowell's life soon after the Indiana All-State performer from Bosse High arrived in southern California. Then, early in Derrick's freshman year, his father died. He had no money for a plane ticket. "The next thing I know, along comes this guy I'd never met, and he introduces himself and asks me what I need," Derrick said.

"I told him about my dad, and within a few hours I had a round-trip ticket home in my hand. Pete took care of me after that. Whenever I needed anything, he got it. Money, clothes, TV, whatever. We used to kid about him among ourselves. After a game, we'd won, we'd all be looking in the stands for Pete so we could shake his hand."

There was something special about this booster's handshakes that made his more welcome than the others'. "Pete's handshakes were warm and firm and contained hundred-dollar bills when we played well," Derrick said. "We loved Pete's handshakes," Derrick said.[25]

The bottom line was that Derrick's comments had reflected poorly on Morrison, Pete's childhood friend, and Derrick would have to retract them or he was off the team and off the dole.

McGee, meanwhile, noted with interest the suspension of a key player as well as the earlier remarks from Tommy Lewis that had hinted at dissension. Soon the rumor mill was busy, reporting that Morrison's job was in jeopardy.[26]

The team had three road games remaining. The first was against Stanford at Palo Alto. The Cardinal crushed the Trojans 85-64.

Right after they got back from that game, McGee told Morrison the rumors were true. "He told me that I was being fired—actually, he said that I wouldn't be coming back as the coach—at a meeting in his office before we left to go up to Oregon," Morrison said. "I didn't tell the team about it and we went up there, and while we lost at Oregon, we beat Oregon State, ruining their Senior Day, in front of a packed house. But it was a bittersweet victory for me. When we came back, I told the team I'd been fired and encouraged them all to stay on at SC."[27]

He had taken the Trojans to two NCAA tournaments and had captured a share of the Pac-10 title only a year earlier. In light of that record, most people assumed that the reports of dissension had been his downfall. In reality, McGee replaced Morrison because he wanted his own person at the helm. The dissension was a convenient excuse, because otherwise, he had no reason to dismiss the Pac-10 co-championship coach who had a young team on the verge of greatness. McGee seized the first opportunity and pulled the trigger.

"I had told him at a breakfast meeting before the season that he was under evaluation," McGee said. "After the last place finish, I decided it was time to make a change.
We had a good conversation, and I offered him a chance to get into administration, and
he accepted."[28]

At the press conference to announce Morrison's removal, McGee praised his contributions to the university and claimed that the "timing was right" for Morrison to step down
as coach to assume a new position in athletic administration. Morrison told reporters he
had resigned, and that was what many printed. But the writers who followed USC knew
Morrison had been forced out and reported "speculation" that he'd actually been fired.[29]

He had been, and assistant coach David Spencer, for one, would never really get over
it. Two decades later, the man responsible for recruiting Hank and Bo remained bitter about
the "backstabbing" dismissal of Morrison and his entire staff. Spence knew better than most
that Hank, Bo, and Tommy were capable of leading USC to great things. The bitterness
that Spencer felt at the denial of that promise is still in his gut today.[30]

CHAPTER
9

THE NEW DEAL

The only remaining question for Hank, Bo, Tommy, and the other returning players lured to USC to play for Stan Morrison was: who was their new coach going to be? That they were upset was a given.

"I want to know the reason why Coach Morrison isn't with us anymore," Bo told Florence. "I have an empty feeling. He did a fine job. I was stunned when he told us he was no longer our coach." Hank was just as upset that Spence had gotten the axe, which Florence assumed (correctly), but had not yet been able to confirm.

Bo reviewed the progress the team had made and how Morrison had inspired them to keep battling to the end of a difficult season. "We were just getting used to all the other players, and now we have to get used to a new coach," Bo said.

Mal noted that Bo and Hank hadn't said that they would transfer, but, the veteran sportswriter added, "They didn't totally rule out the possibility," either. Bo and Hank said they were adopting a "wait and see attitude" and planned to form a four-player delegation to "have some input into selecting a new coach." McGee even told Florence that the players would participate in the decision.[1]

As upset as the two Philly imports were with these developments, Tommy's anger was off the scale. "We all had seen how it had come together at the end of the season. We felt with [Chris] Monk, and maybe Heat, we'd be a Top 10 team next season and now we had no coach," Tom recalled. "We all got together and talked about what had happened. At the first meeting, we all felt we wanted to stay at SC. We talked about how we'd like to see a southern California guy get the job, for a recruiting advantage in the future. Bo, Hank, Rich Grande, and I all discussed the type of coach we'd like to see hired."[2]

"Both Hank and I loved the whole California experience. We loved SC. It was like heaven for us there," Bo would say later. "We didn't want to leave."[3]

Finally, they decided to make an appointment to speak to McGee about their concerns. Naively, the four talented freshmen believed that the man who had just summarily discharged their coach would have an interest in their opinions about a new coach. "We went in there and told him of our discussions. That we felt with the right coach, we'd be very successful next season and beyond," Tom said.[4]

Bo recalls the meeting as one in which McGee displayed a marked lack of interest in what they were telling him. Tom has similar recollections, saying McGee "paid lip service to our suggestions and comments and that was it. When he asked us what we were going to do, Hank and Bo said they'd like to stay. Grande didn't respond at all. I said, based on our discussions, 'We might leave.'"

The meeting broke up with the players feeling very uneasy about what had transpired. They felt that McGee had not treated them very professionally or accorded them much respect. "He concluded by telling us, 'I can't tell you what I'm going to do,'" Tom said.[5] They could only hope that he would hire the "right guy."

"They wanted me to hire Jim Harrick from Pepperdine," McGee said. "I asked them if they'd met with him, and they said they or their representatives had. I did interview Harrick, who wanted the job, but I had my sights set on another guy and pursued him. He turned me down several times. I finally told him, 'This is too important to pass up,' and finally he accepted."[6]

The guy he did hire met none of the criteria that the players had discussed with McGee. And they had never met him—he was from Iowa, for crying out loud, and they wanted someone from California. (In fact, he had been coach at Washington State, a Pac-10 team, from 1972-1983, so he was no stranger to the conference.)

The coach who would inherit Morrison's team of opinionated, high-spirited, superbly talented, blue-chip recruits was George Raveling. Raveling, 48, had become the first black head coach in the Big Ten while at Iowa and had enjoyed success in that highly competitive conference. He was proud of his role as a racial pioneer and for good reason. As a young collegian, he had traveled to Washington, D.C., in the summer of 1963. He was there to participate in the gathering on the National Mall in front of the Lincoln Memorial that would feature a speech by the Reverend Dr. Martin Luther King, Jr.

Arriving early, Raveling volunteered to serve in some way. He was immediately enlisted to provide part of the security detail for King. When King took the podium to address the throng of thousands, as well as television viewers around the nation, Raveling accompanied him and was positioned just behind the civil rights leader as he delivered the "I Have a Dream" speech that would forever be imprinted on the national conscience.

As King completed his description of his soaring and inspiring vision for America, delivered in the classic cadences of the Baptist minister that he was, young Raveling stood riveted at his side. King stepped down from the podium, and Raveling asked if he might have a copy of his remarks. King reached into his coat jacket and withdrew the pages that held his prepared remarks (some of the most eloquent parts of the speech were, in fact, extemporaneous) and handed them to the youngster. "Here—take it," King said. Raveling did so, and he has cherished the manuscript ever since.[7]

Raveling began his coaching career with assistant jobs at his alma mater, Villanova, and at the University of Maryland, before moving to Washington State. There he had taken the Cougars to two NCAA tournaments, including their first appearance in 40 years. So he was hardly an unknown quantity when he arrived to take the helm at Southern California, which was no plum assignment because of the inevitable comparisons to UCLA.

Several other candidates, including Gary Williams at Boston College (inaccurately rumored to be at the top of McGee's list), Jim Harrick, and Bill Mulligan, were rumored to be on McGee's short list. Both Harrick and Mulligan were on the West Coast, Harrick at Pepperdine and Mulligan at UC-Irvine. But they were not, in fact, "real" candidates. Harrick was interviewed but never seriously considered; Mulligan denied any interest in the job and said he was never approached by McGee, and McGee never interviewed Williams.[8]

Mal Florence, ever the consummate reporter, noted that it might all just be a smoke screen to conceal McGee's real choice for the job. As usual, Florence was right.[9]

When McGee emerged from the smoke to announce he'd hired Raveling, the new coach quickly proved himself an equal to Morrison in one important respect: he was an accomplished public speaker and used his quick wit to win reporters over during his first appearance as the new coach. He was coming off a 20-win season at Iowa and an NCAA bid, so he could afford to brag a bit. "If we get a few teams in the Final Four, maybe they'll name the Sports Arena after me. Rav's Place, they can call it," he told them, noting that North Carolina had named its arena after Dean Smith.[10]

The reporters wanted to know if he had a timetable for turning around the USC program. "I'm too smart to answer that," Raveling said. "I'm a product of bussing. I'm smarter than the normal guy." And, no, he wasn't worried that some players might transfer—if they did, they did.

Raveling's comedy routine did not amuse his players, who were waiting to see and talk with their new leader.

What came next was totally unexpected and created such a firestorm that it eclipsed Morrison's firing and dominated the news on the Los Angeles sports pages for weeks.

Tommy Lewis was in Arizona to visit his parents when he heard that Raveling had been hired. "No phone call, no contact, nothing," Tom said. "I heard about [it] on the radio. "A week later, I'm in the gym shooting and an assistant coach, whom Raveling had brought in, came up to me and asked me, 'Are you on the varsity? If you are,' he said to me, 'I want to introduce you to these two guys.' And he indicated two recruits that had come in with him." Tommy, who, like Bo, had been named to the Pac-10 all-freshman team just days earlier, was floored that the assistant hadn't recognized him. Tommy also knew immediately that the presence of two recruits was not a good omen.

"The next week I still had not heard anything from Raveling or McGee. Nothing. I'd never even heard of the guy, but he didn't try to call or anything," Tom said. "The third week after he'd been hired, he called me. I'm thinking, great! I go to his office to meet with him for the first time. He begins by telling me, 'I'm not going to sit here and tell you all about me. If you want to know about me'—and with that he reached into his desk drawer and pulled out a file with about a hundred articles in it—'you can read these.'"

Lewis was shocked.

"Then he told me, 'I need to hear from you by Friday if you are staying or leaving.' This was on a Thursday," Lewis said. "So, on Friday, I call the office. They tell me, 'He isn't here. He is in Iowa. He's moving.' When I told them that he'd given me a deadline, they said that he'd deal with it and me next week."[11]

Hank and Bo had a similar experience with Raveling. It wasn't good. "We went in to the meeting and he sat there and talked about his program at Iowa and how he'd done there, and all during the conversation, he kept referring to me as Hank and to Hank as Bo," Bo said.

"He sat there in this big new swivel chair like Al Pacino and told us he wasn't going to review any film of our games and that everyone on the team was going to have to re-earn their position. It was obvious that, not only did he not know our names, he didn't know our games, either. And that bothered me a lot. Hank was not as upset with the meeting as I was. He wanted to give the guy the benefit of the doubt. He kept trying to talk me into staying. We went over to Pete's and talked to him about it, and later we discussed it with Spence. I told them that I thought Raveling was unprofessional and unappreciative of us. Hank was not so critical. He wanted to stay. But, mentally, I was already gone."[12]

Spence confirms Bo's recollection of that period. "They both came over to my place and were really going at it. Bo was adamant about leaving. Hank kept after him about staying and giving Raveling a chance," Spence said. "But Bo wouldn't budge. Which was very, very unusual. In all their fights and arguing, Hank almost always got his way. Not this time, though. Bo wouldn't give in to Hank on this one. He was leaving. If Hank wanted to stay, he could, but Bo told him he was gone. They went at it hammer and tong for hours, but nothing changed."[13]

Shortly after that argument, Hank, Bo, and Tommy were standing outside their

Russian class on a Wednesday afternoon when someone handed each of them a letter. "The letter said in essence, if we didn't sign the letter saying we were staying at SC by Friday, our scholarships would be revoked," Tom said.[14] (In the early 1970's, the NCAA changed its rules to allow schools to grant athletic scholarships one year at a time. Thus, they became a renewable contract and could be revoked by the coaches at any time for any reason. The NCAA likes to refer to the athletes who hold these scholarships as "student-athletes," and the organization insists that college basketball is played by amateurs.)

"Hank was devastated," Bo said. "He looked like a kid who had just lost their pet dog. We talked to Spence and to Father Dave about what was happening, and they all told us they would support whatever decision we made. I had already decided I was gone. Hank tried once more, half-heartedly, to convince me to stay, but I had made up my mind I wasn't going to play for Raveling, and that was that."

According to Bo, Hank finally, sighed and said, "'We can't break up 'The Hank and Bo Show.' If you're going, I'm going. We came together and we'll leave together.' And that was it," Bo said.[15]

Tommy was as adamant as Bo about leaving. He, too, had lost all respect for the aloof Raveling.

Not one of them signed the letter.

McGee recalls it somewhat differently: "They were given weeks to tell us, 'Are you with us or not?' A new coach has a right to know what he's working with, and that's what George was seeking. When he didn't get it, he revoked the scholarships."[16] McGee quickly informed the teammates that their scholarships would end at the end of the semester. Jeffty Connelly would join the rush out the door by the fourth-best recruiting class in the nation. Only Rich Grande remained. Raveling also inherited Derrick Dowell, who was sitting out the spring semester as a result of "fatigue from the stress of the past season." He would return in the fall, he announced.[17] The suspension by Morrison no longer applied.

Losing so many top players in one class was all but unheard of, and it raised eyebrows among coaches, had reporters' noses twitching, and ultimately roused the NCAA to send investigators to southern California. John Cherwa, then the associate sports editor at the *Los Angeles Times*, said that the transfer of Hank and Bo from USC produced some "interesting nuggets" of information, but "none of it was a headline," and Cherwa knew they couldn't get those nuggets in the paper "without a major hook," which he lacked but continued to watch for.[18]

Asked about the decisions he made as the new USC coach that resulted in the exodus of four highly coveted players, Raveling would offer only, "I wasn't going to have a bunch of 18- and 19-year-old kids telling me how to coach or who to hire."[19]

George Raveling would find little success at Southern California. His jokes would soon fall as flat as his floundering team. But the players he ran off would thrive.[20] Tommy Lewis soon landed at nearby Pepperdine University, where Harrick was only too happy to put the shooting star on the team. Jeffty Connelly found a comfortable berth at the University of Santa Clara.[21]

For Hank and Bo, the decision took a little longer. They planned to transfer together, so they had to reach an agreement. And in all their years together, they seldom found it easy to agree on anything. They checked out Pepperdine and the University of Nevada–Las Vegas (UNLV). They were less than impressed with Harrick, so Pepperdine was out.

"For some reason, Jim just didn't appear that interested in them," said Spence, who had accompanied Hank and Bo to Pepperdine. "He said he was, but he appeared distracted the entire time. When Hank asked him, 'What would you do with my game?' Harrick said quickly, 'I'd teach you to move with the ball better.' Big mistake. That proved to Hank that Harrick knew nothing about him. It was a really lousy visit and Hank let me know about it. 'What the hell are you doing to us, Spence?' he asked me. 'That guy doesn't act like he wants us at all.' Hank was right. Also, Bo didn't really want to go where Lewis was headed. So that kind of eliminated Pepperdine from the list."[22]

They also scratched all the other Pac-10 schools off their list because they'd have to sit out a year after transferring and lose a year of eligibility. That was not an option either player would consider.

Hank and Bo turned to Pete Priamos for ideas and advice. He took them out for a prime rib dinner to explore the options. Priamos vividly remembers the offer from Kentucky. "Their representative showed me a briefcase filled with $10,000 in it. 'Your boys can expect more if they come with us,' I was told." Priamos, a lawyer, never relayed that message.

"Hank, especially, was concerned about finding a place where he would be comfortable in the surroundings," Priamos said of the search. "[Hank and Bo] argued constantly about where they would go and what possibilities they had. They would have heated arguments about it."

Priamos and his son Chris accompanied them to UNLV and took them to a casino to gamble while they were in Las Vegas. Hank ran through the money Priamos had given him to play with. One result of Hank's taste of Las Vegas was his confession to Priamos, that "I can't play here. I like the gambling too much to play in that town. I'd always be broke."[23]

According to Tarkanian, he never made any offer to Bo and Hank because "I felt the team was pretty well set at that point."[24] But Bo's recollection is that UNLV definitely was interested in the pair and claimed, "I saw the briefcase."[25] Tarkanian has long maintained that no player on his teams ever took any payoffs.

By now, Hank and Bo had agreed on one important point: they both loved southern California and wanted to stay there if they could. Hank now sought advice from the man he trusted implicitly, Father Dave Hagan, and the priest eagerly agreed to help.[26]

Although Priamos and Spencer were working diligently to find a California school for Hank and Bo, few options remained. But one jumped out at Hagan right away. Father Dave had known Paul Westhead and his wife, Cassie, when Paul was coaching at La Salle University. After that stint, Paul had become head coach of the Lakers and went on to produce an NBA championship team.[27]

The owner of the Lakers then proclaimed to the world that Paul Westhead was "the greatest coach in the country"—and fired him just over a year later. Westhead then put in one unsuccessful year with the Chicago Bulls and was fired again in 1983. Despite the championship ring on his finger, he was a coach without a team.

He wanted very much to find one.

Eventually, restless, he took a job teaching at Marymount, a small women's college near his home. Westhead was a Shakespeare scholar, and he loved teaching almost as much as he loved basketball.

Almost.

He taught creative writing and a Shakespeare seminar and waited for the offer that would put him back in basketball. And waited and waited and waited. Finally, in the spring of 1985, as Hank and Bo were graduating from high school, an opening was posted at a small Jesuit university near Westhead's home. Loyola Marymount University (which had no affiliation with the women's school), hard by Los Angeles International Airport in a part of the city known as Westchester, was seeking a head basketball coach.

Westhead quickly applied. But when the phone rang at last, he learned that Jimmy Lynum, his friend and former teammate from Philadelphia, had won the job. Westhead now faced the hard reality that teaching the Bard wasn't paying the bills. He needed to coach. He needed a job. He accepted a position as head coach at Ursinus College, an obscure Division III school with an enrollment of just over 1,100, not far from Philly. The Westheads sold their house in Palos Verdes.[28]

It was summer, and the moving van was on the way. Cassie answered the ringing phone. It was Lynum, who told Paul Westhead that he'd been offered an assistant coaching job with the Philadelphia 76'ers. He told Westhead to call James Loughran, president of Loyola Marymount University, immediately, because Lynum was "going to resign that very day, and the job would be open, but that no one else would know about it," Westhead said. All Lynum asked was that Westhead give him time to hand his resignation letter to Loughran.[29]

Meanwhile, the movers were calling Cassie from a nearby pay phone to say they'd be pulling into the Westheads' driveway shortly. "I told them to go and get some coffee and lunch on me. I asked them to call me back later," she said. "I didn't want to tell them I might not need them until Paul found out if he would get the job. I had to do some fast thinking to stall them until we knew for certain what was going to happen."[30]

Lynum also informed the athletic director that he was resigning. Brian Quinn, the AD, hadn't actually started at LMU yet. He was still working as an administrator at a nearby high school. Quinn, in turn, called Loughran to tell him what was going on.

Loughran told Quinn he'd very nearly hired Westhead instead of Lynum. "Then let's try and get Westhead in and hire him," Quinn told the university president. "We need a coach now."[31]

That same afternoon, after a cursory interview that went pleasantly enough, Loughran and Quinn offered Westhead the job and he accepted. Then he called Cassie.[32]

"The movers and their huge van were in the street in front of the house," Cassie recalled. "I was stalling as best I could to keep them at bay until I heard from my husband. Finally, he called, and I told them that we weren't going to be moving after all."

Her husband had a job—and she had furniture on the street and no house to put it in.[33]

The head of the Ursinus English Department canceled the departmental tea he had planned to welcome the new creative writing professor—the one who, strange as it sounded, was also supposed to coach basketball.

Now, a year later, Cassie and Paul were living in a new house in Palos Verdes when Father Dave learned that Hank and Bo were looking for "the right circumstances" to continue playing college basketball.

Father Dave placed a call to Paul Westhead in California.

CHAPTER

10

SETTLIN' IN

God blessed Paul Westhead with Hank and Bo.
—Tommy Lewis

The call would later seem to some to have been providential, but Father Dave was simply doing what he had always done. He was spreading the word in his own inimitable fashion to help two of his flock, and maybe some others, too.

What he told Paul Westhead was that two superb basketball players were wandering around, lost in the desert. They were, fortuitously, nearby. They needed a home.

After he talked to Westhead, Father Dave reached Hank and Bo. He just might have found the place that they were looking for, he told them.

Loyola Marymount University (LMU) was, as it turned out, almost perfect. Located in southern California, where Hank and Bo wanted desperately to remain, it was a Division I school with membership in the West Coast Athletic Conference, as the West Coast Conference was known until 1990. LMU had scholarships available, and it had a former NBA coach—from Philadelphia, no less—who coached an up-tempo style that was tailor- made for their game.

When Father Dave finished extolling the merits of LMU and Westhead, Hank and Bo were eager to meet the former Lakers coach and talk with him about their situation. Pete Priamos set up the meeting through Bob Courtney, a lawyer friend, and accompanied the two players to meet Westhead, but did not join them. Priamos, now persona non grata at USC, was acting solely as driver and adviser to his two young friends.[1] Westhead greeted the young men, then turned them over to an associate for a two-hour cook's tour of the campus. Then they went back to Westhead's office in the gymnasium.

"He put in a tape of his team in action," Bo said. "He didn't say all that much, he just let the tape run. Hank and I watched the tape, and we couldn't believe what we were seeing. It was action that was so fast that we thought he had somehow sped the tape up to impress us. I remember thinking, 'He must think we're a couple of fools that don't know anything about [film] edits.'"[2]

After about five minutes, Hank, shaking his head, jumped up and pointed an accusing finger at Westhead, saying, "You made that up!"

Westhead laughed and said, "No, not at all. That's the way we play here. It's what we call the System. I think it might suit your game."[3]

"The System," he told Hank, was designed to produce a shot every five seconds.

"He got into Hank's head. Bo['s], too," Pete said of Westhead's shrewd selling of LMU.

"He knows my game," Hank told Pete. "He's a Philly guy, too." Hank was excited as Priamos drove back to Pete's Toluca Lake home.[4]

Bo was also impressed. "After the tape show and a few more minutes of discussion, I asked Westhead, 'Where do I sign?'" To Bo, the possibility of playing under Westhead and the System was "a dream come true."

After a brief talk with Pete and, later, with Spence, who earlier in his career had been an assistant coach at LMU, Bo and Hank made their decision. They called Father Dave in Philadelphia and told him what they had decided.[5]

"The Hank and Bo Show" was coming to LMU.

High atop a sun-splashed bluff, overlooking the smog-shrouded skyline of Los Angeles, LMU's modern campus is an island of green serenity far above the bustling metropolitan clamor. Stately palms bend gently in the cool ocean breeze that wafts in from nearby Marina del Rey.

Visible from afar is the spire of the main chapel of the Jesuit school. Beneath it, a verdant hillside rises with three large, whitewashed letters adorning its side and proclaiming to all that this is LMU.

It sood in stark contrast to both the crime-riddled, rundown housing projects of north Philadelphia and the gritty urban campus of the University of Southern California, where a bus-riding burglar could break into a student's dorm room. LMU's campus has such a peaceful, calm air about it that the writer Maryann Hudson would observe, "It felt, standing on the bluff behind the chapel—the sparkling green Pacific in the distance—almost like going to church outdoors."[6]

On this campus of fewer than 4,000 students, Hank Gathers and Bo Kimble would continue their education and their quest for a berth in the NBA. Now they would become the disciples of Paul Westhead, who was spreading a new message, his gospel, to the world:

Scoring 200 points a game is a hell of a lot of fun.

Hank's route to the NBA and Westhead's road to redemption would be the same seldom-used path. Stretching from Oregon to San Diego, the West Coast Conference was one of the many mid-major conferences that would send their conference champion to the NCAA Tournament, where that team would usually serve as cannon fodder for the higher-seeded major powers.

With the exception of the University of San Francisco during the Bill Russell era, the conference teams usually attracted little notice from national pollsters. Their games (played three time zones away from the East Coast media markets) were aired on cable—if they were aired at all—around midnight Eastern Standard Time (EST), when potential recruits were in bed and writers' deadlines had passed. Not a great way to attract attention.

In one respect, it was unique. It was comprised entirely of small, private, church-affiliated schools whose academic reputations overshadowed their athletic prowess. Although schools in the conference awarded athletic scholarships, as a group they were downright old-fashioned, emphasizing the sport of basketball, not its ability to generate revenue for the schools or attention from fans and advertisers. Among all the Division I basketball conferences, it was always at or near the bottom in attendance figures.[7] Loyola Marymount University may have been just a stone's throw from the campus of perennial powerhouse UCLA, but it was a world apart in the importance of the role of basketball on campus.

In most years, only one school from the conference would be invited to participate in the NCAA Tournament (the conference champion received an automatic berth, but the NCAA could invite other teams, too); in some years, another would sneak in, but that was the exception. Usually, an invitation to the less prestigious National Invitation Tournament was the result of a good season that fell short of a conference championship.

Gaining admission to the Dance, however, did not mean a mid-major team would be boogying on a level dance floor. These teams got low seeds, reflecting the poor esteem in which their conference generally was held. So instead of having a fair shot at working its way toward the Sweet Sixteen, a mid-major team usually found itself in a first-round match-up with a major power and en route to an early exit.

Just getting to the NCAA Tournament was the goal for teams in the West Coast Conference. They never even dared to think about making the Final Four, much less winning the championship. Such dreams were not even a consideration—at least not until Westhead, Gathers, and Kimble joined forces. For those three, the Dance was the ultimate destination; and that they had chosen a difficult path to get there didn't faze them at all.

When he was hired the year before, Westhead had inherited an LMU team that was good enough to rate a berth at the National Invitation Tournament in his first season. He had lost a number of those veteran players to graduation, but when Bo and Hank announced on May 9, 1986, that they would be attending LMU, Westhead was getting two players with the talent that he needed to see his system run at its best.

Alas, he would be forced to wait a season before they would be eligible to compete for the Lions of LMU. Under NCAA regulations, the two transfer students were required to sit out one season before they'd be eligible to play. They could practice with the team, but they could not play in any games.

The press had followed the story of Hank and Bo's search for a new basketball home with great interest. While Hank, Bo, and their advisers were figuring out where the players should enroll in the fall, a spate of articles in the *Los Angeles Times* had rehashed the whole story of their departure from USC. The series recounted the controversial moves that Raveling and McGee had made with regard to the freshmen players and the demands that the players meet a deadline for deciding their athletic future. Included was the full text of the infamous letter from Raveling, a self-serving missive informing the players of his intention to recommend the revocation of their scholarships because they had failed to meet his deadline. While the stories offered titillating glimpses of USC's dirty laundry, they provided little new information.[8] Some coverage, particularly one article by Scott Ostler in the *Los Angeles Times* on March 26, gave readers a dim view of four freshmen who were making "demands" of an athletic director. Written in a biting yet somewhat whimsical style, it painted the players in a decidedly poor light. That was an exception.[9]

Although the stories may have been a continuing embarrassment to Raveling, they had little news value after a few weeks, especially after Hank and Bo's announcement that they would be enrolling at LMU, which got wide coverage in the *Los Angeles Times* and the *Los Angeles Daily News*. After that, coverage slowed to a trickle. But a trickle of coverage was more than LMU basketball usually got.

Alan Drooz was the *Los Angeles Times* writer assigned to cover LMU basketball. "At the time we did not give LMU a lot of space in the sports section. UCLA was the main focus, of course, and SC got space, but the other area schools like LMU didn't get that much," he said. "What LMU had going for it, though, was Paul Westhead. He was a former Lakers coach and was well known in L.A. for having been fired after an infamous squabble with his star player, Magic Johnson."[10]

After the press conference, Drooz noted that LMU might be getting a little more ink in the future and recounted the Hagan connection that had led the two former USC players to Westhead and Loyola Marymount. Bo told the reporter truthfully, "It was kind of hard to make a decision, but when we talked to Father Dave, he was very high on Loyola and Coach Westhead and that made the difference." Bo couldn't resist the opportunity to get in one final dig about Raveling: "We found in one meeting with Westhead the feeling that we had been looking for and hadn't been able to find in two or three meetings with Raveling."[11]

In two days, LMU got more coverage in the *Los Angeles Times* than it usually got in two weeks. The *Times* had run an advance story by Randy Harvey on the day of the announcement, and it included the information that Hank and Bo were to "meet the admissions director" at LMU that same day.[12]

In a final but revealing examination of what had led Hank and Bo to LMU, Harvey raised the question that many people were, no doubt, pondering at the time: What is "the responsibility of universities toward student-athletes who have been heavily recruited and the responsibility of those student-athletes toward their universities and the coaches who recruited them?" Harvey's probing question then (and now) produced no satisfactory answer.

Instead, what he found was a classic "failure to communicate," which, he concluded, accounted for Raveling's decided coolness toward Hank and Bo. Noting that Raveling enjoyed a reputation as a great communicator, Harvey reported that the new coach, after six weeks on the job, said he was still confused about what had happened: "For the life of me, I can't figure out where the problem was."

Harvey's lengthy recap (3,500 words) was an even-handed recitation of events that gave Raveling the last word: "I think they are good kids that got bad advice along the way. I'm confused by it all. I think they're confused. I feel sorry for them. I feel sorry for all of us."[13] His felicitous feelings duly recorded, Raveling and everyone else moved on.

Confident that their future was secure and that it promised everything they could possibly have hoped for, Hank and Bo headed back to Philly for the summer. They were welcomed by Doug Overton and other old friends from Dobbins and the neighborhood. Doug recalls the skeptical reception they got from the neighborhood kids:

"The kids on the streets and in the playgrounds would go up to them and say, 'Yo, like, wassup wit' you two? Where you gonna be playin' at now?' And Hank and Bo would say, 'LMU.' The kids would go, 'EL-EM-YEW? Wha's dat? Where dat at? You mean LSU?' And Hank would have to explain to them what and where LMU was. It happened all the time that summer, and Hank would get mad after explaining it so many times and getting looks from the kids on the street that said, in effect, 'Too bad you couldn't get into a real school.'

"He would finally just tell the ones that said they had never heard of the place: 'You will! Me and Bo are going to put that school on the map. You'll see. Everybody will know about LMU before we are through. Everybody!'"[14] It would take a year, but Hank's angry, fearless prediction would come true.

In late July, Stan Morrison accepted a position as athletic director at the University of California at Santa Barbara. At the end of the school year, Taft College disbanded its basketball program. Spence scurried to find a spot for Derrick Gathers and Heat. The dream of seeing all the Dobbins starters reunited at USC had dissolved with Spence's firing.

While playing for Rolland Todd at Taft, the team had gone to UNLV to practice, and

Jerry Tarkanian had gotten to see Heat in action. "Tarkanian wanted me," Heat said. "He told me he wanted me to come up there and play for him. He told me, 'There will be a spot for you.' But Spence had already told me that they had a jersey ready for me at SC, so I was planning on going on down there. Then he got fired and that was the end of that."[15]

Spence was able to place Derrick and Heat at Santa Monica Junior College, which was near LMU. Neither sophomore, especially Heat, had great grades, but they were good enough for admission. They would play there the following season.

After spending the summer at home in Philly, the foursome went back to California as September approached. Heat and Derrick would be playing basketball come the winter, while Hank and Bo could only practice with their new teammates at LMU. They were joined in that misery by another recent transfer.

Corey Gaines had been at UCLA for three seasons, and his playing time had diminished as the years passed. With Pooh Richardson seeing more and more time in the point guard spot for Walt Hazzard's team, Corey was seeing most of the game from the bench, and he didn't like the view. A Los Angeles native and graduate of St. Bernard's High School, Corey had been a McDonald's All-American. He had been recruited heavily but signed with UCLA, where Larry Farmer was then the coach and Cory's roommate was Reggie Miller.

"After my freshman season, Farmer left and Walt Hazzard came in as the coach. I had played for him on the West Side Lakers, an AAU team. I remember thinking at the time that I couldn't be any luckier—Coach Hazzard knows me and knows my game. He liked the street- ball style I played. I was certain he'd let me play my game," Corey said.[16]

His cheery outlook dimmed somewhat when he learned after his sophomore season that Hazzard's prize recruit that year was another point guard. He was from Philadelphia, and he had a funny name—Pooh. And six or seven games into Corey's sophomore season, Pooh Richardson, the former Franklin High standout, started to get the majority of the playing time, with Corey relegated to a reserve role. He was not accustomed to sitting.

"Pooh was good and I liked him a lot. But I wanted to play and I was very unhappy. I thought about leaving a lot," Corey said. "Reggie wanted me to stay. He kept telling me, 'Don't go. Don't go.' He told me to stick it out. But I was really miserable and it showed."

Still, he stayed another frustrating year. "I worked harder in practice than I ever had in my whole life, and still I wasn't playing," he said. "It was during that time that Hank and Bo, who were over at USC, came to visit Pooh. I met Hank that year and we got to know each other and hung out together. Pooh told Hank I was really fast. When we all played some pick-up ball together, Hank and I just clicked. We all became real friendly through school and Pooh."

And Pooh was clearly the player Hazzard was going to use, and that was not good for

Corey. He had only a single year of eligibility remaining and didn't want to spend it on the bench. He knew he could play; he just needed a chance.

"That was just about the time when Hank and Bo decided to go to LMU," Corey said. "My dad was a sheriff's officer in the [San Fernando] Valley and I talked to him about my situation. He told me if I wanted to go to LMU, that was no problem. My dad said, 'If you're not happy, then you have to leave.' He told me I had two choices: I could stay and sulk on the bench or I could decide to do something about it. My dad said, 'The choice is yours. You can be a whiner or a doer.'" And, Corey added, "An assistant coach I respected had told me recently, 'You can play and you're fast. You can go to the NBA. Maybe you should think about leaving.'" Corey got the message. He would take the chance.

Corey decided to go talk with Westhead. "He told me, 'I saw you play when you were younger, and you don't look to me, recently, like you're having any fun now. It doesn't look like you are enjoying the game anymore. I can't promise you anything except this: If you come here, you'll work hard in practice, but you will definitely have fun again. I can promise you that,'" Corey said.

Corey had heard all he needed to hear. He would be joining Hank and Bo at LMU. And so, in the course of just a few weeks, Paul Westhead managed to acquire three bona fide blue-chip players for his unacclaimed school. For now, LMU would remain, as it had for ages, in the shadow of UCLA and USC. In a year, Westhead figured, the Lions would be emerging from those long shadows with a burst of brilliant energy, the likes of which Los Angeles had never seen. Then, Westhead knew, no one would be able to ignore them. After all, it's hard to ignore a speeding comet.

CHAPTER
11
RARIN' TO GO

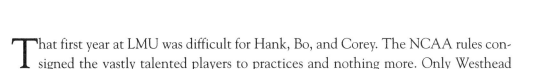

That first year at LMU was difficult for Hank, Bo, and Corey. The NCAA rules con-signed the vastly talented players to practices and nothing more. Only Westhead and his staff would see their tremendous talent and pent-up energy.

"The practices were unbelievable," Bruce Woods, one of Westhead's assistants, recalled. "Hank and Bo and Corey would just tear up the starting team. They would pound them into the floor. It got so bad that Paul had to stop playing them together against the eligible players because they were all losing their confidence, and it showed in the games."[1]

With no games to play and their practices curtailed lest they destroy what was left of the starters' confidence, the three began playing against each other at night. "Sometimes it would be midnight, and we were in there just ballin' like on the street back home," Corey said. "We played with just one light on in the corner of the gym. It became contagious later, and others would join us in there."[2]

The season seemed interminable to the impatient threesome, and Corey often took Hank and Bo home with him. "My mom would cook for them," he said. "She was like a second mother to them. She was always fussing over them. Hank would always be kidding around with her. Hank loved my mom and she loved him."

The three sophomores also went out on the town together. "I had a Datsun 280Z and it was a little two-seater. So every time we'd get ready to go somewhere, the two of them would start arguing over who had to sit in the back. They would go at it like two little 3-year-olds. It was hilarious to me but not to them. They were serious," Corey recalled. "They were like two brothers. It was tough love between those two, and I was always having to mediate."[3]

As with most of their arguments, the 6-foot-4 Bo would inevitably back down and end up scrunched down in the back with his knees up to his chin while Hank sat regally in front, smiling, sunglasses on, his arm resting casually on the window. With his favorite singer, Luther Vandross, blaring out of the speakers, Hank was sure that he was pretty damn cool. Or, more precisely, in West Coast parlance of the day, bitchin', a term that Corey tried, with little success, to explain to the guys from Philly.

Hank and Bo were not at LMU long when Brian Quinn learned that the NCAA might be interested in talking to him about the circumstances of their transfer.

In Indianapolis, Ind., at the headquarters of the monolithic money machine that rules college sports, the press coverage that had attended Hank and Bo's recent activities had somehow stirred the bureaucrats into action. Normally, the arbiters of conduct, ensconced in their comfortable offices, earning very comfortable salaries, were occupied with their seemingly eternal quest to nail Jerry Tarkanian for whatever sin they could dig up. Although that effort took up a large part of the time and attention of the NCAA's enforcement arm, someone had noticed that Hank and Bo had transferred from USC to LMU. That person didn't know anything about it but thought that it looked a bit strange. The NCAA then dispatched investigators to southern California to see if anything untoward was going on at LMU.

The body that is the sole regulator of activity in its member institutions carries a big stick. It writes the regulations and the rules, and it enforces them. It holds absolute power of enforcement, and any noncompliance, should the NCAA discover it, can bring serious sanctions and penalties. It is not possible to appeal its decrees and findings. If the NCAA were a sovereign state (and some working there believe that it is), it would more closely resemble Stalinist-era– Russia than the United States.

The NCAA investigators arrived in Santa Monica to meet with Heat and Derrick Gathers.

"They asked us a lot of questions about money. They wanted to know how two poor kids from Philly could afford to live out here—how we could afford plane tickets and stuff?" said Heat. "We knew that they were really looking at Hank and Bo for sure and not really at us. But we figured we better not say anything about Pete [Priamos] because that could get them in trouble. So we told them that we were getting aid of that kind from Father Dave. That he was supporting us through some foundation or something. It was really Pete, but they must have believed us because they didn't come back."[4]

For Brian Quinn, who until recently had been breaking up spitball fights and counseling truant 15-year-olds, any investigation by the NCAA was very troubling. The rule book was dense and complex, and he hadn't begun to master its nuances. Quinn had been a star athlete at LMU. He was a member of its baseball and basketball teams in the early 60's, and had spent most of his career since in administrative posts in secondary education. With considerable administrative experience, albeit at the high school level,

Quinn had taken the job of administering a collegiate athletic program only a year earlier and was ill prepared for any serious probe. The whole idea made the quiet, scholarly looking Quinn uneasy.

But after the NCAA's team questioned Heat and Derrick, examined Chris Priamos's bank records, and spent some time at LMU, its members retreated to the comforts of Indianapolis, Ind.[5] Nothing amiss had turned up in its cursory examination. For the moment, at least, Quinn was greatly relieved. He could get back to the job he'd been hired to do. And he quickly learned that it wasn't going to be easy.

The outgoing coach, Ed Goorjian, had bequeathed Westhead some good players. Keith Smith and Forrest McKenzie were both outstanding performers who would go on to the NBA. In Westhead's first season at LMU, he had taken the Lions to the National Invitation Tournament. It wasn't the NCAA bid that all schools covet, but for LMU it was a big step. The Lions had defeated in-state power UC-Berkeley and then had fallen to the University of Wyoming in the National Invitational Tournament (NIT).

Despite the Lions' recent success, fan and student interest was way down. Since his hiring the year before, Quinn had wanted to instill in the campus some enthusiasm about its sports program, and now he tackled the problem in earnest. "I decided to start a student fan club to support the basketball team. I circulated flyers all over the campus to generate interest," he said. "Seven kids showed up at the organizational meeting. Seven!

"At the first game that season there were 30 students in the section reserved for them. The gymnasium held more than 4,000, and we couldn't get more than 30 kids to walk over from their dorms to watch a game. It was pretty bad."[6]

This was Westhead's second season, and the team was struggling. It would continue to do so throughout the year. Sparked by juniors Mike Yoest and Mark Armstrong, the Lions used Westhead's fast-paced style. They scored often enough, but they lacked the depth and talent to improve their record.

Early in the season, Alan Drooz had told *Los Angeles Times* readers about the team's prospects. He noted that one problem was defining the personality of the team, and that was partly attributable to the peculiarities of the situation: "There is a whole other team waiting in the wings, some of whom look like the best players in practice," and he named Bo, Hank, and Corey. Drooz also pointed out that in a recent intra-squad game, "Kimble and Gathers scored 46 and 38 points and Gaines added 24." Drooz concluded that LMU's future was going to be very interesting.[7]

When the long 1986-87 season was finally over, LMU had posted a losing mark of 12-16 that landed the Lions squarely in the cellar of the West Coast Athletic Conference. The team had started strong. In mid-January, the Lions were 9-6, but then freshman Jeff Fryer, who was averaging about 8 points but improving with each game, went down with a leg injury, and the Lions dropped eight straight games. Still, they managed to finish strong, winning two of their last three.

Westhead left on a recruiting trip immediately afterward. He told Drooz that he hadn't spent a lot of time reflecting on the season. "I've tried to put it aside and think about the future," Westhead said, displaying the wisdom that comes with scholarship—and the knowledge that Hank, Bo, and Corey were about to become eligible.[8]

Since its founding in 1540 by Ignatius of Loyola, the Society of Jesus, as the Jesuits are formally known, has been recognized and admired by many as an order of fine teachers. The order was also known for producing fiercely independent priests who had driven more than one pope to the Sistine Chapel to pray for patience and several other popes to seek their banishment, ex-communication, and dissolution.

Defiantly ignoring—and surviving— the directives, decrees, and papal bulls of the Holy See, the Jesuits survived all such efforts and pursued their role as educators with barely a backward glance toward the Eternal City. They were far too busy doing God's work as they saw it. If that view conflicted with that of the Vatican, as it often did, so be it.

The order operated a number of prestigious institutions of higher learning in the United States, with universities in Washington, D.C.; Chicago; Baltimore; New Orleans; and Los Angeles, among other major urban centers. The education they provided was acknowledged to be of the highest quality. The achievements of their former students would rival those of any Ivy League school's alumni, and the Jesuit schools' financial health reflected the gratitude of their graduates.

LMU enjoyed a large endowment fund and strong response to every capital-building appeal. The Westchester campus was modern, clean, efficient, and crime free. The small student body and the intimate size of the campus made the university a close-knit community, giving it a hometown feeling that was absent at the mega schools like USC and UCLA.

Loyola Marymount University was the result of a merger of two small schools. The all-female Marymount College, then in financial straits, was folded into Loyola University in the late 1960's. The combined school was never large. It maintained an enrollment of 4,000-4,500 students, including many commuters.

At one time in its history, Loyola had fielded a successful football team that had even yielded a pro, Don Klosterman, who became a well-regarded player for the Los Angeles Rams. But Loyola was too small, and a football program too expensive, to justify the cost, and the university had abandoned its gridiron program in the 1950's.

The school consistently turned out stellar baseball teams and sent many stars to the professional ranks. Brian Quinn, who had played on Loyola's last NCAA basketball team before Westhead's arrival, had also been a standout performer on the diamond. But Loyola's academic reputation largely overshadowed the reputation of its sports teams. That meant that in the major media market of Los Angeles, Loyola—and later LMU—attracted little notice from sportswriters. If Wooden's UCLA basketball dynasty didn't eat up all the column inches allotted for college sports, what remained belonged to coverage of USC's top-notch football squads.

Those who paid attention to such things were well aware that Pete Newell, among others, had attended Loyola. Newell had been a Lions star before going on to a highly successful coaching career, capped by an NCAA basketball title for Cal several decades earlier. Now he would return to the campus each summer to conduct his nationally famous Big Man Camp.

Since the campus was near both LAX and the major Los Angeles sports venues, visiting professional teams often used the LMU gymnasium for practices when they were in Los Angeles. It was not uncommon to see NBA stars on campus as they worked out, in preparation for games against the Lakers and Clippers.[9]

The 4,100 seat gymnasium had been built just before the 1984 Olympic Games, which were held in Los Angeles, and had hosted the weight-lifting competition. The large gray facility was accented in blue across the top of its facade, and it was framed by silo-like turrets at each end. Construction of the building was eagerly financed by a large pledge from a wealthy real estate developer and Loyola graduate who loved the school and its athletes. He had eagerly stepped forward with a large pledge to fund construction. All he asked in return was that the facility be named for his father, Albert Gersten Sr., who had died in 1980. The sign unveiled at the dedication in 1981 read, simply, ALBERT GERSTEN PAVILION.

Albert Gersten, Jr. was a 1969 graduate of Beverly Hills High who then went on to the University of Arizona, where he was a very poor student. "I told my father I wasn't interested in school that much," Al said. "He told me if I wanted to go into business with him, I had to get a college degree." Although his father was Jewish, his mother was Irish Catholic, and young Al ended up at Loyola through his father's connections. He managed to graduate, and the Jesuits managed to influence him.

"I was a political science major, and one of my professors was Bill Fitzgerald, who had been an avid supporter of Bobby Kennedy. [Fitzgerald] took me under his wing and taught me about politics," Al said. "While at Loyola, I worked with him in Watts in a program that we got college credit for—while helping to rebuild Watts after the devastation caused by the 1964 riots. At Loyola, I was inculcated about community service. My experiences with Mexicans and blacks would result in helping me a great deal. I held no prejudices."[10]

Al joined his father's construction business after college and continued his political activities on behalf of the Democratic Party, becoming affiliated with budding California pols Henry Waxman, Howard Berman, and Mel Levine.[11] Gersten benefited from California's surging real estate market of the 1970's and 1980's, building a hugely successful real estate development company. His holdings grew to include restaurants, fast-food franchises, and mortgage companies, and he never forgot his friends at Loyola. Among the summertime employees of one of the mortgage companies was Paul Westhead. "We weren't paying him much at LMU," Gersten said.

Gersten's spectacular business accomplishments would have made his father proud, but the senior Gersten might have looked askance at his son's personal life. His first marriage, to the former Marilyn Mack, lasted 16 years and produced two children, before ending in a divorce. The two remained friends, however, and raised their children together. His second marriage was to self-proclaimed super model Janice Dickinson, who was not, well, publicity shy. "She would later tell Sylvester Stallone she was having his baby, and it wasn't his baby," Al said. "But she was sleeping with almost everyone else and later wrote a book telling the world about it."[12] His marriage to Janice didn't last long. He then married Christine Cushman, whom Al declares to be not only a graduate of Miss Porter's Academy but a classically trained painter and "a wonderful woman." They have twins.

Gersten fils was not only a benefactor of Loyola Marymount University but also an avid fan of its athletic teams. He believed firmly that sports could—and would— bring students to the university, and as a member of its board of regents, he pushed the school to emphasize its basketball program. "The environment that Westhead created at LMU was a positive one," Gersten said. Westhead was "strong on academics" and also produced winning teams. And winning teams inevitably produced fans who would fill the Albert Gersten Pavilion.[13]

With the possible exception of Paul Westhead, no one was happier than Al Gersten when Hank Gathers, Bo Kimble, and Corey Gaines arrived at LMU. Gersten was not yet 40 then, handsome, fit, trim, wealthy, and powerful. His circle of friends included not only political leaders but Hollywood stars and business luminaries. No one who knew him would have been surprised to learn that he quickly became fast friends with Hank Gathers and Bo Kimble. They were winners— and Al Gersten loved winning.

Al Gersten had everything a man could want—everything, that is, but a winning basketball team to fill Albert Gersten Pavilion to the rafters. It had filled few seats for most of the basketball games played there since its opening five years earlier. Now, in the fall of 1987, that was about to change. The waiting was over. The curtain was about to go up at Gersten Pavilion for "The Hank and Bo Show." Even by Hollywood standards, it would be a helluva run.

CHAPTER

12

Runnin' The System

Paul Westhead's coaching style reflected his impressive academic background. He was a calm, cool presence on the sidelines. You would see no wild gestures and antics from Westhead's side of the court. He was a firm believer in positive reinforcement. He had not one ounce of profane temper tantrum in his entire body. His tall, angular frame stayed lean through exercise—he was an avid runner who believed in physical and mental fitness, and practiced what he preached.

He had an unshakable, almost messianic, belief in the system that he'd developed over the years and brought with him to LMU. In its simplest form the System, as it was known, would use a full-court pressure defense to create offensive opportunities. On the offensive end it was designed to produce a shot opportunity within 4 or 5 seconds after an opponent made a basket. In the era of 45-second shot clocks, ball control, and set defenses, his was a lonely voice amid the ubiquitous zone defenses and multiple-pass set offenses.

According to his long-time friend, (Ohio State University's women's basketball coach) Jim Foster, "Westhead's idea of a perfect game was one in which his team would score 200 points. In one game as a professional coach, his team was trailing at the half and the other team had scored 110 points. His assistant, Jimmy Boyle, walking to the locker room with Westhead, said, 'This is just awful. My poor grandchildren are going to read about this tomorrow; it's so embarrassing.' Westhead looked at him and said, 'Jim, we've got them right where we want them.'

"The point he was making was that the System forces other teams to play your style, one they aren't used to and one that they are not well conditioned enough to sustain. Eventually, the System would wear them out, and you, being better conditioned for the frantic pace, would win."[1]

Many mistakenly believe that Westhead's System was nothing more than playground ball on fast-forward. To the unpracticed eye it would appear that way, and Westhead would be criticized for lacking any "real" coaching ability. But in reality, the System was a very clearly defined method of producing points at an unprecedented rate, and most, if not all, opponents couldn't match it. It also removed any advantages brought to the court by an opposing team with superior size. The furious pace would eventually catch up with the bigger men. "We called it TMF Time," said guard Enoch Simmons of the moment when the big men hit the wall of temporary muscle fatigue.[2]

Westhead hardly ignored defense, as his critics would claim; rather, it was an integral part of the System. The harassing, full-court pressure tempted the opposition to take forced shots, risky shots, low-percentage shots. These shots, by their very nature, would often fail. The resulting rebounds would create new scoring opportunities, and within four or five seconds, the whole cycle would repeat.

On offense, the System had a strict structure, even if the critics didn't see it. Every time the opposing team made a basket, the post player would retrieve the ball as quickly as possible. He would immediately release the ball to the point guard, who would race up court or pass the ball ahead up court. There, each of the other players would be in position, in his "spot," the area from which he shot with greatest success.

If you received the pass and were in your spot, you shot.

Simple.

Off a defensive rebound, every player raced up court to his spot. If you had the ball, you never had to worry about the lanes being filled or about where everyone was going to be. You knew that they would be where they were supposed to be every time. If the first option wasn't available, you looked for the second; if your second option was covered, you looked for the third. If all were impossible, the fifth man would be approaching from behind and almost always would be wide open. If all else had failed, you could always drop it off to him for an open shot from the top of the key. There was no such thing as a bad shot in the System.

The best thing about it was that, for players who were accustomed since grade school to being chastised and yanked from the court for attempting a bad shot, all such fear was removed. The players performed free of doubt and concern that a "bad shot" would result in their removal from the game. Consequently, their confidence soared, and with confidence, their performance improved. Relaxed and free, they played at peak performance. Under Westhead's System, if he took you out of the game for any reason, it probably was for not shooting enough. Thus, playing for Paul Westhead was as close to nirvana as any basketball player could get. And no one would be more at home there than Hank Gathers.

Hank was, as Stan Morrison recognized, a great scorer, not a great shooter. In the System, Hank would find more scoring opportunities from conversions than even he could have hoped for. The System produced defensive rebounds by the boatload. As an aggressive, fleet, and immensely strong player, Hank would be the beneficiary of most of those opportunities. At the offensive end, with a shot being launched from afar every four or five seconds, he would have, based on the percentages for those types of shots, numerous put backs and rebounds that he could convert into easy dunks or lay-ups.

When Westhead was at La Salle, he had seen the System bring out the best in Michael Brooks, who flourished under it. (Brooks, who went on to six seasons in the NBA, scored 4,000 points while at La Salle and ranks 12th on the all-time list.)[3]

While Westhead didn't create the System for Hank Gathers, he was made for it and it for him. They were perfect together. For success, the System required unquestioned commitment. Westhead would never find a player more committed than Hank Gathers.

On a trip to Puerto Rico years earlier, Westhead had first seen the possibilities of what he would come to call the System. While coaching on the island, he noticed the free-wheeling run-and-gun style of the players there. As he watched, he also noted their joyful abandon as they raced up and down in the steaming, tropical heat, maintaining a fast-paced rhythm that would have worn even the most nimble steel drum player to a frazzle. They were truly enjoying the game.

He took what he had seen there back to the mainland and began to refine, tinker, and work with it as if it were an academic experiment. He would put the pieces together slowly through the years at his various coaching stops in the college and professional ranks. Sonny Allen, who had adopted a version of the System that was first used and popularized by Cam Henderson at Marshall College in the 1950's, was an early inspiration. By the time Westhead got his opportunity to coach again at LMU, he figured the System was nearly perfect.

In his first two years at LMU, Westhead's System had produced mixed results. He concluded, accurately, that to run the System, he needed topflight players who were totally committed to the program. It wouldn't work with just good players who really liked to play basketball, no matter how great their effort. And when Hank, Bo, and Corey arrived, Westhead had his disciples.

The only remaining glitch, in his estimation, was in the defense. "I knew we weren't creating enough turnovers. Not getting enough steals. I wanted to improve our efforts in that regard," Westhead said.

Did he seek out an experienced, defensive-minded college basketball coach so he could learn the nuances of defensive pressure? Not Paul Westhead. He sought the answer from a football coach. "I went to the Los Angeles Rams," he said. "John Robinson was then the coach, and I told him my problem. He sent me to Fritz Sturmer, their defensive backfield coach. I asked him to show me how his defensive backs defended against the passes thrown their way. He told me it was all in the eyes. They watched—not the receiver's body, legs, or arms—they watched his eyes. The eyes told them where the ball was and when to make their defensive move, he told me."

Westhead spent a week at the Rams' training camp, watching and learning. When he felt confident that he could impart what he had learned, he returned to the hardwood. There he taught his charges what he had learned. He'd fixed the last flaw.[4]

The System was ready. Paul Westhead was ready. Hank, Bo, and Corey were more than ready.

As for the world of college basketball, well, that might take a little while.

"Paul Westhead's greatest strength is his willingness to be different despite what others think. He has an unshakable belief in the System. It doesn't matter at what level. His belief is rock solid, and he conveys that belief effectively. He is engaging, witty, intelligent, and fun to be with," Jim Foster said.

"There is more to him," Foster said of his friend, "than just running up and down the floor."[5]

Paul Westhead was born in Philadelphia and played his college ball there for St. Joseph's under the highly regarded Jack Ramsey. One of Westhead's teammates was Jim Lynum, who would later help Paul land the LMU job. After graduation, Westhead began his coaching career at Cheltenham High School outside Philadelphia, and he enjoyed enough success to get the head coaching job at La Salle University at the tender age of 30. His passion for the fast-paced run-and-gun style of play with the Explorers was rewarded when his star performer, Michael Brooks, eclipsed all the scoring records for the school that had produced Tom Gola.

Westhead managed to win 142 games at La Salle during his nine seasons there, from 1970- to 1979. The other Big Five coaches did not always admire Westhead's tactics—to induce opponents to play his up-tempo style, he would sometimes play only one man back on defense to lure the opposition into taking quick shots—but he enjoyed enough success to be asked to join his friend and former St. Joe's coach, Jack McKinney, as an assistant coach with the Los Angeles Lakers in 1979.

When McKinney suffered near-fatal injuries in a bicycle accident in late 1979, Westhead became the coach. Only 14 games into the season, he inherited a team that included Magic Johnson and an aging, but still effective, Kareem Abdul-Jabbar. Westhead led them to the NBA Finals, where the Lakers defeated the Philadelphia 76ers and Julius Erving. Westhead had an NBA Championship ring.

Jerry Buss, owner of the Lakers and a wealthy real estate tycoon, called Paul "the greatest coach in the country." Westhead was on top of the world, but he soon learned that staying there wasn't easy.

Magic Johnson, arguably the game's biggest star, owned Los Angeles in those days. When he began sniping and griping about his coach and the style of play that Westhead used, the coach's days were numbered.

Westhead had a habit of quoting Shakespeare to his players, which left the NBA stars scratching their heads; most of them had gotten through college on gut courses. But the reserved and taciturn Westhead was no match for the charming and voluble Johnson, who milked his rapport with the press to crusade against his coach. Soon Buss was in an untenable position, forced to choose between his "snobbish" Shakespeare-spouting coach and his wildly popular superstar.

The 1980 season was one of unrest and uneasiness as Magic, suffering nagging injuries, kept up his attack. The second-guessing about Westhead began to intensify when the Lakers fell in the first round of the play-offs to the underdog Houston Rockets. Now Magic even suggested that he would rather be traded than play for Westhead.

Just 11 games into the 1981 season, Buss fired the coach he had proclaimed to be "the greatest" and replaced Westhead with the former television broadcaster whom Paul had hired as his assistant—Pat Riley.

From Los Angeles, Westhead went to Chicago, where he spent a single season with the pre-Michael Jordan Bulls. It was a team that lacked talent, and Westhead's stint in the Windy City was short—he was fired at the end of the season. Humiliated by the treatment he'd received in Los Angeles and stung by Johnson's sniping, Westhead found himself out of basketball as the 1983 season began.

Characteristically, Westhead had chosen to ignore most of Johnson's barbs. The closest he will come to criticism is to say, "We had a different philosophy about the game and how it should be played."

Although he has kept his thoughts to himself, there is no doubt among those who know him that he remained intent on getting back into the NBA.

Thus Westhead and his two prized transfers from USC shared more than a hometown. They shared a need to redeem and restore their reputations after messy exits. They needed a place where their success would be noticed and rewarded by the NBA.

While many questioned Hank and Bo's decision to attend LMU, buried as it was in the mid-major West Coast Conference, it was a means to their end, and not at all as unlikely as some thought. The school was in a major media market with two NBA franchises. It was coached by a former NBA coach who wore a championship ring, and "the System" he was using was sure to garner national attention as the points it produced racked up. The System was a fan-friendly style of play and would provide exciting viewing for the growing television audience, giving the players and coach the exposure they needed. In short, considering the options available to them, it was an excellent choice.

Given the circumstances of Tommy Lewis's recruitment, which had raised eyebrows in the coaching fraternity and at the NCAA, it was not a stretch to conclude that there was something to the stories that reporters kept hearing, the ones that smeared the departed USC stars as a bunch of spoiled teenagers who had sought to dictate terms to a mighty university and were accustomed to special treatment.

When Paul Westhead, Hank, and Bo found each other, all were trying to restore and recover their credibility and, just as important, make it to the NBA. In the sanctified atmosphere of the tiny Jesuit school, whose main thoroughfares are laid out in a cross with the gymnasium at the bottom and the chapel at the top, redemption, restoration, and recognition would be theirs. Together they would be lifted up. At least that was the plan.

The very city where John Wooden had worn the mantle of greatness was ill prepared for Westhead and the System. But that is not to say that Los Angeles hadn't been warned. Alan Drooz's coverage of the new basketball season began with an article on November 26, 1987, that previewed the campaign for his *LA Times* readers and reviewed the events related to the controversial transfers of more than a year before.

"It was a big mess. I was shocked. Hurt and shocked," Hank told Drooz, describing his reaction to Raveling's handling of the situation at USC. Both Hank and Bo said their transition had been smooth and that they had no regrets about their transfer. "There was probably some negative feedback, when all that was going on, that Bo and I were nasty guys, that I was a snob or something like that," Hank said. "The guys (here) saw that it wasn't like that."

Drooz pointed out that Hank and Bo liked Westhead's offense "immensely" and that Hank had scored 60 points in an intra-squad game a week earlier. Drooz concluded by warning that "the smattering of transfers could send the rest of the conference scattering this season."[6] Drooz was referring, of course, to Hank, Bo, and Corey, but another transfer had arrived on campus in September with considerably less fanfare.

His name was Tom Peabody. Born in Philadelphia, where his father, a marine, was stationed at the time, Tom later moved with his family to California's Orange County, where he grew up. A former standout at Mater Dei in Santa Ana, where he had been an integral part of teams that compiled a 59-1 record while he was there, Peabody had accepted a scholarship to Rice University. He was an excellent student as well as athlete, and he had chosen the Texas school that considered itself the Harvard of the Southwest over Fresno State, San Diego State, and Stanford. Two and a half months after he arrived in the Lone Star State, just as basketball practice was beginning, Peabody realized he'd made a big mistake. Despite what Dean Martin sang, Houston wasn't for him.

"I just wasn't mature enough to take it all at once—basketball, school, being away from home," he said. The high school honors student failed his first four exams. Peabody wasn't managing his time well and he knew it.[7] "I wanted to come home. I didn't want to be there. By Thanksgiving I was back in California and enrolled at Orange Coast College, a junior college, in Costa Mesa," he said.[8]

"I finished out the year, coaching the sophomore team at Mater Dei while attending Orange Coast. I played in the JUCO [junior college] summer league that year and was surprised when some recruiters noticed me. I got a call from UC Irvine and Mike Montgomery at Stanford and also from Judas Prada, the number one assistant to Westhead. Montgomery told me he wanted me but that I needed to get some more credits and then I could come there. Prada said they were really looking a year out, and I would be redshirted and then I'd be ready to play," Peabody said. "I decided to go to LMU. When I got there, I found it was a tight-knit community of athletes. Bo and Hank and Corey Gaines and even Pooh Richardson from UCLA and Derrick Dowell from USC all hung out together and played together."

He was pleased with his decision. "As soon as I got there, I knew it was the right fit for me," he said, even though he would not be eligible for another season. For now he could only practice with the team that featured three transfers of some repute. One of those transfers was his roommate in Room 57 in the Hannon Apartments on campus near Gersten Pavilion. He was a big funny guy from Philly named Hank Gathers. After meeting Hank, Tom was even more certain he'd made the right decision.[9]

CHAPTER

13

TAKIN' THE COURT

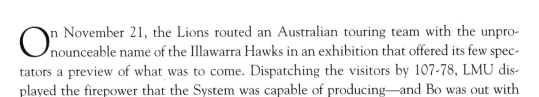

On November 21, the Lions routed an Australian touring team with the unpro-
nounceable name of the Illawarra Hawks in an exhibition that offered its few spectators a preview of what was to come. Dispatching the visitors by 107-78, LMU displayed the firepower that the System was capable of producing—and Bo was out with
an injury.

Westhead called the showing "pretty good, for a first outing." He was pleased with the
fast break and with Corey Gaines's play at the point guard position. Seniors Mike Yoest and
Mark Armstrong joined sophomores Jeff Fryer and Hank in demolishing the Hawks. After
the game, Westhead told Drooz, "I think we can get a lot better."

The Illawarra coach, Dave Lindstrom, had been thoroughly beaten but confirmed the
effectiveness of the System. "There could be a few teams in the country that can run with
them," he said of the Lions. "I'd like to watch the game."[1]

Before beginning their conference season, the Lions would head across the conti-
nent for their season opener in the Joe Lapchick Memorial Tournament, hosted by St.
John's University in New York on the weekend after Thanksgiving. The field for the
1987 edition of the holiday tradition included St. John's, Harvard, Tennessee Tech, and
LMU. Each team played two games, with the winners meeting in the finals at Alumni
Gym on Sunday.

Westhead kept the team in Los Angeles for Thanksgiving, lest the Lions "get spooked"
by the big city. They flew East on Friday, arriving in the early evening. In previewing the
tournament in that morning's *Los Angeles Times*, Drooz had asked, "What's a nice team like
this doing in a place like this?"

A lot of basketball fans were probably asking themselves the same thing. St. John's
enjoyed national respect. It had a long winning tradition, begun by Lapchick in the 1950's
and continued by Lou Carnesecca, the current coach, whose teams were consistently

among the top 20 in the nation. The LMU team, meanwhile, had finished in the basement of the West Coast Athletic Conference against decidedly weaker teams than St. John's, so the Lapchick tourney was hardly the place you'd expect to find the Lions.

Unless, of course, you knew Paul Westhead.

"For us, it's business as usual," he told Drooz off-handedly, deliberately downplaying the significance of the game. "It's not any more than if we're going to Santa Clara."

Brian Quinn was more forthright in his assessment, conceding that while this early season game "wasn't a life or death situation, it's important to do well, impress ourselves on the Eastern writers." Quinn even allowed himself to consider the unthinkable: "If we were to win the tournament, it would be a tremendous accomplishment. It would provide us with a national media base. People would recognize us as a legitimate team. It's a very important game for us."

Even so, Quinn, who admitted to being nervous, was certain of one thing only: "I knew we would be entertaining."

A small alumni contingent had accompanied the team to New York and toured the Big Apple, enjoying Broadway and the Christmas displays along Fifth Avenue. But Westhead confined the team to a hotel near LaGuardia. Westhead wanted no distractions. He knew that a good showing in New York would be a big step for his Loyola Marymount program.

Corey Gaines's parents had made the trip, too. And Lucille Gathers and Father Dave came in from Philadelphia, as did Bo's mother, Hilda.[2] In the opening round, LMU would face Tennessee Tech at 2 p.m., with St. John's taking on Harvard two hours later. The script played out to Hank's satisfaction.

A member of the lightly regarded Ohio Valley Conference, the Golden Eagles of Tennessee Tech, coached by Tom Deaton, had four returning starters from a team that had gone 7-20 the year before. Westhead must have been delighted to learn that the Eagles' average score had been 75 points and that their opponents had averaged nearly 88. As Yogi Berra would have said, "It was over before it was over." The Lions trounced the Eagles 114-78, and Alan Drooz's account began, "It's like they never left."

Corey Gaines accounted for 25 points in his first action since the end of the 1985-86 season. He added 13 steals to his performance, prompting Westhead to say that Corey was "typical of the whole team; once he got his bearing, he was lethal." And Corey told the reporter that he felt "reborn."

Playing in front of his own small but boisterous rooting section, Hank started slowly, shaking off the rust from the lack of competition. In the first half he went only 2-10 from the free-throw line. But in the second half, he shook off the jitters and gave his fans a reason to cheer, throwing down two impressive dunks. He finished with 22 points on 9-16 shooting and added 6 rebounds. Later, he admitted to Drooz that he'd been nervous. "You probably could notice that in my free throws," he said, laughing. "I felt like I was back in high school, missing all those free throws." Hank had nothing but praise for the System: "Once I get myself going, it becomes easy."[3]

St. John's easily turned back Harvard, 105-60. The victory moved LMU into the championship game against St. John's. Westhead invited Louie's Redmen to run with his Lions. "We hope to get into a 100-plus basketball game. Be our guest, see what happens," he challenged.

Lou's reply indicated he might resist the offer. "That fast break I saw today was something I wish my team could do," he said. "That's the best fast break I've ever seen. It resembles the Lakers' fast break." He also predicted the Lions' future: "That is an NCAA (tournament) club."[4]

That Sunday, sports nuts could find tournament action from Anchorage to Maui, but nowhere was it better than in Queens at Alumni Hall. A crowd of 6,008 was on hand to see St. John's take on LMU. The Redmen, who had never lost a game in this tournament, had all they could handle to retain their spotless record. In the end they edged Westhead's Lions by just 3 points as a last-second LMU shot to tie resulted in an air ball.

Carnesecca was not a Hall of Fame coach just because of his gaudy sweaters. He had watched the Tennessee Tech game closely and spotted a way to thwart the LMU fast break. Observing that the System was triggered by the inbounds pass from the post or fifth man to the point guard, Carnesecca instructed his players to try to hold on to the ball after they had made a shot. The strategy worked until nearly the end of the game, when the delaying tactic brought a third technical foul call at a crucial point. After a Michael Porter basket, Mike Brust of St. John's had picked up the ball quickly and walked away from the baseline with it. His delaying tactic drew the technical foul.

The score was 88-84 with six seconds to play. Mike Yoest converted one of the free throws to make it a 3-point game. Now LMU, because of the technical, had possession, and those six seconds remaining were more than enough for the System to produce a shot. Fryer was designated to take it.

Air ball.

Game over.

When the press questioned Westhead about the decision, he said pointedly, "I would have called the same play if it were a 2-point game or a 3-point game. We're going to shoot the three. We're that style. It's a shot we practice. We got what we wanted. We'd do it again if we had another six seconds."

Westhead's words weren't meant just to soothe Fryer's feelings. The coach meant exactly what he'd said. That was the beauty of the System. That was the way it was meant to be played. The missed shot didn't represent failure. It was just another shot. Next time it comes to you, put it up. Sometimes the tactic produces lemonade, sometimes a lemon. But it is never, ever boring.

Hank had played well, making two key, if uncharacteristic, free throws in the waning seconds to keep Loyola Marymount's hopes alive. He finished with 24 points, 18 coming in the second half, and 10 rebounds. He had fastened tassels in LMU's crimson and gray to his white sneakers before the game. When the press questioned the colorful addition, he explained it was in tribute to his hero, Muhammad Ali. "I've been watching a lot of Ali's fights and for the big fights he wore tassels," he explained. "They represent speed and quickness and that's what Loyola's about."

Corey had contributed 20 points, and both he and Hank were named to the all-tournament team. Boo Harvey with 18 and Shelton Jones with 25 had paced the Redmen.[5]

LMU went home 1-1, but the Lions had previewed the System for the New York writers and had given Carnesecca and the Redmen a scare.

For its home opener on December 2, LMU would meet Westmont College, a small school just up the coast in Santa Barbara that belonged to the National Association of Intercollegiate Athletics (NAIA). Westmont proved tougher than the cupcake it was thought to be, but finally succumbed to the pace and fell, 100-84, before 1,250 ticket holders in Gersten, which meant it was more than half-empty. Hank and Corey had continued to play spectacularly well—at one point Hank scored 13 points in a row during a run that began with a steal and reverse dunk and ended with an acrobatic lay-up in heavy traffic. With the score at 71-50, Westhead had substituted freely the rest of the way. The Lions shot 74 percent in the second half and 60 percent overall.[6]

The next day, the student newspaper, the *Los Angeles Loyolan*, carried a small sidebar that urged students to sign up for Brian Quinn's newly formed group of student rooters—the Lions' Pride—which provided members with a guaranteed lower-level seat for the action.[7]

During the previous season the NCAA had added the 3-point line, 19 feet, 9 inches from the hoop, to college basketball, and many purists had bellyached. Westhead loved it.

One reason was Jeff Fryer. The 6-foot-2 sophomore from Newport Beach was a graduate of Corona del Mar High. He was the California beach boy incarnate, a surfer dude with a laid-back, too-cool-for-words, style. His perpetual tan, bleached-blond locks, and sunglasses completed the look. If he'd had an old wood-sided vehicle, he might well have inspired a Brian Wilson tune.

Fryer was also the prototypical 3-point shooter. He was fearless and loved the responsibility that came with his role in the System. He was also smart enough and complex enough to want a shooting coach. He had used one from the time he was in high school, and his name was Tom Marumoto.

By day Marumoto was a hospital pharmacist. By night he gave shooting lessons to players. "I wanted to be a coach but my parents, being Old World Orientals, felt that it was too 'low' a job for one of their sons," he explained. "They wanted us to be professionals." Marumoto dutifully became a pharmacist, but he never abandoned his first love. "I coached behind their backs," he said.

He had been coaching AAU teams in soccer and basketball for years when he met Jeff Fryer in 1980. "He had a passion for basketball. When I met him, he was shooting 600 shots a day," Marumoto recalled. Marumoto, who worked with Jeff throughout his high school career, teaches a three-part process that emphasizes footwork, balance, and timing to produce a naturally harmonious shooting rhythm.

When it came time to select a college, Jeff's mom asked Tom for advice. "His parents were divorced. His dad had gone to UC Irvine and wanted Jeff to go there," Marumoto said. "His mother asked me what I thought, and I told her that LMU seemed like a better choice to me because of Westhead and his style."

Marumoto convinced Fryer that LMU was his best bet, and he continued to work with Jeff throughout his college career, when Fryer's bombs from unbelievably long range would provide a potent outside threat for Westhead's system. Fryer's range was remarkable, and his percentage of success was the envy of all his opponents. "He had a gift. I just fine-tuned it," Marumoto said.[8]

The Lions next faced the University of the Pacific on December 5 and easily dispatched the Tigers from Stockton, 130-103 at Gersten.

Westhead, who felt that anything less than 100 points was a sign that his players needed to ramp up the speed, was happy—the win marked the third time in four games that they had exceeded the century mark.

The Lions, playing before 1,445, started strong and never looked back When they took a 43-19 lead with 12 minutes remaining in the first half, they were on pace to achieve the elusive 200-point game. They dropped off after that, but did manage to break the mark for most points ever scored against the University of the Pacific.[9]

Hank had a total of 25 points and a nearly perfect first half, scoring 11 points in the first five minutes. Corey accounted for 27 points. Westhead rested his starters for much of the second half. The two squads accounted for 172 shots in all. Westhead credited a combination of "sharp offense and defensive full-court pressure." Then he added, "I don't think we've got it really cranked yet. We're still evolving."[10]

LMU's future opponents did not find that analysis heartening. The Lions were averaging 112 points. Westhead explained their success and his system: "Our pressure defense has created more running. We make the opponents shoot. We're not really mad if you make baskets on us because we score better off the score. We just hope you don't take too long to score."[11] The second squad, including Enoch Simmons and Marcellus Lee, spelled Hank and Corey and saw so much playing time that its members were exhausted. But it was a good exhaustion.

The thing about running the System, something that few who observed it would know, was how much running it took to execute Westhead's strategy to perfection. "We ran in practice, and then we ran burners the length of the court after practice. We ran laps and then we ran more laps. The slightest infraction or mistake resulted in more running," Bruce Woods, an assistant coach, recalled.[12]

Starting with the first day of practice in October, they "ran the dune" two or three times a week. Sand Dune Park is located in nearby Manhattan Beach. It is an obscure little pocket park that Westhead had discovered, and it contains a sand hill that rises at a steep 45-degree angle and measures about a hundred yards from bottom to top.

"We ran the dune. Or, some of us ran and others walked," Corey Gaines said.[13] Added Woods, "The idea was to run up the steep dune's deep sand without putting your hands down into the sand. The angle was so steep that your face would be nearly in the sand as you made your way up. Hank loved the punishing runs. He raced up the hill and challenged any and all to beat him." Few did.[14]

The System required a player to be superbly fit. It was essential to its success. The Sand Dune Park drills were part of the intense cardiovascular conditioning that Westhead used to prepare his team to run the System. It was a grueling, grinding program. But it worked. If you were going to play for Paul Westhead, you were going to have to run.[15] And run. And run. "He ran with us," Bo said. "He never asked us to do what he wouldn't do."[16]

The LMU Lions were fit and trim. They were supremely confident that no one could keep up with them. The problem that they faced was inducing the opposition to try. Some teams, usually those that were better coached and prepared, resisted the temptation. One of them was Oregon State, coached by Ralph Miller, who had amassed more than 600 wins. Miller was the nation's winningest active coach and was destined for the Hall of Fame. Miller wasn't easily fooled or lured into a pace of play with which he was uncomfortable.

LMU faced the Beavers on December 9 at spacious Gill Coliseum in Corvallis, Oregon. The Beavers, led by Gary Payton, would play at their own pace. Before shooting, they would take nearly all the 45 seconds allotted, and the Beavers managed to make 68 percent of their attempts in the first half. While that mark decreased in the second half, they still managed to shoot 59 percent overall and controlled the tempo throughout. Ralph

Miller got win number 634 and LMU fell, 84-69.

LMU was in the game for the entire first half, which ended at 39-39, as Hank provided 14 points to keep the Lions competitive. The Beavers' defense bottled up Mike Yoest and Corey Gaines, limiting Corey to only two assists. Westhead summed up the loss: "We were unsuccessful in shaking them out of their pace. It was all a result of Oregon State controlling the pace and our guys getting frustrated it wasn't played at breakneck speed."

Hank led the Lions with 23, and Payton led the Beavers with 13 points and eight assists. Eric Knox, a Beaver who had played with Corey at St. Bernard's, said afterward, "Come January, I'd like to see Loyola Marymount. I'd buy a ticket. They've got a great team."

Miller admitted that the outcome had surprised him a bit: "We had enough patience this time to work for the easy shots."[17] Patience was the antidote for LMU's poisonous pace. Few other teams would figure it out.

Long Beach State University was not one of them. But on December 13, LMU got a surprise. The 49ers won, 117-113, in overtime.

Hank scored 39 points for the Lions as they ran with the 49ers from start to finish. The collapse they expected never came. The game, played before a nearly full house on the Long Beach campus, was made to order for LMU.[18]

The first half saw LMU go on a 23-12 run that put the Lions up 57-35, with little more than four minutes remaining. Hank had 13 points during the spurt. Beginning with a driving dunk, he took command of the offense, and they played the half at a withering pace. "They had one [fast- break possession] that must have taken two seconds," Long Beach State's coach, Joe Harrington, said in amazement.[19]

Hank's performance was impressive, and he seemed able to score in the lane at will, but in the end, his Achilles heel took the Lions down. At the conclusion of regulation play, Hank had two free throws, and he needed to sink both to win the game. With the raucous spectators screaming, "Air ball!" and stomping their feet, he missed both. Long Beach State, which had overcome a 22-point lead, went on to win in the overtime period.

Hank's 39 points were the most scored by an LMU player since Greg Goorjian had 42 in 1983, while playing for his father. Hank's missed free throws mystified Westhead, who knew how much Hank practiced at the foul line. He could sink 10 and 20 in a row at practice—and then, just as quickly, he'd be throwing up air balls.[20]

For the season, he was 57 percent from the free-throw line and 58 percent from the field. His free-throw problems would continue to plague him throughout his career. He would try everything and anything. Nothing ever would work.

14

"The Hank And Bo Show"

The Lions, who were now 3-3 for the season thus far, had a five-day break before they were scheduled to meet Southern California—Southern California College, a small NAIA school in Costa Mesa.

The Vanguards arrived at Gersten from Orange County on December 18 and proved to be as accommodating as the Lions could have hoped. The out-manned and outrun visitors tried to keep pace with their hosts. The result was a foregone conclusion as LMU rolled to a 140-106 win.[1]

The game was notable for two reasons: it produced the second-highest point total ever for a Loyola Marymount team and marked Bo Kimble's return to the court. Bo had suffered a fractured knee cap in late October and had been rehabbing the knee ever since. He had been cleared to practice a week earlier. His return after six weeks would add muscle to an offense that was already first in the conference in average points scored per game at 101.8 and third in the nation behind only the University of Oklahoma and UNLV. Hank was averaging 24.7 points per game to lead the Lions.

Delayed by Bo's injury, the curtain finally rose on "The Hank and Bo Show" before a crowd of 1,100, and opening night lived up to expectations. Hank racked up more than 30 points for the second straight game, finishing with 33 on a nearly flawless 16-18 performance. Bo, in his first appearance since leaving USC, managed 28 points in just 16 minutes. It was like he'd never been away.

The reviews were unanimous: "The Hank and Bo Show" was a hit.

But not everyone was applauding.

One might have assumed that the president of LMU, Father James N. Loughran, would be pleased with the Lions' performance. But on the day that the *Los Angeles Times* ran its account of the debut of "The Hank and Bo Show," it ran another story in which Loughran denied ever promoting LMU as the "Georgetown of the West." "Reporters seem to want to hear me say we'll become the Georgetown of the West. We don't want to be Georgetown athletically or any other fashion," Loughran said. He would simply not concede that the two Jesuit schools had much in common.[2]

In fact, they had a lot in common. Both enjoyed outstanding academic reputations. Both were located in the suburbs of major cities. Both had opted to drop football in the 50's while retaining athletic scholarships for basketball. Both had marquee coaches. Georgetown had John Thompson and LMU had Paul Westhead.

Since his arrival at Georgetown in 1972, Thompson, a large and imposing black man, had used the force of his personality and the backing of the school to turn the Hoyas into a major court power. Westhead had an NBA championship ring and an engaging personality. He used his urbane wit to throw out quotable lines that the press gobbled up. He quoted Shakespeare in the locker room. He was the Guru of Go, the Nutty Professor. He was good copy and he was a winner.

What rankled the alumni and supporters of LMU was that Loughran—who had brought Westhead to LMU—wasn't giving him the support that Thompson, for example, enjoyed at Georgetown. Any appearance money that the Lions earned went into the university's general fund, not the athletic department budget, for example.[3]

"You play to win, but winning isn't the only criterion, maybe not the most important criterion," said Loughran, who seemed to be saying he'd rather have a College Bowl than NCAA championship team. "What happened with the baseball (College World Series appearance). . .was good. (But) if people started evaluating us—the school or the coaches—like that, I would pull back. That's not what we're about."

Brian Quinn, once an athlete at LMU himself, echoed the Loughran line. "We don't have aspirations of being the best basketball team in the West," he said. "The idea is if we do something and invest the money, we should do it well. We do expect to have an excellent basketball program. What I mean by excellent is we are very competitive in our conference, we graduate our athletes and do everything by the (NCAA) law. If we go to the [conference] play-offs, that's a bonus."[4]

The president's attitude disturbed many associated with the university, not least of all, Al Gersten, who wanted a winning program as much as anyone. "They did it on the cheap," he groused. "They never gave the program the financial support it needed."[5] Another person familiar with the position of the administration summed it up succinctly: "The attitude has always been, 'God will look out for us'—and [it] still is."[6]

Fortunately, others didn't share Loughran's attitude. Paul Westhead had a firm hand on the rudder and a clear idea of where his ship was headed, even if Loughran preferred to leave the season in God's hands. A divine lanyard and whistle had no role while Westhead was at the helm.

Not one of his players doubted where Westhead and the Lions were headed. They were moving fast and they were moving up. They knew exactly what course they were on. They had made the commitment to get there together, whatever it took. They never, ever, doubted for a moment that they were on the right course. They just didn't know how fast they'd reach their goal.

Now that Bo was back, the System was running on all cylinders. The ride promised to be a wild one.

"My man is BACK!" Corey Gaines shouted after Bo's debut. "No more losses."[7]

The System did what it was designed to do. It freed Westhead's superbly talented players to play their best. Unfettered, they romped and stomped their way through the rest of the season.

The Lions' next victim was Brooklyn College, and they buried the Kingsmen beneath a never-ending bombardment of 3-pointers—15 in all—to roll to the widest margin in LMU's history, 123-72. Westhead had told writer Alan Drooz after the Southern California game five days earlier that he thought the team was probably two weeks away from being "in full swing." He underestimated his charges: Hank, with 18 points, led six LMU players who scored in double figures.[8]

The Runnin' Ramblers of Loyola of Chicago visited Gersten after Christmas, bringing with them the nation's leading rebounder, 6-foot-9 Kenny Miller, who was pulling down 16 caroms a game. In a very physical game that was not played at the up-tempo pace that the Lions preferred, LMU managed to prevail, by 99-89. The game proved that the Lions could win a physical game and that they could also win without topping 100 points.

The crowd, the largest of the season at 2,780, provided a boisterous backdrop to the action. Hank led the Lions with 19 points and battled Miller to haul in 10 rebounds. Bo provided 17, coming off the bench as Westhead slowly worked him back into the flow. But Mike Yoest, the senior, was the difference, as he accounted for 14 points while grabbing 13 rebounds. Miller fouled out with 5:49 to play and had only nine rebounds.[9]

Holy Cross, the team that once boasted Bob Cousy and Tommy Heinsohn, arrived at Gersten for the last game of 1987. Holy Cross could have used both former Crusader stars—the Lions devoured the Christians, by 127-104.

LMU's total was the most that any team had ever scored against Holy Cross. It was the Lions' fourth straight win and ended their home stand on a positive note. The game was textbook Westhead. As Corey Gaines kneeled at the scoring table late in the game, waiting to return to action, he urged his teammates on, saying, "C'mon, baby, we need 150!"

This was fun. This was the way basketball was meant to be played. "Believe it or not,"

Westhead told Alan Drooz, "this game was decided by defense. Non-believers will have to come see (a game). We played very good defense. We shoot the ball so fast that the other team gets it back fast.

"The scary thing is when the press is working, it makes it look easy. It really isn't. The points go up so fast it looks like a rollover and it wasn't. Holy Cross is a real good team."

With Cousy and Heinsohn, maybe the Crusaders could have prevailed, but not that night. Hank again topped the Lions with 24 points and a game-high 12 rebounds. Bo, coming off the bench, added 23 and, showing his spunk after missing so much time, was involved in three scuffles. Fryer had 20 points. Mike Yoest and Mark Armstrong had 16 apiece as Corey Gaines dished out 11 assists to spread the wealth.[10]

Just before New Year's, the Lions left the balmy California sunshine for frigid Green Bay, where they were to meet the Fighting Phoenix of the University of Wisconsin-Green Bay and then take on Marquette University in Milwaukee. "We're playing good now, we're into a rhythm," Westhead said as they headed East.[11]

The Phoenix were 8-1 as LMU arrived in Green Bay. Wisconsin was averaging about 65 points a game, and in an earlier game neither the Phoenix or their opponents broke 50. LMU, on the other hand, was the nation's second-highest-scoring team, exceeding 100 points in seven games.

But a wind-chill factor of minus 60 and a deliberate pace of play nearly gummed up the oil in Westhead's smooth-running system.[12] Green Bay coach Dick Bennett, who had no player taller than 6-foot-6, knew it would be suicidal to try to stay with the Lions, and refused to be lured into their run-and-gun death trap. He controlled the tempo by using the 45-second clock.

Corey Gaines sank two free throws in the last 29 seconds to give the Lions a narrow victory, 70-67, after a last-second Phoenix 3-pointer fell just short. Hank had a team-high 20 points.[13]

After a day off, on January 7, the Lions met Marquette's Warriors at the Mecca in Milwaukee on January 7. Bob Dukiet's squad was 5-5 but enjoyed a 5-1 mark at home. The Warriors were coming off a win over Kansas State and were averaging about 68 points per game.

The Lions used a ferocious full-court press to spur a 21-8 run after the intermission. They turned back a furious Marquette rally to lead 99-96 with 48 seconds left. Fryer and Armstrong then added crucial free throws, and the Lions held on for a 102-98 win.

Mike Yoest had a great game, making his first 10 field-goal attempts and accounting for 27 points in all. Hank and Corey contributed 21 apiece, as the Lions used a pressing defense to come back from a 5-point deficit at halftime. "The press gave them some problems,"

Westhead said, adding, "anytime we can beat a quality program like this, it helps us. We're trying to send earthquake vibrations that we're around, that our program is improving."[14]

The lingo may have been unfamiliar to the Midwesterners, but they got the message. LMU left for home with two road wins and a six-game streak.

Enjoying warmer surroundings and home cooking again, the Lions would meet Azusa Pacific University on Saturday, January 9, before beginning conference play with contests against the University of San Diego and St. Mary's College the following week.

The fans were catching on. More than 1,800 were in the stands as the Lions took Azusa Pacific with ease, 113-89, and as Mike Yoest tied a school record by making 16 free throws.[15] The Lions would begin West Coast Athletic Conference play with their best record since the 1961-62 season, when Brian Quinn had been on the team.

Indeed, when the results of a preseason media poll were released, Chris Ello of the *Los Angeles Times* was moved to observe that "it appeared as if someone had messed up and printed it upside down." The sportswriters had picked LMU to finish first in the conference.[16]

In the *San Diego Union-Tribune*, Don Norcross picked Bo, Hank, and Corey as all-conference selections along with Tommy Lewis. "Even run-and-gun teams need a hammer inside—your Armon Gilliam types—and Gathers fills the bill," he noted.[17]

Bo was now playing at full speed. He was pain free, making spectacular offensive moves, and playing tenacious defense. The team was using an eight-man rotation and was as close to ready as Westhead could have hoped. As the Lions prepared to face their first conference foe, Westhead told Drooz, "We're right where we'd like to be."[18]

For their first conference game, the Lions faced the Toreros of the University of San Diego. The defending West Coast Athletic Conference champs were never in the game as LMU broke quickly. Hank rode the bench, punishment for missing a team meeting. He started in the second half and quickly made his presence felt—21 points in just 20 minutes. Bo added 18 as the Lions coasted to their 11th win, 115-75. LMU's point total was the most ever scored against San Diego since it had begun playing in Division I in 1979. It was also a school record for LMU in conference play.

Hank, 10 for 12 from the field, told Mark Ziegler of *The San Diego Union-Tribune*, "We can score 100 against anybody. If we get a team that wants to run with us, we can score 180."[19]

Next up were the defense-minded St. Mary's College Gaels. The team was second in the nation in defense, allowing just 56 points per game and never more than 70. Its performance at Gersten, in front of a crowd that had swelled to 3,200, belied its ranking: the soundly whipped Gaels scuttled back to Moraga after LMU blitzed its way to a 98-81 win.

As the second-leading scoring team in the country, the Lions had attempted, late in the game, to hit the century mark again. They began deliberately fouling the St. Mary's players, which led to a bizarre scene: LMU would foul any Gael who had the ball in order to preserve clock time so LMU could score again, a tactic that didn't win any favor with the Gaels' coach, Lynn Nance. "I had never experienced that before," Nance said.[20] Then he added, joking, "If I'd anticipated that, I would have put my good free-throw shooters in. Maybe we'd have won." That wasn't likely, as his team had been trailing by 20 when the Lions' antics began. Yoest and Gaines each had 19 points and Hank had contributed 18 to the winning effort.[21]

Now the Lions left for a two-game trip to the Pacific Northwest, where they were to meet the University of Portland and Gonzaga on January 21 and 23. They found the cool and rainy conditions to their liking as they defeated Portland handily in a high-scoring shoot-out.

Former NBA star Larry Steele was in his first season of coaching the Pilots (5-10) and watched in wonder as the Lions, led by Hank with 34 points, blew his young team away, 134-106. LMU led by only 5 points four minutes into the first half when Hank led a 12-0 run to put the game away. With his performance, he gained the scoring lead for the conference, averaging 23.3 points per game, and the Lions set a new West Coast Athletic Conference scoring mark. The combined total for the game, 240 points, also set a record. To the Pilots' ever-lasting chagrin, the final tally also marked the most points ever scored against that team.[22]

At 13-3 for the season, and 3-0 atop the conference standings (where LMU was tied with the University of San Francisco for the lead), LMU moved up the coast to Spokane to meet the Bulldogs of Gonzaga. The Lions took some time to get their game moving, but when they did, the Bulldogs couldn't keep up. Gonzaga, 7-0 at home, coming in, fell to the rampaging Lions, 85-72, although LMU had shot a pathetic 33 percent in the opening half and trailed by 32-29 at the intermission. With the win, Loyola Marymount claimed sole possession of first place in the WCAC after the University of San Francisco fell to St. Mary's. The Lions kept breaking records, this time returning to Westchester with a school-best 11 straight wins.[23]

Hank was named the conference player of the week for his 56 points in the two wins up North. He was leading all scorers with a 23.2 average.

Whereas the teams in most conferences play each other in succession, the teams that made up the West Coast Athletic Conference played each other in clusters. All the members of the WCAC were religious schools and all had small athletic budgets. So Commissioner Mike Gilleran would design a schedule that made the most of their limited travel budgets. As a result, the biggest factor in determining the schedule was geography. Because Portland and Gonzaga now were headed to the Los Angeles area to play other

WCAC schools, they were the next teams on the Lions' schedule, even though they'd just played each other in Oregon.

By now, the 1987-88 Lions were being compared to the LMU team from the 60's that had done so well with Brian Quinn among its stars. But there was one big difference, Quinn confessed: "We didn't have anyone as good as Gathers."

Brian was heartened to see a line forming in front of the ticket window at Gersten. His efforts to get the student body behind the team, combined with the team's winning streak, were starting to produce the results he sought. The game with archrival Pepperdine, set for February 20, nearly a month off, was already a virtual sell-out, and students would line up on Monday to get tickets for the weekend games coming up.

"We're not lacking for kind words from our alumni—there's a kind of euphoria out there," Quinn said. "It's the community as well. Sometimes I get a little twinge when I see them break the records from our last championship team. But, I say, 'Keep it going, set all kinds of records. It's a new regime.'"

A fan, as well as an administrator, Quinn warned, "If people want to come to our games, they'd better get their tickets. We're becoming a hot item." Having confirmed the popularity of "The Hank and Bo Show," Quinn and his staff now faced the unfamiliar task of dealing with traffic and parking problems. It was a problem LMU hadn't seen since the Olympic Games, but Brian wasn't complaining.[24]

As LMU prepared for the games of January 29 and 30, the Lions were breathing down the neck of the University of Oklahoma for the national lead in scoring. Less than a point separated the Sooners and Lions as the Lions began to play against Gonzaga.

Late in the first half, the fans were treated to a taste of "The Hank and Bo Show" at its best when Hank fired a behind-the-back pass to a streaking Bo for a lay-up that he quickly followed with a 3-point basket from way down court. The Rolling Stones couldn't have rocked the place any louder than Hank and Bo rocked Gersten Pavilion that night as they delivered a 116-100 win. Gonzaga had shot a blistering 69 percent, but LMU had taken 101 shots to Gonzaga's 59. "Our guys really got after it tonight," a satisfied Westhead reported. "Our defense is much like our offense. It's simple and absolute and there's no middle ground."[25]

The next night, the Lions picked up where they had left off, running a fast-break clinic for the Pilots of Portland. In front of an appreciative crowd of 2,830, LMU chalked up its 13-straight win, 122-109, and moved to 16-3 and 6-0 in conference play. By the end of the game, the students occupying the Lions' Pride section were chanting "We're Number One!"—well aware that the national lead in scoring would belong to LMU after the game. When it was over, the crowd gave the team a two-minute standing ovation.

Westhead conceded that leading in scoring wasn't a priority for him but that "it means our fast break is working. This is what we do. This is what we teach. I've been running it for a long time—but we've never defended before. Our defense is as pressure oriented as our offense."[26]

Now, though he didn't dare say it, Westhead had the total package. It looked just the way he always knew it would. Westhead allowed himself a smile but resisted the temptation to say "I told you so" out loud.

15

WILDFIRE SPREADS

I f Paul Westhead wasn't the type to brag, no matter. On February 3 the *Associated Press* Poll revealed that the country was beginning to notice what the coach already knew. The LMU Lions received 30 votes from sportswriters in the balloting for the top 25 teams in the country—the first time that LMU had been included. The Lions were the only team from California that was able to garner any support from the sportswriters.

Now the Lions also made their first appearance in the rankings of the *USA Today/CNN* Poll, debuting in 24th place in the poll of coaches and writers. The word was getting out, and in his cramped quarters at Gersten, Barry Zepel, the sports information director and the only full-time person in the sports public relations department, noticed that the phone was beginning to ring.[1]

Next up for the Lions were the Dons of the University of San Francisco (USF). The decades since Bill Russell, Sam Jones, and K. C. Jones had ruled the basketball world had been less than kind to the Dons. They could have used some of their old teammates' magic as LMU rolled into the Bay Area and blew the Dons away. The final score was 128-111, and it really wasn't that close.

USF coach Jim Brovelli had decided to try sending in waves of substitutes to try to keep up with LMU's frantic pace.

Bad idea.

For the first half, the Dons stayed in the game until the clock was running down, and so were they. LMU put together a 10-0 run that had the Dons panting as they headed to intermission. The second half saw LMU put together another 10-0 run with the score tied at 77. It was, literally and figuratively, the Dons' last gasp.

Later, Brovelli explained his strategy: "What we wanted to do was outnumber 'em and attack the basket," he said. "What was critical was decision making. We made poor decisions, then it snowballed. We took the quick shot when we shouldn't have." No one bothered to explain to Brovelli that he had become yet another victim of the System. He never knew what hit him. The Lions had scored the most points ever scored against USF, a record that Brovelli probably would not boast about. Fryer was hot in the second half and hit five 3-pointers to finish with 22. Mark Armstrong pulled down 19 rebounds, many in the second half, which helped LMU pull away. Hank had 25 points and Bo 24. LMU's nation-leading scoring average increased to 109.2.[2]

Zepel's cramped office was coming under siege. In the past week USA Today and then Sports Illustrated had called. Even ESPN wanted to interview Westhead. Barry put out an urgent request for additional staff. He'd have to get by with student interns, he was told. He did, and together they tried diligently to keep pace with the media demands, which were increasing with each win.[3]

The next stop for the Lions was Santa Clara, where they took on the University of Santa Clara. The going was a lot tougher there. The Broncos so extended the Lions before a loud, hostile, sell-out crowd that keeping the winning streak alive came down to a last-second free throw by Mike Yoest.

The veteran stepped to the line with just :02 on the clock and the Santa Clara crowd roaring in his face. In the stands his father, Dave, almost couldn't bear the tension. A friend told him not to worry, saying, "Mike will be all right," to which the agitated dad replied, "But, I won't."

At the line, facing the bedlam behind the backboard, Mike kept telling himself, "'It's going in. It's going in.' I was a little nervous but I was confident. Anyone who isn't nervous in that situation is either lying or frozen." Westhead liked to say that Yoest was "as reliable as the sunrise," and he proved to be just that. The senior captain calmly sank the first of two shots, breaking a 93-93 tie.

As the din grew to ear-splitting proportions, Hank stepped over the line into the lane. The refs immediately assessed a lane violation against LMU, denying Mike his second shot. Fortunately, his first proved good enough—Santa Clara failed to score, and LMU held on to win, 94-93.

"I knew it was going in," Mike said later. "This is what you practice in your back yard as a kid—no time left, tie score, you're at the line."[4]

LMU left the chilly Bay Area and headed home. The Lions were now 8-0 in the conference and held a two-game lead over Santa Clara. Their overall mark was now 18-3, and they had moved up a ranking in the AP Poll.

Hank had told the San Francisco- area sportswriters, who, like the rest of the nation, were now showing an interest in LMU, about the Lions' practice sessions. "Our practices aren't fun," he said. "We run for two hours, with two one-minute breaks. We work really hard. The games are the fun. We know we can run 40 minutes. The 45-second clock doesn't even enter into our game."

Now even Westhead was bragging a bit. "Our decision to press has proved correct. Our defense ignites our offense," he told the reporters. "Among coaches, they say it's impossible. Proponents of full-court pressure say you can't do both. They (the players) have to agree to play hard."[5]

Westhead, who had been running a version of the System since high school, had never seen it work so well. But, then, he'd never had the array of talent he now had, and that proved his theories. Over the years, many had said he was crazy, but his faith had remained unshakable. Now his perseverance was being rewarded at last.

Although the Lions had just played USF and Santa Clara, they were next up on the Lions' card.

Santa Clara arrived at Gersten, seeking to avenge its narrow loss of 10 days before. The sight that greeted the Broncos as they tumbled from their bus in the parking lot on February 12 was as unfamiliar to them as it was to Brian Quinn and Al Gersten. Scalpers were hawking tickets outside Gersten Pavilion. Even more odd was that people were eagerly grabbing them. Some reportedly paid as much as $50. "The Hank and Bo Show" was going to produce a sold-out Gersten Pavilion, and the 4,156 who squeezed inside were so eager to see the action that they were willing to pay scalpers' prices.[6]

As he pulled into the parking lot before the game, Al Gersten was grinning widely. Quinn's youngest daughter, Maureen, accompanied her father to the game and couldn't quite believe what she saw—not a single empty seat as the Lions took the court.[7]

The Broncos were known for physical play, and they did not disappoint. The Lions emerged from the bruising contest with a 108-89 win, but the victory was costly. With the score at 69-66, Corey Gaines had gone down hard in the lane while driving to the basket. Santa Clara's Jens Gordon also fell, landing on top of Corey, who left the game with an ankle injury so severe that he required the assistance of trainer Chip Schaeffer to get off the court, and Gaines wouldn't return.

The Lions fed off Corey's injury. After Jeff Fryer took and converted Corey's two free throws, the team put together a 12-0 run. Bo sank two 3-pointers, and Enoch Simmons, replacing Corey at the point, added two baskets as the Lions pulled away to notch their 19th win of the year. Westhead, who pronounced the game "a good clean one," was concerned about the loss of Gaines, saying, "I don't know if we can win without Corey Gaines. He's that valuable to the way we push the ball."[8]

When Brigham Young fell to the University of Alabama-Birmingham on February 13, LMU owned the nation's longest winning streak.

As USF and LMU faced off the next night, Corey Gaines watched in street clothes.

His ankle was badly sprained but not broken. He was confident that Chip would have him ready for the game against Pepperdine the next week.

The Lions felt Corey's absence that night, especially after they lost Mark Armstrong to fouls in the second half. USF climbed patiently back from 100-75 and got within 6 points at 108-102 before LMU pulled away. The final score was 118-109.

The chant that rose from the packed house—"EN-SEE-AY-AY"—was serious stuff, and Westhead was delighted, quipping, "I can't remember the last time I won 20. I think it was with the Chicago Bulls. We won 28." He was joking, of course, about the paltry record that his Bulls had compiled during an 82-game NBA season.[9]

Alan Drooz, meanwhile, was noticing that his editor, Bill Dwyre, was giving him more and more space in which to recount the Lions' accomplishments and tell readers about developments in the story. And it wasn't just the *Los Angeles Times* that had taken notice. *Washington Post* readers learned of the transformation taking place "on a hillside overlooking the lazy harbor of Marina Del Rey," where once "only parents and [players'] girlfriends and the opponents' fans had turned up. . . . Now lines [were] forming" for a chance to see the high-scoring Lions.[10]

The Lions were now 20th in the nation in both the AP and UPI polls.

Westhead told Matt Lait of the *Washington Post* that the lure of the NBA wasn't as strong as it once was for him. "Happiness is when your scheme is working and the players have bought into it," Westhead said. He had seen the System sputter in the professional ranks when players failed to buy into it. "It only works when you buy the whole system," he added. "Without buying in like that it becomes very mediocre. This team has good quality and commitment to the scheme. They really believe [the System] is invincible." No one believed more than Westhead, who told Lait that he was following the advice of Mark Twain: "Put all your eggs in one basket and watch that basket."[11] Westhead was as content as any mother hen.

After all, even the venerable *New York Times* had noticed the commotion that Loyola Marymount was stirring up. The story rehashed Magic Johnson's unhappiness with Westhead—Magic said that Paul was too conservative and stodgy—which had resulted in Paul's dismissal from the Lakers, despite having led the team to the NBA title.

"The irony is inescapable," the *Times* writer opined, noting that the stodgy coach now had a team that was scoring 109 points a game. "My style has always been the same, the running game, shoot within seven seconds," Westhead told the paper. "Sometimes, people can see things differently. First and foremost, I'm a running coach. I don't mind being hung out for my weaknesses, but not running is not one of them."[12] Westhead would say no more about the highly publicized confrontation with Johnson. He would remain ever politic and proper in public—the public could make up its own mind.

Next up was Pepperdine, LMU's hated rival from tony Malibu.

Jim Harrick, who had landed Tommy Lewis while allowing Hank and Bo to get away, warily welcomed the Lions for the 100th meeting of the two schools, saying, "I don't know if we can stop them, but we can contain them some." Westhead said simply that he was expecting a high-scoring game. "I know we've had a few," he said with a smile.[13]

Tommy Lewis was averaging 22.7 points, which was now tops in the WCAC. The Waves were 16-7 and 8-2 coming into the game. Tommy did not enjoy the same level of team support that Hank and Bo were getting at LMU, and Lewis and Pepperdine lacked the depth to run with the Lions.

They tried, but the result was predictable: LMU pounded the Waves harder than the winter surf visible from Firestone Fieldhouse, taking the game, 107-95. Corey Gaines had returned to action with his ankle heavily taped and "played to near exhaustion," according to Westhead. "Without Corey, it would have been a different game," he said.

Mark Armstrong was especially pleased, saying, "I've been a part of a lot of new things at Loyola. I think we're setting a foundation. When I came here, Pepperdine was king of the hill. Now, I think there might be a new king of the hill." Mike Yoest, also a senior, added, "I've been beaten by these guys too many times here. I'm 1-3 here. This was our year."

As Corey iced his aching ankle, he said he'd be ready for the rematch three days hence.[14] No one doubted that he would.

After the game, Harrick called LMU "the best WCAC team we've faced since I've been in the conference. They not only deserve their ranking," Harrick said of the Lions, who were still ranked #20, "they should be #15."

During the game, the refs had warned both Bo and Tommy about throwing elbows.[15] Bo, who had no love for Tommy after USC, where he felt Morrison favored Lewis, scored a career-high 32 points. So this win was especially sweet for Bo, even if his rival had scored 27 points in the losing effort. Among the spectators in the stands was Stan Morrison.[16]

Four days later, the two teams met again at Gersten Pavilion for the game that would determine the conference title. When the game was over, Jamie Sanchez, the tennis coach who doubled as the facilities manager, scrambled to find a tall step ladder so the Lions could cut down the nets, keepsakes of their 142-127 victory. LMU had turned back Pepperdine in a nonstop basket blitz that had the new scoreboard flashing like a strobe light as Prime Ticket, the cable network serving the Los Angeles area, beamed the game live to its subscribers.

Pepperdine had held its own in the first half, and the game was tied at 86 when Dexter Howard picked up a charging foul. Several scuffles broke out, and after the referees restored peace, LMU raced out to seal the win. Pepperdine's Levy Middlebrooks, a 250-pound center, blocked the lane with his considerable bulk and challenged every Lion who dared enter. He had a 40-point game, but it wasn't enough. Hank had 32 for the game.

Bo, eagerly facing Tommy Lewis again, poured it on and accounted for a career-high 36 points. The crowd, which had become unruly when the scuffling broke out on the floor, had taunted Lewis with a barrage of "Lewis sucks!" every time Tommy touched the ball. Brian Quinn found the chant embarrassing, and he tried to quell the obscenities from the student section, with little success.

Confirming the growing popularity of the Lions in Los Angeles was the presence of Dancing Barry, a frenetic performer who was a regular at the Forum for professional games. After a lull, he'd get the crowd going again with his spastic dance routine. The carnival atmosphere only added to the discomfort felt by Harrick at the loss to LMU.

"Kimble may be the best player in the country," Harrick said. "We've faced Danny Manning (Kansas) and nobody has done to us what Bo Kimble did tonight."[17]

With the public address system blaring James Brown's "I Feel Good," and the Rolling Stones's "Satisfaction," Brian Quinn watched with Maureen as the record crowd of 4,525 (several hundred had sneaked in) stood and cheered each Lion in turn as he climbed the ladder to cut down the net.[18]

It had been a long climb for Brian, too. He'd seen support for the team grow from seven mildly interested students to the thousands who now vied for a ticket. A beaming Brian, his flushed face nearly as red as his hair, watched Westhead cut the last snippet of net off the rim and thought about what a long, long way he and Westhead had come together. Clutching Maureen's hand tightly in his, Brian flashed an impish Irish grin and thought, "And the best thing is, it isn't over yet. It's just the beginning."[19]

Now the Lions were #15 in the UPI poll and had passed Georgetown to become the nation's top-ranked Jesuit basketball power. Back in north Philly, no one was snickering and asking, "EL-EM who?"

Having clinched the conference title, LMU—the first team in the conference to go from last to first in one year—traveled to Moraga to meet St. Mary's. The 22-3 Lions were now averaging 110 points a game and leading the nation, but the defense-oriented Gaels were allowing only 54 points per game and ranked fifth in the country.

The Gaels had not forgotten their last meeting, when LMU substitutes had tried desperately to break 100 points as the Gaels tried to stall. Westhead knew this could be a dangerous game for LMU: the Gaels would be fueled by an urge for revenge, and the Lions, having clinched the conference title, might see this game as anticlimactic.

He was right to be concerned. Playing fiercely on their home court, the Gaels refused to fold. And they were getting great support from the hometown crowd in the stands, where supporters lofted a banner that read "Top 20? My Butt!"

The Gaels disrupted the LMU offense and stayed with the Lions throughout. As the game clock wound down, it appeared that the bells of St. Mary's might well ring with the joy of an upset victory. With only 11 seconds left on the clock, St. Mary's held a 94-93 lead before 3,500 screaming Gaels fans ready to celebrate.

St. Mary's had just edged the Lions on a short jumper from Robert Haugen (22 points). LMU headed up court, eschewing a time-out to set up a specific play. Mike Yoest got the ball on the left wing and fired, sinking the 3-pointer. LMU won, 96-94.

"Surprisingly, it felt real good. It felt like the best jumper of my life," Yoest said, adding, "When you're on a roll, things just seem to come your way."

The crowd stood in stunned silence as the Lions celebrated on court. Mike's buzzer beater had capped a furious LMU comeback. The Lions had trailed by as many as 7 points with 1:35 to go, but they had kept on shooting. Trust the System, they'd been told time and again. They did and pulled out their 20th-straight win.

St. Mary's had shot an incredible 70 percent in the second half and had held a 13-point lead at one point. LMU never backed down. Hank had brought the Lions back into contention by miraculously hitting three 3-pointers. After the game, Westhead confirmed for Drooz that "we did make a decision not to call a time-out. We're a running team, we had to shoot on the run. That was an incredible game. Yoest, that shot was. . .wow."

Lynn Nance, the disappointed St. Mary's coach, said, "That's the hardest this (St. Mary's) team has played. If Loyola is not the best team in the West, I don't know who is."

As a relieved Westhead and the team headed to the locker room, Dan McKillop, the St. Mary's athletic director, intercepted Paul. Extending his hand, McKillop said, "That's the best game ever played in this building."[20]

Certainly much of Loyola's success was attributable to the System and using it to perfection, but there may have been an additional reason. The team was enjoying a training table for the first time. A dietitian, Lisa Strong, was supervising the Lions' caloric intake. She wouldn't take any credit for their success, but she had tried to improve their stamina with a healthier diet. Strong noticed that the players had a tendency to skip breakfast or eat high-cholesterol foods, like sausage and eggs. She encouraged them to eat cereals and tried, with some success, to get them to cut back on red meat. She served them chicken and pasta three times a week, kept the fruits and salads coming, and encouraged them to load carbs on game days.

Most players found that such an eating plan worked in their favor, as marathon runners had long since discovered. Not all bought it, though. "Bo had three Burger Kings before the last game," Jay Hillock, one of Westhead's assistants, remarked of one failed convert.[21]

The regular season would conclude in the band- box gymnasium at the University of San Diego, where the seventh-place Toreros would try to spoil LMU's perfect conference mark. The game was sold out as LMU took the court in front of a standing-room-only crowd of 2,500 fans in the San Diego Sports Arena. In what would become typical of him, Hank Gathers responded with a sparkling performance to lead LMU to victory. Although San Diego's Marty Munn scored 35 points in his final home game, LMU outgunned its hosts to win, by 141-126.

Afterward, Westhead said, "Hank Gathers can control a game. He's such a force on the boards, at times he truly is 'The Bank.'" This was the first time that Paul's nickname for Hank appeared in print, but Paul had been using it for some time because he could bank on Hank's shooting ability close to the hoop. He had nicknames for everyone. Usually it would be something like E-Man for Enoch Simmons or M-Man for Matt Yoest, but with Hank it was always, "The Bank" or "Bankman."

"He was the difference in the game," Westhead said and, indeed, Hank's 34 points and 13 rebounds had dominated LMU's scoring.[22]

Ahead was the WCAC tournament, which the Lions would enter with 21 straight victories to their credit. The tournament would be held at Santa Clara, and the first day's action would feature four games—two in the afternoon and two at night. The semifinals were scheduled for the next night, and the winners would meet for the title and automatic NCAA bid on the third day, Monday, March 7, 1988.

Although the Lions would probably be invited to play in the NCAA Tournament even if they didn't win the WCAC, Westhead wasn't counting on it. He'd be using all his guns. Corey Gaines, though still hobbled, was on the game roster. "Resting him didn't even cross my mind," Paul said of the gimpy Gaines. Westhead explained at a media luncheon that because his players ran so hard and so long, missing games and practices hurt their conditioning and disrupted the substitution patterns. "It may be a weakness, but we can't afford to protect [rest] a valuable player," he told the press.[23]

ESPN would televise the finals live for the first time, and the Lions were ready for their close-up.

They managed to keep their winning streak alive, turning back Larry Steele's Portland Pilots and then Pepperdine in close games. LMU beat Portland by only 6 points, 110-104, and Hank scored a tourney record of 33. Pepperdine made it even closer before losing 109-106 in a rough-and-tumble contest. "We were a little sluggish," Hank said of the Lions in their first two contests.[24]

But LMU survived to face the Broncos of Santa Clara for the crown, and a national audience would see the System for the first time, thanks to ESPN. The Broncos had gone 14-1 at home during the season. The only loss had been to LMU on Mike Yoest's miracle shot at the buzzer.

This time, it didn't take a miracle. LMU clinched an NCAA berth with a 104-96 win. Hank scored 24 points and was named the tourney MVP. The Lions, who played catch-up in every game in the tournament, got a gutsy performance from Corey Gaines, "maybe his best game of the year," Westhead said. At the intermission, he had told Corey, "Whatever you did in the first half [when he made six shots in six attempts], just keep doing it." He did, and the Lions prevailed, despite the best efforts of Hank and Bo's former teammate Jeffty Connelly, who scored 20 points for Santa Clara.

Named to the WCAC All-Tournament team were Corey Gaines, Hank Gathers, Bo Kimble, Tommy Lewis, Jeffty Connelly, and Levy Middlebrooks. The win also marked a milestone for Paul Westhead, his 200th career win.[25] It was only fitting that the present he'd receive was what every college coach wished for, an invitation to the Dance. They would have to wait five days, till the NCAA called, to learn where the Dance would be held.

In his popular column in the *Los Angeles Times*, Mike Downey noted that 1988 marked the silver anniversary of the NCAA title that had been claimed by another Loyola, the Ramblers of Chicago. "Don't look now, but lightning is back in the sky," Downey warned, "…because here comes Loyola again." This time it was "Paul Westhead's Loyola Marymount Lions, the rip-roaringest, high scoringest, hottest little basketball team you ever did see."

Rehashing the season that Alan Drooz had covered with ever-increasing column inches, Downey opined that the LMU ticket, which was once the coldest ticket in town, was "bigger in Los Angeles than USC and even U Know What over in Westwood."[26] With such praise from the popular columnist, no one could doubt that the Lions had arrived.

As John Cherwa, then the associate sports editor of the *Los Angeles Times*, explained many years later, "Westhead was a celebrity before [as Lakers coach]. The coming together of the three of them [Westhead, Hank, and Bo] was an improbable story—but then L.A. is a city of improbable stories. [Unlike Hollywood,] this one, though, was real." The story of LMU's rise was "an important one for the *Times*," which was why he pretty much gave Drooz his head and authorized increased coverage as it unfolded.[27]

The smaller *Daily Breeze*, in Torrance, which served communities strung along the coast of Los Angeles and Orange counties, also had followed the Lions' success closely. The *Breeze* had a full-time reporter assigned to the team, and columnist Mike Waldner gave the Lions increasing attention as the season wore on. LMU was now a major story in southern California and a growing one nationally.

Perhaps the strangest fan redoubt was the bayou country of Louisiana, where the popularity of Westhead's team rivaled that of crawfish pie and Dottie West. An all-sports radio station, WIBR in Baton Rouge, had begun to notice LMU. The host of one show, Bob Brodhead, had contacted Barry Zepel when the Lions first cracked the Top 20. Before long Zepel, and later Mark Armstrong, could be heard doing live interviews on the 4 p.m.-6 p.m. drive-time show in Louisiana.

"I had been watching this team and got interested. My daughter, Mindy, who produces the show, said, 'Let's get in touch with them,'" Brodhead told Drooz. "It has been a lot of fun. The U.S. loves a Cinderella. Everybody loves an underdog." Brodhead, a former LSU athletic director, added that his call-in volume had increased significantly since the ESPN telecast. Mindy Brodhead explained the team's appeal to Louisianans by noting, "We've kind of hyped it as an Everyman's hard-working team."

The Brodheads and others at the station regularly wore LMU sweatshirts, and Mindy, who said LMU now had a cult following in the area, added that Louisiana fans might just be able to offer the Lions more than moral support in the NCAA Tournament: "We're gonna get a voodoo in the swamp and send it to the team."[28]

When Westhead learned the pairings and sites for the NCAA Tournament, it was clear that LMU, winner of the lightly regarded WCAC championship, was getting the Rodney Dangerfield treatment from the committee. The Lions were going to appear in Salt Lake City. Worse, one of the teams they'd be facing in the regional was none other than the University of North Carolina, a storied basketball power coached by the legendary Dean Smith. Maybe the Lions' Louisiana fans could conjure (legendary New Orleans voodoo practitioner) Marie Laveau, herself, on their behalf. This was serious stuff.

Although the Associated Press had LMU ranked 16th, the NCAA had made the Lions the 10th seed in the West Region. Their low seed meant that, in the NCAA's eyes, they were no better than 40 in a field of 64. Westhead ignored the slap in the face and told the *Los Angeles Times*, "I'm not surprised by anything the NCAA does. I'm very excited about the NCAA Tournament. Now, we'll just gear up for an extra- special running game."

Hank was a little more forthright, if not original, in his statement about the shabby treatment of LMU: "Our new phrase on this team is, 'We're gonna shock the world,'" he said, borrowing the line made famous by his idol, Muhammad Ali. "Loyola Marymount intends to let everyone know just exactly who we are," he added in a visceral reaction to the NCAA's dissing of his team.[29]

Between Sunday and game time on Thursday, Hank would use that line to fire up his teammates.[30] First up were the seventh-seeded Cowboys of the University of Wyoming, and fans everywhere were looking forward to the match because, as Billy Donovan, the last coach to take the Lions to the NCAA Tournament, said, "They're fearless and fun to watch."[31]

Not everyone was so sure about Westhead and the System. John Wooden's teams at UCLA had used a version of the fast break, a controlled fast break, and that was the only version that any Pac-10 team used during the Wooden era. "Defense usually makes a champion," Wooden said, adding, "While I'm very fond of Paul Westhead, I would be greatly surprised if they won it all."

The more popular, if less eloquent, opinion of the Lions' appeal was voiced by a balding, one-eyed former coach who was the fledgling ESPN network's resident basketball guru. "Run, baby, run!" said Dick Vitale at full volume. Vitale, who was often wrong but never in doubt, added, "This is going to be the style of the '90's."

Although Tom Davis, Iowa's coach, noted that if Westhead were to win the tournament, he "might be surprised at how many coaching clinics he'd be doing," critics continued to point out that the Lions gave up almost as many points as they scored, which the critics cited as evidence of Westhead's disdain for any semblance of defense.[32]

They missed the point.

Coaches who earned plaudits for their defensive genius—Wooden, Dean Smith, Pete Carrill at Princeton, and even John Chaney at Temple—would assert a strategy that was designed to "defend" their basket against attack by the opposing team. Whether a zone defense or a man-to-man defense, all "good" coaches deployed one, the purists averred.

The LMU defense was as tenacious as any in the country. The guards picked up the opposition as soon as they made a basket and harassed and shadowed them like a swarm of angry bees. The result often was that the Lions forced their opponent to make bad passes and turnovers, and they created yet another scoring opportunity for LMU. At worst, the opponent would rush to take a bad or low-percentage shot. So, yes, they were playing defense, just with different tactics. Sure, Westhead sometimes resorted to gimmicks if the Lions couldn't lure their opponent into his running game trap. Sometimes, he placed only four men, sometimes even fewer, in the defensive end, leaving one or more players behind and hoping the mismatch would lead the team with the numbers advantage to shoot faster. He did that only when all else failed, but it would mark him as a coach who cared little for defense. The blot on his reputation was something he would never be able to eradicate, but, then, he didn't particularly care to. With all due respect to John Wooden, either you got it or you didn't. The System was staying.

No matter where fans stood on the defense question, nearly everyone agreed with Donovan: LMU was fun to watch. People were attracted to the team's fast and furious style, and basketball fans would be watching in huge numbers as the Lions took on the Cowboys in the first round. As Robyn Norwood told *Los Angeles Times* readers in her preview of the tournament, "LMU vs. Wyoming" was one of "the Games to watch."[33]

Going into the tournament, senior Mike Yoest, who had been supplanted as conference scoring king by Hank, said, "We really feel confident. We know what we can do." Mike confessed that the 1986-87 team had gone into games hoping not to lose, but with Hank, Bo, and Corey on board, "Now we go out expecting to win, by a lot."[34]

Wyoming's coach, Benny Dees, declared that he was "bitterly disappointed about the seeding"—and Paul Westhead understood why: the Cowboys had won their conference, were better than a seventh seed, and shouldn't have had to face, in their first outing of the tournament, the nation's top-scoring team riding a 24-game winning streak.[35]

The Cowboys had tried using the running game themselves, early in the season, and got it "stuffed down our throats, [so] we had to change a few things," Dees said. Slowing down the pace had worked for the Cowboys, who, with Fennis Denbo and center Eric Lechner, finished the season on a 11-1 run. After Dees and an assistant watched some LMU tapes, though, they "decided we could run with them. We had two [future] NBA first-round draft choices on our team, and we felt pretty confident going in that we could stay" with LMU, Dees said.

That confidence soon proved to be badly misplaced. "It was like watching the wind-shield wipers on your car in a torrential downpour, watching them go up and down the floor," the Wyoming coach recalled. In the early going, Wyoming took a modest lead. "I knew we were in trouble when Hank came by our bench after a free throw at one end and said to a teammate, 'We've got 'em juiced. We've got 'em right where we want 'em,'" Dees said.

Firmly within the jaws of the deadly LMU trap, Dees tried everything to slow the game down. "We told our kids to hold the ball, get back on defense, take only good shots, but we got sucked in. You could see it happening, and there was nothing I could do about it. We started out conservative, and pretty soon, after a few long rebounds, bang, they're gone. We were in a horse race we couldn't win. Before long, we started leaking a little and it was over. We wore out two basketballs," Dees said.[36]

The game ended at LMU 119, Wyoming 115. The combined score set a new NCAA Tournament record, and Loyola Marymount owned the record for most points in a first- or second-round game. Westhead, who had told the press before the game, "We don't care if you score, just don't take too long to do it," had gotten exactly what he wanted.[37]

LMU had used a pressure defense against Wyoming to force 15 turnovers in the first half. At one critical stretch near the end of the first half, the Lions had made two steals of inbounds passes and scored 6 straight points to take the lead at 63-52 at halftime. "That did us in," Dees said later.[38]

The CBS announcer signed off by calling it "the best game I've ever seen."[39]

As a reward for their effort, the Lions got to face North Carolina.

The UNC coach, Dean Smith, was a disciple of Phog Allen's, for whom he had played at the University of Kansas, and fundamentals were important to him. So was winning and adapting to win. He wasn't headed to the Hall of Fame for nothing. Smith was convinced that to beat LMU, he would need to take the Lions out of their offense.

He devised a game plan that used Carolina's tremendous depth to thwart the LMU fast break. He used a full-court trapping defense to prevent Corey Gaines from pulling the trigger that ignited LMU's scoring arsenal. Wave after wave of players came in to keep fresh legs and arms in the face of the harried LMU guard, and it worked. After a slow start, with J. R. Reid holding sway beneath the basket, the pressure and the frigid LMU shooting (13-51 from the field in the first half) did them in.

While LMU couldn't have thrown one into the ocean, Carolina was scoring on every attempt. The Tarheels shot 78 percent to LMU's 25 percent in the first half and made their 65-40 lead hold up. The final score was 123-97. LMU, the sentimental favorite battling the big-time ACC program and legendary coach, was sent home. For the game, UNC shot a resounding 79 percent, and its 123 points broke the tournament record.[40] It wasn't even close.

The winning streak and the long dream season ended with a resounding thud in Salt Lake City. The Lions headed home. Cinderella was dancing no more.

The students who had embraced the Lions' run warmly welcomed them back to campus from the glitz and glamour of the tournament. In his column in the *Los Angeles Loyolan*, marking the end of the season, Keith Cameron, who had covered the team all year, spoke for the vast majority when he wrote, "Thanks for the memories. Next season is only eight months away."[41]

At the graduation ceremony in May, LMU bestowed an honorary degree on its most illustrious graduate, Pete Newell. Somehow, after the year that the Lions had enjoyed, it seemed appropriate.

In late spring, Brian Quinn was in Stillwater, Oklahoma, for a regional NCAA baseball tournament, when he realized the wide impact that the Lions' run had made. "I was in the lobby of the hotel and heard people talking about our basketball team. People knew of us all over the country," Quinn said in amazement.[42]

Hank Gathers wouldn't have been, at all, surprised. He had delivered on his promise. Everyone now knew where, and what LMU was. And the Lions weren't through.

CHAPTER
16

A HEAVY LOAD

The spring of 1988 brought bizarre highs and lows for Paul Westhead.

At the end of March, the U.S. Basketball Writers Association (USBWA) announced its All-America picks, and Westhead saw three of his players named to the team for LMU's district. Balloting was by district, and the voters were the writers who actually covered the games in each district. They had seen the players in action. The USBWA choices, as opposed to those of the other, more widely disseminated, news services were known to be more accurate because they were based on personal observation and comparisons, not press clippings or an occasional glimpse of a game on television.

The District 8 writers selected Sean Elliott, University of Arizona; Pooh Richardson, UCLA; Hank Gathers, LMU; Brian Shaw, UC-Santa Barbara; Todd Lichti, Stanford; Ricky Berry, San Jose State; Steve Kerr, University of Arizona; Anthony Taylor, University of Oregon; Gary Payton, Oregon State; and, in a three- way tie for the final spot, Bo Kimble and Corey Gaines of LMU and Trevor Wilson of UCLA.

Lute Olsen was voted Coach of the Year in District 8, and Sean Elliott, of Olsen's Arizona Wildcats, was named Player of the Year.[1]

In May, *The Arizona Republic* reported that Jerry Colangelo, owner of the Phoenix Suns, was interested in hiring Westhead as a coach for the struggling NBA franchise. Reached for his reaction, Westhead told the paper, "I don't know what to say because I haven't heard from the Suns. I haven't talked with them at all. In general terms, I really love the college game, especially with what we did this year."[2]

Then, in June, Westhead learned that a troubled former player, Spencer Haywood, had considered killing Westhead in 1980 when Haywood was addicted to drugs and in the depths of a depression. Haywood told *People* magazine that, with his brain scrambled by drugs, he had somehow come to believe that Paul, who'd suspended him during the NBA play-offs, was responsible for Haywood's financial and professional problems. Haywood revealed that he had hired a hit man from Detroit, who flew in to Los Angeles with a friend to kill Paul by sabotaging his car. Haywood's mother had persuaded him to call the whole thing off.[3]

Westhead seemingly took it all in stride, well aware that the previous season was just the beginning of his Lions' success and that with it would come still more celebrity.

Hank and Bo had come West to USC with academic preparation that left them better able to infuse your air conditioner with Freon or spot weld its frame than to cope with the rigors of academia at topflight institutions.

They had received coaching on good study habits while they were at USC and had maintained a grade-point average high enough to ensure their eligibility to play basketball. But Loyola Marymount University was not USC. It was a university that was as proud of its high academic standards as USC was of its Heisman Trophy winners.

"I was the first person that they met here," said Lane Bove, then the head of student affairs at LMU, who is known to all as Laney and whose surname is pronounced Bo-VAY. She was a native of Indiana, so she grew up with a Hoosier's love for basketball. At LMU, she would be the person responsible, along with Olivia La Bouff of the Learning Resource Center, for the academic performance of Hank and Bo.

The Learning Resource Center was housed on the second floor of the Von der Ahe Library. "We had a study- hall room, and there were smaller offices for tutorial work, and another area for student-to-student work," Bove said. "I met with them each week for at least a 15-minute session, to check in with them. It was a mandatory meeting, and Hank never missed. I'd ask about their progress, any problems, attendance, and what we could provide to help."

For the most part, the Jesuit institution was appreciative of the positive attention that the basketball program had brought to the school. But that did not mean, however, that the players would be getting a free pass academically. They were required to do the same work as the other students. Scoring average and rebounds didn't count in the classroom. No exceptions.

When they arrived at LMU, Hank and Bo "had an almost animal instinct, as inner-city kids, to sniff things out, to know if you're being straight with them," Bove recalled. "We made certain that they knew from the outset that if they wanted to play basketball here, they were going to have to bite the apple. There was not going to be any b.s. They understood quickly that if they wanted to play, they had to work in the classroom.

"Coming from where he came from, I knew it wouldn't be easy for Hank here. But I let him know we were here to help him. We earned his trust, and it became a 'we can do this' type attitude that got him through. It was never easy, and we knew it wouldn't be, but if it took extra hours, and it often did, then that's what we did. But they got it. They got that we were about being there for them. That we had concern for them."

Warming to her subject, she continued, "There are two Jesuit education tenets that you need to understand. The first is *cura personalia*, or personal care, and the other is *magis*, or more [greater good]. The Learning Resource Center was the embodiment of those tenets, and in practice, for Hank, it meant the difference between failure and success. I told him on many occasions that we will work together to get that paper done. No matter what it takes or how long it takes.

"Hank saw himself as a basketball player, it was who Hank was. When he got pushed up against the academic load, it was hard for him."

On numerous occasions during his years at LMU, the demure 5-foot-2 Bove would gaze up, up, up into the concerned brown eyes of the 6-foot-7 Hank Gathers and quietly but firmly say, "Sit down, Hank, and we'll get this done together," and he would comply without hesitation.

Lane Bove and Olivia La Bouff were all about the greater good, and Hank was the beneficiary of their care and attention.

Hank and Bo were both in the Communications and Film School, interested in preparing for a career in television journalism after their basketball days were over. Their course load was rigorous, and often Hank would simply be overwhelmed by the demands of his studies.

"In many ways, Hank was like a sponge, soaking up all the information eagerly. But, when he froze—boy, did he freeze," Bove said.[4]

Hank Gathers was acutely aware of the need to remain eligible academically. His entire life plan depended on it. Failure in the classroom would mean he couldn't play basketball. If he couldn't play college ball, he wouldn't be drafted by the NBA, and he would be a failure. His mother, brothers, and son would remain in the projects. He couldn't allow that to happen—wouldn't allow that to happen.

Hank's greatest asset was his indomitable will to succeed, no matter the long odds. It had carried him to great heights on the court. In the classroom at LMU, that force of will needed some help. As Bove said, when faced with a deadline for a paper he felt ill prepared to complete, he would literally freeze with fear. The fear of failure and the certain knowledge that failure would end his dream were more than he could bear.

Cassie Westhead, meanwhile, was taking advantage of her husband's position on the faculty at LMU to complete her degree. She was in several classes with Hank. "Most of the players would come in and sit way in the back, hoping to avoid notice and hoping they wouldn't be called upon by the professor," she said. "Hank walked in and sat right up front. Often he'd sit right next to me. He called me Cassie. The other players all thought I was a plant, just there checking up on them. Not Hank. I would watch him and his open eagerness to learn and to take it all in. In the history class we had together, I would be writing my lecture notes as fast as I could to keep up. I would end up with three or four full pages, and Hank would have only a page or so of notes, but they were beautifully written and organized.

"Our professor, Father Rolfe, would kid Hank. When he gave us a quiz, he'd tell Hank, 'Try to beat Cassie.' Once, when he did better than I did, Father Rolfe asked me if he could announce it. I said, "Sure.' When he did, Hank was so proud."

Cassie also witnessed the fear. "Once, after class, I walked over to Paul's office. When I walked in, I saw Hank lying face down on the floor. All 6-foot-7 of him, just lying there, all stretched out, with his head buried in his arms. I didn't know what to do. I mouthed silently to Paul, 'What's the matter with Hank?' He just shook his head and said, 'He's got a paper due and he is afraid he can't finish it on time.' He really did care and wanted to do so well. I was really impressed with that."[5]

Hank would get through those paralyzing moments only because of Olivia La Bouff and Lane Bove. It was a combined effort that was never ending, but they were his academic life-support system. With their help and care he would make it. But it was never easy. For Hank nothing ever was.

Paul Westhead's LMU basketball program was headed in the right direction. He had taken the Lions to the NCAA Tournament, and he was confident that he could do it again. He had a nucleus of returning talent that he was comfortable with. He would lose Corey Gaines, Mark Armstrong, and Mike Yoest to graduation. But Tom Peabody would be eligible, and Westhead had added some other promising recruits. The one returning senior was Enoch Simmons, if he returned.

Simmons was a highly valued sixth man in Westhead's rotation, and with Gaines lost to graduation, the coach was counting on Enoch to trigger the offense. But Simmons was also a standout performer on the baseball diamond: he'd been a fourth-round pick of the Oakland A's and had spent the summer in the A's rookie league. He'd hit .307 for the short season in Arizona.

After much debate and discussion with Westhead, he decided to return for his final year of eligibility. He had seen the power of the System, and the chance to be the point guard was more than he could resist. The A's would have to wait. E-Man was coming back to run the System.[6]

Westhead had managed to recruit another point guard as insurance—Terrell Lowery, who had been an all-star performer in high school for Oakland Tech, a San Francisco Bay Area power. His arrival on campus was important.

Hank took an immediate liking to Terrell, a feisty kid who came from a tough inner-city neighborhood in predominantly black Oakland. "Hank adopted him and treated him almost like a little brother," Bruce Woods, the assistant coach, recalled. "He would say of Terrell, 'Just as soon as his game catches up to his mouth, he'll be real good.'"[7]

Another new face on the team came with a mouth that talked a bit slower and had a slight foreign accent. The mouth belonged to Per Stumer (pronounced Steemer), a Swede who was 6-foot-7 and played forward/center for the Swedish national team. The 21-year-old had been coached abroad by a former LMU player, Brad Dean, who had sent him on to Westhead with high praise. Per came with tremendous raw power and a soft shooting touch. He arrived at LMU in September, and after surviving the Hank Test in Gersten, he was deemed to be "tough enough" and ready to play.

Per, who missed a steady supply of pickled herring, developed, instead, a strong liking for chocolate chip cookies. That wouldn't ordinarily have posed any problems but, as he eventually learned, Hank enjoyed them as well.

Per kept his cache of cookies in the apartment that he shared with Hank and two others. When Per noticed his supply seemed to be dwindling faster than he thought it should, he asked if anyone could identify the cookie thief. When he found out that Hank was the cookie monster, he just laughed it off and bought enough for both of them. Hank, in turn, liked Per almost as much as his cookies.

Hank attempted to convince the big Swede that in California, a community property state, its marital laws extended to refrigerators. "He thought everything I put in the refrigerator was community property. He told me that. He told me that if it was in there, he was entitled to it," Per recalled, laughing.[8]

Hank had stayed in California that summer; it had flown by, and he'd had plenty of company. Heat, now out of school because of his poor grades and attendance, had spent much of the summer with Hank. So had Derrick, who was now a student at Cal State–Northridge with a scholarship that Spence had arranged. When school started again in the fall, Heat headed home to Philadelphia, afraid he was becoming an imposition.[9]

Hank had kept in shape over the summer by playing at the beach and against NBA rookies who were participating in the NBA's Southern California summer league, which was based at Gersten. It was top-flight competition, and he retained his competitive edge. He watched the NBA rookies with interest, gauging his prospects against what he saw and tested himself in one-on-one competition with the more reckless ones. The experience told him what he needed to do to get ready for the next level, and he simply set out to work even harder.[10]

Bruce Woods was often the assistant coach who was around the gym when Hank began a lifting program to add strength and power. He was about the same age as Hank, and they became very friendly through their shared workout routine. Bruce spotted for Hank and watched in awe as he did hundreds of reps with heavy weights. His benchwork and curls were countless. Then he would do push-ups until his veins bulged from his arms. Bruce was also there when Hank ran sprints and when he ran laps. "Hank was a dynamo in the gym. He was tireless and as strong a player as I've ever seen," Bruce said.[11]

But as Cassie Westhead knew from their history course, Hank Gathers wasn't all brawn. Nor did he intend to be the Ted Baxter of sports broadcasting when his playing days were over. Both he and Bo recognized that Los Angles offered the two communications majors a perfect opportunity to gain some experience.

Ed Arnold was the weekend sports anchor at KTLA-TV, Channel 5, the top-rated independent station in Los Angeles. Ed had met Hank and Bo in the course of his reporting duties and took both on as summer interns.

After their transfer to LMU, KTLA had made a conscious decision to accord the school more coverage. "We were already trying to cover UCLA, USC, Long Beach State, Pepperdine, and UC—Santa Barbara, in addition to the Lakers and Clippers, so we were stretched pretty thin," Arnold said. "But Jeff Wald, our news director, was close to Al Gersten, and Jeff told me to give more coverage to LMU, with Westhead and Gathers and Kimble. The rest of us in the sports department kind of laughed, because we all had decided already it might be a developing story. We followed their first season closely, and as they enjoyed more success, we gave them more and more air time."

Before long, Arnold said, "I knew, and everyone else knew, that they were special. They ran a fast break. I called it a rocket break—it was that fast. I had never seen anything like it. It was a thing of beauty. The great appeal was in The Little Engine That Could aspect of the LMU story."

Having Hank and Bo at the station was an eye- opener for Ed. "They were both so interested in the workings behind the scenes. Hank wanted to know about the business. He was very serious about it," he said, noting the intellectual curiosity that Cassie Westhead and Lane Bove had spotted. "Hank was eager to learn from the people working there. He didn't care if it was editing or location work, he ate it all up. He wanted to learn it all."

Hank was popular at the station, too. "He was so magnetic and so funny. Everyone at the station loved him. He was a great mimic and full of life and fun. People just wanted to be around him," Ed said. "He would look at me and say, 'Ed, I'm gonna have your job,' and then he'd laugh.

"I've never dealt with two athletes like them," Arnold said of Hank and Bo, "nor will I ever again. Not just their ability to play basketball but their ability to deal with people. Their personalities were different. One reminded me of a ladies' man, and the other was a clown. Hank, around people, was so great. He adored kids. If he could make a difference in a child's life, it was something special to him. The student body loved him. There was no 'big star,' 'prima donna,' attitude about him at all.

"The relationship they enjoyed with the Westhead family, Cassie and Paul, was great for them. The whole family loved them. And Paul was the right man and the right coach for those two."[12]

After their summer of learning the ropes at KTLA, Hank and Bo returned to LMU for their second season of play. *The Los Angeles Loyolan* reported that the starting salary for a communications major was $18,200. The NBA paid better.

Practice began in mid-October. Hank could barely wait.

David Spencer was back in Los Angeles after a stint as an assistant coach at the University of Hawaii, and he got in touch with Bo and Hank. "They were still my guys," he said.

Spence had some posters for Hank and Bo. He had made them himself and intended them as motivators for the coming year. Hank's was all about rebounds and how he could improve on that aspect of his game this season. Spence had listed on both posters the names of the likely top draft picks in the NBA in the class they would be in.

"I explained to Hank that with all the shots LMU took in a game, there was no excuse for him not to lead the nation in rebounding. I told him if he wanted to attract the attention of the NBA scouts, that was what he needed to do," Spence said. Hank took David's poster and taped it on the ceiling directly over his bed. It was a constant reminder of what he needed to do.[13]

Attracting the NBA's attention was vitally important to Hank and Bo, and in that regard, they had an advantage this season that they hadn't enjoyed the previous year. LMU and its high-scoring offense were going to get regular TV exposure this season. Network executives had quickly spotted the spike in the Nielsen ratings whenever LMU and its fast-paced style had been telecast. The Lions were slated to make a dozen appearances on local cable and on ESPN, USA Network, WGN, and CBS nationally. The local college radio station, KXLU, invested money to improve its signal, so listeners throughout the nation's largest media market could now tune in to LMU games. John Goodwin and Joe Washington would handle the broadcasts. The Z Channel, a cable television network that reached 115,000 subscribers in the metropolitan area, would be televising a package of five games with Tony Hernandez, the outlet's sports reporter, doing play-by-play and Ann Meyers, the UCLA and women's Olympic basketball star, providing color commentary.[14] "The Hank and Bo Show" was going prime time.

Vol. V No. 2   Los Angeles, California

SPIRIT

Summer 1

L O Y O L A   M A R Y M O U N T   U N I V E R S I T

17

A FEW STEPS BACK

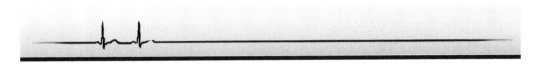

B o was less than ready.

He had begun to feel discomfort in his knee almost from the start of practice. He'd be all right at the beginning and then, as they ran more and more, his knee would start to throb with pain. "I had stopped the weight training after I came back last season. It was a mistake," Bo said.

The knee kept bothering him, and he was examined several times. The doctors thought it might be some cartilage damage, but they weren't certain. Finally, they told him to rest it for a month to see if that would do the trick. "I thought, 'This can't be happening to me,'" Bo said.

Hank, who never thought anyone was working hard enough, especially Bo, was suspicious. "He thought I was doggin' it. Just not pushing myself hard enough," Bo said.[1] Their often strained and stormy relationship now was stretched to the breaking point as Bo sat out practice and the team prepared for what Hank regarded as their showcase season.

"Later, I learned that although he was angry with me, behind my back, he was concerned. He was talking to Father Dave and to Spence about me. He was afraid I was not taking care of myself properly," Bo said.[2] The concern was as real as the anger and frustration he displayed to Bo's face. Hank knew that, despite their fierce rivalry, they were better together than apart. After all, they were "The Hank and Bo Show."

When pain would prevent Bo from continuing in practice, Hank would get in his face and scream, "Come on, you pussy, you aren't ready for the show, come on, you aren't ready!"[3] But Hank's yelling couldn't banish the throbbing pain that Bo was experiencing. It was real, whether Hank believed it or not, and Bo knew it wasn't good. Their showcase season, their chance to strut their stuff for the NBA scouts and viewers nationwide, was set to begin November 28 against Azusa Pacific College.

An intra-squad game on November 12 had produced a score of 172-148 and offered a preview of what was coming. Hank, leading the "Crimson" squad, had scored 58 points, and his back-up, center Chris "Blade" Knight, a 6-foot-9, 180-pounder, had led the "Gray" team with 50.[4]

After the Lions beat the Czech national team with Bo, Jeff Fryer, and Hank (with a slight groin pull) all sitting out, Alan Drooz told *Los Angeles Times* readers that while the Lions might not match the previous year's 28 wins, "it looks like they'll have some fun. And so will those watching."[5]

When the United States had lost in a shocker, in a semifinal round, to the Soviet Union in the 1988 Olympic basketball game that September, some were ready to concede that Westhead's style of play might have some merit. The 3-point shot had sunk the U.S. team in the Olympics, and the Brazilians had used it to defeat the Americans in the Pan-American Games a year earlier. "The rest of the world plays with a higher priority on the 3-point shot," Westhead said.[6] The change in the rules in 1980, to award 3 points for a shot made from beyond the 3-point line (set in 1986 at 19 feet, 9 inches from the basket) altered the game. It provides a way for a team not blessed with great height to compete effectively by using the high-risk, high-reward shot. It gives teams that are decided underdogs based on talent, a chance to succeed by hitting their 3's. When used successfully, the shot can change the momentum of a game, and it creates excitement for the fans, who love it. Success from the 3-point line inevitably stretches the defense, which has to come out to defend against it, thus opening up numerous easy opportunities to score inside that would not occur against taller defenders.[7]

While the stodgy U.S. team was losing, Westhead was winning international converts. And at least one coach in California was a convert for a while. Bill Mulligan at UC-Irvine decided to adopt Westhead's approach. But then the Anteaters (not especially noted for their speed in the wild) lost to Georgia State in their opener, 109-84, and Mulligan scrapped the plan.[8]

As the Lions were getting ready to play, Westhead decided it was time for his players to run the dune. The trip to Manhattan Beach was a surprise to the newcomers. After struggling to the top for the third and final time, Per Stumer looked at Bruce Woods and, panting, asked, "What the hell am I doing here?" Then he declared, "That's the hardest thing I've ever done in my life," and broke into his version of a Rocky dance at the top of the steps. Terrell Lowery was judged the overall winner of the timed competition, and Hank, grinning at the sweat-drenched Lowery, said, "Terrell needs a T-shirt: 'I survived the Dune.'"[9]

It was all over in 15 minutes, and the newcomers were exhausted and impressed by the daunting experience they had just endured. In the wacky world of the System, it was an essential part of the program. Professor Westhead knew tired legs couldn't run the System. His players had to learn to play through fatigue, and one sure way to learn that was by running the dune. The dune had gotten their attention.[10]

The team, ranked anywhere from #17 to #40 in the nation, in the preseason polls, opened at home against Azusa Pacific with Bo still in pain and Fryer limping from an ankle sprain. Students were wearing T-shirts emblazoned with "Repeat Guaranteed" on the front.

Hank had told Drooz before the game, "Last season is over with. We're a new team. It's a whole new ball game. We'll play as hard as we can. We'll run as fast as we can. If we don't win 25 we'll be close. We're gonna win a lot of games. We still have the system and good guys who can run it. The system makes players better. I think we are the best at pushing the ball."[11]

No one would argue with him about that.

In addition to his other motivations, Hank was determined to prove himself to some who recently had not, in his opinion, shown him proper respect. And as a product of the projects, Hank placed a premium on respect, or a lack thereof.

Georgetown's John Thompson, who coached the 1988 Olympic team, had not even bothered to invite Hank to the trials. Hank felt slighted. He didn't say much publicly at the time, but being dissed like that hurt. He wanted to send a message that the Thompsons of the world couldn't miss.[12]

Although Hank had not been a member of the U.S. Olympic team, he was an active participant in the early spring in the Special Games, a series of athletic contests for physically and mentally disabled youngsters from the Los Angeles area. Each participant was teamed with a student for the competition, an event that brought out a large crowd of parents, students, and supporters.

Hank Gathers was there to meet and greet the young contestants. He would approach them with an easy, ambling gait and warm smile, often asking, "'Who's your favorite player?'" said Kristin Ramage Nelson, who was a cheerleader for LMU. "If they showed any hesitation, Hank supplied the answer for them: 'It's Hank the Bank, isn't it?'" The 6-foot-7 giant would let out a hearty laugh while kneeling to be at eye level with the wide-eyed youngsters. "Hank loved the kids and they loved him," she said. He signed their programs and T-shirts and hats without complaint and chatted warmly with all who approached. "His affection and concern were genuine," she added. "He loved them and the effort they put forth."[13]

The spirit and spunk the children displayed by competing, despite their disabilities resonated with Hank. He knew all about being told "you can't" and of beating the odds to prove to people that "yes, I can." He'd been doing it all his life. If he could help the youngsters in their battles, he would do so gladly, without publicity or fanfare or recognition.

Their smiles told him all he needed to know.

The man whose sharply chiseled body and snarling all-out effort on the court could cause an opposing player's legs to tremble like a Chihuahua's was a gentle Pied Piper to children. His affection and concern for them was real, and their love of him was evident.[14] "I always said Hank had the biggest heart of all the players Paul ever coached," Cassie Westhead said.[15]

As the season got under way, WCAC Commissioner Mike Gilleran said, "I can tell you our [WCAC] stock went up immensely (last season). When I go back East now, people know our name."[16] He was, of course, referring to the attention that LMU had brought to the conference.

The season opener showed that the 1987-88 season had been no fluke. With nearly 2,000 spectators on hand, the Lions received their conference championship rings and then ran rings around Azusa Pacific. When it was over, they had rewritten the record book with a final score of 164-138, having established new marks in total points scored, most scored by one team, and most scored by a losing team. It also marked only the second 300-point game in college basketball history.

Hank, with 33 points in just 19 minutes, led the Lions, which had six players who scored in double figures. Sixteen LMU players contributed to the score, and only one played more than twenty minutes. Walk-on Tom Morley, the 16th LMU player to see action, scored the final points with, fittingly, a 3-pointer with 20 seconds to play.[17]

Next, they headed up the road to face Santa Barbara and a date with reality.

Bo had played only 10 minutes in the easy romp against Azusa Pacific, but the Lions would need him to play for more than that against the Gauchos. Westhead could only hope that Bo would be ready.

Santa Barbara had opened with a win over Colorado, 71-70, and Coach Jerry Pimm knew it would be a survival test for his team. Just staying awake might be a problem. To accommodate ESPN, the start of the game had been pushed back to 9:25 p.m., P.S.T.[18]

An enthusiastic, sell-out crowd of 6,000 packed the Events Center for a rare chance to watch their Gauchos perform on national television. They wouldn't need any No-Doz. They got everything they could have hoped for in the dramatic 95-94 win. Halfway through the second half, LMU was trailing by as many as 17 points and put a scare into everyone—as the Lions rallied furiously to come back. Led by Hank's 35 points, they fell just short. The Gauchos had used their own pressure defense to disrupt the Lions in the first half, as they forced 13 LMU turnovers while racing out to a 32-19 lead. Hank and Jeff Fryer then brought LMU to within 4 points at the half, but Santa Barbara quickly rebuilt a double-digit lead that just barely held up as Stumer sank a 3-pointer with two seconds left. Per had gotten them close, but it was too late.[19]

The loss to Santa Barbara was troubling enough for the Lions without the obstacles they faced for their next game, against Oregon State. This was Coach Ralph Miller's last season, and his Beavers had given LMU a defensive clinic the previous season, winning 84-69 and holding LMU to its lowest output of the season. Gary Payton was leading the Beavers, who were 2-0 coming in to the game at Gersten. In those two contests, they had held their opponents to an average of 59 points.[20]

Bo was still hobbling along and not feeling any better. As the Lions took the court on December 7, Bo, nattily dressed in slacks and a cream sports coat, settled his gimpy knee on the end of the LMU bench.

Barry Zepel and Brian Quinn had arranged a pregame presentation for Miller. Westhead presented the coaching legend with a commemorative mug. The Beavers presented their coach with his 655th win, mugging the Lions, 100-90.

Hank had tried desperately to make up for Bo's absence. He scored 34 points and pulled down 17 rebounds. The Lions shot only 34 percent, though, in the second half. Jeff Fryer made only 4 of 18 attempts. Even with Gary Payton benched for a long stretch with four personal fouls, the Lions couldn't overtake the visitors. Oregon State had scored 7 unanswered points and launched a 21-9 run while Payton sat. When he did return, they held a 10-point lead and LMU couldn't make it up. LMU went the last 2:24 without a basket, which may have been a record for a Westhead-coached team.

Hank had made some key steals and some critical baskets to keep it close early on, but he had gotten little help. "When we're under 100, that usually means trouble for us," he pointed out.[21]

A nationally televised date with the University of Oklahoma was only 10 days away. Without Bo, who had been averaging 20 points per game, LMU was in trouble. In the loss to Oregon State, four players had accounted for all but 3 Lion points. "We need a healthy Bo," Westhead told Alan Drooz. "He's an important player to us. But he has to be healthy to be important."

Chip Schaeffer, the team's trainer, tried to put a positive spin on the situation, saying, "Kimble is doing real well. He could have played (Wednesday). I feel confident he'll be 90 percent plus by Oklahoma." As Drooz wryly noted, without Kimble, the highly anticipated "Hank and Bo Show" was slipping in the ratings.[22]

Next on the Lions' card was an exhibition on December 10 against Athletes in Action (AIA), a faith-based organization of former collegians, before LMU had to play the Sooners. Westhead used the AIA game to test his new players. Tom Peabody responded with an impressive performance. He had been eager for a chance to show the coach what he could do, and after the long lay-off from competition, he enjoyed his minutes on the court. John O'Connell, a freshman whom Westhead had recruited from

Philadelphia, saw action as well. He earned the praise of his teammates as he played the second half with four stitches in his lip without complaint. The Lions won the shoot-out, 146-137. Officially, they were still on a two-game losing streak, but the win helped lift their spirits, if nothing else.[23]

As the Lions prepared for the game against the University of Oklahoma, Hank was leading the nation in scoring (33.7), and LMU was averaging 116 points, while Oklahoma was close behind, at 102.

The good news for the Lions was that Bo was going to play. He had tested his knee on the Cybex machine with Chip watching, and the knee had shown marked improvement. Still, no one knew how well his knee would hold up in a game that was likely to be a race-horse affair. The Sooners' coach, Billy Tubbs, told the press it might be a 300-point game, adding, "I just hope we get 200 of them."

Westhead was predictable in his prognostication: "We're gonna shoot it whether you play good defense or not. It depends on them. If their offense has the green light, the score could be a lot like last week's game" [against Athletes in Action]."[24]

On the day of the game, December 17, *Los Angeles Times* readers learned that the NCAA investigation of USC had yielded some reprimands by the Pac 10 in connection with four violations of NCAA rules involving the 1985-86 Trojans. The story stated that two former USC players—a USC source told the paper they were Hank and Bo—had received plane tickets and meals from a Trojan booster, who had also paid for their long-distance phone calls, without the knowledge of former Trojans coach Stan Morrison. The article noted that the booster, whom the *Los Angeles Times* did not iden-tify, was no longer associated with the university.

Bo acknowledged to the *Los Angeles Times* that a booster, whom he did not name, had provided him and Hank with airplane tickets ($300 each) so they could return to Philadelphia for Christmas three years before. "We paid him back when we got back," Bo said. "We borrowed the money from Father Dave. Father Dave wanted us to come home for Christmas. We weren't trying to hide anything. We could have lied about it. But we told the truth. I'm surprised that they're even talking about it now. Morrison had nothing to do with it. We didn't tell him anything."

Mike McGee told the paper, "This has been a very complex investigation on the part of the Pac-10 and NCAA. While it is troubling that the things occurred, we consider the matter closed because none of the individuals are currently at the university."[25]

If the NCAA and Pac-10 investigators had been examining the relationship between Hank and Bo and Priamos for three years and had found only the plane tick-ets, a few phone calls, and meals, it becomes clear why it takes those investigators years to uncover blatant wrongdoing. The investigators assigned to the case must have been the most inept in the country until the Boulder, Colorado, police began searching for the murderer of Jon-Benet Ramsey.

In any event, USC got its wrist slapped and everyone promptly forgot about it. Pete Priamos acknowledged years later that he had sighed in relief that Hank and Bo had "kept me out of it."[26]

Like it or not, ready or not, the spotlight was on the Lions as they headed for Oklahoma. The contest would pit two remarkably similar coaches against each other.

Like Westhead at LMU, Billy Tubbs got little respect for his success at Oklahoma. His high-scoring Sooners were often criticized for their inattention to defense. It rankled Tubbs as much as it did Westhead, which is to say, not a lot. Tubbs had his own prism through which he viewed the world outside his office in Norman. When Tubbs left his alma mater, Lamar University, in 1980 and arrived to coach the Sooners' basketball team, he recognized immediately that there were pluses and minuses.

Barry Switzer's football team played to packed houses of 75,000 as it battled for the national title. Far from being discouraged at playing second fiddle to Switzer's gridiron program, Tubbs saw advantages. "I love it when the football team puts 75,000 in the seats because it helps our budget. Football is our ally. We're not in competition. Being against football around here," Tubbs sagely offered, "is like being against motherhood."

When football season ended (often in a New Year's Day bowl game), Tubbs told Alan Drooz, "We're 'number one' in the state when it comes to basketball season. Besides, what would I do with 75,000 people if we didn't have football? (It) keeps 'em out of my hair, which I don't have much of anyway."[27]

ESPN's Dick Vitale had made Tubbs a member of his "All-wacko" team, but the coach, engaging and quotable, was also a workaholic who prepared his team with an attention to detail that belied his flippant comments. He had taken Lamar to two NCAA tournament appearances. When he arrived, the Sooners had had only two 20-win seasons in their history, but after his second year at Norman, the Sooners never had fewer than 22 wins and won the Big Eight title three times. When Tubbs had Wayman Tisdale on his roster, he took the team to the Elite Eight twice. Tubbs, explained a former assistant coach, was "in the entertainment business. People would much rather see a 115-100 game than a 66-58 one. He understands that." Vitale, whose "wacko" characterization did little to enhance Tubbs's credibility, added, "I've found him to be a fun-loving kind of guy. But, he's also a fierce competitor. His style aggravates some people—he's his own man."[28] He could just as easily have been referring to Paul Westhead.

The two high-octane teams met in Lloyd Noble Arena for what USA Today had dubbed "the run-and-gun match made in heaven." Barry Zepel, LMU's sports information director, told the *Los Angeles Loyolan* that he had handled requests for interviews and back-ground information from *USA Today*, Curry Kirkpatrick at *Sports Illustrated*, and so many others that week, he'd lost count. Zepel had been at his post since 1979, and the Lions' recent success had been a welcome development to a man who had tried in vain for most of his tenure to get publicity for his school. The success came at a price, though. "It's great to have, but it's exhausting," he said. "It's tough to be creative when everyone wants some-thing different. But, I've waited 10 years for the chance and it's great for the school."[29]

For the 11,534 Sooner fans and the national TV audience, the game lived up to the hype. LMU managed to stay with the Sooners in the first half and trailed by just one, 64-63, at the break. During halftime, Stacey King told his teammates, "This is for bragging rights. We want to keep them down. We want to keep them under 100."[30]

The Sooners did just that. Oklahoma, led by Mookie Blaylock and King, sent the Lions reeling back to California on the short end of a 136-103 final score. The Sooners were 6-1, and LMU had fallen to 1-3. After the half, Tubbs had switched to a half-court, man-to-man defense and pressured the LMU guards with Blaylock. The Sooners blasted away and maintained the lead throughout.

"They (LMU) were talking a lot of stuff before the game that we couldn't run with them; that they were in the best shape. We wanted to show them who was in the best shape. A game like that, you forget you're tired," said King. History and geography would suggest he had never seen a dune to run.

Hank had 27 points and a career-high 18 rebounds. Enoch Simmons and Jeff Fryer had scored 28 points each to lead LMU. No other Lions reached double figures. The Sooners got a career best of 31 from Blaylock, Tyrone Jones added 33, and King had 28.

Hank summed up the experience succinctly: "It was definitely fun. If I had to, I would do it all over again." No doubt, he meant he'd do it with a different ending. Without Bo for most of the game the Lions had shot a pathetic 40 percent and just 34 percent in the critical second half. That, and the harassment by Blaylock, was their undoing.[31]

After Oklahoma, LMU headed East to play in the Old Style Tournament in Chicago. The tournament, held over two days, owed its name to a brewery that produced a local beer of the same name. In the first round, the Lions would meet the Governors of Austin Peay College, who were 6-3 for the season thus far, while the local host team, DePaul, took on North Carolina A&T. The sponsors undoubtedly were hoping for a DePaul-LMU match-up for the final.

The Lions had all they could handle in turning back the gutsy Governors from Clarksville, Tenn., by 94-93. Enoch Simmons gave the Lions their first win of the month when he sank a jumper with five seconds remaining. The Governors had forced numerous first-half turnovers and led the Lions, 56-50, at the break. Bo, playing hurt, put the Lions within one point—with less than a minute to go—with a jump shot that set up Simmons's game winner.[32] Thus the Lions escaped what would have been an embarrassing loss and moved ahead to face the Blue Demons of DePaul, who had easily vanquished North Carolina A&T. Superstation WGN would televise the final.

Despite scoring 111 points, the Lions fell to DePaul. The host team managed to put up 115 points, the most important of which came on a 3-pointer by Brad Niemann with 40 seconds to play. The Blue Demons were trailing, 109-108, when Niemann's shot dove home. The Lions tried to foul to have a chance to come back, but DePaul converted and it was over.[33]

Hank had fouled out with 2:46 to play after scoring 32 points to lead LMU. At one point in the first half, he made nine straight points to put LMU in front, 25-16. Bo was scoreless, perhaps for the first time in his career.[34] Not a good sign. Feeling as bad as an Old Style hangover, the Lions headed home, 2-4.

They soon learned the worst: Bo was out indefinitely. The doctors had taken another look at his knee and decided that surgery was in order. He could wait until the end of the season or have it repaired now. In pain and unable to perform at anything near the level he needed to, he opted to have the operation right away. It would mean he would miss at least six weeks, but it might allow him to return for the end of the season. It was a devastating blow to Bo, but he had little choice.[35]

Between Christmas and New Year's, he had arthroscopic surgery to remove torn cartilage, and Hank visited his dejected teammate. "He was very quiet," Bo said. "No typical Hank talking. It was as if he didn't know what to say. He knew I was hurt and I was depressed about it. He offered his best wishes and after half an hour or so, he left," and went to the gym to play.[36] For the first time since ninth grade, Hank was facing basketball without Bo. No one knew how long Bo would be out of action.

After Bo's operation, Hank underwent a transformation that surprised Bo and everyone else. "It was as if he was playing for both of us," Bo said. "He took the responsibility for the team on his shoulders from that point on."[37]

Marist College made the trek from New York to Gersten, hoping that the dejected and depleted Lions would be easy game. The Red Foxes brought with them a 3-3 mark and their 6-foot-11 center from Yugoslavia, Miroslav Pecraski, for the December 28 game. The visitors could have used the Yugoslavian army and they still might have lost. The Lions found the first home game in three weeks to their liking—as they hounded and ultimately ran down the Red Foxes, 131-107.

The first half saw LMU build a 70-54 cushion on 12 3-pointers, and the familiar LMU fast-break offense and pressure defense forced Marist into a running style the

Foxes couldn't sustain. Hank led the Lions with 39 points and 13 rebounds. Fryer had 28 and Simmons added 20 points and 10 assists as 11 LMU players scored.

"We really had our offense going," Westhead said. "I think they couldn't quite keep up. We played with some good energy." He didn't say so, but he was especially impressed by Hank's forceful inside game, which helped the Lions gain control of the game in the first half. Hank played with a fierce intensity as he battled the taller Marist players. The team responded to his leadership, built a 16-point halftime lead, and coasted home.[39]

The publicity the school had been receiving as a result of the extensive television exposure and Barry Zepel's efforts did not make everyone on the Westchester campus happy. WGN had repeatedly referred to the school as "Marymount" during its coverage of the Old Time finals. Other papers and magazines had used "Loyola of Marymount."

Zepel was asked to put out a press release explaining the school's proper name and asking that journalists and announcers avoid all other designations. Don Ott, a publicist for the West Coast Athletic Conference (WCAC), saw an opportunity for additional exposure and churned out a whimsical press release that said, "What would Dame be without its Notre or Forest without its Wake? What would Rock be without Slippery or Little? Never leave your Dickinson without a Fairleigh and avoid a Marymount without a Loyola."

Despite the win against Marist, Westhead found little reason to smile. "The absence of Bo is stretching me," he told Alan Drooz. "We don't really have another (shooting guard). Against Marist, we used Terrell Lowery and he seemed to like it."

Saying it was still too early to gauge the effect Bo's absence would have on the team, Paul said, "The guys recognized his inability to play weeks ago. The next three or four games, we'll see the results and learn if someone will step forward in the wake of his absence."[40]

He got his answer in the very next game.

18

STRONGEST MAN ALIVE

H ank had a charming habit of proclaiming to anyone and everyone around the team, always with a smile of self-assurance, that he was "the strongest man in the world."

He said it with such regularity and with such disarming sincerity that it became a part of his persona. It was his way of both affirming his tremendous athletic ability and convincing himself, as much as anyone else, that he was, indeed, the strongest man in the world.

Because of his role in the System, he needed to be no less than that to succeed and for the System to succeed. Wimps could not run at full speed for 40 minutes, nor could most 6-foot-7 power players. He needed every ounce of his considerable strength when his role called for him to battle bigger, heavier, post- position giants for the numerous rebounds the System produced. Whether he really believed it or not (most would agree that he did), he needed to act like he truly was the strongest man in the world.

Besides, Hank also loved the appellation. It reminded him of Superman. And everyone, including Hank, loved Superman. If ever the Lions needed a quick-change artist to emerge from a phone booth and come to the rescue while Bo was flat on his back with his leg in the air, it was now.

On Friday, December 30, LMU took the court in Reno to face the Wolf Pack of the University of Nevada-Reno. Hank had had some luck in the Reno casinos on Thursday, and the Lions were hoping his luck would rub off, as they attempted to get to .500 for the season. A crowd of 7,640, fifth-largest in the school's history, was on hand. The Wolf Pack, at 6-3, was a high-scoring team that averaged about 93 points a game and was 5-1 at Lawlor Events Center. The Lions, meanwhile, were 3-4 and averaging 112.4 points per game while surrendering 112.

Scoring a career-high 49 points and tying an LMU record, Hank took the team with him on a mad run through the Wolf Pack that would have had the craps shooters downtown whooping with joy. He pulled down 26 rebounds to lead the Lions to a 130-125 win.

Not that it hadn't been a nail-biter at times. The Lions had been down, 62-57, at the half, causing Westhead to challenge his team: "We asked for it (the pace). What are we gonna do about it?" Later, he told Alan Drooz that he wasn't actually worried at that point because "we still had Hank the Bank."[1]

"Whenever we got it to Hank in the paint, it was as good as money in the bank," he explained.[2]

And on this night, in the Silver State, Hank had been as good as gold. Responding to Westhead's challenge, Hank had taken command of the Lions' offense and scored the first three baskets of the second half. LMU built leads that reached 13 points at times and withstood a late Reno charge. When both Enoch Simmons and Jeff Fryer were lost to fouls, Hank simply stepped it up another notch. His fellow cookie lover, Per Stumer, scored 16 points, as Hank lifted the entire team to another level by his example. Tom Peabody and Terry Mister filled in admirably, both scoring 12 points and hitting critical shots down the stretch as LMU held on to win.[3]

That night, Hank displayed the form that became his signature. His domain was in the crowded key, where his put backs, short jumpers, lay-ups, and dunks brought scoring opportunities. And what dunks they were. They were both beautiful and vicious at the same time, depending, of course, on your perspective. Each sent a message to opponents and brought the crowd to its feet. His calling card was a tomahawk dunk thrown down through the net cords with every ounce of energy he could muster. "Look at me! Notice me! I'm the leader!" it said with every rim-rattling, backboard-shaking dunk. No one watching an LMU game could miss No. 44.

Sometimes, as in this game against the Wolf Pack, Hank would display the lessons he had taken as a youngster from Heat and Doug Overton—he would grab a long defensive carom and take off up court. With astonishing speed and grace for a 6-foot-7 player, he would dribble-drive, changing hands to evade a defender, and go coast to coast, finishing with a dunk that began from just in front of the free-throw lane as he launched his muscular body skyward with ease.

A despondent and depressed Bo Kimble listened to the game on the radio. The game was already under way when he tuned in. "I heard Hank had 20-some points, and I figured the game must be almost over. It was only the beginning of the second half," Bo said. He spent the rest of the game grinning and silently cheering his teammate on. Hank had let loose the monster within, Bo thought. He'd be impossible to stop now.[4]

Bo also knew Hank would be impossible when he returned to recap the game for his ailing teammate—detail by hyperbolic, hysterical detail—all delivered with his dead-on Howard Cosell impersonation. But, thought Bo, "This time it will be O.K. because he's playing for both of us."[5] Bo's recovery started right then and there. This show was too good to miss. He needed to get back.

Meanwhile, leadership of the Lions fell to Hank, who had always been a vocal leader. Now he became even more so. He was an unselfish, driving force on the floor; his sense of mission resonated with his teammates, and they responded.[6]

The 1988-89 season was about to begin in earnest. The Phoenix of Wisconsin–Green Bay were coming to Gersten on January 2, and Xavier would follow two days later, on the fourth, and both presented formidable problems for LMU.

Loyola Marymount barely survived the visit by the Phoenix players, who found the southern California sun to their liking in the middle of a Green Bay winter. But Enoch Simmons calmly sank two free throws with two seconds to play, giving the Lions a narrow 85-83 win. Hank had 33 points.[7]

Coach Pete Gillen and Xavier University arrived next, and this time LMU wasn't as lucky. The Musketeers handed LMU a 118-113 loss. "Hank was just about unstoppable that night," Gillen said. "We had to slow the pace down. I told my team to make five or six passes before taking a shot; of course, the crowd booed us for that. We had Tyrone Hill and he was about 6-foot-9, and we had Derek Strong, 6-foot-10, another big man. Both went to the NBA. But Hank scored at will. He was just muscle on muscle with my guys and he won. He was a 6-foot-7 stud with a chiseled body, and he wouldn't back down," Gillen said.

The major factor in the tenacity that Gillen had witnessed was not the need to make up for Bo's absence, or simply Hank's love of the game, but his determination to make it to the NBA. Scouts were watching with a critical eye. Some declared him to be too small, others too limited in range. Hank would simply show them—as he had shown doubters all his life—that he would outwork, out-hustle, and out-muscle his way into the professional ranks. "I'll get through you, around you, over you, and you can't stop me," was the message his every move telegraphed to his opponents in every game he played. The scouts read that message too, and to many of them, Hank's incredible will and competitive nature overcame all his perceived shortcomings.

Against the two big men of Xavier, Hank managed 34 points and 16 rebounds. Gillen, who left both Hill and Strong in the game despite early foul trouble, explained, "I didn't want to go to the graveyard with my best players on the bench."[8]

After the game, Pete saw Hank outside Gersten as the Xavier team headed for the bus. "He was dressed in a white silk sweatsuit, and he was just a tremendous physical presence. We talked a few minutes about the game, and I could tell he just enjoyed the game so much," Gillen said.[9]

The loss to Xavier put the Lions at 5-5 as they headed to San Diego to face U.S. International University (USIU). Despite the name, it was a small school of 3,500, mostly commuters, and best known for scoring a lot of points in basketball games. The

Soaring Gulls wore their reputation on the court as a badge of honor and hoped no one would look too closely at the school's curriculum.

The Gulls' home court was the downtown San Diego Convention Center in Golden Hall, and the Lions met them there on January 7 in what everyone knew would be a scoring bonanza.

"One thing about Westhead is that he refused to compromise, even a little bit," said his long-time friend Don Casey, himself a former coach. "Paul was bright, even brilliant, [as] a scholar, but when he steps on the court it's like another button is pushed. It was score or be scored upon. He was absolutely committed to his dribble, fast-break, concept."[10]

In U.S. International, Westhead would find an opponent easy to lure into a running game. Coach Gary Zarecky had been at USIU for three seasons, and while his school was not that successful while playing as a Division I independent (29-55), the Gulls did have a pronounced proclivity for fast-paced play. Among Zarecky's favorite coaches were Oklahoma's Billy Tubbs and Westhead.

LMU was more than happy to give the Gulls the type of game they wanted. The two teams tore through the game and the NCAA record book in the process. As buckets rained down on sunny San Diego, the Lions turned back their accommodating hosts 162-144. The contest established a new mark for most points in a game, 306, and LMU tied the mark held by UNLV for most points scored by a team, 162. Hank led the Lions in the romp with 40 points and 23 rebounds. Simmons added a personal best of 38 points, and Jeff Fryer chipped in with 30. The records that fell included the most points by a losing team.

"It was a fun game to be in," Zarecky told Alan Drooz. "This is the kind of game I've thought about for 25 years. But it's more fun if you're on the other end. People are coming up and congratulating me. I'm not sure what for."

Of the records his team set, Westhead dismissed them with, "I don't really get into that (record) stuff that much. I'm into it this much—I would like to see our team play the perfect game, run the perfect break every time. That would be up around 240 (points). So 160 is just kind of dabbling with mediocrity."[11] But his mediocre Lions now had a positive momentum for the first time in a long time, at 6-5 for the season.

On January 11, the Dons of San Francisco traveled down to LMU. With nearly 3,300 on hand, the Lions prevailed, 113-95. Hank had 36 points and 11 rebounds, while leading the victors in the first conference game of the year.[12]

Another conference game followed on January 12th, against Santa Clara. Led again by Hank, with strong support from Per Stumer, the newly energized Lions started slowly but forced 29 turnovers in front of more than 4,000 ticket holders to record an 87-80 win.[13]

Stumer had started every game, and the big, likeable Swede was fitting in better than Westhead could have hoped. Per was finding the System to his liking.

Hank, Bo and Jeff Fryer, a dangerous threesome.

Hank at the mike. Ed Arnold said of the aspiring sportscaster, "He wanted to learn everything. He was funny and he would have been very good at it."

Running The System.

Hank at the free throw line where he always struggled but never stopped trying to improve.

ALBERT GERSTEN PAVILION
Loyola Marymount University

SUNDAY 5:00 P.M.

WEST COAST *CONFERENCE* TOURNAMENT **SEMI-FINALS**

MAR
4
1990

Admission
Student

$12.00
$10.00

Sun., Mar. 4, 1990 · 5:00 PM

Weldon, Williams & Lick, Inc.

LOWER LEVEL
103 N 3

103 N 3
LOWER LEVEL

PARTICIPANT

WEST COAST
CONFERENCE
TOURNAMENT

Gonzaga
Portland
San Francisco
Saint Mary's
Santa Clara
Pepperdine
Loyola Marymount
San Diego

LOS ANGELES
MARCH 1990

LOYOLA MARYMOUNT UNIVERSITY
GERSTEN PAVILION

Saturday, March 3
Session 1 • 12 Noon and 2:00 p.m.
Session 2 • 6:00 and 8:00 p.m.

Sunday, March 4
Semi-Finals • 5:00 and 7:00 p.m.

Monday, March 5
Championship • 8:30 p.m.

THE
A COPLEY
LOS ANGELES
NEWSPAPER

Daily Breeze

STREET EDITION
March 5, 1990 25¢
Torrance, California
96th year/Number 64
©1990 The Copley Press Inc.

MONDAY

Doctor prescribes steady diet of walking
Fitness leader speaks in Torrance

Jerry Dunphy makes news in prime-time
Veteran anchorman heads KCAL's new 3-hour effort

UCLA ends regular season with victory
Bruins beat visiting Washington

| HEALTH | A10 | LIFE/ARTS | C1 | SPORTS | D1 |

LMU star player collapses, dies

Eric "Hank" Gathers was a top scorer, rebounder.

By Chris Long and Eric Stephens
STAFF WRITERS

Eric "Hank" Gathers, a standout center for the Loyola Marymount University basketball team, collapsed on the court during a game Sunday night and later died at Daniel Freeman Marina Hospital.

Gathers was 23.

Dr. Mason Weiss, the cardiologist in attendance at the hospital, said the cause of death was unknown.

Brian Quinn, LMU's athletic director, said Gathers had a heart arrythmia that was being treated medically. Gathers also collapsed during a game on Dec. 9.

"Hank Gathers sustained a syncopal event tonight while playing basketball at Loyola Marymount," Quinn said. "Cardiac resuscitation was performed by the physician in attendance and he was transported to Daniel Freeman Marina Hospital where resuscitation was continued. At 6:55 p.m., he was pronounced dead.

"Mr. Gathers had a previous syncopal episode in December of 1989, which had been determined to be caused by a heart arrythmia, which ws treated medically," Quinn said. "He was cleared to participate in all athletic events."

Gathers collapsed on the court at 5:14 p.m. He was attended to by LMU team trainer Robert Schaefer until paramedics arrived.

Lucille Gathers, his mother, and Carol Livingston, his aunt, had flown in from Philadelphia for the West Coast Conference Tournament, which was being played at LMU. Also in atten-

dance was Derrick Gathers, his brother, who is a basketball player at Cal State Northridge.

They immediately ran down to the court when Gathers collapsed.

Gathers was taken to the hospital by ambulance where further resuscitation efforts were unsuccessful.

"We continued resuscitation measures for over an hour," Weiss said. "He was awake, then he completely passed out. His heart rhythm was not compatible with life.

"He was conscious on the

floor. The physician got some response, then apparently some seizure activity occurred, which

PLAYER/BACK PAGE

IN ADDITION

- **Players, friends** react to the tragedy./D1, D6
- **Sports Editor** Mike Waldner remembers Gathers./D1
- **West Coast Conference** tournament canceled./D6

Los Angeles Times

CIRCULATION:
1,118,649 DAILY / 1,433,739 SUNDAY

MONDAY, MARCH 5, 1990
COPYRIGHT 1990/THE TIMES MIRROR COMPANY/CC† /100 PAGES

DAILY 25¢
DESIGNATED AREAS HIGHER

COLUMN ONE

Schools Put to Bold Test in N.Y.

■ Joe Fernandez dropped out of high school. Now as chancellor, he has set out to turn around the nation's largest public school system.

By KAREN TUMULTY
TIMES STAFF WRITER

NEW YORK—Back in the early 1950s, the New York City school system failed with Joe Fernandez. Or maybe it was the other way around.

There were probably teachers who tried to reach him, but none made much of an impression. Of all of them, he can remember only one by name: Mrs. Brown from third grade, who took him on his first trip to a museum.

As a teen-ager in East Harlem, he hung out with a gang that called itself the Riffs. Afternoons would find them cutting class and sneaking into the Paramount Theater on 42nd Street. They experimented with drugs and got into fights. Some of Joe's friends ended up in jail.

At 17, Joe saw what lay ahead of him in Harlem, and decided he had to escape. He quit school over his parents' objections and joined the Air Force.

Almost 40 years later, this high-school dropout has returned to New York hoping to turn around a troubled educational program that is awash in scandal and literally falling apart. In January, Joseph A. Fernandez, the son of Puerto Rican immigrants, became chancellor of

Middle-Class Backlash Hits at Panhandlers

By DAVID TREADWELL
TIMES STAFF WRITER

NEW YORK—When a federal court judge here struck down a long-standing ban against panhandling at the Port Authority bus terminal, James Benagh could not wait to apply for one of the new begging permits transit officials began issuing to comply with the ruling.

"I put on my best suit and tie, shined my shoes and shaved—everything—and got the very first permit," the 52-year-old New Yorker proudly recalled.

But Benagh had no intention of using the permit to wheedle spare change out of the thousands of travelers and commuters who daily pass in and out of

Please see BEG, A10

L.A. Marathon — a Block Party 26 Miles Long

By SHERYL STOLBERG
TIMES STAFF WRITER

Nearly 19,000 runners trekked through the City of Angels on Sunday, and the city they saw during Los Angeles' fifth annual marathon was as colorful as their sweat-drenched T-shirts and as alive as a jogger on a high.

The race turned Los Angeles into a 26.2-mile-long block party.

On Olvera Street, a mariachi

Loyola Marymount's Hank Gathers after he collapsed; he was later pronounced dead at hospital.
GARY FRIEDMAN / Los Angeles Times

Gorbachev Sees Voters Holding Key to Reform

■ **Soviet Union:** The Kremlin leader goes to the polls, hopes elections will bring new faces into government.

Gathers, Loyola Basketball Star, Collapses, Dies

By JIM HODGES
TIMES STAFF WRITER

Rebel Clash Puts Aquino in New Crisis

■ **Philippines:** The battle leaves a dozen dead, including a general. The renegade governor who supported December coup attempt escapes arrest.

By BOB DROGIN
TIMES STAFF WRITER

MANILA—A major new crisis loomed Sunday for President Corazon Aquino's struggling administration after Philippine troops battled a renegade governor's heavily armed supporters in northern Luzon and a senior military official was shot to death.

Government troops backed by helicopter gunships later stormed a seedy hotel in Tuguegarao, a provincial capital about 250 miles northeast of Manila, and rescued an Aquino Cabinet secretary and about 50 other officials and guests trapped by rebel forces since dawn.

Suspended Gov. Rodolfo Aguinaldo, who has been charged with supporting last December's failed coup against Aquino, was still at large early today. But officials confirmed the death of Brig. Gen. Oscar Florendo, 51, chief armed forces spokesman and head of the military's civil relations branch.

More than a dozen other people were reported killed and 10 wounded in the fierce battle around the Delfino Hotel.

"The act of cowardice and treachery of Aguinaldo's followers will not go unpunished," Aquino vowed in a statement here. "We will see that the fullest force of the law is meted out to them.

"I call on all our people to

Death silences Lions' roar

Mike
Waldner

Memories of
a kind Lion

I want to remember Hank Gathers with the big smile on his face and the friendly "Hi, howyadoing?" greeting.

I want to remember Hank Gathers rattling the entire building with one of his monster dunks.

I want to remember Hank Gathers telling everyone after Saturday's game about how he was responsible to set an example for his teammates by grabbing rebounds in the West Coast Conference Tournament and then in the NCAA Tournament.

I will never forget watching Gathers crumple to the court early Sunday evening at Loyola Marymount University during a meaningless basketball game against the University of Portland.

I will never forget watching Gathers go into convulsions on the floor.

I will never forget watching the medical people trying to save his life on the cold concrete slab outside Gersten Pavilion. There they treated him before they took him by ambulance to Daniel Freeman Hospital.

This strong young man — this very strong young man — had a weak heart.

Gathers had been treated for a heart problem after he collapsed Dec. 9 during a game against UC Santa Barbara.

The doctors tested and tested him. They tested him some more. They tested him some more. They could find no medical reason to prohibit him from playing.

So they gave him medication to control the beat of his heart. And they let him do what he did so well. They let him play basketball. That's what he was doing Sunday in the WCC Tournament.

The medication made him weak, so he asked to be reduced to cut down the dosage, which they did.

After that, he insisted he felt fine. Strong. Healthy. He had no problems. His play gave no indication at all of any reason for concern.

Gathers died Sunday at 6:55 p.m. in the hospital.

They did the right thing when they stopped the game and told everyone to go home.

Fans in the stands, who had remained in stunned silence, applauded the announcement.

Should they cancel the tournament?

They also did the correct thing when they called off the tournament.

Should LMU end the season without playing in the NCAA Tournament?

The immediate urge is to scream that they should forget all about basketball.

But that's a decision the players should make, with input from university officials. They should make their decisions without the rest of us putting in our two cents.

WALDNER/ BACK PAGE

Hank Gathers, with his arm twisted behind him, is laid back on to the court by LMU trainer Robert Schaefer, kneeling right, after Gathers collapsed. Lions Coach Paul Westhead looks on from the background.

BRUCE HAZELTON/STAFF PHOTOGRAPHER

GATHERS' CAREER

Year	School	Games	Points	Rebounds
1985-86	USC	28	8.3	5.1
1987-88	Loyola Marymount	32	22.5	8.7
1988-89	Loyola Marymount	31	32.7	13.7
1989-90	Loyola Marymount	24	28.8	11.2
Totals		115	23.1	9.7

LMU left
stunned
by death

By Eric Stephens
and Chris Long
STAFF WRITERS

Hank Gathers, the leader of the Loyola Marymount basketball team and one of the top scorers in NCAA history, died Sunday night at Daniel Freeman Marina Hospital in Marina Del Rey.

Gathers, a 23-year-old senior center for the Lions, had been taken to the hospital after collapsing to the floor during the first half of the West Coast Conference Tournament semifinal game against Portland at LMU's Gersten Pavilion.

Family and close friends were in the hallway outside the room where Gathers was being treated. Two teammates — point guard Tony Walker and reserve Chris Knight — waited in the emergency waiting room.

Derrick Gathers, Hank's brother, had telephoned close family friend the Rev. Dave Hagan in Philadelphia at about 6:25 p.m. and told him that Hank did not have a pulse.

"He called me from the emergency room," Hagan said. "I'm very, very surprised. I just hope he's still alive. We're all praying."

Thirty minutes later, Gathers was dead.

At 6:58 p.m., a male voice screamed repeatedly and pounded on the wall outside Gathers' room. One minute later, Gathers' aunt, Carol Livingston, ran out of the emergency lobby and outside to a nearby telephone booth repeatedly yelling "He's gone, he's gone."

Livingston then contacted relatives in Philadelphia, Gathers' hometown, and told them the news of the All-American's death.

Gathers was pronounced dead by hospital staff at 6:55 p.m.

Knight and Walker, though, sensed the outcome earlier after Livingston burst through the waiting room. Knight went outside and screamed, while tears streamed down Walker's face.

Both walked out to the parking lot later in the evening and would not comment about the loss of their popular teammate.

"It is a tremendous loss for our university," said Brian Quinn, Loyola Marymount athletic director, in a news conference in the hospital's main lobby. "He was an outstanding young man. We're all going to miss him and we are truly grateful for the opportunity to be friends. How deeply we will miss him."

Other players, including Bo Kimble, the nation's leading scorer, and reserves Terrell Lowery and Marcellus Lee were there, while LMU Coach Paul Westhead arrived shortly afterward.

GATHERS/ BACK PAGE

Somber mood shrouds Laker game

By Mitch Chortkoff
STAFF WRITER

Pooh Richardson and Hank Gathers were close. Both had left Philadelphia to become college basketball stars in Southern California. They had planned a reunion for Sunday night.

Gathers would play for Loyola Marymount in the West Coast Conference tournament early Sunday evening. Then he'd come to the Forum, where Richardson, the former UCLA point guard, was playing for the Lakers.

Other members of the Gathers family would be present. Gathers' mother was in town from Philadelphia.

Gathers never made it to the Forum. Thirty-five minutes before the NBA game was to begin, Gathers died at Daniel Freeman Marina Hospital in Marina del Rey.

As the Lakers progressed to a routine 115-96 victory, Richardson played the first half without knowing about his friend.

He found out at intermission although it was the plan of Coach Bill Musselman to keep him from knowing until after the game.

Lakers center Mychal Thompson was the informant.

"I told (Wolves' forward) Tyrone Corbin and he told Pooh," said Thompson. "I also told the Laker players."

LAKERS/ BACK PAGE

This dunk off a Terrell Lowery pass came just seconds before Hank Gathers collapsed.

BRUCE HAZELTON/STAFF PHOTOGRAPHER

In loving memory of

Hank Gathers

February 11, 1967
March 4, 1990

Funeral Mass
March 6, 1990
Loyola Marymount University

March 6, 1990. Hank's silver casket rests near the spot where he fell to the court during LMU Memorial Mass at Gersten Pavilion. The service was so emotionally moving, Chris Myers, then a young ESPN reporter, was unable to remain in the building. "There wasn't a dry eye in the place."

Hank Gathers, 1967-1990

Lucille Gathers Cheeseboro holding Hank's jersey. Lucille acknowledges the cheers of the crowd at LMU's 2000 ceremony retiring Hank's #44 jersey. Paul Westhead and LMU Athletic Director Bill Husak look on. Hank's son, Aaron Crump, is in foreground.

A somber Bo Kimble looks on as Hank's jersey is raised to the rafters where it hangs next to his own.

As the post player, or fifth man, in the System, his role was clearly defined. He retrieved every one of the opponents' made shots and, as quickly as possible, fired the inbounds pass to Simmons or Lowery at the point, who then took off up court. More than once, Per got a chance, when everyone else was covered, to take a short dump-off pass as he came up court, trailing the others. Invariably, the 6-foot-7 Stumer would put up a soft 3-point shot. The result was usually nothing but net, driving the Lions' opponents crazy and delighting the fans. Per was per-fect for the System.[14]

The Lions now hit the road, traveling to Chicago to meet the DePaul Blue Demons again on January 14. In front of about 10,000 spectators and a national TV audience on CBS, the Lions fell to Joey Meyer's team, 122-108. LMU trailed by 16 at the intermission and couldn't make it up. Fryer put up 42 points and was named Chevrolet player of the game. Hank, probably feeling the pressure of the national television audience (and NBA scouts) as much as the Blue Demons' smothering defense, started 1-11 from the field. He did manage to finish with 26 points, a season low, and chipped in with 14 rebounds.

Meyer had three—and sometimes four—players collapsing on Hank throughout the game. With 7-foot center James Hamby and 6-foot-7 Stanley Brundy of Crenshaw High School in Los Angeles all over him, Hank had to battle continuously. "I told him at half-time if he was triple teamed to pass it off or take all three to the hole. I wouldn't ever tell him to back down," Westhead said. "The third (defensive) player was a new dimension for him. It was a learning experience."[15]

In the *Los Angeles Times* that day, Alan Drooz had told readers about Hank Gathers in considerable detail. The profile ran nearly 2,200 hundred words and recounted the events that had put Hank at LMU with Westhead and the System.[16]

Hank was averaging nearly 35 points per game and was leading the nation in scoring and in rebounding. He might just be the perfect player for Westhead's System, Drooz observed. "Blessed with a combination of strength, quickness, jumping ability and speed, the seemingly tireless Gathers more often than not accomplishes his task of finishing off the fast break he is expected to start with his rebounds," he wrote. Drooz had watched every one of Hank's LMU games and noted that, for all his physical skills, his main attribute may be "his intense desire on the court. His attitude goes well beyond blue-collar, closer to a warrior, last-one-standing attitude."

After he wasn't invited to the Olympic trials, the story revealed, Hank was determined to do as Westhead advised and "show 'em this year." And, said Hank, "I'm showing 'em."

Bo agreed with Drooz's assessment that his [Kimble's] absence had probably speeded Hank's emergence: "In a way, me being out has raised him to this level. He's kind of in a groove. He's programmed himself. The funny thing is, if I was playing, he'd still be scoring, but he wouldn't be leading the country. I've never seen Hank play like he's playing this year.

Right now, he's in a class by himself. And I've seen where he's come from."

Westhead, who had benefited as much as Hank had from his move to take over the scoring responsibilities in Bo's absence, said, "I think the future of Hank is, he'll become a much more poised player, which we're already seeing. Then he'll become really lethal."[17]

Home once more, LMU faced Gonzaga at Gersten, six days later. A near-capacity crowd of 4,000 was on hand as the Lions got back on track. Fryer continued his hot streak, putting in five 3-pointers and accounting for 37 points to lead LMU. Hank pulled down 13 rebounds and added 31 points as the Lions rolled to a 113-104 victory. "Our pressure defense was a key factor," said Westhead.[18]

Bo was on the bench, cheering his teammates on. His rehab was going well, and he was looking forward to returning to action. In the meantime, he watched in awe and appreciation as Hank continued to push, pull, and carry the Lions along with him. Without Bo and his outside shooting threat, Hank was drawing more and more defensive attention. Instead of being unproductive, he had become even more intense, and the results were evident. Hank led in scoring or rebounds in every game, and in most games he led his team in both. When the opposition collapsed and double-teamed Hank, Fryer was free to fire at will and did so. The team was feeding off Hank's intensity and responding to his forceful leadership. The Lions were turning around a season that looked like it might be a disaster when Bo went under the knife in December. With "Superman" leading the charge, they were playing with abandon; the System worked best that way.

In recognition of his efforts, Hank was named the WCAC player of the month for January, and the current edition of *Sports Illustrated* named him Player of the Week.[19]

The night after the Lions put away Gonzaga, a struggling Portland, led by Terrell Lowery's older brother, Josh, who was averaging 14.5 points a game after transferring from San Diego State, came limping into Gersten at 1-15.

At half-time, the score was 45-43, and Hank vented his dismay and anger in the locker room at the lackadaisical play. The Lions started the second half on a 15-4 run and sank the Pilots, 100-90. LMU had moved to 10-6 and notched another WCAC win.[20]

Next up were back-to-back games against the Waves of Pepperdine. The first game was televised in Los Angeles by the Prime Ticket cable network from Firestone Field House in Malibu. But the Lions, who had been on a streak of 19 straight conference victories, were stopped cold by the Waves, who prevailed, 104-79. Hank's 25 points weren't enough as the Waves, led by Dexter Howard and Tommy Lewis, handed the Lions their seventh loss. "They held the ball well, used the clock well, and rebounded well," Westhead said. "After that, there's not much left to do."[21]

The rematch at Gersten took place four days later before a capacity crowd of 4,350 that greeted Lewis and the Waves with a loud chorus of boos. The Lions got their revenge, despite Lewis's 26 points. At one point, a frustrated Lewis was charged with a technical foul for slamming the ball to the court in anger. Hank had led LMU on a run in the first half with the score knotted at 13. He scored the next 8 points in a row, with the last basket coming on a "sweet reverse slam dunk" that brought the fans to their feet in appreciation.[22]

In Bo's absence, Tom Peabody had filled in at small forward and at guard. The former Mater Dei star had brought a degree of unbridled enthusiasm to the game that stood out—even amid the frenetic activity of the Lions—quickly making him a fan favorite at Gersten. Against Pepperdine, Tom had nearly come to blows with Craig Davis. After a violent collision between the two, Tom had gone to the dressing room, returning later with five stitches and the same reckless abandon. His stats for the game would read four assists, three rebounds, two floor burns (abrasions suffered when the hardwood scraped his skin), and one cut eye—a typical Peabody performance.[23]

On a team whose members had all earned a nickname, Tom's would be more, well, colorful than most. Actually, his nickname matched the varying colorful hues of black and blue covering his otherwise skinny white body. "The Human Bruise" was as fitting a description as one could attach to Tom.

His hustle and enthusiasm made up for any deficiencies in skills, and his willingness to sacrifice his body won him plaudits from the staff and cheers from the crowds. Tom had leaped, crashed, careened, and skidded across the court, over the scorers' table, into the crowd, and against the padded stanchion supporting the basket. He kept Chip Schaefer occupied nearly full time as he ministered to Peabody's various cuts, bruises, contusions, and sprains. Tom spent so much time in the trainer's room that he could have had his mail delivered there.

Tom's mother, who attended most games with Tom's brother, Terry, a physician, could barely stand to watch.

"He was always an active child," Delores Peabody recalled. "I asked him once how he managed to sit still in class, and he told me that he was able to do so because he knew that after the class came recess, and he would be able to run then, and that's all he thought about. He was always bruised and cut up as a youngster. He looked so bad so often that my husband worried that the neighbors might think he was inflicting the damage." She would sit in the stands with her eyes covered. For those who could bear to watch, Tom was quite the sight, and he had become an integral part of the lineup.[24]

On the nation's highest-scoring team, Tom Peabody seemed out of place—or, more precisely, all over the place. In 23 games, he'd attempted an average of only three shots a game. Yet his scrambling, aggressive style of play made him a fan favorite, even if it drove his mom to shield her eyes.

"With all the talent we had, my role was to create opportunities for Hank and Bo and the others. I played aggressively and tried to create as many steals as possible on defense to set the others up," Tom explained. "I only knew one style—all out for 40 minutes."[25] Tom's value to the Lions wasn't in offensive production but in creating havoc and harassing the defense. His performance was measured in floor burns and bruises, not in points. If he ended up in someone's lap in the third row of seats, so be it.

Still, his antics made even some of the most partisan Lions fans cringe. "You had to admire his hustle, but you don't want to see someone get hurt," Barry Zepel said.[26]

Since his surgery in late December, Bo had recovered rapidly under the rehabilitation program designed by the Kerlan-Jobe Orthopedic Clinic in Los Angeles. The world-famous clinic, known for its development of the revolutionary "Tommy John surgery" that had saved the career of the Dodgers pitcher, and so many others since, was located nearby.

The Kerlan-Jobe orthopedists were the team physicians for the LMU Lions, and you would be hard pressed to find a better orthopedics clinic anywhere. The half-dozen young doctors on fellowships at the clinic routinely attended the Lions' games.[27]

Bo had been in the best hands for someone trying to come back from a knee operation. He was monitored by the clinic, and his rehabilitation, under the watchful eye of Chip Schaefer (who had worked at Kerlan-Jobe before coming to LMU), was ahead of schedule. Bo had begun to participate on a limited basis in practice and was ready and eager to test the knee under game conditions. He was given clearance to return in late January, only a little more than a month after the arthroscopic procedure.

As Bo prepared to return to action, the Soaring Gulls of U.S. International arrived at Gersten on a wing and a prayer on January 31. The visit would be a memorable one.

When the lights finally stopped flashing on the new scoreboard that Al Gersten had bought, the final tally was Loyola Marymount 181-U.S. International 150, and it broke NCAA records all over the place, including the records both teams had established less than a month before: most points by a winning team and most points by a losing team. The longest stretch between baskets was 56 seconds.[28]

Hank had accounted for 41 points and a school record of 29 rebounds to pad his national lead in both departments. The game nearly met Westhead's criteria for perfect. Only 19 more points and it would have. "We could easily have scored 200 if the starters had played longer, without any bizarre things happening," said Westhead, whose definition of bizarre must have been different from the standard meaning. He added, "We made some nice steals and forced turnovers."[29]

The record-breaking game made headlines all over the country. *The Washington Post* ran Alan Drooz's story in its entirety, and even *The New York Times* carried two hundred words of it.

Lost in the coverage was Bo's return to the lineup. As he took to the court to spell Tom Peabody, Bo was greeted with warm cheers from the crowd. "Bo was a big plus factor for us," Westhead said. "We wanted to give him some minutes before we put him into league play." Bo had played about 18 minutes and had 20 points, including a 3-pointer to end the first half.[30] He was back, and if his knee still wasn't up to 40 minutes of play, his shooting touch had not suffered from the lay-off.

The Lions had reason to be optimistic about the rest of the season. Bo was back, Hank had never been better, and the other players were all filling their roles with increasing comfort and productiveness.

As LMU prepared to meet St. Mary's, the sports section of *The Washington Post* featured a story about Hank and his success to date. Written by C. L. Smith Muniz, it recounted Hank's travails at USC with Raveling and offered some opinions on the star who was leading the nation in scoring and rebounding.

Rick Pitino, who had hoped to get Hank for his Providence team, only to lose him to USC, was now with the New York Knicks. He had recently run into Hank at an airport and had told the player, "Just keep it up. I'm watching." What Pitino was observing was a man intent on proving others wrong.

"Actions speak louder than words," Hank said. "My play shows I should have been invited to the [Olympic] trials. That I should have played at USC. I've done it quietly. That's the classy way to do it. . . . But I must admit when I didn't get invited to the trials, I was pretty ticked."

Smith Muniz said that Westhead called Hank a "baby Barkley" after the Philadelphia 76'ers one-man wrecking crew. Like Sir Charles, Hank was no shy guy, and he liked the comparison. "Barkley, Muhammad Ali, Sugar Ray Leonard, Magic Johnson, and me," Hank said. "Hell of a team. You wouldn't need a center. You wouldn't necessarily have to play basketball, either."

So intent was Hank on getting the Lions into a winning groove that he hadn't realized he was leading the nation in scoring "until a few weeks ago. It caught me by surprise. It would be a pretty nice thing to hang on my belt. But. . .I want to lead in rebounding. That's my bread and butter. . . .Everyone can learn to pick up a ball and score. Not rebound. It comes straight from the heart."[31]

Next up for the Lions were the Gaels of St. Mary's, due at Gersten on February 3, followed by the University of San Diego the next evening. Both conference games were critical—only eight games remained before the play-offs. LMU was tied with Pepperdine and St. Mary's at 5-1 as the Lions took the court against the defense-minded Gaels.

St. Mary's was second in the country in defense, allowing only 54.7 points per game, while LMU had the highest average score nationally, 113.4 points per game. Something would have to give. Surprising the 4,366 on hand, it was the Lions. St. Mary's beat them at their own game. The Gaels, belying their reputation for defensive dominance, triumphed by an uncharacteristic 116-104.

"We've been running well all year," Lynn Nance said of his Gaels, who moved to 18-2, and 6-1 in conference play. "People who have played us have been trying to stop us from running, because we've been very effective. It's too bad we're stereotyped (as all defense). We've been scoring quite a few points."

Hank had tallied 39 points to lead LMU, but failed to get the support he needed. He had a terrific 18-24 shooting night and added 18 rebounds. But it was not enough. The Lions managed to shoot only 45 percent, while the Gaels were hot at 64 percent. Hank was complimentary. "They surprised us," he candidly acknowledged. "They went straight at us. They played the game to win instead of not to lose. They did an excellent job of capitalizing on our mistakes."[32]

Now 5-2 in conference play, the Lions met San Diego at Gersten the following night. With another capacity crowd causing Brian Quinn to beam proudly from the stands, LMU turned back the Toreros, by 139-104, against a team that hadn't been outscored by more than 20 points in any previous conference game.

LMU took control early in the game. Hank, still leading the country in scoring and rebounding, displayed the ball-handling skills he had been honing since the days on the north Philly streets with Heat and Doug Overton. Hank put on a sharp passing display that resulted in 9 assists to accompany his 30 points and 14 rebounds.[33]

Bo was playing his way back into shape. He managed 22 points in just 21 minutes and had a steal that he finished off with a leading high pass as Hank streaked past, then threw it down with authority as the crowd went nuts. Everyone contributed: Per Stumer made two consecutive 3-pointers at the eight-minute mark, and Fryer and Simmons accounted for 29 and 25 points, respectively. "It's nice when we have it greased," said Westhead about the accurate shooting.[34]

LMU moved to 6-2 in the conference and prepared to square off against San Diego again six days later. The location was different but the result the same. LMU came away with a 104-88 win on the road.

The next night, the Lions trekked northward again, this time to Moraga, to take on St. Mary's. The Gaels turned back LMU, 95-81, in front of 3,550 pleased partisans. Hank had 37 points and 13 rebounds, but the effort was not enough. "We let it get away tonight," he said. "We beat ourselves. We let it slip away." Tied at 62, the Lions had gone ice cold for the next five minutes and were outscored, 14-0. Hank hit a jumper with just under seven minutes to go, which brought the Lions within 6 points, but the Gaels quickly pulled away again, completing their sweep of the Lions in conference play.

After the disappointing loss, Hank issued a challenge: "In the Tournament, St. Mary's has got to prove themselves again, just like we did last year. I think we're the best team in the league. We're just not playing like it. I still think we're going to win the tournament. Our guys have just got to realize how serious this is."[35] He would make certain that they did.

LMU returned to the far friendlier Gersten Pavilion for two contests over the weekend, February 17 and 18, against the University of Portland and Gonzaga. Gersten Pavilion was packed as Lions fans welcomed the team as it faced off against the Portland Pilots. With Bo starting for the first time since December, the Lions quickly jumped out to a 10-4 lead. LMU scored in rapid bursts, racking up 9 points in just 90 seconds. With the score at 24-15, Bo stole the ball and sent it to Simmons, who made a great lob pass to Hank, who jammed home a slam dunk. Stumer nailed a 3-pointer, Bo added a bucket, and the Lions were off and running. The dazed Pilots, without the services of Josh Lowery, who had been suspended after an off-campus fight, committed 30 turnovers. LMU shot 70 percent from the field in the first half and never looked back.[36]

"I'm pleased with Bo," Westhead said. "I was tempted to start him against St. Mary's, but I didn't." Hank had 32 points, including a "monster reverse slam" that made the LMU lead 42 points, the biggest margin of the year, and added nine rebounds.[37]

The following night, the Gonzaga Bulldogs offered some stiffer opposition. The Zags took a 7-point lead at 27-20, after Hank had scored 12 points in the first four minutes. Then it became the Bo Show for a while. As Keith Cameron reported in the *Los Angeles Loyolan*, Bo "put Gonzaga guard Mike Winger in the popcorn machine and nailed a 3-pointer. Then he nailed another and added an eight-foot jumper to make it 28-27 LMU."[38] Gonzaga shot an astounding 62 percent in the first half, hitting 12 of its 13 shots at one point, and fighting back to lead by 3. But then "The Hank and Bo Show" appeared, scoring 17 points to give LMU a 61-50 lead at the half.[39]

Peabody was stellar on defense, and Hank and Bo each poured in 40 points to lead the Lions. Gonzaga's Doug Spradley tallied 40 points, as well, prompting Westhead to quip, "I keep saying, 'Come to Loyola, you'll get 40, with us or against us.'" The final score was 147-136, as LMU closed out its home schedule. It was the most points ever scored in a WCAC game.[40]

19

HEART OF A LION

While Hank was known for his kindness to children, it was not so evident in his treatment of the tropical fish he kept in his apartment.

Hank's stewardship of the tropical fish he kept in his apartment brought out his fighting spirit, as well as his compassion.

"Hank and I got these tropical fish, and we each had a tank of them in our rooms," Tom Peabody said. "When the California weather turned cooler in the winter evenings, he decided they might be too cold. Out of a concern for the exotic and colorful fish, he turned up the heat in his aquarium tank. When we got back from a trip, they were all floating belly up in the water. He'd poached them.

"His favorite fish he had named 'Bank,' and Hank was so upset when he died that he insisted on burying him. He put him in a plastic bag and used a tissue to make a small pillow for him. Then he used a soup spoon to dig a grave for the fish outside our room. He put flowers over the spot. Afterwards, we went to an L. L. Cool J concert, and Hank couldn't stop talking about the loss of his fish."

Long after he had moved off campus, every time he passed the spot where Bank was interred, he'd say respectfully, "That's where the little guy is."[1]

That wasn't the end of the fish stories, though. "We had gone out and replaced those fish," Tom said, "and while mine were all rather attractive, interesting, and docile species, Hank bought two [of an] ominous-looking, orange-accented fish called an Oscar, a ferocious fighting fish. The two didn't get along in his tank, so he took one out and threw him in with mine."

Oscars can grow to 14 inches in length and are aggressive and territorial. They require at least a 55-gallon tank in which to establish a territory and be happy. Anything less than that and the Oscar will tend to be grumpy and aggressive. Unfortunately, Tom's tank was not that big.

"The damn thing ate up every one of my fish in the tank," Tom said. "Hank thought it was hilarious and that my fish were just a bunch of pussies that got what they deserved."[2]

Hank respected in fish what he respected on the court.

The basketball uniforms of the late 80's were a far cry from the long, baggy, mid-calf shorts of today. The trunks, especially, were short and tight. The players called them Daisy Dukes, after the type of shorts worn by the Catherine Bach character in the Dukes of Hazzard, a TV series. Hank, with his enormous bulging thighs, would jump center to begin every game. He would approach the center circle slowly, extend his muscular arm and hand, and greet the opposing player with a vise-like grip. Dropping his hand, he'd look that player in the eye, hike up his Daisy Dukes to reveal the tree-trunk thighs, and mutter as ominously as he could, "Get ready to go to war."[3]

Hank's intimidation was always backed up by his play, and there was no lack of effort on his part in any game. He played each minute at full speed, with no quarter asked and none given. He was as fierce a competitor on the court as that cannibalistic Oscar fish in Tom Peabody's tank.

For most players, going to war with Hank was to be a goldfish with an Oscar bearing down.

Two road contests remained for LMU as the season drew to a close.

The Lions were headed North for weekend games with Santa Clara and the University of San Francisco on successive nights. The Lions, at 9-3, trailed Pepperdine and St. Mary's, both of which stood at 10-2.

The final weekend of regular season play began for the Lions in front of a standing-room-only crowd of 5,000 in Toso Pavilion at Santa Clara. The Broncos stood at 10-2 at home.

Hank and Jeff Fryer each had 32 points as the Lions rolled over the Broncos, 112-101. The combined point total set a new Toso Pavilion record and left Coach Carroll Williams shaking his head. "We just had too many turnovers. We didn't want to take a quick shot. That was our game plan. We were too frantic and out of control in the first half," Carroll said after watching the System lure yet another victim into its trap. The win, coupled with a loss by Pepperdine, pulled LMU into a second-place tie with the Waves, heading into the final game of the season.

Fryer had made the difference for the Lions, Westhead said. "His shooting was uncanny. A couple of times, most of the people and a few of the players didn't know the ball was inbounds and he was shooting the 3-pointer," Paul said of Jeff's quick-draw shooting display.[4]

Alan Drooz was getting more and more space to write about the Lions and their growing popularity. He used some of it to profile another colorful character in the cast that Westhead had assembled.

Jeff Fryer was the first recruit Paul Westhead had signed after being named head coach at LMU. "The thing I remember the most was he asked me if the NCAA was going to have the 3-point shot," Westhead told Alan Drooz. "I said no way. Then, out of the blue, they added the rule the next week. It's like he's psychic. I called him and said, 'Your stock just went up.' He was a terrific 3-point shooter in high school."

The blond, tanned, laid-back Fryer was the antithesis of Hank Gathers, yet he was an essential ingredient in Westhead's System. Fryer rained 3-point shots like one of those machines that tennis and baseball players use for practice—they just kept coming. He was a fearless shooter in a system that encouraged shooting.

"He's a hired gunner," Westhead said. "He knows that. He fits the crucial two-man (off guard) position in our system—shooting any time you get your hands on it. We knew he could shoot coming out of high school. We didn't know how tough or hardworking he was." Alone and far away from the basket, the 6-foot-2 Fryer had nerves of steel and an unflinching belief in his own ability. He fired at will and moved on. Without that ego, such long-range shots will clang harmlessly away.

He was yet another of whom it could be said, accurately, that he and the System were made for each other.

"This has been the perfect place for me," he told Drooz.[5]

The Lions' final regular season game was against the enigmatic Dons of (the University of) San Francisco (USF). The Dons had beaten Notre Dame, and both Pepperdine and Saint Mary's, yet had fallen to San Diego and had been clobbered by Santa Clara at home. No one ever knew which team would show up when the Dons took the court.

Unfortunately, for the Lions, the Dons were on their game and scored an upset 123-109 win in the season finale before 5,220 on February 25. "Our goal was to peak at the end of the season," explained a happy Jim Brovelli, who obviously thought they had.

Hank had 34 points in the losing effort, while Enoch Simmons contributed 26. The game was decided in a four-minute stretch midway through the second half. LMU held a 76-71 lead when USF mounted a 19-8 run that all but finished LMU's chances. "We were pressing and trapping pretty well but we didn't get the turnovers," Westhead said. USF shot a stunning 72 percent in the second half, breaking LMU's press and the Lions' backs.[6]

Because of various tie breakers, LMU finished the season as the team seeded third when the WCAC tournament pairings were announced. Play was to begin in San Francisco on March 4. If they were to repeat as conference champs, the Lions would have to run the table.

The sole senior not in the starting lineup was John Veargason, who was 6-foot-10. The first front-court reserve had shown flashes of brilliant play in the past, but as his playing time increased during his senior year, he had blossomed. He had several rebounding efforts in double figures and had provided some key blocked shots. "It's kind of been a difficult last couple of years," John told Alan Drooz. "Things just finally came. Maybe slower than people expected. Maybe slower than I expected."

With each season, in limited playing time and battling injuries, John had gotten more comfortable in his role. But he had gotten down on himself and had seen a sports psychologist. "The psychologist helped me a lot—thinking about stuff—and not thinking about stuff," John said. Battling for rebounds, he had even taken one away from Hank and had drawn some respect from Hank and praise from Westhead for his efforts.

Although Veargason had averaged fewer than 4 points per game in his final season, he had provided key relief for Hank and Per. As John's playing career was drawing to a close, he reflected, "I just try to stay in the role I've been given here. Every now and then, there might turn out to be a little bit more, but I just try to stay within myself."[7]

The WCAC Tournament was a minimarathon. It required the winner to win three games on three consecutive days.

LMU squeaked by Gonzaga, 101-98, and then turned back Tommy Lewis and Pepperdine 112-98, setting up a meeting with Santa Clara for the conference title.

Lucille had arrived in California to watch Hank in the play-offs.

"I took her to a mall before the Santa Clara game," Pete Priamos said. "We were just walking through, just window shopping, when she saw a coat she liked. It cost $80." Lucille "made it very clear that she expected me to buy it for her. I did," Pete said.[8]

People who knew Lucille would not have been surprised. Her co-workers at the hospital knew her as someone who could be "loud and obnoxious—she thought she ran the place," said one of the hospital's registered nurses of the hefty housekeeping aide whose responsibility was mopping floors and emptying waste baskets.

That attitude and Lucille's assertive, take-charge demeanor were in full flower in her son, but without the rough edges. It wouldn't be much longer, and she'd be taken care of by her "Hankie," not Pete Priamos. It was just a matter of time.

The championship game was close throughout, and was played at less than breakneck speed. The Lions found themselves in a battle as the Broncs tied the game at 63 with only 2:50 to play. Jeffty Connelly hit a jumper with 60 seconds left to put Santa Clara up by 2 points.

Hank responded with a 10-foot jumper to tie and then stole the inbound pass. He fed Enoch Simmons (playing with a badly injured left finger that would later require surgery), who put up a 25-footer at the buzzer that rimmed out.

The two teams went to overtime and a battle of free throws. LMU prevailed, 75-70, as Fryer and Simmons converted their opportunities.

Hank was named to the All-Tournament team with Bo and Jeffty Connelly and was named the tournament MVP. Hank had 30 points and 16 rebounds in the win.

"It was a tough game. We didn't play our best, but we hung tough and pulled out a good one," Bo said. Per wasn't that sure, saying, "We played our worst game of the year and will have to play better in the NCAA's."[9]

In the *Los Angeles Loyolan*, Keith Cameron noted, "It might not have been a pretty dance but the Lions are going back to the Ball. Their clock hasn't struck midnight yet."[10]

The clock began ticking a little louder after the pairings for the NCAA Tournament were announced.

LMU was assigned to the regional in Indianapolis, while St. Mary's, a team the Lions had beaten en route to their conference title, was accorded a favorable spot and stayed home in the Western regional.

Waiting for the Lions in the spacious Hoosier Dome were the Razorbacks of the University of Arkansas. The Hogs were about as ugly a partner as you could imagine. They had won the Southwest Conference title by dispatching Texas, 100-76. As LMU's opening-round opponent, they would provide no cakewalk.

"It should be pretty fun," Per Stumer said when he learned that the Lions would be facing Nolan Richardson's squad, thus displaying what a lifetime of dark Swedish winters had done to his ability to assess American basketball. Bo had a more enlightened response, saying, "If Arkansas is a running team, then I'm fine with playing someone like that." Hank's response was typical: "I don't care where we go. I'm just happy we're still playing."[11]

But Westhead had a big problem. Enoch Simmons was hurt and couldn't play. As point guard, Simmons's job was to trigger the offense. His loss was a devastating blow. "Peabody will start at guard," Westhead said. "And we are revving up Terrell Lowery and [Terry] Mister [a sophomore reserve] to back him up. We hope to get 20 minutes from Tom at point guard. We need him at other spots too."[12] The only thing Westhead knew for sure was that Tom would give all he could and then some. The coach could only hope it would be enough.

Hank had been nominated for the prestigious John Wooden Award as the nation's top player, and he had become only the 12th Division I player in the history of the game to score more than 1,000 points in a season. "I'm pretty happy about the Wooden Award (nomination). It's unexpected. I did not expect to lead the nation in scoring and rebounding, but that helped (in getting) the nomination," Hank said.[13]

Hank's record-breaking season—he was only the second player in history to lead the country in scoring and rebounding (Xavier McDaniel had been the other)—landed him a profile in USA Today , as the Lions prepared for action in Indianapolis.[14] Noting that Hank had always had the ability to make others laugh, writer Michael Hurd observed that where Hank had grown up, there was little to laugh at: "Drugs, gangs and all the other inner city sociological nightmares."

"I wanted to get out of Philly. It didn't matter where. I thought, 'There has to be a better life than this,'" Hank told Hurd. "I lived in a high-rise all my life. There was trash all over the place. I was never into drugs and drinking. I tried it, but it wasn't my thing. I'm on a natural high."

Father Dave told Hurd about Lucille. "She's a tough lady," Hagan said, crediting her for her sons' survival. "Most of the kids never get out of (Raymond Rosen). This is the only world they know. Hank is kind of an exception in that he got through it."

Hank was cautious about his future. "I can't begin to think I'm sitting on top of the world because I'm on top of the NCAA stats," the ever-candid Hank said. "I have a hell of a way to go."[15]

On March 16, in front of 37,322 fans and a national TV audience, the Lions met the Razorbacks—and got tusked. The Hogs won, 121-101, not even close.

Arkansas arrived at the tournament, 24-6 for the season, averaging more than 90 points a game and riding a seven-game winning streak. Momentum was with the Hogs as they swept LMU away, pigging the Lions' own style. Led by Mario Credit, the Razorbacks built a lead of as many as 18 points in the first half, while LMU could barely find the basket. "Credit really hurt us in the first half. I didn't expect that," Westhead acknowledged. He told Alan Drooz, "Our shots just wouldn't go down. We generated enough shots, played hard but just couldn't get over the hump."

The Lions had lost Fryer and Lowery to fouls, and Peabody finished with an ice pack strapped to his badly bruised leg. They went down with guns blazing, but they went down.[16] LMU shot only 35 percent for the game. Hank had 28 points and 17 rebounds, but it was not enough. Twice, the Lions clawed to within 6 points in the second half, but each time Arkansas responded.[17]

"The ball is finally over. The clock has struck midnight," wrote Keith Cameron in the *Los Angeles Loyolan*.[18]

For the season Hank Gathers had scored 1,015 points, an average of 32.7 points per game. He had also averaged 13.7 rebounds a game. He had just completed his junior year and was at the pinnacle of the college basketball world.

He had little left to prove to NBA scouts. He could leave college and enter the NBA draft. It was what Magic Johnson had done after leading Michigan State to the NCAA title. Others had also left early, and they hadn't been nearly as successful as Magic.

"Magic told [Hank] he should leave," Heat said. "He said he should go now and not come back."[19]

Predictably, in making his decision, Hank turned to many people, especially the two people he trusted most. David Spencer and Father Dave Hagan both told him he should stay in college, but their reasons were different. Pete Priamos also offered an ear. The former USC booster had stayed close to Hank, becoming a fixture in the stands at LMU home games. His presence left Brian Quinn slightly unnerved, because investigators from the NCAA and WCAC were always sniffing around. Once, Brian had asked Priamos to leave the arena.

"The NCAA was investigating Hank and Bo and how they were supporting themselves," Priamos said. "Quinn asked me to leave the arena. I told Hank and Bo, and they said I should stay. I didn't want to cause trouble and was ready to leave. Hank said, 'Fuck 'em—if you go, I'm going with you.' That was the end of that. I stayed."

Other activities of Pete's and Hank's would have left Quinn totally unhinged had he known about them. "I used to take Hank to the track at Los Alamitos," Pete said. "I would give him $40 or so to gamble. He loved to gamble. If he got a little ahead, he was thrilled. People were always coming up to him at the track, giving him tips and tickets they had bought for him."

So after Hank called, Pete met him at Charlie Brown's restaurant, where they reviewed a small pile of basketball magazines together. "We went over each player and where they might go in the [NBA] draft," Pete said. "I didn't tell him what to do. I just helped him see what his chances were of going high [in the draft] this year as opposed to next year."[20]

Spence was also comparing the two classes of draft picks with Hank. Spence had joined the agency of Leonard Armato, an Los Angeles attorney who was representing athletes, and Spence had every expectation that he would represent Hank and Bo when they turned professional. Spence drew up a detailed analysis of the probable draft-pick order and showed it to Hank. "There were just so many more top picks this season than next that it looked obvious to us that he should stay put for one more year," Spence said. "Hank's chances of going in the lottery next season were much better, and the money that would bring was so much more, it just made good sense."[21]

Hank also consulted Paul Westhead. Paul had been an NBA coach, and he knew Hank's game and his deficiencies better than anyone. He, too, counseled Hank to stay at LMU for another year. He told Hank it would give him time to improve his shooting range and that would make him even more valuable to the pros. Hank seldom shot from beyond 10 feet. He had incredible power and a quickness that enabled him to convert rebounds and crash menacingly through the lane. There were no baby sky hooks or 15-foot jumpers. Hank lived "in the paint."

Westhead was convinced another season was the best choice for Hank. "My impression is, you get famous first, then become a lottery pick the following year," Westhead explained. "The amazing thing is he wasn't one of the top 94 players invited to try out for the Olympics. The progress he's made in a year is immense. I think the year was used up getting a reputation. For that reason, I think another season is important. You evolve as a star, then need the year on Broadway."[22]

Obviously, Paul Westhead had a vested interest in Hank's returning to LMU. But the scholarly side of him would have pushed Hank to stay for his degree, and he was very close to Hank. He and Cassie treated him almost like a member of the family, and Hank felt the same way about the Westheads and their children, spending time with all of them.

"Of the hundreds of players that Paul coached though the years, Hank was my favorite," Cassie said. "He'd come off the court after a game and see me sitting there and yell out to me, a big grin on his face, 'Cass, who's your favorite player?'"

"I always told him, 'You are, Hank.'"[23]

One can safely assume that Paul Westhead, with his unique knowledge of the way professional teams assess players, gave Hank his best advice and that he'd have given the same advice even if Hank hadn't had a year of eligibility remaining. No one who knows Westhead doubts for a moment that Paul gave Hank the same advice he'd give his own son. They were that close.

Thus, despite the siren song of the NBA and what Magic had advised, Priamos, Spencer, and Westhead had provided compelling basketball reasons for Hank to stay in college for another year. But those were not the only reasons, though, that he was considering staying at LMU for his senior year.

Father Dave and Lane Bove, as well as Ed Arnold, all gently urged Hank to stay the course, as difficult as it was, and become the first in his family to earn a college diploma. "It would mean getting a degree and a better pro contract, Father Dave told him," John McNamee said. "He told him to stay put."[24] On the other hand, "cashing out"

would have been easy—and perhaps a smart move: it was unlikely Hank could dupli-
cate his record-breaking season by staying in college for another year. His NBA value
was firmly established, and it is hard to imagine that he really could have enhanced his
value by playing college ball for another year. On the other hand, staying in school and
earning his degree in communications would mean that his perpetual struggle in the
classroom would continue.

But Hank had yet another reason to stay: he wanted to win two NCAA Tournament
games before he turned pro. After his fabulous year, he had set that as a goal for himself and
the Lions in his final year. Shooting for the Elite Eight or Final Four seemed unrealistic,
even to Hank, but two tournament games should be within their reach.

And so the player who had put together the greatest single season in NCAA history
since Xavier McDaniel in 1985 decided to stay in school for one more year. The NBA
would still be there. His chances of landing a first-round-lottery-pick contract were much
greater if he waited. He would be able to get Lucille and his brothers out of the projects and
move his son to Los Angeles. And he'd have his degree and maybe two NCAA
Tournament wins to boot.

The only risk, Spence had pointed out, was any injury that might hamper his career.
That could be taken care of by purchasing an insurance policy that would pay if Hank suffered such an injury. The policy was for $1 million, and Dana Morck, a Torrance insurance
broker, arranged for it. The policy was issued by Lloyds of London, and a friend of Hank's
arranged a bank loan of $6,600 to pay the premium.[25] Now all Hank had to do was to con-
tinue to play the way he always had, and he would realize the dream he had harbored for
more years than he could remember.

If Hank didn't make it as a pro, maybe he could have a future in stand-up comedy.
While he was still undecided about his career decision, he was tapped to serve as the
emcee at the awards banquet at season's end. While Westhead handed the Lions watch-
es to commemorate their NCAA appearance, Hank was handing out barbs. He spared
no one, and they all thought it was hilarious, although it was one of those you-had-to-
be-there events. Below is an excerpt of Hank's words.

On John Veargason: "John's kind of lazy. If John could get a remote control to tie his
shoes, he would."

On Enoch Simmons (who had sat out the Arkansas game with an injury): "I just have
one thing to say to Enoch: Thanks for ruining our season."

On Terrell Lowery: "If his legs ever catch up with his mouth, he might become as good
a player as he thinks he is."

Hank also introduced himself: "Now, the man you've all been waiting for. . .please rise."

He also took shots at himself: "One thing—I used to be a good free throw shooter before I got here. It's all that running. And the Santa Ana winds don't help."

Westhead didn't escape unscathed. Hank warned his coach that his "prominent ears could cause some confusion with a Disney cartoon elephant."[26]

Hank had stayed up late the night before, working with reporter Alan Drooz and LMU sports information pro Barry Zepel on his routine.[27] He prepared for the banquet the same way he prepared for a game. He worked at it and worked at it until he felt he was ready.

Hank had them all laughing out loud. He was totally at ease in front of the mike and loved the spotlight; he loved laughter and making people laugh. His teammates laughed loudest. They knew it was his way of saying thank- you for all they had done.[28]

During the last week of April, Hank called a press conference at LMU to announce his decision. May 13 was the deadline for entering his name in the draft. He had consulted with Jerry West of the Lakers and Marty Blake, who ran an NBA scouting service. Both had advised Hank to stay in school.

Hank strode to the mike while cameras whirred and flashbulbs popped. Scowling seriously as the reporters held their pens to their notebooks, he deadpanned into the cameras, "I've decided to give up basketball totally—and go into boxing."

The crowd broke into laughter.

When the laughing stopped, Hank announced that he was staying at LMU and was at ease with the decision he'd made. "It would be difficult to leave. I truly have a love for the faculty, students, my teammates and the coaching staff," he said. Later, he told Alan Drooz, "My family has been in poverty since I can remember. My mother's O.K. One more year won't make much difference."

Westhead applauded the decision, too: "That's the sign of a player who saw his career—his life—at some distance: 'There's the instant and there's the better things if I wait.' I think his talents will now unfold closer to the maximum."

There was yet another reason for remaining in school. It was a bit too early to bring down the curtain on "The Hank and Bo Show." "I don't think I want to give that up now," Hank said. "We've been through thick and thin together." And Bo had to play another season of college ball so the scouts could get a good look at him with a healthy knee.

Hank was facing a busy summer. He was slated to pose for *Playboy's* preseason All-America team photo, as well as *Street and Smith* magazine, and he was going home to play in the Sonny Hill summer league.

As Alan Drooz concluded, Hank was clearly a bank with no fear of failure.[29]

CHAPTER

20

GETTING IN GEAR

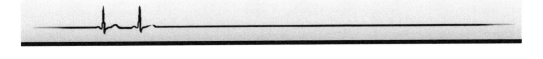

Hank had been sending money home to Lucille in Philadelphia via Western Union since he had arrived at LMU. His youngest brother, Charles, or New-New, as he was called, would collect the money. It was never much—$40 or $50 or so, sometimes more. New-New would have to supply a password to pick up the money at the Super Fresh Convenience Mart at 22nd and Lehigh. New-New soon became such a familiar face that the clerk no longer asked him for the password.[1]

Father Dave also assisted the family, in accord with his long-time habit. But now, even the sleepy NCAA was keeping a half-lidded eye on the priest's activities, lest he break rules against giving players money. Father Dave didn't care—he believed that he had every right to help the family and would send money to Hank and give some to Lucille, as well.

"He saw nothing wrong with giving her money to buy a plane ticket to Los Angeles to see her son," Father John McNamee said. "After all, he felt that a mother should be able to visit with her son. If her economic circumstances prevented her from doing so, he saw nothing wrong with helping her."[2]

Father Dave was doing what he had always done, and Hank and the family were benefiting from his concern.

While the flow of money from Hank to Philly was regular, it increased in volume and frequency after he decided to stay at LMU for another year, according to Father Dave.[3]

Hank's decision to stay at LMU meant that Lucille and Charles, the only son still living at home, would have to endure the row house in the Raymond Rosen projects for another year, until Hank landed a lucrative NBA contract. But she wouldn't have to be uncomfortable in the interim.

Cleo Jackson, who lived near Lucille in the projects, recalled that "one morning Lucille came down [stairs] to discover all her kitchen furniture was missing. She thought she'd been robbed. "A couple hours later, there it was, new kitchen furniture. Another time she comes downstairs and there's nothing in the living room. Sure enough, Hank bought her all new stuff for that, too. There was nothing that boy wouldn't do for his mother."[4]

Father Dave had helped with the living room furniture caper. He "lured her out of the house while Hank and his friends loaded the new furniture into the house so that she would come back and be surprised," he said.[5]

Lucille had been the oldest of 13 children and had known only poverty all her life. After her marriage crumbled, she was the sole source of support for her four children. She did the very best she could, but in the bleak Raymond Rosen Homes, there was little to cheer her.

A bout with hepatitis left her on disability and welfare as Hank began his senior year.[6] Some of his brothers were doing well, but Chris was not. Lucille's firstborn had succumbed to the life of the streets and now faced serious prison time on a robbery charge.[7]

Derrick, still in college and doing well, had once taken a stray bullet in the abdomen while in the front yard of his mother's row house. The scar he bore was a vivid reminder to Lucille of just how deadly a place this was for her family. Charles, now in his late teens, was still living there with her.

Hank, or Hankie, as she called him, was her pride, her joy, and her salvation. He was his mother's son in every way, with her strong will and determination as well as her infectious laugh and joyful outlook—despite the bleakness of their circumstances.

Hank was her hope and her dream. He told her constantly that he would take her, his brothers, and Aaron, his son, out of the projects. He was going to take care of them all. She knew he would. She loved Hank and he loved her. They shared a special bond that went beyond mother and son. Hank had been her rock ever since his father had disappeared into his various addictions. Hank's assurances that he'd take care of her, that he'd provide everything she needed or wanted, were the only solace she had in an otherwise dismal existence.[8]

Hank's generosity toward his mother while he was in college was evidence of what was to come. It might take another year, but he would make good on his promise to get her out of there. And she knew he would—she had waited this long, she could wait a little longer. Everything was going to be just as Hank always said it would be.

Lucille wasn't the only person enjoying a new prosperity. Since the press conference, Hank had moved to a new off-campus apartment near school. The rent was more than $1,000 per month for the two-bedroom unit. The place was furnished, and when Aaron came to visit during the summer, he particularly enjoyed running up and down the circular staircase to the second floor. Vernell Ritchey, Hank's girlfriend, was there frequently.

Hank was madly in love with her and told everyone he was going to marry her as soon as he got out of school.[9]

He also was driving a new sports car.

"I had bought him an old clunker [the year before] for about $2,000," Pete Priamos said. "We went down to pick it up at the Hawthorne police station [Pete bought it from the impound lot]. It wasn't much, but it was transportation for him. He didn't have it long before he and Bo were racing on the Santa Monica Freeway one night, and he ran into a truck with it. That was it for the car."[10] But in the fall of 1989, Hank was driving a new car, a Mercury, and it was no clunker.

Back in Philly, even Father Dave noticed a change in the Gatherses' circumstances. Now, when he asked Lucille—still disabled by the hepatitis—if she needed any money, she would reply in the negative. Once Father Dave sent Hank a gift of $100 through a credit card, and Hank never picked it up.[11]

The NCAA enforcement officer at the time was David Burst. "There were questions raised about Father Dave at the time the two of them [Hank and Bo] transferred from USC," Burst said. "But it never resulted in an investigation here, that I can recall. There were no violations found."[12] Although [LMU athletic director] Quinn, [LMU sports information officer] Zepel, and others clearly remember having a sense of being watched by the NCAA while Hank was at LMU, the man who would have been doing the watching, Burst, denied that he was conducting any investigation.[13]

Clearly, Father Dave's relationship with Hank preceded his enrollment at LMU, thus exempting gifts from Father Dave from the NCAA rules barring financial assistance to student-athletes beyond their scholarships. So if any of Hank's well-heeled friends chose to funnel some assistance through Father Dave, it would be difficult for the NCAA to act. But according to Burst, though, no one at the NCAA was even asking questions.

What is clear is that Hank had a little help from his friends and that the NCAA's chief investigator says there was no investigation and the organization found nothing wrong at the time.

By the summer of 1989, only the playground hangers-on would see Heat's prodigious talents; he had washed out of school the year before and now split his time between Philly and Hank's apartment in California. Derrick had left junior college and was enrolled at Cal State-Northridge, thanks to some help from Spence. Derrick was at Hank's apartment much of the time—it was within driving distance of Derrick's school—and both Tom Peabody and Bo recall that Derrick spent a lot of time around LMU.[14] Hank would include Derrick in the weekend and summer pick-up games, and Derrick often partook of the social scene at and around LMU. His older brother was well known and well liked.[15]

Although Derrick's temperament was more volatile than his brother's and his talents not quite so refined, he could play basketball. His grades, while better than Heat's, had not been good enough for admission to a Division I program.[16] (At the time, Cal State-Northridge was a Division II school.) During the previous season, Derrick had been an important part of Cal State-Northridge's 16-11 basketball team. He had averaged nearly 17 points and 7 rebounds to lead his team, and was named its most valuable player. He was a California Collegiate Athletic Conference (CCAC) second-team selection.[17]

Bruce Woods was especially aware of how serious Hank was about the coming season.

"He asked me to meet him in the weight room at 6:30 in the morning to help him work out," the assistant coach recalled. "He would do leg curls and squats and work mostly on his leg strength. He would always greet me with a smile and say, 'Woodsey, I've got to defend my title. I need you, man.' He was not too concerned about his scoring title. It was the rebounding title that he really cared about. He felt that was the most important thing for him. It would prove to the pros he could compete at the next level."

No one could outwork Hank Gathers. If someone wanted his rebounding title, he'd better be ready to work for it, because Hank was not going to surrender it without a fight. Hank, who had been watching boxing films with Tom Peabody for years, was getting ready to come out swinging.

Woods, who was only 25 at the time, was often the foil for Hank's humor. Hank enjoyed ribbing everyone and never missed an opportunity to embarrass Bruce. "We would be in the gym practicing free throws. Hank was absolutely awful at it in game situations, and he asked me to help him work on technique. Once, while we were in there, my girlfriend, Stacy, came by to pick me up. We'd been dating for a while, and Hank knew it," Woods said.

As the pretty strawberry blond strode across the floor, Hank yelled out, "Hey, Stace. Watch this. If I make 10 in a row, Bruce is gonna have to marry you!" While Stacy laughed, Bruce cringed in embarrassment. "I knew I was pretty safe, though," Bruce said. "Hank was a terrible free-throw shooter. But he never would stop trying to get better."

Hank also appreciated all the extra time that Woods was putting in at ungodly hours to help him. "In early September, a photographer arrived to do a photo shoot with Hank for the *Street and Smith's College Basketball Preview* magazine," Bruce recalled. "It was the bible of college basketball, and Hank was going to be on the cover. He got on his uniform and, after posing for a while with the photographer, asked the guy to take one more, of the two of us together.

"It was taken in the same place and shot at the same angle as the cover shot. Hank had it framed, and he gave it to me. On it he had written in his neat handwriting, 'To Bruce Woods—No one helps me produce like my main man, Bruce! Thanks for your help. The Bank Man.' And he signed it 'Eric "Hank" Gathers #44.'"

Years later, Bruce would say, "That was typical of Hank. He'd imitate Muhammad Ali with a poem about you that made you smile, but you would know he meant it from the heart."[18]

Jay Hillock was another of Westhead's assistants, "the enforcer" on the coaching staff. "I was always the guy that had to tell [the players] they had to run extra laps for being late or missing class," Hillock explained. He had been a head coach at Gonzaga for four years, going 60-50 at the Spokane, Wash., school before leaving to return to his native southern California. Jay joined Paul's staff at LMU for the 1985-86 season, and by the 1989-90 season, he had spent 11 years in the West Coast Athletic Conference.

LMU was "a school searching for an identity. They were trying to decide if they were going to be an academic-type place like Santa Clara or loosen up like Pepperdine," said Jay. "There was always a debate over the athletics versus academics," Jay said. "When we first got there, we only attracted about 500 people to a game, so the debate wasn't really meaningful. Later, it all changed.

"Hank was as competitive as anyone I ever saw. He loved to play, much more than Bo. He could jaw with the best of them. He had a little street in him, and he'd get a chip on his shoulder for me when I'd be checking up on his classes. But he was witty and charming, and you couldn't help liking him."[19]

The other assistant was Judas Prada, whom Hank would kid unmercifully. Prada was always the first at the table for meals in the team training room. "He would eat as fast as he could so he wouldn't be there when Hank arrived," Bruce Woods said.[20]

During the summer of 1989, Hank had again been an intern for Ed Arnold at KTLA, an informal arrangement that allowed Hank to spend time at the station, whenever possible. He also attended the Ray Englebrecht Sportscasters Camp for young hopefuls, that was held at LMU. Recalled Arnold, "He was given a scholarship to attend so that they could use his presence to attract other kids," Ed Arnold said.

Hank was serious about broadcasting. He was the host of a halftime show that he taped in advance and that aired on the cable channel that televised the LMU games. "He was quite good," Arnold said. "He was both articulate and funny. He had a segment which he called the 'Hank Gathers Moment of Truth,' where he'd pause dramatically and pose a question to his guest. It was usually a humorous one and he did a good job. He even had his mother on the show. He questioned her about her weight and exercise regimen."

Arnold, who was as close to Hank as any Los Angeles television reporter covering the Lions, added, "Hank had a flair for it and would have been very good at it."[21]

Mike Waldner, a columnist for the *Daily Breeze*, covered Hank throughout his time in Los Angeles. He, too, got to know the player quite well during that time. "He was intensely concerned about doing things right. If I interviewed him, he'd ask me after[ward] if he had given a good interview," Mike said. "He was interested in how I prepared [for interviews] and how I worked. It was a genuine interest, and he was serious about becoming a broadcast journalist. Of course, that would be after basketball, but he was still very serious in learning as much as he could about it."[22]

Basketball would come first, though, and everyone was eagerly anticipating the 1989-90 season.

"Al Gersten told me before the season started that LMU was going to have one of 'the greatest teams in the land,'" Ed Arnold said. Al would be the first to acknowledge his tendency toward hyperbole, but there was a sense that something special was happening at LMU. There was, said Arnold, "magic in the air."[23]

Hank's record-smashing season of 1988-89 had made him a figure of national interest. His picture graced the cover of *Sport Magazine* (which ceased publication in August 2000, after 54 years), in addition to *Street and Smith's* Yearbook. Barry Zepel's thorough and informative LMU Basketball media guide featured a color photo of Hank finishing one of his trademark dunks. He and the team were profiled in *Sports Illustrated* and countless other periodicals. Hank was, in the opinion of many, the number one player in the country heading into his senior year. His team had generated a loyal, even fanatical, following from coast to coast, with its exciting, fast-paced, high-scoring style.

Hank Gathers and tiny LMU were media darlings, a Cinderella-on-fast-forward story that had captivated the country. The Lions would be featured on national television, and a large contingent of reporters would cover their games and document their every move. *The Los Angeles Times'* Alan Drooz would have plenty of company on press row. He and Mike Waldner would be fighting for elbow room in a press section that they were accustomed to having pretty much to themselves.

Bo Kimble was healthy at last; Hank was out to defend his title. With "The Hank and Bo Show" at full strength, it was curtain time for the final act of their college career, and it promised to be one hell of a show. It would begin on November 15 on national television with the preseason National Invitation Tournament, amid the glitter and glamour of Las Vegas, where the Lions would face off against the UNLV Runnin' Rebels of Jerry Tarkanian.

All the national attention was paying dividends on the LMU campus. The Lions' success had met with great approval from students and especially from alumni. LMU now ranked first in the nation among universities for voluntary contributions received, $26.8 million, which was $2 million dollars ahead of Wake Forest University. The current capital fund drive had met its goal. Winning had undoubtedly helped, as had the checks from the NCAA. For the Lions' 1988 appearance in the first round of the NCAA tournament, LMU had received $250,000. Schools that advanced to the Final Four in Seattle each got $1.25 million.[24]

"The team brought a sense of pride to the student body. It was true for the faculty and students alike," said Lane Bove, now senior vice president for student affairs at LMU. "Before Hank and Bo got here, you would see students dressed in UCLA or USC sweatshirts on campus. No one wore LMU shirts. After those first two seasons, everyone was wearing LMU sweatshirts. And it wasn't just here. We had a terrible time keeping sweatshirts in stock in the bookstore. We got mail orders from all across the country for sweatshirts and tees. We had kids coming in at night to fill the orders and keep up with the demand."

But not everyone, though, was thrilled with what basketball success had done for LMU. Bove served on a committee that the Reverend James Loughran, the university's president, had formed to "determine the direction of the basketball program." It was pretty clear to Bove what Father Loughran thought that direction should be, "Father Loughran didn't think it was right for a Jesuit school to be a basketball institution. Division III was ideal for him," she said.[25]

"LMU had grown steadily in size and academic reputation," Father Loughran said years later. "In my opinion, that growth had little, if anything, to do with the 'success' of the basketball team."[26]

In the end, only three people on the committee supported Father Loughran's view. The rest favored staying at the Division I level.[27]

"It was a great experience for the school. For me, seeing how proud and energized the students became in all aspects of the institution, was really impressive," Bove said. "With Hank and Bo here it was a magical time for the school."[28]

Said Terry Lanni, who then served on the board of trustees, "The direction of the program was a subject of debate around that time. On balance, I believe most of the trustees thought that the exposure the team was giving the university was a positive force. It certainly helped in the fund-raising efforts. There were some that wanted LMU to be known for academics, as a university, not as a basketball power. But there were a number of us on the board who thought in terms of Duke and Boston College and Stanford. We didn't see it as mutually exclusive. We strongly believed that we could have both.

"As a graduate of USC, I was convinced by my experience there that money usually followed athletic success. I also knew you could have good academic standards and athletic success. It [the discussions about the direction of the basketball program] was at a time at LMU when we were launching our Campaign for the Future, and I am certain that the success of the team was instrumental in making that campaign a success."[29]

Bo had spent the summer in Philadelphia, competing in the collegiate division of the Sonny Hill League and proving that his knee was fine. Indeed, he led all scorers, averaging 33 points per game. Lionel Simmons, La Salle's star player, was second.[30]

For the most part, Hank had stayed on the West Coast that summer. In June, he had participated in the trials for the U.S. team at the World University Games. His work-outs had impressed pro scouts, and Westhead, who was on campus for part of the summer, said that Hank was "certainly everyone's equal" and "clearly in the plans" of World University Games coach Bobby Cremins before back spasms sidelined Hank. "The spasms took a few days to cool down. It's really nothing serious. He's back lifting weights," Paul told Alan Drooz in June.[31]

For the *Playboy* photo shoot, Hank had flown to Florida, where he met Simmons, his old high school competitor and friend, in July. They talked about old times and about the game between their schools that was set for January in Philadelphia.[32] Also in Florida for the *Playboy* shoot were other members of the magazine's 10-man All-America team—Derrick Coleman of Syracuse, Georgetown's Alonzo Mourning, Gary Payton of Oregon State, and Dwayne Schintzius of Florida.

Hank had attended Pete Newell's Big Man Camp on the LMU campus in late July, and he'd spent August hanging out at Gersten, playing pickup games.

Rumors had swirled all summer that Westhead was leaving for another pro or college job. Paul, meanwhile, was coaching on a tour of Australia and Taiwan with a team of NBA players, including his old Lakers star Kareem Abdul-Jabbar. Westhead denied all the rumors and on his return, conducted a fast-break clinic in Great Falls, Montana.[33]

September found him back at LMU along with Hank and Bo. It was show time.

Despite Hank's decision to stay in the college ranks for another year, he was convinced that he could run with the big dogs now, that he could play against anyone in the NBA and hold his own. He would back down from no one, not even the league's superstar, Earvin "Magic" Johnson of the Lakers.

The Lakers and the Clippers, as well as other NBA teams, used Gersten Pavilion as a practice facility. The LA Summer Pro League played its games there. Although the league was mainly for rookies, it also attracted veterans who lived nearby and used it to stay in shape or who were trying to catch on with another team. Gersten was always full of friendly pickup games of pros and LMU players who were around the gym. Well, if Hank was playing, it wasn't always so friendly.

"Hank was playing in a pickup game in the late summer against a team of pro players that included Magic," Bruce Woods recalled. "Hank called a foul on Magic and demanded the ball from the Lakers star."

Here's how Bruce described their exchange:

"That's not a foul," Magic complained.

"It's a damn foul," Hank demanded. "Gimme the ball."

"No damn way is that a foul," Magic protested.

"It's a foul 'cause I said it's a foul," Hank insisted.

"What gives you the right to say it's a foul?" Magic responded.

Hank, his anger and voice rising, glared at the NBA superstar and yelled, "'BECAUSE YOU'RE IN MY HOUSE NOW! THIS IS MY HOUSE!"

The gym was dead silent as everyone turned to watch the confrontation.

"Ball up!" Hank barked at Magic, indicating that play would resume.

"Ball up!!" he repeated, now inches from Magic's face. Magic just shook his head and backed off.

"Then it was over," Woods said.

Hank had served notice. Gersten Pavilion was his house. If you entered, you did so at your own risk. He would defend his house to the end and not even Magic Johnson could stop him.

Woods, who had seen it all, said, "I knew then it was going to be a memorable season."[34]

TAKING CENTER COURT

The team officially began practice on October 15. Also joining the Lions were Tony Walker, a speedy transfer from Ventura Junior College, 6-foot-9 forward Chris Scott, a freshman from Logan High in Union City, California; and walk-on guard Greg Walker, from San Jose, California completed the squad.

All of the players were given physicals before being cleared to practice. The exams were conducted by the Kerlan-Jobe Orthopaedic Clinic, whose doctors served as team physicians for LMU.

Dr. Ben Shaffer was one of seven young physicians, out of hundreds of applicants, who had won coveted fellowships at the world-famous clinic. Under the direction of the clinic's cofounders, the fellows would receive specialized training in the growing field of sports medicine. Young, athletic, and darkly handsome, his black hair worn slightly long, Shaffer had graduated from the University of Florida and then its College of Medicine, from which he graduated in 1984. He did an internship at Mt. Sinai Hospital, in New York, followed by a four-year residency program at the New York Hospital for Joint Diseases and Orthopedic Institute. He completed his training there in 1989.

The spot he had won at the renowned clinic in sunny southern California was a dream job for an aspiring sports medicine specialist. Dr. Ben Shaffer, 31, couldn't have been prouder or happier as he headed to Los Angeles. "Sports medicine was a specific subspecialty that had to do with taking care of athletes, surgical procedures, and management of patients who had athletic-type injuries," he said.[1]

Dr. George Kerlan had become the Dodgers' team physician when they moved to Los Angeles in 1958. He also taught at the University of Southern California School of Medicine, and was increasingly called upon for consultations by teams and individual athletes in other sports. Dr. Frank Jobe, who had known Dr. Kerlan when they were both on staff at Los Angeles County General Hospital, offered to help his friend with these requests. Together they founded the Kerlan-Jobe Orthopedic Clinic, then known as the Southwestern Orthopedic Medical Group, in 1965 near the Hollywood Park racetrack. The revolutionary surgical procedure that Jobe performed on pitcher Tommy John, in 1974, was what had made the clinic world famous.[2]

"When I got there, they were taking care of the Lakers, Dodgers, Rams, Angels, Anaheim Ducks, and three colleges, one of which was Loyola Marymount University," Dr. Shaffer said. "As a fellow, I was designated as assistant team physician for all the pro teams and attended all the games. The only thing that we were full physicians for, with full responsibility, was the three college teams. I was one of three fellows who shared the responsibility for the athletic care at Loyola Marymount. Dr. Clarence Shields and Dr. Ralph Gamberdella were listed as responsible—they were partners at Kerlan-Jobe, well-established practitioners, but they didn't attend any games. We [the fellows] did all the work. We were their agents and attended the games on a rotating basis. Kind of a luck-of-the-draw sort of arrangement as to which doctor went to which game."

The actual examination of the LMU basketball players fell to Dr. Ben Shaffer on the appointed day. "I performed the preseason physical exam. It involved a fairly full medical history, about two pages long, that the players were asked to fill out before I did the clearance. The physical examination I did on Hank and the others that day was a standard assessment," Dr. Shaffer said. "I did an orthopedic exam of his neck, back, shoulders, knees, and elbows to see if there were any orthopedic problems. I listened to his lungs with a stethoscope, and then I listened to his heart. I listened for any abnormal rhythm, any abnormal sounds— bruits, murmurs, or any unusual sounds. I did the blood pressure test and a hernia examination. I reviewed the questionnaire to determine if there were any flags there that needed to be followed up on."

"Interestingly," Dr. Shaffer said, "on Hank's questionnaire, written next to the last question, which dealt with any heart problems, he had scrawled in large letters. 'HELL NO!'"

Dr. Shaffer found no problems, cleared Hank to play, and signed the form.[3]

The intrasquad game between the Crimson and Gray teams was a high-scoring event, 150-141, that produced no serious injuries to anyone. Hank scored 52 points for the losers.

Brian Berger, who covered the action for the *Los Angeles Loyolan*, reported, "It was quite a sight. Bo Kimble was phenomenal and had no signs of a bad knee." Berger would be doing the play-by-play for KXLU, the LMU radio station, along with color analyst Keith Forman. In the *Loyolan* Berger warned, "Hang on to your hats. This could be the season 'The System' comes of age."[4]

Among those observing the LMU practices was a short, courtly Asian, the coach of South Korea's national team, Jung Myung Lim. Pete Newell, who had told the *Los Angeles Times*' Alan Drooz that fall that "Loyola (Marymount) is changing the game," had made the arrangements for the South Korean coach's visit.[5] The popularity of the System was spreading around the globe.

After the Lions' game against UNLV in the NIT, the LMU schedule called for the team to play UC-Santa Barbara, Oregon State, and Oklahoma—all before Christmas. The New Year would bring a homecoming trip to Philadelphia for Westhead, Hank, and Bo, with the Lions slated to meet St. Joseph's, Paul Westhead's alma mater, and then the nationally ranked La Salle Explorers, whom he had coached with much success, before joining the Lakers.

The 1989 NCAA Tournament had ended with the thrilling Michigan single-point overtime victory against P. J. Carlesimo's Seton Hall Pirates. Before the NCAA could sit back, though, and enjoy the growing audience (nearly 20 million households and fully one-third of all television sets were tuned to the game—the most since 1979's Magic-Bird match-up), scandals and accusations rocked college basketball once more.

It was an all-too-familiar story. Fans had stayed away in droves after the point-shaving scandals of the early 1950's, until a gangly 6-foot-9 farm boy with the headline-friendly name of Bevo Francis brought spectators back to the arenas. Playing for an obscure Southern Ohio school with fewer than 100 students, Francis had become the all-time leading college scorer, the stuff of Hollywood movies. During the 1953-54 season, the nation was captivated when he and his Rio Grande College teammates embarked on a cross-country tour that pitted them against the basketball giants of the era. Newspapers and magazines, including *Life*, covered their ups and downs. At a time when fewer than one-third of American households had a television set, movie theater newsreels featured the scoring sensation. Bevo became a national celebrity and tiny Rio Grande College a household name. Interest in their Cinderella story is widely credited with saving the faith of college basketball fans.

Slowly, but steadily, the crowds returned to college games. In the coming years, there would be temporary setbacks, as gamblers would continue to seek youngsters willing to shave points for a few extra bucks—and usually found them—but the damage was always temporary.

As the 1989-90 season was about to unfold, coaches at Syracuse, Maryland, and North Carolina (NC) State were defending themselves and their programs against accusations of recruiting and other violations. Kentucky was reeling from the revelation that one of its boosters had sent $1,000 in cash in an Emery Air Freight envelope to the family of recruit Chris Mills. Only three years earlier, the *Lexington Herald-Leader* had won a Pulitzer Prize for investigative reporting after detailing cash payoffs to University of Kentucky basketball players.

The myriad accusations would claim the coaching careers of Jim Valvano at NC State (he would find a new career in television) and Lefty Driesell at (the University of) Maryland, and eventually led to the departure of Eddie Sutton from (the University of) Kentucky. Their names were some of the biggest in college basketball, and it was not the kind of publicity the NCAA was looking for.

To make matters worse, the NCAA's favorite whipping boy, Jerry Tarkanian at UNLV, had a team that was being touted as a title contender. The NCAA could not have been pleased at the prospect of handing its championship trophy to Tark the Shark that year.

Meanwhile, the LMU Lions were poised to become media darlings, the feel-good story of a badly tarnished sport. They would soon find themselves, and their wildly popular, high-scoring games, a staple on television. Their schedule would be a strong national one, and they would attract large viewing audiences with each appearance. The Lions, and their star player, Hank Gathers, a leading candidate for Player of the Year, were expected to do much to overcome the negative publicity.

However, the team was not receiving much respect, from the basketball polls. The Lions had enjoyed a top-20 ranking in 1988-89, but now were not on any preseason top 40 list. The highest that the team appeared was at number 48, in Dick Vitale's basketball magazine.[6]

As Westhead dryly remarked to Alan Drooz, "There must be a lot of good teams out there if there are 30 or 40 teams better than us."[7] While he didn't say so, Westhead was reasonably certain that his Lions would shake up the ratings just as thoroughly as the Loma Prieta earthquake had shaken the Bay Area in October.

Hank was still trying to cure his woeful free-throw shooting (56 percent), Drooz reported in the *Los Angeles Times*. Hank had continued to struggle with free throws all the previous season, when the coaches had had to talk him out of trying to shoot left-handed.[8] "He was a natural born left-hander," Priamos said. "He told me his father had struck him as a child when he used his left hand, and he was forced to change to [being] right-handed."[9]

Hank had been shooting left-handed in practice and was making as many as 80 percent. He had shot left-handed in the scrimmage game and intended to continue. The coaches were uncertain whether to encourage that tack, Drooz reported.[10] Hank would ultimately settle on shooting as a lefty, but it was not much help. He continued to struggle from the line, and his success rate was barely more than 50 percent.

To get ready for their opener against UNLV, the Lions took on the Australian national team again. The Aussies offered a good test. Made up of former Olympians, including

Andrew Gaze (who had nearly brought a national championship to Seton Hall against Michigan the year before), the Aussies were no cupcakes, as the Lions quickly found out.

Before you could say, "Throw another shrimp on the barbie," things started to go wrong. Terrell Lowery, who was slated to replace Simmons at the point guard slot, was taken to the hospital before the game even started. He had been complaining of stomach pains all morning. Then, the team that usually thrived on 3-point shots made only 9. The Australians made 14. Gaze accounted for 6 of them, and he had a game-high 37 points, as Australia won, 117-104. Hank had 28 points to lead the Lions, and engaged in several shoving matches with the more experienced Aussies.

Lowery recovered rapidly from his abdominal distress and was soon back on campus.[11] The Lions would have to recover as well. Coming up was the team that almost everyone thought was the best in the land. The Runnin' Rebels of UNLV and their coach, Tark the Shark, were waiting at Thomas and Mack Arena in Las Vegas, which was always packed with rabid Rebel rooters.

With the television cameras greased to swivel as fast as they could, the two highest-scoring teams in the history of basketball met on November 15. The glitz of the pregame introductions rivaled that of any Vegas extravaganza. A single spotlight followed a mechanical shark as it circled the top of the pitch-black arena, accompanied by ominous Jaws-like music. Amid smoke and blaring music, the UNLV players would emerge from the darkness with a blazing white spotlight trained on them. Other spots danced around the audience as the announcer dramatically introduced each player. It was pure Vegas theater, as impressive as a performance by David Copperfield. The introductions for the opposing team, however, were similar to those for any game in any other arena.

"We will not be (intimidated) by the glitter," Westhead declared. "We are an experienced team."[12] With all due respect, the atmosphere inside Thomas and Mack was meant to intimidate and to impress and, for the most part, through 17 seasons under the Shark, it had done so.[13]

The 1989-90 team that Tarkanian had assembled included junior-college transfer Larry Johnson, who was 6-foot-7, and Stacey Augmon, at forward. David Butler was out until mid-December, because of academics. In the backcourt were Greg Anthony (who had played against LMU as a freshman, at Portland, before transferring) and the hot 3-point shooter Anderson Hunt, who had dropped 12 3-point bombs on the Soviet national team in an exhibition game. As they began their sixth season at Thomas and Mack, the Rebels record there was 86-6.[14]

With sharks circling, strobe lights flashing, and music blaring, the Lions ran onto the court.

As the centers faced each other for the jump, Hank, who knew a thing or two about intimidation, hiked up his crimson shorts, glared at the imposing Johnson, and snarled, "Get ready for war!" What followed very much resembled a war: shouting matches, pushing and shoving, and even bomb threats—as the two fast-paced teams went at it in front of 18,000 fans.

LMU trailed early but then went on a 20-2 run. Tarkanian called a time-out and chewed out his team. Bald head glistening, bare arms waving, droopy eyes flashing, Tark screamed, "I can't believe you can be this bad. You're not playing any defense at all. We've got to stop these shots!" ESPN's cameras and mikes caught the entire tirade.[15]

Steve Carp covered the game for the *Las Vegas Sun* and recalled it quite clearly, more than 15 years later: "It was very intense. There was a lot of trash talking during the game. It was a very physical contest."[16]

Tarkanian's tirade failed to rouse his team, and Loyola Marymount pushed out to a 41-34 lead.[17] "There was a stoppage of play. No one knew why," Carp said. "Then, after a minute or so, the public address system informed us that 'a suspicious package has been found in the building.' We were told on press row that it was being examined. It might contain a bomb."[18] Play was stopped at the 5:41 mark, and so was LMU's momentum, as both teams retreated to the locker room to await the bomb squad's findings. It turned out to be a student's utterly harmless backpack.[19]

But the damage had been done, though. Play resumed after about 10 minutes, and LMU never regained its momentum. During the break, Sugar Ray Leonard, one of Hank's idols, and Andre Agassi had fled for the exits. Though LMU held on to a 54-52 lead at halftime, UNLV had regrouped during the bomb scare and went on to win 102-91.[20] Neither Hank nor Bo played particularly well. Bo had 19 points and Hank 18, although he had managed to welcome Larry Johnson to Division I play by sending the UNLV star's first shot about three rows up into the crowd.[21]

As the two teams headed up the narrow tunnel leading to the locker rooms after the game, the pushing, jostling, and jawing became intense. "There was a lot of mouthing-off and some scuffling," Carp said. "The assistant coaches got between the players and kept it from getting out of hand."[22]

Hank was incensed that play had been stopped, convinced it was a trumped-up excuse to stop LMU from running away with the game.[23] Were Hank's anger and suspicion justified?

Well, as Steve Carp said, "There's never been a bomb scare since." The reporter who covered Tarkanian during all his years at UNLV said, "I wouldn't blame [Hank] if he felt that way. It wouldn't surprise me [if it had been faked]. In dealing with Tarkanian, I learned never to be surprised by anything that happens."[24]

Westhead was stoic, telling the *Los Angeles Loyolan* reporter, "We have the whole season left. Time will tell if we manage to respond in a positive way. We have eight or nine days off and will use it to get ready."[25]

Tark the Shark's comment to the press afterward was revealing: "I wouldn't want to play them again."[26]

Was that a trace of red on his teeth?

Bitten by the Shark and the nation's number one team, the Lions had time off to recover and prepare for the Silver State's other team, the lesser-known but equally ferocious Wolf Pack of Nevada-Reno.

The Lions sent the Wolf Pack skulking back to its den with a few furtive backward glances to be certain they weren't being followed. LMU trounced the Wolves, 145-102, in front of nearly 3,700. Hank had 17 rebounds in defense of his title and added 28 points. Bo poured in 31 in less than 30 minutes as the Lions coasted to their first win. "It was a fast-paced game, which we thrive on," Westhead said. "Our press kind of helped create the pace. Even though we got 145 points, we'll get sharper."[27]

LMU headed to Florida for the Gator Bowl Tournament, which was played in Jacksonville. The two-game weekend event would be televised live by Sports Channel America on December 1 and 2.

Per Stumer had been racking up the frequent-flyer miles. He had made two round trips to Sweden to play in two of the three qualifying games for the Swedish national team. He had left after the UNLV game and returned for the Nevada-Reno contest. Then he flew back to Sweden and returned just in time for the game in Jacksonville. Red-eyed and jet-lagged, he was on the court and ready on December 1.[28]

LMU faced Stetson in the first round and had little trouble with the Hatters, prevailing, 125-95.[29] Hank had 38 points in the win, smashing the Gator Bowl tournament record in the process (the old mark was 36, by Auburn's Chuck Person, in 1983, against Villanova). Hank also pulled down 16 rebounds.

The Lions had built a 34-point halftime lead as Bo hit eight 3-point shots on his way to a 35-point game. "Hank was very effective offensively, slicing through the lane. He was playing up," Westhead said of Hank's aggressive and dominating performance.[31] The win put the Lions in the championship game against the Dolphins of Jacksonville on the host team's home court.

Drowning the Dolphins required a string of 15 consecutive points as time was winding down. In securing the 115-114 victory, Hank managed 32 points to lead the Lions, 17 coming in the second half. Chris Knight accounted for 12 important points in limited play. It was Terrell Lowery, though, who sank a crucial free throw to break a 105 tie, and then blocked the inbounds pass to thwart the Dolphins. Hank was named the tournament's MVP for his two strong performances.[32] With Hank clutching yet another trophy, the Lions returned home on December 4, 3-1 for the season, thus far.

The Soaring Gulls of U.S. International University would host the Lions at Golden Hall in San Diego on December 7. The Gulls had played Billy Tubbs and his University of Oklahoma team earlier in the year and had surrendered 173 points, losing to the Sooners by 62 points. Was Westhead's elusive dream—in which one team would score 200 points—possible?

As the Lions and the Gulls squared off, the scoreboard over the court at Golden Hall bore the hopeful phrase "History in the Making." The Lions found themselves locked in a tight game as they committed numerous turnovers that the Gulls converted.

Hank controlled the boards throughout the first half, putting up 23 points and accounting for 11 rebounds, but LMU couldn't pull away, and held a slim 75-72 lead over the tenacious Gulls at the break. The System finally began to click in the second half, and LMU went on a 24-4 surge to pull away. The final score was 152-137.

Hank finished with 37 points and 27 rebounds in a dominating display of raw power.[32] "His play was as strong as it could be," Bruce Woods said. "He swept the boards with authority, and his offense was dominating in the paint."[33]

"I think [a record] was on our mind, but my guys didn't really have that 200 look on their faces," Hank told Alan Drooz. "USIU did a good job of smacking us and making us wake up."[34]

LMU had a day off before taking on UC-Santa Barbara at Gersten on Saturday, December 9. It was a game that would change everything. Santa Barbara was coming off a week's rest. The Gauchos were 3-1, having lost by only 6 to Iowa in the finals of the Amana Classic, and had made their way into the top 20 of several polls. In the 1988-89 season, Jerry Pimm's charges had defeated LMU, 95-94, at Santa Barbara.[35]

Hank was averaging 29 points per game to lead the team, with Bo close behind at 27.5. Peabody had been filling in admirably for an injured Fryer, and Terrell Lowery was leading the conference in assists.[36]

Gersten was packed for the Santa Barbara game. The Lion's Pride, which Brian Quinn had begun five years earlier with a paltry 15 members or so, was now 1,000 members strong. Five hundred members received tickets behind the Lions' bench, where, armed with their rooter rags of crimson and gray, and wearing LMU T-shirts, they provided constant vocal support.[37]

The game was close as Hank stepped to the free-throw line early in the second half. He shot his first of two free throws and then slowly collapsed onto the court.

A week later, he would tell the respected newspaper columnist Mike Downey what had happened: "I noticed that I wasn't breathing well. I was getting short breaths while I was running and I'm probably one of the best runners we've got, if not the best. I was kind of tired, unusually tired, when Eric McArthur fouled me and I stepped to the line.

"I wiped my face off, took a deep breath, and suddenly I felt a little light- headed. Felt a rush coming on. That's when I blacked out. For a second of time, I could feel myself falling, real slow. When I was on the floor, I was awake. My memory's picture- perfect about everything else, but I lost a second or two somewhere on the way down. I remember I got up, but a couple of my teammates grabbed me. I wasn't so much frightened as confused."[38]

Dr. Dan Hyslop, LMU's staff physician, was only ten to fifteen yards away and rushed to Hank's side.[39] On the other side of the gym was Dr. Nick Di Gioviane, an orthopedist, from the Kerlan-Jobe clinic. He saw Hank drop and thought he was just goofing around, until Di Gioviane's wife, a registered nurse, said, "He's hurt—you better get down there."[40] When Dr. Di Gioviane got to Hank's side, Dr. Hyslop was already there, and so was trainer Chip Schaeffer, whose first reaction also had been that Hank was clowning around. As Schaeffer reached Hank, he was trying to sit up as Dr. Hyslop tried to take his pulse.[41] It was irregular, so the doctors and Schaeffer decided to take Hank to the trainers' room behind the stands for further evaluation. Dr. Di Gioviane and Schaeffer helped him off the court.

In the trainers' room, Hank's pulse was still irregular. Dr. Hyslop and Dr. Di Gioviane checked his pulse and heart rate every five minutes or so.[42] "Anyone who takes care of athletes can look into their eyes, and the eyes will tell you if they are hurt, even when the athlete denies it," Dr. Di Gioviane said. "I looked into Hank's eyes and I saw uncertainty there." Dr. Di Gioviane decided a consultation with an internist was in order and contacted Dr. Michael "Mickey" Mellman, who was affiliated with Centinella Hospital Medical Center, and had worked with the team before. Dr. Mellman arranged to have Hank admitted to Centinella, and Dr. Di Gioviane summoned an ambulance.[43]

Hank balked. He insisted that he was fine and wanted to go back into the game, not to some hospital. Dr. Hyslop nixed that. Hank was so angry and frustrated that he pounded a cabinet in the trainer's room with his fist.[44]

By the time Pete Priamos got to Hank, his rage had turned to fear. Priamos found the player on his knees on the floor, his head buried in his arms on one of the cabinet tables along the wall. He was crying.

"I blew the NBA," a weeping Hank told Priamos.

"You didn't blow anything. You just had a little fainting spell," Priamos told him. "It will be O.K." Somehow, Priamos was able to calm Hank, and he stopped crying.[45]

Next to arrive in the trainers' room was Stan Morrison, who was now the athletic director at UC-Santa Barbara. Hank told Morrison that he was scared.

"Hank, just do whatever they tell you to do," his former coach advised.

"I will, Coach. I'll do whatever they say."[46]

Dr. Mellman, who received Dr. Di Gioviane's call through his service, took control of Hank's case. He ordered that the player be admitted, instead of being treated in Centinella's emergency room.[47]

When Dr. Mellman got to Centinella, he introduced himself to Hank. Dr. Mellman had been the internist for the Lakers, Kings, Dodgers, and the LA Express since 1981. He was a consultant to Major League Baseball and attended to all teams playing at the Forum. He was a graduate of Mt. Sinai School of Medicine (in New York) and had done his residency at Cedars-Sinai in Los Angeles.[48]

Dr. Hyslop had given the paramedics a handwritten note to take to the hospital that explained what had happened at Gersten—the fainting spell, followed by twitching legs, difficulty breathing, and light-headedness. Hank's pulse had been 54 and irregular, the note said.[49]

Dr. Mellman said later he did not recall seeing the note. The internist ordered tests to determine the cause of Hank's fainting, or syncope, as the doctors called it. The tests included the standard stress test while he was on a treadmill, and an electrocardiogram. The tests were inconclusive, although Dr. Mellman was able to rule out central nervous system dysfunction, as well as any illegal drugs.[50]

(That the tests turned up no illegal drug use was no surprise. Hank loathed drugs of any kind, as well as alcohol, aversions that were a product of his upbringing. He had seen how they had destroyed his father and the lives of others in his neighborhood. Hank drank only cranberry juice—never a soda, and especially not a cola, because of the caffeine. And his friends knew that if they were drinking alcohol during an evening on the town with Hank, he was likely to harangue them about becoming teetotalers.)[51]

Lane Bove spoke with Hank by telephone. He assured her that the doctor had said that everything was "going to be okay" and that he would soon be able to return to school. She asked Hank to contact her when he got back.[52] Morrison called Hank, too, and Hank made a joke about his free-throw shooting, how he shouldn't have tried to do it sitting down.[53]

During the testing, Bove was in constant contact with Brian Quinn; based on those conversations, she felt confident that the school was doing everything it should to ensure that Hank was getting the best care possible.[54]

Hank was discharged from Centinella on the 11th, and a follow-up visit was scheduled for the next day. During that visit, Dr. Mellman advised Hank that he would need to undergo additional testing, and he submitted to a thallium stress test study while on the treadmill, to determine how well blood was flowing to his heart muscle, but it too was inconclusive. Dr. Mellman also hung around his neck a Holter monitor, an ambulatory electrocardiography device, and told him to wear it everywhere, including practice.

However, all the tests but one showed abnormalities. The test that was normal was the echocardiogram, and Hank hung his hat on it, although he should not have. Although Dr. Mellman later would be unable to remember specific dates and times of their meetings, between Hank's discharge from Centinellla and New Year's Day, he did recall that Hank was very specific on one point: Dr. Mellman could speak to only a few people about the player's condition and what the testing was showing.[55]

During the testing, Hank arrived at practice one afternoon in his sweats and reported with pride that the doctors couldn't find anything wrong with him.

"I broke their damn machine," he said, referring to the treadmill test that had failed to produce a heart rate high enough to be of value.[56] Indeed, because of the physical conditioning that Westhead required of his athletes, the testing showed that Hank's resting heart rate was similar to that of a marathon runner.[57]

"There's nothing wrong with my heart," he said loudly to the team, adding, "I'm still the strongest man in America—I have the heart of a lion!"[58]

"Looking at him, the self-proclaimed 'strongest man alive,' you had to believe him," said Tom Peabody.[59] Although everyone wanted to know how Hank was doing, on this day, as on many subsequent ones, Hank would say the tests were inconclusive and he was doing fine. What Peabody didn't know—what none of them knew—was that Hank was doing what he had done in Vegas, Reno, and the Los Alamitos racetrack: he was gambling.

CHAPTER 22

ROLLING THE DICE

On December 14, Dr. Mellman referred Hank to Dr. Vernon Hattori, a cardiologist at Apex Cardiology, as the practice was called, for further evaluation. Dr. Hattori met with Hank that day.

Hattori told Hank that he had reviewed the test results and had spoken twice with Dr. Mellman. Hattori's opinion of the tread mill test results was that they were unremarkable except in terms of the ST segments (in his electrocardiogram), which indicate ischemia (a restriction in blood supply), but that there were some ventricular arrhythmias (abnormal rapid heart beats, originating in the lower chambers of the heart).[1] However, the tests had failed to conclusively identify what was causing the problem.[2]

The insurance agent who had arranged for Hank's $1 million policy with Lloyd's of London reached him by phone while Hank was undergoing the testing. Dana Monck believed that Hank had a case for collecting the money, but Hank wasn't at all interested in talking about it, lest the NBA get wind of it.

"He said he was fine. It seemed he didn't want to talk about his condition that much," Monck recalled.[3]

Dr. Hattori consulted informally with a colleague at Apex Cardiology, Dr. Charles Swerdlow, in case the medical team decided to bring him in for a formal consultation. Dr. Swerdlow was an electrophysiologist and arrhythmia expert who had headed the electrophysiology lab at Stanford University for five years before joining Apex as a consultant. He had written nearly a dozen articles in the previous eight years about the treatment of periodic ventricular tachycardia—the formal diagnosis of Hank's problem, though no one had determined what was causing it. Standard treatment was a drug, Inderal.[4]

On December 17, Mike Downey reported in his *Los Angeles Times* column that he had recently visited with Hank, who had just returned from a visit to the doctor's office.

"Looks tired. No pep to his step. He's been prodded and poked, X-rayed and wired to machines. He's had his heart examined. Had his heart checked. So far, so good. He feels fine. Feels strong as a lion. He's sick and tired, all right—sick and tried of being tested," Downey wrote.[5]

While waiting for clearance to play, Hank had been attending Clippers games with Ed Arnold so he could observe Ed's interviewing technique, Downey reported. Indeed, his broadcasting career seemed to be much on Hank's mind. He told Downey he'd wanted to be a sportscaster ever since he'd heard the late Dave Zinkoff introduce him during the high school championships in Philadelphia.

At the young broadcasters' camp the previous summer, Hank had called an Angels-Mariners baseball game and was so bad that everyone had laughed when they played the tape back. He was already doing spots, though, for Sports Channel, which was using them during the LMU games that the cable channel was televising that season.

Hank told Downey that his doctor had not yet determined what the problem was. "He's tested me for everything. I'm glad he's being careful," Hank said, "But, we've got to get me back in the game." As eager as Hank was to return to playing, the university was being very cautious. "I told Brian Quinn that Hank could not practice and could not step one foot back on our court until we had a release from the doctors," Lane Bove recalled. Until the release arrived, Hank would have to wait. On that, Bove said, "there could be no debate."[6]

At some point that third week in December, Dr. Hattori told Hank that he would have to be admitted to Daniel Freeman Memorial Hospital, for additional testing, explaining that none of the tests thus far had told the doctors why his heart kept racing. Hank was admitted on December 18, for an angiogram, which Dr. Hattori would perform, and the electrophysiology (EP) test, which would be done by Dr. Swerdlow.[7]

The day Hank was admitted, Dr. Hattori spoke with Hank and his family—Derrick was there, and Lucille had flown out two days earlier—explaining the procedures and the dangers involved. The EP test was necessary, Dr. Hattori said, to determine whether Hank's heart had any detectable structural or electrical problems. Dr. Swerdlow was hoping that this test would finally reveal why Hank's heart kept going haywire.[8]

Dr. Hattori did the angiogram that same day. This test involves threading a catheter through the femoral artery via an incision in the groin. Dye is then injected through the catheter, and the dye is visible on an X-ray, showing how blood is flowing through the vessels. Dr. Swerdlow later said the angiogram showed an "incidental abnormality."[9]

The next day, Dr. Swerdlow conducted the EP study on Hank, who was awake for the procedure. The test is risky because the cardiac specialist conducting the test is trying to determine how electricity flows through the patient's heart and uses chemical and electrical means to stimulate it to a very high rate.[10]

While increasing Hank's heart rate, Dr. Swerdlow induced ventricular fibrillation (quivering, or uncoordinated, rapid contractions of the ventricles of the heart). Hank lost consciousness for about 15 seconds. Before the study began, self-adhesive defibrillation panels had been applied to Hank's chest. On Dr. Swerdlow's order, the nurse pushed a button, and the panels administered a shock of 200 joules, the standard initial shock strength. Hank's heart converted to a normal rhythm.[11]

In the waiting room were Lucille, Pete Priamos, and Vernell Ritchey, Hank's girlfriend. Lucille would later testify that she wasn't aware of the risks associated with the EP test and that she had consistently tried to talk Hank out of continuing to play.[12] Others recall a much different attitude, though. "She pushed him" to get back on the court, Priamos said.[13] None of the physicians involved ever mentioned hearing Lucille raise any objections to the testing or the subsequent decision to allow Hank to play again.[14]

While Hank was hospitalized, a social worker spoke with Vernell about Hank. She told the worker that basketball was "his whole life" and that his current fears were related to the possibility of this "devastating loss." The social worker's notes also indicated that Hank was eager to return to his usual activity and showed no apprehension about resuming competitive basketball. On the contrary, he appeared to have "downplayed" the importance of the follow-up care outlined by the physicians.[15]

The scary EP test proved inconclusive. Dr. Swerdlow wanted to do more extensive testing. Because of Hank's unexplained syncopal episode, Dr. Swerdlow suspected that Hank was suffering *high-risk* arrhythmias, which would mean the end of his basketball career.[16] But the cardiologists discharged Hank from Daniel Freeman Memorial the next day and sent him home to rest.

Dr. Swerdlow told Dr. Hattori that he suspected that the abnormally high heart rate had caused the fainting episode on court. Hank would not be able to play until the suspected arrhythmia was diagnosed and under control. Dr. Swerdlow also told Hank that he needed further evaluation because they had not yet determined what was causing his heart to race periodically, even when Hank was at rest. Swerdlow minced no words, telling his superstar patient that his heart was abnormal. Later he would characterize Hank as "very sad to hear. . .that he had definite heart disease."[17]

After Dr. Swerdlow laid out his findings and concerns, Dr. Hattori spoke to Hank in Dr. Swerdlow's presence and the electrophysiologist listened as Dr. Hattori "minimized the abnormalities identified. Specifically, he (Dr. Hattori) continued to emphasize his opinion that there was a "higher probability" that Hank's heart problems were the result of dehydration "and possibly the 'flu,'" rather than anything more serious. "As we walked out of the room, I told Dr. Hattori that I disagreed with his approach, believed he was misleading the patient, and [was] doing the patient a disservice," Dr. Swerdlow's notes say. "Hattori indicated to me that he believed that I had taken away too much of the patient's hope and that the patient and his family were 'devastated' by my direct approach."[18]

Pete Priamos was present during one of Dr. Hattori's discussions with Hank about his condition. "I was there when Hattori explained the possible side effects [of medication] to Hank. He was insistent on playing again as soon as possible. He was pushing Hattori to let him play again."

Pete also recalled something Hank had told him once about his history of miserable free-throw shooting. "He said when he got to the free-throw line, instead of his heart slowing down, it would start to speed up or race," Pete said. "That's why he had a hard time concentrating on the shot. Later, I asked him if he had told his doctors about that. He said, no.'"[19]

As everyone who knew Hank was aware, he was relentlessly persistent. Whether he was snarling his war challenge at the center jump or backing Magic Johnson down at Gersten, Hank was not going to be denied. Hank certainly wasn't about to let some skinny doctor stop him. He had to show the NBA that he was back and as strong as ever. He would pester, badger, and beg, but he was going to play.

Dr. Swerdlow also discussed his findings with Hank's internist, Dr. Mellman, on December 19. According to Dr. Swerdlow, the internist agreed with the need for further evaluation, said Hank would not play again until the arrhythmia was under control, and thanked Dr. Swerdlow for his assistance. At that point, neither physician knew how long it might be until Hank could play again, if, indeed, ever.[20] The next day, Wednesday, December 20, Dr. Hattori, the Apex cardiologist, decided that Hank should be benched indefinitely.[21]

On Thursday, though, just two days after Dr. Mellman and Dr. Swerdlow spoke, and a day after Dr. Hattori, the cardiologist, had grounded Hank, Dr. Mellman, the internist and the only physician in contact with school officials, wrote the university a letter in which he cleared Hank to resume playing basketball, so long as he submitted to continual monitoring and assessment. Dr. Mellman would later say that he considered the letter a conditional release to play—Hank was allowed to suit up only if his cardiologists and coaches agreed that he was fit to play. Dr. Mellman would also say that he wrote the letter only because he was asked to, by Barry Zepel, the LMU sports information director, who was acting on behalf of Brian Quinn, the athletic director. Zepel testified that he did not recall asking for it. Quinn clearly recalled receiving it.[22] (The letter survived and was introduced as evidence during the trial that followed.)

Meanwhile, Hank called Dr. Hattori and asked if he could just practice shooting. Dr. Hattori told him he could shoot but nothing else.[23]

The university received the letter from Dr. Mellman the following day, December 22.[24] The university was covered: a doctor had signed off on Hank's fitness to participate in varsity basketball. He was under the active care and monitoring of a cardiologist. LMU had provided for its player.

In his story in the *Los Angeles Times* that day, Alan Drooz reported that Hank had been cleared to begin practice. [It was just 15 days since he had collapsed at Gersten. His tests had been inconclusive and his doctors still were not sure what had caused the episode.]

"All the tests they did indicate that I'm in great physical condition. I feel fine and I am still the strongest man in the country," Hank told Drooz. "I'm still sore from all the testing. . . . I guess what happened to me was just one of those things."[25] Clearly, Hank was hoping the NBA scouts would buy his story.

After Hank collapsed, the Lions had won the game, 104-101, against UC-Santa Barbara. While Hank was out being tested and evaluated, Loyola Marymount had beaten nationally ranked Oregon State, with Bo accounting for 53 points in an important road win. Then the Lions lost to the University of Oklahoma, 136-121, at Gersten Pavilion. Bo led the losing effort with 46 points and 14 rebounds.[26]

The day after Christmas, the doctors hooked Hank up to the Holter monitor for 90 minutes to play one-on-one basketball.[27] A nurse with a defibrillator stood at courtside.

Dr. Hattori, his cardiologist, read the Holter results on December 27. Unlike the previous test, these results were diagnostic. The recording made during basketball practice showed that Hank's heart rhythm was drastically abnormal. During the single basketball practice session, he had experienced 188 episodes of ventricular tachycardia, any one of which, had they not stopped on their own, could have degenerated into fibrillation and killed him; at times, his heart raced at nearly 200 beats per minute (Lance Armstrong's maximum heart rate in competition was 201 beats per minute).[28] Further, of all Hank's heartbeats recorded by the monitor while he was playing, 26.6 percent were abnormal. Dr. Hattori considered the test results so bad that he believed that, even if Hank never played basketball again, he would need treatment for the demonstrated cardiac arrhythmia. Dr.

Hattori would later testify that he was not aware that Dr. Mellman had already sent a letter to Brian Quinn, clearing Hank to resume playing basketball.[29]

Dr. Hattori reported the results to Dr. Swerdlow and asked for his treatment recommendations. Dr. Swerdlow reviewed the Holter results and recommended Inderal, the medication that was the standard treatment for arrhythmia at that time.

Inderal has a number of side effects, including several that would be especially repugnant to a 23-year-old college athlete: fatigue, drowsiness, and sexual dysfunction. Dr. Hattori discussed all the side effects with Hank, explaining that the doctors were going to start him on a high dosage, so the side effects would be especially pronounced at first. Per Dr. Hattori's prescription and directions, the next day, December 28, Hank would begin taking 200 mg in carefully scheduled increments, every 24 hours. Dr. Hattori also scheduled the player for another Holter test two days hence so they could assess whether the Inderal was going to help him. Dr. Hattori planned to see how Hank responded to the Inderal before deciding whether he could play basketball again.[30]

On December 29, Hank wore the Holter to basketball practice. Medical personnel were at the court as he played a simulated game. The testing even included a number of breaks to shoot free throws, which Dr. Swerdlow insisted upon, because Hank had been shooting free throws when he collapsed. The test went without incident.[31]

Several hours later, Hank returned to Dr. Hattori's office in the cardiology department at Daniel Freeman. By now, Dr. Hattori had consulted with Dr. Swerdlow about what the Holter results showed: the Inderal had produced dramatic improvement.[32] Only about 1 percent of Hank's heartbeats were abnormal now, and the ventricular tachycardia was also greatly improved. Dr. Swerdlow still thought that Hank should not be playing basketball and advised Dr. Hattori that if he were to clear Hank to play, it would have to be with the proviso that he continue to take the high dosage of Inderal and continue to have follow-up Holter tests. During their conversation, Dr. Hattori told Dr. Swerdlow that the university wanted to buy a defibrillator and asked him to recommend a machine. Dr. Swerdlow said that buying one was a good idea for any sports venue because of the risk of a fan's collapsing from an arrhythmia, but added that his views about Hank's playing had nothing to do with whether the arena had a defibrillator or not.[33]

Dr. Hattori now told Hank that his Holter results were very much improved and that he could start playing basketball again. He encouraged Hank to start out slowly, emphasizing a gradual return. Hank expressed a strong desire to play the next night, December 30, against Niagara, to show people (presumably NBA scouts) that he was back in action. After some discussion, Dr. Hattori cleared him to play. Dr. Swerdlow recalls that there were conversations about the Holter results, which he too reviewed, and he agreed that Hank could play so long as he was taking the 200 mg of Inderal as prescribed. Dr. Swerdlow's conversations with both Dr. Mellman and Dr. Hattori took place on December 30 and 31.[34] Dr. Hattori intended to keep a close eye on his patient, with further Holter tests and other checks to monitor his therapy.[35]

The college bought a Life Pak 200 defibrillator—Lane Bove approved the $5,200 expenditure—which was both portable and billed as being as simple to use as the then-ubiquitous Instamatic camera. The defibrillator was in the trainer's kit when the Lions took the floor against Niagara. A nurse in the Apex practice had arranged for Chip Schaeffer to be trained to use the device, which was to be kept at courtside. She subsequently informed Dr. Hattori that Chip knew how to use it. "I was shown a video in which they spent about 45 minutes demonstrating how the device worked," Chip recalled.[36]

Hank returned to action against Niagara, and he was awful. The effects of the medication had slowed considerably his once-swift reaction time. He did manage 11 rebounds, but during his 24-minutes of play, he exhibited none of the fierce intensity and competitiveness that had marked his every game as a collegian. Still, LMU managed to turn back the Purple Eagles, 122-87.

"Hank did about what we expected," Westhead told Alan Drooz. "He showed flashes of playing well; at times he was off. I thought he played well. But from past performances, that wasn't the Hank you see all the time. It wasn't bad, though."[37] But it wasn't good.

On New Year's Day, Dr. Mellman, Dr. Hattori, Hank, Paul Westhead, and Chip Schaeffer all met in Westhead's office so the doctors could explain the test findings, the medication, its side effects, and other information that the athletic department needed. The meeting lasted almost 90 minutes and focused on how long Hank could play at a stretch, not on the medical ramifications of his condition.[38] Dr. Swerdlow was not invited to the meeting and did not know that it was being held.[39]

Hank was beyond adamant about playing. He was desperate to return, to prove to the NBA scouts that he was just fine.[40]

With the maximum dosage that Dr. Hattori had prescribed, Hank was receiving therapeutic benefit—the drug was keeping his heart from racing out of control. He had been tested under game conditions and at practices, as well as on the treadmill. He was experiencing no problems with fainting or rapid uncontrolled heartbeats.[41]

The problem with the treatment was not with its efficacy but with Hank's inability to perform at his best while taking the drug. Two competing interests were at play: the treatment and safety of the patient and the performance of the athlete. Ideally, the two could be managed, with the athlete continuing to play while being observed for any problems. If he was responding well, perhaps the doctors could adjust the dosage, allowing his performance and energy level to improve. It was a delicate balance, though, especially because he had been diagnosed with a heart arrhythmia and would be engaging in extreme exercise. Some might say it was risky.

Even after Hank returned to the lineup after his December 9 collapse, the courtside physicians were the young orthopedic fellows from Kerlan-Jobe. Kerlan-Jobe was as good as it got for treatment of sprains and broken bones, muscle tears, and ligament problems. Its physicians were second to none in the country in dealing with the vast array of orthopedic problems presented by athletes in competition. But they were not cardiologists.

The Kerlan-Jobe fellows were aware that Hank was under the care of a cardiologist, but were not informed or apprised of his treatment, progress, or prognosis. All they knew was that he had been medically cleared to play.[42]

Neither Dr. Hattori nor Dr. Mellman saw fit to attend the games.[43]

By early January, Dr. Swerdlow was no longer actively involved in Hank's case. He was available as a consultant and had told Dr. Hattori that if Hank's dosage were reduced, which Dr. Hattori was considering because of Hank's persistent lobbying, Hank should still take at least 80 mg of short-acting Inderal "in the late afternoon" before a game, because he was at the greatest risk during a game.—Dr. Swerdlow wanted Hank to have "a high blood level of [Inderal] prior to basketball."[44]

One day, Dr. Swerdlow was walking by Dr. Hattori's office when the cardiologist spied his colleague and summoned Dr. Swerdlow to come in to talk with Hank, who again was complaining about the effect of Inderal on his basketball performance. Dr. Swerdlow told him point-blank: "Better a live sportscaster than a dead basketball player."[45] His comment, he recalled, disturbed Hank a great deal. From that early January conversation on, Dr. Swerdlow had no more active involvement with Hank.[46]

Dr. Swerdlow would later say that he and Dr. Hattori had a legitimate difference of opinion, not unusual among doctors, as to the course of treatment for Hank Gathers. Dr. Swerdlow said, "Vernon and I disagreed. It isn't uncommon. He is an excellent doctor."[47]

How good was he as a sparring partner, though? The patient, Hank Gathers, was a young man with an imposing physical presence and a habit of forcing his will and frame on much bigger, stronger opponents. He was not used to being denied. He refused to be denied. That characteristic was his strongest asset, the one most responsible for his success.

So in one corner stood Dr. Vernon Hattori, the tall, thin, bookish physician. In the other stood the self-billed "strongest man alive."

It was no contest.

Hank knew he needed to play at the highest level to impress the NBA scouts. His fainting episode had already raised all sorts of questions, and he felt an urgent need to demonstrate convincingly that he was fit and ready to perform as always. Standing in his way was the sluggishness, the most pronounced side effect of Inderal that Hank suffered. "At the time, my father was also taking Inderal," Chip Schaeffer said. "I told my mother, who was an RN, about the dosage that Hank was taking and she said, 'Wow, it's a wonder he can even walk.'"[48]

In short, on Inderal, Hank was relatively safe—and a zombie. He wasn't the agile and aggressive player who had led the nation in scoring and rebounding only the year before. Not even close. He was slow and uncoordinated, and no one was more disturbed about this than Hank.[49] While Dr. Hattori oversaw Hank's medical treatment and monitoring, the day-to-day oversight of his conditioning fell to a dedicated 28-year-old athletic trainer. Chip Schaeffer would use his expertise to help Hank Gathers, dutifully icing and tending to his arthritic and aching knees and to his other sprains and bruises, just as he did for Bo, Tom, and even Kristin Ramage. As for Hank's particular problems with his heart, Chip deferred, as all trainers do, to the opinion of the doctors regarding an athlete's fitness to play.

Chip Schaeffer said that, after the doctors cleared Hank to play, "it never entered my mind" that his condition could be life threatening.[50]

The trip that followed the Niagara win and Hank's return would take the Lions East to meet Xavier University of Ohio on January 2, and then to play the much-anticipated two-game series in Philadelphia on the 4th and the 6th of January that was to be a homecoming celebration for Paul, Hank, and Bo.

"I went up to where Hank was sitting on the plane," Alan Drooz recalled. "I was going to ask him a few questions about his condition, but he was asleep. It wasn't the cat nap that many of us take on planes. He was totally zonked out. He was so out of it that I didn't bother him at all. He stayed asleep the whole time."[51]

His coaches and teammates now noticed that Hank, always a fanatic about working out, had a new routine. Before a game, he jumped rope furiously in the gymnasium. When he finished, he was dripping with perspiration from the effort.[52] He was, in fact, doing what his doctors had told him to do because the medication slowed his heart rate. The exercise would get his heart rate up, which the doctors considered essential to avoid a serious decrease in his resting heart rate while on the medication.[53]

In the game against Xavier, Hank played a total of 30 minutes, 6 more than he had against Niagara. The extra minutes only proved even more conclusively that on Inderal, he was not himself. Hank, who normally sank about 50 percent of his shots from the floor—or more—went 7-23 against the Musketeers. He managed only eight rebounds.

The Musketeers boasted two future NBA stars, the 6-foot-10 seniors Derrick Strong and Tyrone Hill, and that could account for some of the poor performance. Throughout his career, though, Hank had almost always responded with a big effort to the challenge of going against bigger and supposedly better players. It was his way of proving himself and showing the NBA scouts he could compete with the best.

Hill finished the game with 38 points and Strong hauled down 24 boards. Despite another fine effort by Bo, with 38 points, LMU lost, 115-113.[54]

Out-muscled and out-hustled, Hank was not happy. "Hank looked like he had drugs in him," Pete Gillen recalled. "He was definitely not 100 percent . He was still sharp but not himself. But even at 80 percent he was still better than most people."[55]

Better than most wasn't nearly good enough for Hank Gathers.

In preparing the schedule, Westhead had arranged what he had expected to be a triumphant return to Philadelphia for Hank and Bo. After all that Hank and Bo had achieved, they'd earned an opportunity to showcase their talents before family, friends, and the fans who had followed their exploits since Dobbins and the Sonny Hill League.[56]

Paul had arranged a game with his alma mater, St. Joseph's, and then, after a day off, the Lions would take on La Salle University, where Paul had coached. The Explorers had an unblemished record and featured Lionel Simmons and Doug Overton. The two-game showcase series was the talk of Philly.

Hank was really looking forward to it. "He kept calling me, telling me how they would run us off the floor," Lionel Simmons said. Doug recalled that "Hank called me a lot to tell me we'd never be able to keep up with them."[57] The friendly jibes that Hank directed at his old teammate and former foe were perfectly in character for Hank. He was keeping in touch with old friends while serving notice that the sheriff was on his way back to town. He'd be ballin' and they'd better be ready.

"Hank wanted to put on the show of his life," Yank said.[58]

The Alumni Memorial Fieldhouse at St. Joseph's was sold out for the January 4 game. A record crowd had claimed all 3,200 seats to see the return of the two local stars. A banner taped to one wall read, "Welcome Back Coach Westhead."

The Lions struggled against the Jimmy Boyle-coached Hawks of St. Joseph's, who were having a terrible season (1-8). Hank played only 26 minutes. In the stands were his son, his mother, his brother Charles, Yank, Sonny Hill, and Father Dave.[59]

Hank finished the game with 11 points, having shot 5-11 from the floor, and he managed seven rebounds. He was extremely lethargic and moved a step too slowly all night.[60] It took a miracle 35-foot shot by Bo to pull out a win for the Lions as time wound down.

LMU students Brian Berger and Keith Foreman called the game over KXLU, and their wild exuberance, as much as the Hail Mary shot by Bo, led sportscaster Len Berman to replay the action on WNBC in New York, the network's flagship station.[61]

Film of the game shows Hank hanging off to the side while a throng of players and fans surrounds and congratulates Bo.

Then, as the team made its way into the locker room, Hank's pent-up anger and frustration boiled over. He had played embarrassingly poorly in front of his friends and family, and to make matters worse, he'd been upstaged by Bo. It was more than he could handle.[62]

"He trashed the room," Tom Peabody recalled. "He knocked over a row of metal lockers and kicked at a bathroom stall wall. He was terribly upset and angry."[63] His volcanic and violent eruption in the locker room replaced the grins of victory with frowns of fear and concern.

"He said he felt like he was drunk," Heat said. Hank told him, "I can see [what I need to do] but can't react fast enough."[64]

Through tears of frustration and anger, Hank screamed, "I ain't taking no more fuckin' medicine!"[65]

Everyone on the team witnessed Hank's tirade, and the Lions watched helplessly as he took out his frustration and anger on the walls and lockers lining the dressing room.

"Hank was a proud man," said Chip Schaeffer, explaining the outburst as a by-product of Hank's wounded pride at his poor showing in front of his family and friends. Yank thought it was about more than ego: "He knew if he was sick and taking medicine, he wouldn't be drafted by the NBA."[66]

"He was a totally different player on those drugs," Terrell Lowery said. "Even in practice, it showed. He was missing shots, his rebounding was off. He was slow getting to the ball. You could see it in his eyes. There was something different there."[67]

Terrell's was an astute observation. Rebounding is a matter of attitude. Scoring is about talent and ego and practice, but rebounding is all about attitude. Otherwise, the tallest players would get all the rebounds. If you believe you deserve the rebound, you have a better chance of getting it than anyone else. That fiery competitive determination, the hallmark of Hank's game, was gone. The Inderal had evened out his heartbeat, sure, but it had also flattened his attitude. His spirited possessiveness—"This is my rebound!"—had disappeared along with the arrhythmias and fainting episodes. Now Hank's game was marked by uninspired, lethargic play and his dull, drugged eyes.

He was just going through the motions. He never stopped trying, but not even Hank's indomitable will could overpower the side effects of the massive dosage of Inderal. The drug had extinguished the fire in his belly and the spark in his eyes.

Not even a year earlier, a young *Washington Post* sports reporter had written six words on deadline that described perfectly Hank's ability to dominate the boards: "It comes straight from the heart."[68] Now that very heart, medicated into a somnambulistic state, was preventing Hank from playing the way he could. He could take no more.

Sonny Hill and Father Dave got to the locker room as fast as they could, and both tried to console Hank. He was angry at his performance, despondent over the drug's effects on him. More important, he was dreadfully scared of what it was doing to his NBA prospects. For Hank Gathers, that was not acceptable. He would do something about it. Right away.

According to both Terrell Lowery and Heat, Hank and several other players went back to Father Dave's house after the game.[69] "Hank and Father Dave talked together, alone, for hours," said Heat. It was more than hours, according to Chip Schaeffer, who recalled that "we kind of lost track of Hank for about a day."[70]

Father Dave had always been a source of comfort and aid to Hank and his family. He was one of the few people Hank knew he could approach for help and he would get it. Father Dave was keenly aware of what Inderal was doing to Hank and knew, perhaps better than anyone, that Hank thought he needed to succeed on the basketball court if he was going to help his son, his mother, and his brothers out of poverty.

Hank Gathers was one of the few success stories that Father Dave had seen in all the years he had worked in the slums of Philadelphia. Hank was an example of someone who had beaten the odds of his circumstances and had made something of himself. He was a Horatio Alger in basketball shorts, a shining example that if you worked hard enough, you could beat the odds. You didn't have to give in to crime and drugs and indifference. If Hank Gathers could do it, then you can do it, Father Dave could tell the youngsters coming up.

While Hank was undergoing the initial tests in early December, Father Dave had spoken with Dr. Hattori, who had minced no words with Father Dave, for the priest recalled that the cardiologist had told him that the dosage was high because Dr. Hattori "didn't want Hank to have a heart attack." Father Dave would say later that he regretted not following up on that comment and asking what the possibility of a heart attack was. But he didn't, though. He did discuss the Inderal dosage with a friend of his who was a cardiologist. His friend told Father Dave that if Hank was on 200 mg of Inderal, he "probably had a serious problem."[71]

Father Dave later confessed that "he didn't want to know what [Hank's risk of a heart attack] was. He wanted so desperately for Hank to succeed that he was afraid to ask any questions which might deter Hank from his goal."[72]

While Hank was holed up with Father Dave on January 5, Chip Schaeffer put in a call to Dr. Hattori's office back in California. Chip explained Hank's poor performance in the St. Joe's game and his upset at what the Inderal was doing to his ability to play. According to Dr. Hattori, Chip—no doubt relaying a request from Hank—asked if Dr. Hattori could reduce the dosage. The cardiologist said he told Chip he didn't see how that was possible, given that he was 3,000 miles away from his patient.[73]

Dr. Hattori said he also heard from Paul Westhead, who asked if it was medically safe to do anything to help Hank play better. Hank was embarrassing himself, and if he couldn't play better, the coach might have to bench him.[74] Dr. Hattori explained, as he had just done in his conversation with Chip, that he couldn't do anything to help Hank from 3,000 miles away. Paul then asked Dr. Hattori to call Hank at his mother's house, which the cardiologist agreed to do.[75]

When he and Hank spoke, Hank told Dr. Hattori that he "felt shitty" and that the medication was making him "feel like a robot."[76] He was feeling uncoordinated shortly after taking his morning dose of Inderal.

Although Hank had been on Inderal since December 29, this was the first time that Dr. Hattori had discussed with his patient how he felt on the drug.[77] Dr. Hattori had explained the potential side effects when he prescribed the drug initially and recalled that he told Hank at that time that they might be able to reduce the dosage at some unspecified point in the future if it looked like it would be safe to do so.[78]

For Hank, the future was clearly now. If he couldn't get the dosage reduced, he had no future in basketball. His dream would be over. Hank pleaded his case to Dr. Hattori, vigorously and animatedly for a long time.

Like Bo, Heat, Doug, Magic, and countless others before him, Dr. Hattori gave in to Hank's relentless arguments. He cut Hank's morning dose of Inderal in half, from 80 mg to 40 mg. Dr. Hattori later would explain that he did so because the game against La Salle was so important to Hank—his family and friends would be there, and it was being televised.[79] That meant that Hank's daily dosage was 160 mg instead of 200.

Dr. Hattori never spoke with Chip or Paul about the reduction in the medication. He did tell Hank, he said, about the importance of taking the pills three times a day—morning, midafternoon, and night—and on time. He would see Hank again when he returned on January 8 and would reevaluate the dosage after another Holter monitor test.[80]

While the team was still on the road, Dr. Hattori mentioned to Dr. Swerdlow, in passing, that he was going to decrease Hank's Inderal to 80 mg daily. Dr. Swerdlow recalled that he advised his colleague, "I'd be very sure to document efficacy."[81]

Aaron Gathers met Tom Peabody and the other players while Hank was in town, and the boy spent a lot of time with his father. It was an exciting time for the six-year-old, and he later drew pictures of his father and his other favorite players. Tom and Bo and his uncle Phil Crump—"Sub" as he was known—who played for San Jose State, were portrayed and prominently displayed in Marva's apartment in the Rosen Homes.[82]

When Hank picked Aaron up at Marva's one day, he decided his son's hair was too long. Aaron returned home sporting a new crew cut, exactly the same buzz cut as Hank's.[83]

Hank had assured Aaron that he would be bringing him out to Los Angeles as soon as he turned pro, right after the season.[84] Aaron was excited about going back to Los Angeles and the festive atmosphere that surrounded his father during the visit to his old neighborhood. Everyone, it seemed, loved his dad.[85]

Hank had taken his former roommate Tom Peabody home to meet Lucille. As they approached the Raymond Rosen Homes, Hank turned to Tom and said, as he had to Tommy Lewis, "The only reason you're still alive is because you're with me," and he wasn't kidding.[86]

The La Salle Explorers and the LMU Lions met at the Civic Center in Philadelphia on January 6 for a game telecast nationally by ESPN. Lucille, Charles, Yank, Heat, Father Dave, Aaron, and Marva were in the crowd. After the St. Joseph's game Hank was especially eager to show the NBA that he was back at peak form.[87]

Jeff Fryer's injury was healed and he was ready to play. Terrell Lowery had a new look, a shaved head, the result of a haircut gone awry, and he was scoring more than 16 points a game. Bo was playing superbly at full capacity, but the Lions still missed the dominating play of their inspirational leader.[88]

La Salle had not lost a game, and the Explorers featured two fearsome players: Lionel Simmons, one of the nation's best and a certain first-round draft choice, and Hank's old teammate from Dobbins, Doug Overton. The game was an ideal setting for Hank to prove he was, indeed, back.

The day before, Steve Berkowitz of *The Washington Post* had explained the System for his readers: "The System is what makes Loyola Marymount the runningest, gunningest, highest-scoring team in college basketball history, or, as Westhead described it, 'Gasoline on fire.'" Recounting the success of the System at LMU, Berkowitz asked Paul what would happen after his two stars, Hank and Bo, left the team. "Maybe we've already done more than is ever possible," Paul said. "But, who knows?"[89]

With his Inderal dosage reduced, Hank's playing improved immediately. Against La Salle, Hank played his best since the fainting spell in early December.

Number 44 was back.

Going into the game, the Explorers were undefeated and ranked #17 in the latest poll of sportswriters. They decided to accept the Lions' challenge: They would run with LMU.

It was a mistake.

Hank scored 27 points and hauled down 12 rebounds. Bo added 32 points as the two former Dobbins Tech stars paced Loyola Marymount to a 121-116 win over La Salle before a sell-out crowd of 10,004. Lionel Simmons had 34 points but was held scoreless for the last

5:40 of the game, and by the time it was over, Doug Overton was sitting on the bench with five fouls. LMU improved to 9-3 while La Salle fell to 9-1.

"Obviously, we're distraught," said La Salle's coach, Bill "Speedy" Morris, who had hoped (despite his nickname) to slow the pace down and keep the score in the 60's. "I made a decision to run with them and play schoolyard ball. You can go to any playground and see this kind of basketball." Not unsurprisingly, he added, "I don't like it."

Simmons was a victim of the pace. He put up three air balls from the foul line late in the game and struggled to the end. Hank, on the other hand, "was gratified he was able to shake off the effects of the medication he has been taking since fainting on Dec. 9," Alan Drooz reported. Hank had led LMU with a 19-6 burst in the first half, and the Lions led by as many as 11 points before taking a lead of 59-55 to the locker room. Hank had 16 points at the break.

When Hank, who had missed his first six free throws, made the front end of a one-and-one near the end of the game, he turned, grinning, and pointed into the crowd. "I was pointing to Father Dave Hagan, who's been on my back since grade school to make free throws, and my mom," Hank explained. "She tells me, 'Make three bounces and shoot,' and it will always go in." Of his poor showing using that approach, he added, "She's not always right."

Drooz noted that Hank played 30 minutes, making 12 of 20 shots. He glowered when-ever Westhead rested him, Alan noticed. "I feel three or four times better than I did Thursday night (against St. Joseph's). It was like two different people," Hank said, pleased with the energy the reduced dosage had produced. "It feels super to be able to come home and play one decent game."

Bo said he watched Hank in warm-ups and noted, "That look on his face—I knew he was gonna be back and have a great game."[90] Bo had no idea that Dr. Hattori had cut Hank's dosage.[91] Westhead said Hank "had to play above his dilemma. What you saw tonight was only a 10th of how good he is. It has begun to reverse itself. Hank took one step forward."[92]

Father Dave saw Hank after the game, just before he left Philadelphia. Although they had talked about the medication into the wee hours only days before, the subject never came up again, the priest said. He and Hank chatted briefly before the player climbed into a van to go to a postgame party that a booster was throwing to celebrate the win. Throughout the rest of the season, Hank and Father Dave would talk frequently. Hank always called after a game, and they would review his performance. But the priest never saw his young friend alive again.[93]

THE COMEBACK KID

Afteter the Lions returned to the West Coast, Dr. Hattori performed another Holter monitor test on Hank on January 7, to gauge the effectiveness of the lower dosage of Inderal. The next day, the cardiologist dropped the dosage to 120 mg, at Hank's request.[1]

Dr. Hattori said that he consulted with Dr. Swerdlow about the reductions in the Inderal and recalled that his colleague was "very uncomfortable." After reviewing the results of the Holter test, Dr. Hattori said he felt "that the arrhythmia suppression seemed adequate."[2]

The Lions' next game was three days later, against Santa Clara. They turned back the Broncos, 113-100, before a standing-room-only crowd of 5,000, at Santa Clara. Bo had 35 points, and Hank contributed 22 in 27 minutes of action. Hank's energy level had improved considerably. He added several "thundering dunks" in limited playing time.[3]

The Lions won their fourth straight game on January 13 against San Diego, 119-112.[4] Hank played better, leading the team with 32 points, the first time he had led the team in scoring since December 9. Bo, who was leading the nation in scoring, accounted for 28 points, 9 fewer than his average. LMU was now second in the nation in offense, averaging 117.6 points per game, and had scored 100 or more for the 12th time in 14 games. LMU's 11-3 start equaled the Lions' best ever.

Despite the time he had missed, Hank was closing in on some milestones. He was 20 points away from Forrest McKenzie's 2,060 career scoring total, which was tops in the conference, as well as the best mark for an LMU player. Hank also was on track to join the elite group of players who had amassed 2,500 points and 1,000 rebounds.[5]

There was also another Lion who was closing in on various records. In only his fifth year as coach, Paul Westhead was one win short of the 91 posted by former LMU Coach John Arndt in seven seasons at the helm.[6]

Although his game had improved considerably, Hank continued to bitch about the effects of the drug. Dr. Hattori tried another tactic. On January 18, the day before the Lions were to play Gonzaga, he put Hank on a long-lasting version of Inderal, Inderal L.A., and told the player to take 120 mg once a day instead of 40 mg three times a day. This regime lasted only two days. When Hank complained that "he hated it," the cardiologist told him to go back to the 40 mg three times a day.[7]

McKenzie's scoring record fell on a furious slam dunk against Gonzaga at Gersten Pavilion. "It's kind of appropriate (Hank) went over the top for a follow-up slam dunk (for the record)," Westhead said. "That's what Hank stands for: You shoot it, I'll get it."

The Lions coasted to an easy 144-100 victory. The highlight was Hank's record-breaking basket 12:25 into the game. The game was halted, and the crowd gave him a standing ovation as he received the ball to commemorate his achievement. Hank would later say he wasn't even aware of the record until David Spencer mentioned it to him in a conversation on the morning of the game.

"I told him he shouldn't have called me. It ruined the surprise," Hank said. Westhead added, "For all they've done here (the three seniors), it is a tribute that one of them stands atop (the WCC)."

The Lions' next victim was Larry Steele's Portland Pilots, the team that was in second place in the conference standings, in a game scheduled for the following night, January 20. The score was decisive, 131-106.

The Pilots were outrun and outgunned by LMU, despite 27 points from Josh Lowery, Terrell's brother, and 29 from William McDowell. In the second half, LMU ran away, never leading by less than 18 points. Hank accounted for 27 points in 29 minutes of action and added nine rebounds, as he joined the 1,000-point club with 1,006 for his career.[8]

The LMU Lions were once again the highest-scoring team in the land, averaging 117.7 points per game, with no score under 90 in any contest. Even so, some still thought that LMU was all offense. "We kind of encourage that (thinking)," Westhead said. "We like the idea that you think it's gonna be all fun and games." As Oklahoma coach Billy Tubbs observed, "Those of you who think Loyola doesn't play defense, think again."

LMU's defensive pressure was forcing 23.4 turnovers a game. When the Lions' offense had sputtered on occasion, they fed off their relentless press to convert turnovers into points.[9] What made their press so effective was that they used a strenuous denial on the inbounds pass. These were the lessons Paul had learned from football coach Fritz Shurmur and the Rams' defensive backs, to intercept passes and create turnovers. The tactic was relentless and very demanding of the players.

Jay Hillock said, "The only hard and fast rule the coaches say is that every player has to hustle. All the guys have got to be committed. If one player isn't doing his job, it can really expose your weaknesses."

"I'm subbing more than I ever have," Westhead explained. "Our whole gig is we don't wear out."

By using this tactic, LMU was averaging nearly 14 steals a game. It was a relentless, swarming assault that went full tilt for 40 minutes. It required excellent athletes and excellent conditioning to work effectively. "You've gotta run it down," Hillock said. "You can't give up."

Hank said of the defensive scheme, "I like the press. I like to get into it. . . . We have such good chase down. The attitude now is, 'Think up, not back.' We know we can run the ball down now. We've got some guys who can flat out get after it." And, he added, the tactics was giving the Lions "the extra edge we need." Tellingly, Hank did not include himself in that appraisal.

"When he (Westhead) first started it, the first couple of weeks, we were saying to ourselves—no way, we can't do it; it takes too much energy. We thought, 'It's like you've got to be in superhuman shape,'" Hank told *Los Angeles Times* reporter Drooz.[10]

Hank, of course, was playing under heavy doses of medication in this extremely demanding defensive scheme. Inderal was slowing his step and sapping his stamina. It was like trying to run with a sack of cement on your back. Speed and stamina were the staples of the System. Without them, you were a hindrance, not an asset. Hank knew it, and he knew better than anyone just how "off" he was. It was why he kept battering Dr. Hattori for further reductions.

As hard as Hank worked at convincing Dr. Hattori to cut his dosage, he worked just as hard, maybe harder, to convince the other players and his coaches that the medication was not affecting his play.

Westhead had a long-standing policy of punishing players for missing classes and failing to turn in assignments on time: they had to run laps on the cinder track outside Gersten.

Terrell Lowery thought the coach was being hard on Hank after he missed some classes or was late to them.[11]

In fact, Westhead was treating Hank like every one else. If Westhead had been fully informed and aware of Hank's condition, would he have had his star player running extra laps as punishment for petty offenses? That he continued to enforce the rules, making Hank run those laps, is compelling evidence of just how little the coach knew of Hank's condition.

What he saw on the court was a player slowed by medication. That was apparent. Beyond that, all he knew was that doctors had cleared Hank to play and they were monitoring his "condition."[12]

So Westhead's concerns were the concerns of a coach: Might a different type of medication improve the player's performance? Was there anything else that they could try? Could they consider some other approach?[13] These were among the questions that Westhead asked Dr. Hattori when they spoke in late January. The coach said that Hank was still playing poorly and told Dr. Hattori that at this level of play, Hank was jeopardizing his future as a pro. According to Dr. Hattori, Westhead said that if he were a pro scout, he would not be interested in Hank Gathers.[14]

Although Hank was on a team that ran a fast-break offense and a full-court-pressing defense that required superb conditioning, no one warned Westhead of the risks of exercise to his star player. He had no reason to believe that the high energy level required by the System was any more taxing for Hank's heart than it was for any other player's.[15]

In fact, Hank had figured out that exercise also improved how he actually felt. The more he exercised after taking the drug, the better he felt. At the end of a rigorous practice or game, his stamina was better than at the outset. He thought he was metabolizing the drug through the exercise and believed that vigorous exercise could reduce its side effects.[16] Although he had been told to exercise vigorously before a game, no one was monitoring what he was doing.

Hank would never admit to Paul that he was tired. In fact, he objected vehemently whenever Paul tried to limit his playing time.[17] Hank couldn't quit. He would keep running the System as hard as he could for as long as he could.

The NCAA asked Hank to film an antidrug message for use during the NCAA championship tournament in March. "I'm excited," Hank said. "I always wanted to do something like that."[18]

Toward the end of January, Dr. Hattori reduced Hank's medication yet again. Hank was not pleased with his performance, and the cardiologist agreed to lower the dosage, from 120 mg to 80.[19]

Dr. Hattori scheduled a Holter test to be done within 48 hours after Hank began taking the lower dosage. The test would not be done, though, until February 20, nearly three weeks—and nine games—later. According to Dr. Hattori, Hank missed several appointments and had a cold when he finally showed up on February 7. Dr. Hattori decided that, because of the heavy cold, he wouldn't get true results from the Holter and asked Hank to return when he was over the cold.[20]

Dr. Hattori said he again conferred with Dr. Swerdlow about the reduction to 80 mg of Inderal. Dr. Swerdlow, whose recollection is that Hattori "briefly informed me in passing" of the planned reduction, expressed his concern about such a decrease and stressed that Dr. Hattori should make sure to document that the lower dosage was effective.[21] In other words, he should run Holter tests to demonstrate that the lower dosage was indeed suppressing Hank's arrhythmia and fainting. Yet for three weeks and nine games, Hank played on the lower dosage without any Holter evidence to support the efficacy of that dosage.

At the lower dosage, Hank was feeling better. Now, in his last season of collegiate competition, Hank considered it paramount that he play to his full potential. In only a few short months, the season would end, and he needed those months to prove he was in top form. The NBA scouts would be watching his every game. The pressure to perform—to prove that he was still the player who had led the nation in scoring and rebounding—was increasing with every passing day. It was constantly on his mind, and he would continue to badger Dr. Hattori about the medication level in order to get back the stamina and speed he knew he needed.

Westhead asked his friend Don Casey, coach of the LA Clippers, to talk to Hank during this period. Casey assured Hank that he would be a "desirable addition" to several teams in the NBA that used a running style. Casey was aware of the fainting spell and still felt Hank would be a first-round pick.[22] Dr. Hattori would later say that he did not think that changing Hank's dosage increased his risk of dying. The cardiologist said he told Westhead that it was important that Hank continue to take his medication, but that it also was important to help Hank achieve his goal of playing effective basketball.[23]

Dr. Hattori said he felt very strongly that Hank was able to communicate his medical condition.[24] Hank's communiques were, of course, designed to get his dosage reduced and thereby improve his performance. But Hattori relied on Hank's self-reports.

The Lions' season was going well. And, just as Hank had done when Bo's knee failed him the year before, Bo was now carrying the Lions. He was leading the nation in scoring, healthy and able to play to his full potential for the first time since coming to LMU.

The odds that two high school teammates, playing for the same college, could lead the nation in scoring in two consecutive years are long indeed. Yet it was happening, and "The Hank and Bo Show" was the talk of the country.

Bryant Gumble had selected them as Sportsmen of the Week, and Hank and Bo appeared with him on the popular *Today Show*. They chatted about growing up together, and when Gumble asked Hank about his health, Hank assured him that "everything is going just fine." Asked about his chances of making it in the NBA, since he was a little small for the post position and not a true power forward, Hank answered, "I'll be O.K. I have the heart of a lion."

Even at less than 100 percent, Hank was still a potent force. Hank's efforts, combined with Bo's scoring, made the Lions one of the top 25 teams in the country, one that many felt would do extremely well at the NCAA Tournament. Gonzaga's coach, Dan Fitzgerald, was among them: "With the right draw, they're capable of winning a couple of games (in the NCAA Tournament), maybe making the final 16. Their leadership is good. They're senior oriented. Their chemistry is real good. You don't like to see anybody get hurt, but I think Hank (Gathers) going down (he fainted in a game in early December) and them continuing to win helped their confidence."

Fitzgerald was looking ahead when he told Drooz, "You just don't get transfers like Kimble and Gathers. That's once in a lifetime. You don't get two first-round (NBA) picks normally. Loyola will be decent again next year. But they'll be back breathing the same air as the rest of us."[25]

For their next game, the Lions would fly to the Pacific Northwest to take on Portland on January 25 and Gonzaga on January 27.

Hank scored 31 points against Portland and then 34 against Gonzaga, in a 15-19 performance, and was on the floor for more than 30 minutes in each contest. The win over Gonzaga, 99-88, was only the third time that LMU had failed to crack the century mark in the 1989-90 season. "My team was a little flat footed," Westhead told Alan Drooz. "The pace of the game wasn't to our liking."[26]

Even so, LMU was a perfect 6-0 in the WCC.

The Lions' schedule would next take them on a hectic trip that would begin with a WCC game against St. Mary's on February 1, followed by a game in Baton Rouge against Louisiana State University that CBS would air, and then another flight West to meet San Francisco—all in three days.

The Lions pounded the Gaels of St. Mary's, 150-119, racking up the most points ever scored against a St. Mary's team and breaking their own conference record of 147, set the previous February.

At the lower dosage of Inderal, Hank had his "biggest performance in nearly two months," scoring 44 points and grabbing 13 rebounds, Drooz reported. Hank had converted 18 of 22 shots from the floor. Hank's aggressive play had put the entire St. Mary's front line in foul trouble by halftime, and LMU coasted home with leads of as much as 30 points. The Lions' performance left the St. Mary's coach dazed. He told Drooz, "We're going back to the hotel and say some rosaries and try to wipe this out of our minds."[27]

While the Gaels were praying, the Lions were flying to Baton Rouge to meet LSU.

A national television audience would be watching the LSU game on February 3, so it was vitally important to Hank that he perform well. He would play the highly publicized game and a number of others on the lower dosage, with no evidence from Holter tests that it was safe for him to do so. Nevertheless, he was permitted to play.

The LSU game offered Hank an opportunity to display his ability to compete against a team that featured two future NBA big men, Stanley Roberts, who was 7-foot-1, and a 17-year-old freshman, the 7-foot-tall Shaquille O'Neal.

LSU had a deep bench, with another wide-bodied player, Wayne Sims, who spelled O'Neal and Roberts. The setting was ideal for Hank to show that his quickness and desire enabled him to compete against the type of players he would face in the NBA. The game was expected to attract a large audience as CBS was airing it as a lead-in to the Pebble Beach Pro-Am Golf Tournament.

Of all the games Hank played while at LMU, none would define him better than the game against the Bayou Bengals. Played at the jam-packed Pete Maravich Assembly Center (named after the late LSU star, who had also worn number 44 and who had died of a heart attack during a pick-up game), the LSU game told you everything you wanted to know about Hank Gathers.

Writers, coaches, and players use a term to describe the elusive, intangible asset that some athletes possess and others simply do not. It is, ironically, what they refer to as heart. Heart was what enabled heavyweight champion Floyd Patterson, bludgeoned by Ingemar Johansson's right hand, to rise, senseless and staggering, seven times from the canvas to fight on. The Swiss marathon runner Gabriella Andersen-Scheiss displayed heart to millions as she entered the Los Angeles Coliseum in the 1984 Olympics. Suffering from severe heat exhaustion, she reeled drunkenly around the 440 meters of the stadium track. Her skin a ghastly white, her arm bent grotesquely across her twisted body, she refused all assistance. It took her six long, agonizing, stumbling minutes to complete the circuit. As she did so, the crowd of 80,000 stood and cheered each excruciatingly painful step until she collapsed across the finish line.

There is no way to describe precisely what heart is. Either you have it or you do not. On February 3, 1990, Hank Gathers proved to one and all—even if his own heart was not functioning properly—that he indeed possessed heart.

The twin towers of Roberts and O'Neal blocked, altered, and stuffed back in his face Hank's first six shot attempts. At the first time-out in the LMU huddle, Hank screamed at Tony Walker, playing the point, "Give me the fuckin' ball! You hear me? Give me the ball!"[28]

Players who have had their first six attempts blocked, embarrassingly, humiliatingly, usually react by retreating into an ineffective, intimidated shell, drawing silly fouls and becoming a nonfactor. But Hank Gathers was anything but normal. As his coach would say of him, "Hank Gathers was a walking thunderbolt. There was nothing ordinary about Hank Gathers."[29]

While James Brown, who was doing the play-by-play, and Quinn Buckner, who was providing commentary, chatted about Hank's desire to prove to the NBA that, despite being at least five inches shorter, he could more than hold his own against the big players, Hank Gathers took over the game.

After the time-out, Hank went right back up against the two imposing LSU big men and scored, prompting Brown to comment that "Gathers is not being intimidated by O'Neal."[30] As the game progressed, Hank took the scoring load on himself. LMU struggled from the perimeter with Fryer going 1-7 during one stretch, but Hank kept the Lions in the game.[31] His thunder could be heard even through the roaring din of the capacity crowd.

Dale Brown, the LSU coach, said, "I had to decide: Would a loss playing a running game be as bad as slowing down the tempo and admitting we couldn't play with them?" Brown used his own brand of psychology on Stanley Roberts, who was not a swift-footed player by any stretch of the imagination. Brown said he had told Roberts at practice the day before the game, "'Stanley, I don't know what time it is in California, but I'll bet you that Westhead is telling his team right about now that 'Roberts can't run with us.'

"I decided," Brown said, "to run with them." I told Stanley, 'Westhead is telling his team, "'If they try to run with us with that old, slow Stanley Roberts, we'll run them off the court.'"[32]

Whatever works. At one point, Roberts was 10-10 from the field.[33]

The game was played so fast that "it was like watching a sock in a clothes dryer drum, back and forth—faster than a Japanese ping-pong game," Brown said. "Our kids were all whipped, and we thought we were in great shape."[34]

Chris Jackson, LSU's premier point guard, had a great offensive and defensive performance and kept Bo under control for most of the game. But Hank fought on. Toward the end of regulation play, James Brown told the television audience, referring to Hank, "The [NBA] scouts have to be impressed with him."[35]

The Lions had an opportunity to win the game in regulation, but Lowery missed a free throw with 10 seconds to play. Hank got the rebound but his put-back fell short.

In overtime, Hank hit the first two LMU baskets to put the Lions ahead by 4 points, but ultimately LSU's depth, and the Bengals' made free throws, prevailed. The final score was 148-141. Hank had scored 48 points, despite the denials of his first six attempts.[36]

He had shown two future NBA stars, the capacity crowd, a national television audience, and the NBA scouts who were watching everything he wanted them to see. Maybe he had a problem with his heart, but there was certainly no doubt that he had heart. Indeed, as he liked to proclaim, he had the heart of a lion. Now he was ready for all the seven-footers the NBA could throw at him.

The Chevrolet MVP awards that CBS made after each televised game went to Shaquille O'Neal and Hank Gathers. After the game, Hank called Father Dave in

Philadelphia, as he always did, and screamed proudly, "I scored 48 points against O'Neal and Roberts!"[37]

Nearly two decades later, Brown said, "People still come up to me and say it's the best game they have ever seen."[38]

After the grueling overtime game with LSU, the Lions boarded a flight back to California. They arrived in Los Angeles close to midnight. The next day, February 4, they would meet the University of San Francisco (USF) at Gersten Pavilion at 5 p.m. It would mark their third game in four days.

If the Dons thought they were going to catch the Lions in a jet-lagged stupor after the LSU game, they would be shocked to learn that these Lions weren't sleepy. Despite the hectic schedule and grueling travel, the Lions exploded against USF and roared to a 157-115 win. Their 157 points gave LMU its second conference scoring record in four nights, eclipsing the 150 the Lions had scored against St. Mary's.

"This was a good test of a team," Westhead told Alan Drooz after the game. "You can have a grueling day and come back and act like you've been off for a week. It's more a tribute of our team wanting to show a hard, tough loss would not have any negative effect. I mentioned that I thought it was important to play hard."

Apparently, the Lions listened. Bo bounced back with another 50-point game, his fourth this season. Hank added 30 points and 13 rebounds in another strong effort, even though he played only 25 minutes. Westhead, who had watched the games from the bench, said of the schedule, "Winners smile, losers say deal. Heck, I like playing the next day."

The Lions now had five days off before they returned to action, in San Francisco, against the Dons—in a rematch on February 9, then they would meet St. Mary's, the following day.

LMU blasted the Dons in front of a sellout crowd of 5,387 in Memorial Gymnasium. The host team didn't go down without a fight. The Dons were as close as 6 points with 4:27 to play before finally being worn down. The final score was 137-123.

Hank was incensed at what he thought was a deliberate attempt by USF, and the Dons' coach, Jim Brovelli, to injure him. He had taken an elbow to the face early in the game and, even after a foul was called, remained animated and angry. He yelled at the officials about the foul's being intentional, and Westhead had to remove him from the contest until he cooled off.[39]

After the game, Hank told Alan Drooz it was the most physical game he'd ever played in and accused Brovelli of sending in waves of less talented players to try to injure him. "I'm a player with NBA possibilities, and they're messing with my future," Hank complained, betraying where his thoughts always lay.

Hank managed only three rebounds in 26 minutes of play and added 28 points. He went to the free-throw line a season-high 17 times, which shows he was right about how physical the game was.

Informed about Hank's complaints, Brovelli said Hank was the most physical player in the conference and should be "able to take some of what he dishes out."[40]

Jeff Fryer was in the zone and nailed all seven of his 3-point attempts to finish with an amazing scoring line: 33 points on 12 shots. "I'm getting less shots this year, with the other guys scoring so much," he said. "I take what they give me." Bo had 37 points as the Lions maintained their perfect record in conference play at 9-0.

The Lions roared into McKeon Pavilion at St. Mary's the next night. A sell-out crowd of 3,500 awaited the conference leaders. The Gaels, decimated by injuries, were forced to start a team that averaged fewer points per game than Bo Kimble was scoring all by himself.

McKeon Pavilion records—for points in a half, and in a game—fell as the Lions rolled to a 139-110 victory. Hank scored 30 points to tie Bill Cartwright's record of 1,065 points in a conference career. Hank also had 13 rebounds. He was playing with his old desire and determination, as evidenced by Westhead's critique of his performance: "It's a good thing they have a high ceiling in here. When he goes after the ball with that kind of energy, it transmits to the whole team."[41]

On Valentine's Day, Pepperdine arrived at Gersten Pavilion to find yet another sell-out crowd, but no flowers or candy. The Lions mauled their rivals, 131-116, and clinched at least a tie for the conference title with the win. LMU trailed only once, at 8-6, before running off a 14-0 streak, led by Fryer's 3-point shooting. Jeff hit five in the first 6:40 of play.

Tom Lewis, who was having problems relating to Pepperdine coach Tom Asbury, sat on the bench for most of the second half and still finished with 19 points. His former teammates, Bo and Hank, had 36 and 29 points, respectively. Hank also added 12 rebounds.[42]

Pepperdine's Waves got their revenge on Saturday night, at a sold-out Firestone Fieldhouse, in a game dedicated to a badly injured player. Waves sophomore center Mark Georgeson had been involved in a serious auto accident on his way to his parents' home after the loss to LMU on Wednesday. He was still listed in critical condition at game time.

"We played with great emotion tonight," Tom Asbury said of the effort his team put forth to turn back the Lions by 131-123. Pepperdine set a school record for scoring and snapped LMU's 11-game winning streak in the process. "Pepperdine earned the win," Westhead said.

The loss to a team not ranked in the top 20 was the first and only blemish on the Lions' conference record. It also denied Paul his 100th win at LMU. Both Bo and Hank scored

32 points in the losing cause. They combined to shoot only 7 of 25 in the first half, allowing Pepperdine to build a lead.[43] "I don't like them very much," Jeff Fryer said of the Waves after the game. "I'd like to face them again."

Hank was more philosophical, but also anticipated a rematch in the WCC tournament, saying, "They got one. We'll see them again. We split last year and bombed them in the tournament, so we'll see."[44]

On February 18, the *Chicago Sun-Times* carried a feature about Bo, by Bernie Wilson, that quoted an obviously more mature and gracious Hank. Of Bo's national scoring lead, Hank said, "If there is a person you would want to lose it to—and nobody wants to lose their title—(Bo) would be that person. I'm very happy for Bo. He's got great skills. I'm not surprised by anything he does. I knew both of us had the ability to lead the nation."[45]

In *The Denver Post*, Todd Phipers told his readers that an appropriate line to describe the LMU Lions' style might be found in MacBeth: "If it were done when 'tis done, then 'twere well / It were done quickly."

Westhead explained the success of the System, saying, "And what happens is that teams, despite their great intentions of keeping ahold of the pace and not letting it become frantic and quick, all of a sudden find the game is out of their hands. . .gone."

After reviewing the irony of Westhead's firing from the Lakers because of complaints that he was slowing down the pace, Phipers asked Paul if the System was the future course of college basketball. Paul explained why he thought it definitely was not. "You have to play so hard. You have to be in an absolute sprint to the spots 100 percent of the time," he said. "Our guys are grooved. They wouldn't know how to walk down the court. They'd trip, or they'd stumble, or they'd go to sleep or something."[46]

The improvement in Hank's performance on the court since the St. Joe's game in early January was no accident. The improvement in his stamina and quickness, which accounted for his improved scoring and rebounding, was in direct correlation to the reduction in his dosage of Inderal and his pregame routine of vigorous exercise—jumping rope or running sprints, which he thought would flush the reduced dosage out of his system. Although his doctors had told him to do this vigorous exercise, they may not have taken two hallmarks of Hank's belief system into account: if a little bit is good, a lot is better; and sheer hard work will get you through any tough situation. They undoubtedly were unaware, as well, of his penchant for gambling. On top of that, as the dosage was reduced, Hank felt better and better; in his mind, how he was feeling was confirmation that the drug was keeping him from playing well.[47]

Although he clearly had been told that he had to take the medication in whatever dosage prescribed in order to play, what is less clear is whether Hank obeyed that requirement.

Dr. Hattori had set out to monitor Hank closely by putting him on a treadmill with a Holter monitor around his neck after each dosage reduction, but Hank had stalled and otherwise blocked the doctor's plans. Hattori was frustrated by Hank's failure to come in as scheduled, yet he continued to allow him to compete without determining whether the new and lower dosage was doing its job.

Since Hank associated the drug with his poor performance, he was not in the least interested in having Dr. Hattori determine that the dosage was too low. The drug kept him from playing his best. He would do whatever he could to avoid any testing that might lead to an increase in dosage. Besides, time was on his side. Only a handful of games remained before the WCC tournament and then the NCAA Tournament. Hank had to stall or put off the testing for only a little while longer.

Dr. Hattori finally got Hank to take a Holter test on February 20 and was pleased with the results. But as the play-offs, and the increased attention that they brought, drew closer, Hank pleaded for Dr. Hattori to cut the dosage even further.[48]

Only two contests remained before the conference tournament.

On February 23, San Diego came to Gersten Pavilion and was rudely trampled by the hosts, 131-119, before another sold-out crowd. Bo scored 47 points, Hank added 35, and Jeff Fryer contributed 33. Paul Westhead got his 100th win at LMU against only 47 losses.[49]

The final regular season contest was the next night against Santa Clara. It was also Senior Night, a traditional farewell to the graduating players. Lucille was there, along with Charles, and with her sons, she proudly strolled out on the court, clutching a bouquet, to the cheers of the throng in Gersten. Hank, his arm around his mother, beamed proudly as he accepted the handshake of Brian Quinn at center court.

As the game got underway, Lucille, sitting in the stands, held aloft a hand-made sign that read GO HANK.[50] Hank, and the rest of the Lions, did as she asked and rolled to a 117-81 win. Hank had 29 points and Bo added 35 (his mother, Hilda, was there, too), and the two Philly imports combined for 26 of 37 attempts from the floor to pace the Lions.

In the early going, Santa Clara, paced by Jeffty Connelly, opened an 8-point lead, and the Lions went to a new defensive scheme. "We went to a press we never used," Westhead said. "It's a very chancy defense. Usually you tire after three minutes. We used it for 23 minutes. I think it turned the game round." Hank agreed, saying, "It was one of the best games we've played. We did something a little different and it speeded up the game. The team's energy level was real high."[51]

Of Hank's performance, Westhead said, "The energy of Hank was way up tonight. He sent a message to everyone on the team. For better or worse—and most of the time it has been for better—Hank is the leader of this team."[52]

The message Hank was most interested in sending was to the NBA: I'm back and as good as ever. "I'm not even tired—I don't even feel like I've played a game," Hank declared after the furiously paced contest.[53]

Although Hank's energy level and performance had steadily improved as his dosage was decreased, no one could be certain, though, that he was following the directions that Dr. Hattori had given him, to take two doses a day—or even if he was taking any doses, at all, on game days.

What was clear was that after Dr. Hattori reduced Hank's dosage again in late January, Hank had steadily climbed back to nearly the same level at which he had been playing before his collapse on December 9. Hank was still not happy about being on the medication and continued to plead with Dr. Hattori to reduce it even further. Hank knew that he needed to be at his best during the play-offs and the NCAA Tournament, when the NBA scouts would be watching with an especially keen eye.

On February 26, Dr. Hattori relented and lowered the dosage yet again. Now Hank was supposed to take 40 mg of Inderal daily, in two 20 mg doses, or one-fifth of the original prescription.[54] "It is a dosage that would be prescribed for a young child. Not a 6-foot-7, 235-pound man," Dr. Swerdlow remarked years later, characterizing it as "an amount you'd give a rabbit."[55]

The season would end with the WCC tournament's final round on March 5, which would be televised nationally on ESPN. As always, Dr. Hattori insisted that Hank be tested at the new reduced dosage by working out on the treadmill, while wearing a Holter monitor, to determine whether the Inderal was still suppressing his arrhythmias. The test was scheduled for the afternoon of Wednesday, February 28, two days after he began taking the reduced dosage.[56]

Hank did not show up.

He couldn't risk having the test show the dosage to be too low to suppress the arrhythmia, because then he would have to take a higher dosage, at a level that slowed him down and showed him at less than his best. Everything he had worked for depended on his performance in the few remaining games.

Everything.

When Hank failed to show up for the Holter test on Wednesday, Dr. Hattori asked his nurse to get hold of Hank and reschedule it for the next day, March 1. Hank blew off that appointment, too.[57] The tournament was to begin on Saturday. Dr. Hattori would testify that he was extremely aggravated at Hank's failure to show up for the test. He said he called Hank's apartment repeatedly, without reaching him.[58]

Dr. Hattori also called Westhead on Friday, March 2, and left a message for Paul that it was imperative that Hank come in and see him. Several hours later, either

Westhead or Chip Schaeffer called Dr. Hattori back (the physician wasn't sure who called), and Dr. Hattori said that he was irate that Hank had missed his tests. He told Westhead/Schaeffer that it was imperative that he speak with Hank—and if he didn't speak to Hank within the next 12 hours, he'd ground him.

Dr. Hattori later conceded that his threat not to let Hank play that weekend was made simply for its "shock value," and that he never intended to prevent Hank from competing. He had made the threat simply to get Hank to return his calls so he could discuss his medication with him. Dr. Hattori said later that he knew it was logistically impossible to have Hank tested before the tournament because the weekend was already upon them, but he said that he was considering restoring the dosage of 40 mg twice a day, which had proved successful at suppressing the arrhythmias in the past.[59]

Finally, at about 6 p.m. on Friday, Hank called Dr. Hattori, who was in the coronary care unit at the hospital. Dr. Hattori said he explained to Hank how aggravated he was that Hank had failed to come in for his tests. According to the cardiologist, Hank claimed that he was pressed for time—he'd had a lot of interviews to do and was very busy with the press. He was apologetic about missing the tests and offered to come in right away to be tested.[60]

Dr. Hattori told Hank that was not possible because the hospital was not staffed for running tests on weekends. Consequently, Dr. Hattori told Hank, he would have to go back on the 40 mg twice a day in order to play.

"No, no, no—everything is fine—I can feel my heart, it doesn't race anymore," Hank protested.[61]

Dr. Hattori said that Hank explained emphatically that he could tell when an arrhythmia or fainting spell was starting and promised to take himself out of the game if he felt the symptoms. "I promise," Hank told his doctor.[62]

Based on this assurance from his patient, that he could feel the onset of both the arrhythmia and fainting, and that he would voluntarily remove himself from the game when he experienced symptoms, Dr. Hattori agreed to let Hank play on the reduced dosage of 40 mg a day in two 20 mg dosages.

Hank had won another argument. Dr. Hattori didn't call either Paul Westhead or Chip Schaeffer to say he had decided to allow Hank to play on the reduced medication (40 mg daily) without being tested.[63]

The tournament began the next day, Saturday, March 3. Dr. Hattori headed East on I-10 to a weekend-long bachelor party in Palm Springs.

CHAPTER 24

TIME RUNS OUT

"I used to look up at those housing projects near where I lived in North Philly and think to myself, "There's got to be more to life than this."

—Hank Gathers

The West Coast Conference Tournament began on Saturday, March 3, at Gersten Pavilion. The format called for a series of single elimination games to be played over the weekend, with the conference championship game to be played on Monday, March 5, and televised nationally on ESPN.

LMU had won the season championship outright and was a virtual lock for an NCAA bid. The Lions were ranked 22nd nationally in most polls and would be playing in the NCAA Tournament no matter who won the WCC tourney. On March 11, when the NCAA was scheduled to announce its tournament field, the only news for the Lions would be how high they were seeded and where they would play. The rest of the conference teams were hoping for an upset of the Lions and an automatic invite to the NCAA Tournament as champs of the West Coast Conference Tournament.

The weekend began with a gala banquet, held at the Hilton Hotel near the LMU campus, to welcome all the participants.

"I found myself seated next to Paul Westhead at the banquet," Larry Steele said. "I asked him during dinner, if he wouldn't mind, I would like to speak with Hank. He said it would be fine."

The Portland coach had a special interest in Hank Gathers. "I had been diagnosed with Wolf-Parkinson-White syndrome, or WPW, and had been taking medication for the condition," he explained. "I knew from my own recent personal experiences the dangers of interrupting the medications that were prescribed for heart conditions. I wanted a chance to talk with Hank, to warn him about the dangers based on what had happened to me."

Steele's heart problems were congenital and had begun at the University of Kentucky when he was playing for Adolph Rupp's Wildcats. Nevertheless, he had been able to turn pro and had played for the Portland Trailblazers from 1971-1980, including the year they won the NBA championship. Steele was the recipient of Bill Walton's outlet passes that ignited the Trailblazers' fast-break attack. Throughout his career, Steele had suffered a series of incidents, about eight or nine times, when his heart would race wildly at rates of more than 280 beats per minute. They were always related to exercise and vigorous physical activity. Four or five times, the incidents put him in an emergency room.

Finally, he was diagnosed with WPW and placed on medication. The alternative was open heart surgery, and Steele wasn't ready for that.

"After 10 months on medicine, I stopped taking the medication. I stopped taking it for three days. I'd had it with the sluggishness and side effects the medicine caused. I noticed immediately how much better I felt without the medication. I felt like I was superhuman as soon as I went off the medication," he said. "But the racing heart rate returned, and I ended up in another emergency room near death. I went reluctantly back on the medication.

"I hated the medicine and how it made me feel. A couple months later, I had had it with the medicine and went back to my doctor and asked him to schedule the open heart surgery. I felt I would rather die than keep taking that medication."

Steele found a physician who was experimenting with surgery to correct the problem and scheduled the new and risky procedure in Oklahoma City. He was only the 55th person in the world to undergo the procedure, and it proved successful.

"But I knew as an athlete what it felt like to be on the heart medication, and I also knew the dangers associated with going off the medicine," he said. "I wanted to talk to Hank about my own experiences and perhaps tell him maybe the doctors had missed something with his diagnosis. I was mainly concerned, after the experience I had, that he would stop taking his medicine, and [I] wanted to warn him of the danger that presented."

Westhead readily agreed to arrange for Steele and Hank to talk.

The banquet concluded, and the teams and players dispersed to their respective hotel rooms. Steele didn't talk with Hank that night, figuring there'd be time after the tournament, which began the next day.[1]

The opening round contest would find LMU facing a struggling Gonzaga team in front of a friendly crowd at Gersten Pavilion.

The Lions grabbed a quick 27-11 lead, to the delight of the 3,875 in attendance at the afternoon game. Gonzaga coach Dan Fitzgerald thought that his team "would have to play a perfect game" to pull off an upset. Instead, "the opposite occurred," Fitzgerald moaned.

The Lions took a 59-33 halftime lead and never looked back. LMU set WCC tournament records for points (121), rebounds (66), field goals (48), and attempts (96). The final score was 121-84.

"They still go 100 miles an hour," Gonzaga senior Jim McPhee said of the Lions. "(If) you don't play hard against them, forget it. It's not even funny."

The Lions were led again by Hank, who had 28 points and 11 rebounds. Jeff Fryer added 25, and Bo chipped in with 21 as the Lions improved to 23-5. Westhead told the *Los Angeles Times'* Drooz his strategy for the tournament: "We're gonna play all out and hope we have enough energy left to play Monday (in the Finals). Full throttle."[2]

The win put LMU into the semifinals on Sunday against Portland, which had turned back Santa Clara.

In an interview after the game, Hank told Brian Berger of KXLU, "Everyone knows I'm the leader of this team. I'm also the spiritual leader of this team. As Hank Gathers goes, so goes the team."[3]

Sportscaster Ed Arnold was in Al Gersten's motor home in the parking lot after the Gonzaga game.

"Hank and Bo both came in and we were talking. Hank was admiring a souvenir watch I had received from the conference, and he, joking around, said he wanted it. I told him he'd probably be getting one when the tournament was over. He said he liked mine and wanted me to give it to him. I just laughed at him and said I'd think about it," Arnold said.

"I had to get back to the station and do a telecast. I gave them both a big hug. I wished them luck and told them I'd have someone covering the game tomorrow. I had to teach a class at UCLA the next night and couldn't be there myself, but I told them I'd be at the finals and would see them then."[4] The game with Portland would begin at 5 p.m., P.S.T.

Against Gonzaga, Hank had played extremely well down the stretch. He was close to being the same Hank Gathers who had led the nation in scoring and rebounding the previous season. He was very nearly the Hank Gathers who had dominated the WCC and had graced the cover of *Street and Smith's* Basketball Preview. Hank had come back so well from the December 9 incident that Westhead saw little difference in his performance now. Hank was displaying the old energy, enthusiasm, and quickness that had made him one of the top players in the country.[5]

The improvement in Hank's performance correlated directly with the reduction in the level of medication he was taking. The lower the dosage, the higher his energy level and the better he performed. As Larry Steele had discovered with nearly fatal consequences, if you went off the medication, you "felt like Superman."

We do not know definitively how faithfully Hank was following his doctor's orders in taking even the dosage that was then so low that Dr. Swerdlow characterized it as "appropriate for a small child."[6]

Hank rose late on Sunday morning and prepared to meet the Pilots of Portland. No one knows whether he took his Inderal. The day began with a few light sprinkles. It was cool as the crowd of runners massed on Figueroa Street downtown for the start of the Los Angeles Marathon.

As the day wore on, Hank and his family decided to attend the Lakers game that evening. Pooh Richardson, Hank's friend and former rival from Philadelphia, now with the Minnesota Timberwolves, provided the tickets. He left them at the will-call window at the Los Angeles Forum.

Lucille, Derrick, Charles, and Hank's aunt, Carole Livingston, would all be at the tournament. Lucille, who had gained more weight since she'd stopped working, wore a new bright yellow dress with a floral print. The family was in a festive and cheerful mood as they made their way to Gersten to cheer Hank on in the late afternoon game.

Only one more WCC tournament game remained after this one, and that one would be on ESPN where their "GO HANK" signs would be visible to the nation. Then it would be on to the NCAA Tournament, more television exposure for Hank, and then, finally, the NBA draft. It was all so close now.

WCC Commissioner Mike Gilleran was pulling into a reserved parking spot in front of Gersten Pavilion when he noticed someone in sweats running around the track next to the gymnasium. It was, he realized, Hank Gathers.[7]

As Chip Schaeffer was tending to her balky knee, LMU cheerleader Kristin Ramage saw Hank enter the training room. He greeted her with his usual easy smile and cheery hello as he walked by the training table.

Kristin was a psychology major, and she had talked with Hank at some length on several occasions. After his collapse during the UC-Santa Barbara game, she had noticed a subtle change. "He was still very nice but much more quiet and focused after that. He still joked around with me but seemed more determined," she said. "From our conversations, I sensed that he felt he was letting people down. From what he said, I felt he was feeling a lot of pressure. People—his family—were coming out [to California], and he was afraid he was letting them down."

As Hank walked through the trainer's room that afternoon, Kristin noticed something odd. "Hank was dripping wet with perspiration. He had a sweat suit on and was soaked clean through," she said. "I knew he always jumped rope before the games, but this was even way before [game time]."[8]

Hank had been out on the cinder track surrounding the soccer field outside Gersten. He had been running laps and doing wind sprints for about 40 minutes.[9]

Hank knew he needed to be at his best in the tournament because NBA scouts would be watching, and the doctors had told him to warm up enough to elevate his heart rate before a game. He would still jump rope before the game, but he had come to believe that running would flush the medicine out of his system. He had done it before and it always worked. He wanted to be certain he was at his physical best for the game against Portland.

Back in early January, when Dr. Hattori had summoned Dr. Swerdlow from the hall to come chat with Hank, he had complained about Inderal's effect on his playing. Dr. Swerdlow had told Hank that he could change the medication, but Hank would have to be hospitalized. Hank nixed that idea, Dr. Swerdlow wrote later, a "combination of a natural dislike for hospitals, his game schedule, and his desire not to appear ill while he was a prime NBA draft choice were the reasons."[10]

Dr. Hattori planned, once the season was over, to convert Hank to another drug with less debilitating side effects. To do that, though, Hank would have to stop playing while the doctor ran tests of the new drug's efficacy. Hank had not been willing to do that during the season because it would mean missing some games. Dr. Hattori figured that after the conference tournament, but before the NCAA Tournament began, when there was a break long enough not to interfere with any games, he could switch Hank to the new medication. Hank was aware of Dr. Hattori's plan.[11]

Hank Gathers ran out onto the court at Gersten Pavilion to a smattering of applause from the early arrivals.

On the sidelines, Portland coach Larry Steele watched as the Lions warmed up. "While I stood there watching their team warm up, I couldn't help but notice Hank," he said. "My assistants and I just stood there as he warmed up in front of our bench. He was absolutely going for it all."[12]

Steele had watched Hank play against his Pilots for three seasons. "The first time I ever saw him, it was so obvious that he was a man playing against boys. He absolutely looked like he had been in the NBA for five years, working on his game and physique," Steele said. "You noticed his physical presence first, and then, once play began, it was apparent he was the team's leader and committed to their aggressive style of play. He displayed great ability and effort on the court."

Now Larry Steele watched Hank with growing interest and more than a little concern. "As I watched Hank, I was projecting my own experiences and concerns about how I had felt when I stopped the medicine and what had happened to me," Steele said. "There was a very unusual situation going on. Their warm-ups took place right in front of our bench.

Hank was going in for lay-ups like he was going for the winning basket with the score tied and time running out. He was using all of his physical presence and his mental focus as if the game was about to end—not like it was just the beginning of warm-ups. He came out ready to go, and it was very noticeable."

Steele, former NBA star that he was, recognized what was going on with Hank professionally and suspected what was happening medically: "Hank was in the very first stage of increasing his worth over the next four to five weeks. He was going to be increasing his value to the NBA, starting with that game.

"I knew from experience that when I went off my medication, I felt just like Superman. I had such absolute tremendous energy because I was really back to normal. I had gone from a reduced being, mentally and physically, back to normal, and it put me in another state. The effect of stopping the medication was that, while you were only returning to normal and feeling more like yourself, you felt a tremendous surge of energy.

"I thought," said Steele, "as I watched Hank in the warm-ups, and saw that he appeared to be on cloud nine, that he had stopped taking his medicine."[13]

Steele wasn't the only person to notice a difference in Hank.

Mike Gilleran watched the pregame warm-ups from the stands. "Hank was much springier in the warm-ups than he had been in months," he said.[14]

Per Sturmer remembers that it was a beautiful, sunny Southern California day—one of the many benefits of being in Los Angeles instead of his native Sweden, where March was a cold and dreary month.

He noticed something else, too: "In warm-ups that day, Hank looked like Superman."[15]

Was it what Steele feared, that Hank had gone off his medication? Or was it simply, as Hank had told Spence the night before, that he knew just how close he was to realizing his dream?[16] The NBA draft would be held in June and he would be a high first-round draft choice, making him a millionaire. His mom and son, Aaron, would be taken care of. It wouldn't be long now.

As he arrived for the game, Brian Quinn surveyed the growing crowd in Gersten Pavilion and paused to wave and acknowledge boosters and fans. His daughter, Maureen, clutched his hand tightly as they made their way through the crowd. Her favorite player was Hank Gathers. She was 12, and her room at home was adorned with the usual dolls and stuffed animals of a preteen girl. But prominently displayed on the walls and dresser top, though, were pictures and things that Hank had given her.

"She just adored him," Brian recalled. Hank was special and she was excited to be there to see him play.

"On the bus trips she went on with the team, [Tom] Peabody was always teasing her, kidding around with her. Hank took care of her," Brian said. "Hank was fascinated by her math homework. On the bus, he'd sit with her while she did the problems. She loved Hank."[17]

March 4 was Lane Bove's birthday. Her husband, David, had arranged a small birthday brunch for her at their home. All their friends were present, and they planned to head over to Gersten for the game after they ate.

"David knew I loved champagne and had offered me, along with the other guests, some of the bubbly with brunch. When I declined the drink, he looked at me quizzically. I said, 'I don't know why, but I don't think I should have anything to drink. I have a strange feeling I might have to work later,'" she said.[18]

Al Gersten had procured the large motor home specifically for the conference tournament and had set it up for a mobile cocktail party. The oversized vehicle was parked conspicuously in front of Gersten Pavilion. Inside, the mood was festive and upbeat as Al and his friends enjoyed a late afternoon drink and some hors d'oeuvres before they went to the game. Al expected Hank and Bo and some others to join the celebration after the game, as they had the day before.[19]

Cassie Westhead joined her Palos Verdes neighbors Paul and Kay Conrad in the stands. Paul and Kay were season ticket holders, even though Paul, a Pulitzer Prize-winning cartoonist for the *Los Angeles Times*, could have easily scored a free media pass.

"Our son, David, had attended LMU, and when Paul [Westhead], who was our neighbor, became coach, we continued to go to the games as often as possible," Kay Conrad said. "We had gone to a number of games that season. We were both big fans, and Hank was the biggest star."[20]

Alan Drooz arrived for the game early and found his place along press row. He and Mike Waldner and Joe Resnick were joined by a score of others covering the game for their television stations and newspapers. They all received the press kit that Barry Zepel had assembled for the afternoon's action.

Zepel had seen interest in his little Jesuit school grow from one or two local reporters to a national following in just the past three seasons. "I was working harder than ever just to keep up with the growing interest. It was tiring and stressful, and I loved every minute of it," he said. His once largely ignored Lions were a national item, and he was the font of information about them. This was as good as it got for a sports information director. And the best, he was sure, was yet to come. The Lions were a legitimate national championship contender. "Who would have ever imagined that?" he thought, as he watched the warm-ups.[21]

Dr. Dan Hyslop, the LMU school doctor, was wearing a red ball cap as he scurried around, trying to score a game ticket for his brother-in-law. He wryly recalled when you couldn't give away a ticket to an LMU game.[22]

Dr. Ben Shaffer had drawn the assignment to attend the game on behalf of the Kerlan-Jobe clinic. His jeans and running sneakers were topped by a blue sports coat and dark, open-necked dress shirt. He stuck the yellow laminated participant pass in his jacket pocket and took his seat several rows up from the court.[23]

Peter Priamos planned to go to the game—he usually attended LMU home games—despite the misgivings about his presence that some had had in the past. Hank and Bo had always urged him to be at their games—he was one of their oldest friends in Los Angeles. Today he would be joined by their relatives in cheering on the two Philly kids who had brought the LMU Lions to the pinnacle of basketball success. Priamos genuinely liked and cared for the two former USC recruits. No one was happier than Pete about how well they had done. He couldn't help remembering how he had bought them underwear when they first arrived on the West Coast, so ill prepared had they been for the world beyond inner-city Philadelphia.

He'd seen them battle injuries, the mess at USC, and their transfer to a new school, and how they overcame it all to be among the top players in the land. They had come a long way together, and Pete was very proud of them and his role in helping them get to this point. He was running late today—he would get there, but he would miss the beginning of the game.[24]

In 14 years as the public address announcer at LMU, Bernie Sandalow had seen all the highs and lows of LMU hoops. This, he felt, was most decidedly the high point of his tenure behind the mike.[25]

Derrick Gathers and a friend of his from Philadelphia, Lawrence Lawhorn, were in the second row, right behind the LMU bench. Seven or eight rows up were Lucille and Charles, along with Hank's girlfriend, Vernell Ritchey, and Bo's mom, Hilda Moody.[26]

Spence sat nearby. The man who had brought Hank and Bo to Southern California was at Gersten to see the culmination of their college careers. Certainly, he had hoped it would be under different circumstances, but he wouldn't have missed this game for anything. By now, Spencer was working as a sports agent for Leonard Armato in Los Angeles, and he expected to be the agent for both Hank and Bo after the season ended.

"I had been there at the first-round game the day before," Spence said. "After the game, Hank said to me, 'Come on, Spence, let's go out to dinner.' I said, 'No, Hank, I don't feel like it tonight.' Hank, being Hank, who never took no for an answer, insisted that we go to dinner together. I am so glad that he did, because I got to spend that night before the game with him." After he had dropped Hank off, Spence noticed that Hank had left a jar of cranberry juice in the console cup holder. "Hank had only taken a sip or two, so I decided to take it in and save it for the next time he came over." He slid it onto the top shelf of the refrigerator and closed the door. The next day he and his wife went to the game together.[27]

A continent away Father Dave Hagan eagerly awaited the phone call he knew he would get from Hank about the game. In the East, it was already past eight o'clock and much colder than in Los Angeles. The priest had braved the chill night air to grab a light dinner and a Black Russian or two at Rembrandt's. He knew he would be back in plenty of time for Hank's call.

The nationally ranked La Salle Explorers, still sporting only the single loss suffered at the hands of Hank and Bo's Lions, were preparing for their own Metro Atlantic Conference play-off game at Knickerbocker Arena in Albany, New York. Doug Overton and Lionel Simmons were on the court, battling Siena College for their own NCAA berth.

In Philadelphia, the best point guard that Hank and Bo—and many others—had ever seen was watching television. Heat was home in the neighborhood while others, far less skilled than he, were performing in front of packed houses and national television audiences. He'd spent the day watching some televised games and then played in a Sonny Hill League game at the Moylen Recreation Center in front of a dozen or so spectators. He was rooting hard for his friends from Dobbins, but that was all he could contribute now. There would be no more firing perfect, instinctive, no-look passes to them. He'd lead no more fast breaks for them. He could only root silently for his friends who were still playing college ball and wonder what might have been. They were still in his heart and mind and, often, in his dreams. He fell asleep early.[28]

In their neatly kept apartment in the otherwise dismal Raymond Rosen Homes, Marva and her mother, Phyllis Crump, gave in to Aaron's pleadings and said he could stay up later than usual to see ESPN's late sports show to learn how his daddy and his team had done.[29]

The game with Portland began on time at 5 p.m. and was broadcast over KXLU-FM, the Loyola Marymount college radio station. No other area radio or television station was covering the game. The signal, though, was strong enough to be received throughout the Los Angeles metropolitan area, and thousands regularly listened to the broadcasts as they followed the Lions' fortunes.

As they had all year long, Keith Forman and Brian Berger brought the action to their listeners from the station's courtside broadcast booth at Gersten Pavilion. It was located at floor level and just to the left of the LMU bench. They were so close to the action that the assistant coaches would often check Berger's stats sheet to ascertain the correct number of personal fouls on their players.[30]

Because the championship game was scheduled to be televised live by ESPN the next day, a free-lance cameraman, Carter Trigg, who would work the final game, was on hand, checking lighting and angles. His camera was rolling from the opening tip. High above the stands, the Loyola student operating his camera for the coaching staff began taping the game for Westhead and his assistants to review.[31]

As he did before every opening tip-off, Hank Gathers pulled up his shorts and growled to the Portland center, "Get ready for war!" Hank controlled the tap, and play was underway. Heavily favored LMU pulled out to an early lead over Larry Steele's much improved, but still outclassed, Pilots.

Josh Lowery, Terrell's 6-foot-five brother, was the Pilots' leading scorer; the game against his trash-talking little brother was the last time that they would face each other. Josh hit a few early buckets to keep Portland close.

The thousands of listeners throughout Los Angeles and the San Fernando Valley heard Forman and Berger's call of what happened right in front of them, midway through the first half. The score stood LMU, 18-Portland, 11.

FORMAN: Fryer, 3-point attempt. That is good!

BERGER: First 3-pointer for Jeff Fryer. He's usually the guy that starts the Lions off. Those are his first 3 points. Bo Kimble with 10 early points.

FORMAN: Two 3-pointers for the Lions so far. One for Bo, one for Fryer.

FORMAN: Foul away from the ball after the shot. That's on Per Sturmer. His first, the second team foul, on the Lions.

BERGER: Not too many fouls called early in the game. The officials are letting them play for the most part.

FORMAN: Lowery inbounds the ball to Spoelstra. Erik gives it right back to Lowery across half- court. Three-pointer on the way. That is off the front of the rim. Gathers, powerful rebound! (Crowd reacts.) Hauls it in and dribbles out of the backcourt all by himself. Now to the free-throw line. Coast to coast. Got it! (Crowd reacts loudly.) Up and in.

BERGER: Hank wants to be known as a man who can handle the ball. He showed he was there. He took it right down the court, all the way in, for two.

FORMAN: Twenty-three to eleven. Lions have led the entire way. Fourteen [minutes]-fifteen [seconds] to go in the first half. Spoelstra dribbling in the backcourt gets it across to Lowery. Lowery versus Lowery. Pass inside to Hutchinson. Shot is good. Twenty-three to thirteen—Lions lead by ten. Lowery pulls up for a 3. On the way. That's no good. Rebound Hutchinson. Doing it at both ends of the court. Long baseball pass to Josh Lowery. Three-pointer from the corner. That's off the rim. Mobley with the rebound, then loses it to Terrell Lowery. Terrell brings the ball up the backcourt, running down the left sideline. Alley- oop to Gathers! (Crowd explodes noisily.) NBA play. Unbelievable! (Crowd still screaming.)

BERGER: Great pass by Terrell Lowery. He was on the left side at half- court. He threw it up. A perfect pass. Hank caught it in stride and jammed it! (Crowd still buzzing excitedly over the play.)

FORMAN: Hank was right in position. It wasn't even a lob pass—he just rifled it up there. That's got to be one of the quickest alley- oops— (A gasp from the crowd is audible in the background.)

BERGER (breaking in): Hank collapsed!

FORMAN: Hank Gathers on the floor, collapsed. He was standing right beyond half-court, and all of a sudden he just fell down. The trainers are all on the court. Hank's mother is rushing on the court. Hank is trying to get up.

BERGER: He's still down. Trainers are out there. A doctor has come out of the crowd. Chip Schaeffer is rolling him over. He wants to get up but—

FORMAN: He's now going into, it looks like—his body is kind of—it's hard to explain. He's lying on the floor. He's trying to get up. Everybody is trying to keep him down. Obviously, it's pretty silent.

BERGER (in a hushed voice): He was going into convulsions. And right now his brother Derrick is walking out onto the court. Coach Paul Westhead is out there. You could hear a pin drop in here right now.

FORMAN: Thirteen–thirty-four on the clock. Lions lead it 25-13. This happened right after Gathers got the alley-oop dunk from Terrell. He was walking away. Hank's mom visibly upset. [Actually, it was Carole Livingston who was wailing audibly, not Lucille, as Keith assumed.] Lots of people out there tending to him. This is pretty much a shock to everybody.

BERGER: This is very surprising because Hank was celebrating with Terrell after he made that nice play and was just walking, going back to set up for the press and. . .(voice trails off).

FORMAN (voice subdued and flat): We're going to take a break. We'll be right back. You're listening to KXLU Los Angeles. (Fade out to music.)[32]

What the two young LMU communications majors had just described to their listening audience took place in front of a crowd of nearly 4,100 and at least three video cameras. The crowd, which had risen as one to excitedly cheer Hank's slam-dunk basket, was reduced in a matter of seconds to a shocked and stunned silence by what was happening on the court. The people remained standing, silent and transfixed. A man was dying in front of their eyes. The cameras that were recording it all left a visual record of what happened.[33]

It was 5:14 p.m., P.S.T.

After Hank slam-dunked Terrell's alley-oop pass, he had landed nimbly in the blue-painted key beneath the quaking basket and headed up court, exchanging a hand slap with Terrell, giving him a pat on the rear, and telling him, "Good pass, Buck." Nick Schneider, LMU's 12-year-old ball boy, was seated directly beneath the basket when his hero threw down the thundering dunk. "I was at the bottom of the hoop looking up, and I remember the feeling of the entire basket shaking and rattling. It felt like I was on a ride because of the force that literally jarred me from my seat," he said.[34]

A referee's whistle had stopped play momentarily, then the ball was in play once more. As Hank turned to move back on defense, past Per Sturmer, Hank's hands were on his thighs. Then he staggered in an awkward, jerky, reeling motion and fell heavily to the court. He landed hard on his left side and rolled onto his back, just to the left of the crimson and gray LMU logo at center court. The players will never forget the sound Hank's body made as it thwacked the hardwood floor. "It sounded like a tree crashing to the ground," Per said.[35]

Portland's Eric Mobley reached out in an act of sportsmanship to take Hank's arm and help him up. But Hank's arm hung limply in Mobley's hand and he dropped it abruptly; it fell heavily to the floor, and Mobley backed away, fear visible on his face.

Chip Schaeffer had rushed from the LMU bench to Hank's side almost immediately. Carole Livingston had climbed quickly from the stands, bursting through a row of folding chairs to get to her nephew's side. Her sudden emergence and subsequent wailing had led observers to assume she was Hank's mother.

Within seconds of his fall, his heart racing wildly and chest heaving hard enough to raise his back off the floor, Hank had struggled to get up. Resisting Chip's urgings to stay down, Hank had managed to lift himself halfway up, and he continued to fight for a few more seconds. In defiance of all medical odds he fought desperately on. His racing heart had precipitated a sudden loss of blood pressure, and the lack of blood and oxygen to his brain were disorienting and disabling his muscular body. Struggling to his left side, propped on one arm, his eyes open, he stared in unfocused confusion toward the side court.

"Where we were seated at courtside, just a few yards away with no obstructions, I saw Hank's eyes staring directly at me," Brian Berger said.[36]

"I was only about 15 feet away," LMU cheerleader Kristin Ramage Nelson recalled. "He was breathing very fast, as if he couldn't catch his breath."[37]

Rolling to his left, he got to his hands and knees before Chip gently pushed him back. And Hank Gathers, the strongest man alive, no longer possessed the strength to resist the trainer's gentle hands. He rolled back over onto his back. His left arm was pinned beneath him. The man who proudly claimed that he had the heart of a lion had been betrayed by his own heart.

Seconds after Hank fell, Dr. Ben Shaffer ran onto the court. At first he thought Hank was having another fainting episode like he'd had back in December.[38] But as he neared the spot where Hank had fallen, the player's body went into violent, spasmodic convulsions, in full view of his horrified family and the crowd. Hank's right leg and then his left jerked wildly in a scissor-kick. His arms and chest twitched violently as his body reacted to the deprivation of blood and oxygen. Less than 30 seconds had elapsed since he had fallen to the court.

Chip urged Hank to take deep breaths and to stay calm as his body jumped and twitched beneath his hands. As Dr. Shaffer joined them, the activity ceased. Westhead, who had quickly moved to Hank's prostrate form and was bent over to look at his player, backed away, gently urging Dr. Shaffer closer with a hand on the doctor's back. Chip's hand was on Hank's chest, gently restraining him from trying to get up, as the trainer talked to Hank.

Dr. Shaffer, on one knee as he observed Hank, knew this was no bruised thigh or bloodied nose, a blown-out knee or torn Achilles. This was much, much worse than anything the young orthopedist had ever had to face.

The scene remains vivid in his mind: Hank's head leaned back and "was almost on my knee," Shaffer said. "I had my finger on his carotid pulse and I thought I could feel a pulse. Hank was somewhat 'arousable.' He had the glazed-over eyes of someone who had just experienced a seizure. I told him to take a deep breath and to relax. He was breathing fast, rapid breaths."[39]

Tom Fregoso, the Portland trainer, who was certified in CPR, had also rushed over to help. As Dr. Shaffer took Hank's carotid pulse, Fregoso reached for Hank's arm and took a radial pulse. He told Dr. Shaffer that Hank had a radial pulse, and he observed that Hank was breathing.[40]

Dr. Shaffer found Hank's pulse to be very rapid, "over 100 beats per minute."

"I said, 'Hank, take a deep breath,' and he responded to my command. His breathing was spontaneous and all seizure activity had ceased. His eyes were open and glazed,"

Dr. Shaffer said. He told Hank on two more occasions to take a deep breath and Hank did so.[41]

"At first, Hank was responsive to our directions," Chip said. "Then, Dr. Shaffer told me to get a stretcher to transport him from the court. I ran to the training room and got one."[42]

By now, Derrick and Charles had reached Hank and Carole Livingston. Derrick knelt at his brother's side, while Charles stood nearby, hands jammed in his pockets, a look of horror on his face. He wandered anxiously back and forth around his brother's prostrate form.

As Dr. Shaffer tried to assess what was happening to Hank, his aunt sent up a wailing howl as she knelt on the floor. Bo, who was standing over his teammate, tried to calm her. She pushed him away, shouting, "Get away, leave me alone!" Her loud, hysterical wailing eerily filled the otherwise silent gymnasium, intensifying the sense of foreboding and dread that had enveloped the crowd.

Lucille, hampered by her weight, was slower to react than the rest of her family. She soon managed, with the assistance of Derrick's friend, Lawrence Lawhorn, to make her way to her son's side. She peered over the shoulders of the doctors who were working on Hank. What she saw caused her to instinctively recoil, her hand clutching at her bosom, as if she had been struck by an invisible blow from her fallen child.

While Lucille watched with growing concern, she had the presence of mind to chastise her keening sister. Swatting at Carole Livingston with a slap or two, Lucille admonished her, as if she were an unruly child, to stop her wailing and to pull herself together. It didn't work. Livingston would continue her theatrics, which culminated in a loud scream and wild flailing at the floor as Hank was moved to a stretcher.

The medical personnel and Chip were joined by Terry Peabody, Tom's brother-physician, and Jamie Sanchez, the facilities manager and LMU tennis coach.

As the doctors had begun to work on Hank, Westhead had gotten out of the way, walking back toward the bench. He paused a few steps away from Hank and looked back at his fallen star. When he turned away, his face was ashen and his head was down. Visibly shaken, Paul moved slowly and mechanically to the bench area.

Brian Quinn said that when Hank fell, "at first I thought it was like the Santa Barbara game. Then, when he failed to rise and the trainer and doctors began to work on Hank, LMU's president, Father James Loughran, turned to me and said, 'I think you'd better go down there.' I quickly went down to the court."

As he passed through the press row, Brian asked someone to dial 911.[43]

Gary Jones, who was covering the game for the Los Angeles Daily News, made the call. It was 5:17 p.m., P.S.T.

Focused intently on the gravity of what was unfolding in front of him, his hands nervously pawing at his face, Brian watched wide-eyed, as they worked on Hank. In the stands where Brian had left her, young Maureen looked on in horror as her favorite player's body convulsed and jumped. She was too young to know what it meant but old enough to know it wasn't good. What she saw frightened her and left her staring, now alone and confused, at her hero.

Lane Bove hurried from the stands to help with crowd control and to get people to clear the way so Hank could be moved outside. "It happened right in front of me," she said. "I went on automatic pilot. My administrator persona took over, and I operated purely on instinct."[44]

Chip got back with the stretcher, and those tending to Hank lifted him onto it. Chip said that he found Hank "in a much worse condition. I grabbed the defibrillator and went with him as they carried him outside."

At that point, Dr. Dan Hyslop sprinted onto the court, summoned by his sister from the lobby, where he had gone to get their brother a ticket.

Fregoso had helped to lift Hank and recalled that he observed that Hank was breathing as he was moved from the court.

"I told him to take a deep breath and he did," Dr. Shaffer remembered. "His eyes were open at the time."[45]

Per Sturmer was at the front of the stretcher and helped to carry Hank toward the long, narrow corridor that led to the trainers' room. Bo and Terrell trailed behind, followed by Vernell, Derrick, and Charles.

Paul Westhead put a comforting arm around Lucille. She held Paul's hand as they walked away from Hank and those attending to him. Her other hand was raised to her face and it was trembling.

The trainers' room was behind the stands. As they came off the court and approached the corridor, Dr. Shaffer was watching Hank and he "appeared to have deteriorated clinically." The gym's glass exit doors were right in front of them. They had gone less than 70 feet.

"His arm flopped off the stretcher and went limp," Dr. Shaffer said. "At that moment, as I looked down, I knew his heart had stopped."[46]

As they got to the double glass doors, Dr. Hyslop said, "Let's go outside."[47]

Dr. Shaffer yelled at someone to open the door and set him down.

Within five seconds the stretcher crew had set Hank gently on the concrete apron outside the glass doors. Westhead, standing nearby, watched helplessly.

Dr. Shaffer felt for Hank's carotid pulse and found it to be "thready [weak] and barely palpable. He was having intermittent respirations—and within seconds he no longer had a detectable pulse. At that point, I delivered a precordial thump [to the chest] and started CPR," Dr. Shaffer said.[48]

As Dr. Ben Shaffer was giving Hank mouth-to-mouth respiration and pumping his chest, he instructed Chip to get the defibrillator charged and the leads applied. Dr. Shaffer still wasn't getting a pulse. Dr. Dan Hyslop and Chip readied the defibrillator. All were absorbed by the acute medical crisis, struggling to do everything they possibly could to help Hank hold on to life.

Dr. Shaffer ordered that Hank be rolled off the stretcher and onto the concrete so he could get better compressions. At that point, Dr. Hyslop said, "Let's get that thing [the defibrillator] on Hank."

"Rip that shirt off," Dr. Shaffer ordered.

"Hold on, hold on. Come on, Hank, baby. Hold on, hold on. Breathe! Breathe, Hank!" Dr. Shaffer implored, then continued his count of the chest compressions: "One, two, three, four, five. . . give a breath. . . okay.

"Good job, Hank. Keep breathing. . . I'm with you, baby. C'mon!"

As Dr. Shaffer continued with the CPR and mouth-to-mouth, everyone would pause periodically to check for a pulse.

They found none.

After about three minutes of feverish CPR activity, they applied the defibrillator, and it refused to deliver a shock because it thought it detected a heartbeat. Dr. Hyslop soon realized what the problem was—the CPR and chest thumping were fooling the machine into thinking Hank's heart was beating when it was not.

"Get back!" Dr. Hyslop yelled.

Hank's muscular form rose under the force of the 200 joules of current applied to his chest and then fell to the concrete, still. In the background Lucille's anguished scream pierced the early evening.

"No! No! No!" she shrieked in despair. Lawhorn and Derrick moved her away from Hank.

"Hold on," Shaffer urged Hank, as Dr. Hyslop and then Fregoso continued the manual CPR. They still could detect no pulse.

"C'mon, baby!" Dr. Shaffer cried out as Dr. Hyslop prepared to deliver a second shock with the defibrillator, about a minute after the first.

"Hold, on—let me feel," Dr. Shaffer said.

"Have anything?" Dr. Hyslop asked.

"I don't have a pulse," Dr. Shaffer replied.

"O.K., let's go. Give him a breath. Five pulses and a breath," Dr. Hyslop instructed.

"Tilt his head back a little bit. Tilt it back," Dr. Hyslop said.

"One, two, three, four, five. One, two, three, four, five," Dr. Shaffer counted, then pressed his mouth to Hank's lips in an effort to breathe life back into his patient.

Now they could hear a siren growing louder as it approached the grim scene outside Gersten. The paramedics were arriving.

"Stop for a sec. We're going to juice one more time here," Dr. Shaffer advised.

"C'mon, babe," he urged Hank.

"O.K., stop moving him so we can see if he's got a pulse," Dr. Shaffer instructed.

Nothing.

"O.K. Everybody clear," he ordered. This time he sent the maximum charge of 360 joules surging through Hank's heart.

Still nothing.

Dr. Hyslop and Dr. Shaffer continued their manual CPR as the paramedics of Rescue Ambulance 5 of the Los Angeles Fire Department in Westchester made their way to Hank's side.

It was 5:21 p.m., P.S.T.

The paramedics quickly hooked up their own monitor and an intravenous line.

They administered yet another shock to Hank.

Still no pulse.

The paramedics used a long, slim needle to give Hank an injection of lidocaine. The drug elicited no response, either, and the paramedics moved him into the ambulance.

He had been outside on the ground for almost 10 minutes, during most of which there had been no discernible signs of life.

Dr. Shaffer instinctively climbed into the ambulance with his patient and continued to assist the paramedics with CPR. The ambulance pulled away, headed to Daniel Freeman/Marina Mercy Memorial Hospital in Marina del Rey.[49]

As the ambulance left, siren wailing and lights flashing, the others could only stare after it in numb disbelief.

It was 5:34 p.m., P.S.T.

Rescue Ambulance 5 speeded down Loyola Boulevard, carrying within it the lifeless form of the young man who had boasted to all that he was the strongest man alive.

CHAPTER
25

THE REST IS SILENCE

As the ambulance left, WCC Commissioner Mike Gilleran gathered the athletic directors and coaches around him.

"We decided quickly to suspend the tournament and the game," he said. In the stillness of the fast-emptying Gersten Pavilion, Bernie Sandalow announced the decision.[1]

Jamie Sanchez recalled that Gersten emptied out in what "seemed like a matter of seconds. . . . No one was there. It was deadly silent. It was as if time had stood still."[2]

As trainers Tom Fregoso and Chip Schaeffer, who had attended the University of Utah together, made their way back into the nearly empty gym, Fregoso placed a comforting arm around Chip's shoulders and softly told his former classmate that he was "almost certain" Hank was gone.[3]

Dr. Dan Hyslop's sister drove him to to the hospital.

The players had first gone to the small LMU locker room. Then Father Loughran came in and said a prayer, and they moved to the larger trainers' room. "A lot of the parents were gathered there. It was very somber in there," Tom Peabody recalled. Some players left for the hospital to get more information.

"I didn't see that as an option," Tom said. "I thought we might still be going back to play. I asked my brother, Terry, 'Did you see him?' He said, 'Yeah.'"

"How is he?"

"Well, you have to remember, he's young. If anybody's got a chance, it's him."

"When he said that, it was the first time that it occurred to me that he might not make it," Tom said.

Then Terry told Tom, "I had a heart rate, we were doing CPR, and I had a heart rate, and I thought he had overcome it, and then we lost it. Then the paramedics arrived."

Tom said, "We sat there a long time, and Westhead was in and out, and Bruce Woods was with us, and we were talking, and things were quiet in there. My brother at one point said, 'The longer we're in here, the better.'

"Then the phone rang in Chip's office, and Westhead went in to take the call," said Tom. "They closed the door, and it became very, very quiet. When he hung up the phone and he came out, he was shaken. He said, 'Hank,' and he kind of lost it, then he said, 'didn't make it.' Then he turned and walked out. Greg Walker's father was in there with us, and he let out this god-awful scream. My father, who hadn't heard what Westhead said, asked what had happened. I told him Hank had passed away. My father was crying."

Tom left for his room shortly after that. "As loud as that gym had been, as I walked out across the campus, it was the saddest and quietest walk I ever had from that gym back to my apartment. You could see everyone was out. They were out on the balconies out of their windows. Out in the quad. When we walked out of there, there wasn't a sound."[4]

Jamie Sanchez had left the gymnasium, as well, and experienced much the same thing. "It was," he said, "as if a shroud had been draped over the entire campus."[5]

Kristin Ramage had watched as Hank was carried off the court. "I knew something was terribly wrong," she said.

As the stretcher moved off the court, Kristin's hands flew to her face and her fearful eyes brimmed with tears. At precisely that moment a photographer captured her image.

"Hank had an awesome presence about him. He just filled a room even if he was quiet," Kristin recalled. "I couldn't imagine that anything so bad could happen to a 23-year-old," she said. Kristin watched through the window with growing concern as Dr. Shaffer, Fregoso, and Dr. Hyslop worked on Hank.

"I said to everyone, 'Something's very wrong,'" she said. "I called my mom, who was a nurse, and said, 'I think he's dead.' When I got back home, the TV news told me he had died. I burst into tears."[6]

Paul and Cassie Westhead went to the hospital, as did several LMU players and coaches.

Brian Quinn and Barry Zepel were already there, as were most of the reporters who had seen Hank collapse on the court. The small waiting room area outside the emergency room was overflowing with reporters. "I quickly commandeered one of the few phones in the lobby and called the office," said Joe Resnick, who had covered the game for the Associated Press. "I stayed on the phone with an open line, dictating whatever happened back to the AP office."[7]

Chris Myers of ESPN's Los Angeles bureau was dressed casually because he'd been called in from a weekend off. He borrowed a sports coat from another reporter and prepared to do a live remote telecast from the hospital.

"I had been to a movie, *Born on the Fourth of July*, with a friend. After the movie I had checked my messages and found one directing me to go to Gersten Pavilion. It said Hank Gathers had collapsed," Myers recalled. "On our way, I asked my friend, who was in pre-med, a few questions to prepare myself. We got there after [Hank had] been transported, so we went on to Daniel Freeman."[8]

Television crews from all three network affiliates and KTLA, where Hank had served as an intern, soon arrived as well.

Keith Olbermann had been at the Los Angeles Coliseum covering the marathon. When he was told that Hank had collapsed, he left immediately.

The ambulance had arrived at the ER at 5:38 p.m., P.S.T. Despite the frantic efforts to revive him at the scene and throughout the short trip with an injection of lidocaine and three more electric shocks, he was not responsive.[9]

ER nurse Dottie Sukova began to work on Hank immediately. She had no idea who the patient was. Dr. Mason Weiss, a cardiologist who was a colleague of Dr. Hattori's, was on call for Apex. He was in the ER when the paramedics and Dr. Ben Shaffer arrived.

For the better part of an hour, Dr. Weiss and the ER staff worked on the stricken athlete, still in his uniform, lying on the cold steel table. His jersey had been ripped open down the middle of his number 44. The sneakered feet of the 6-foot-7 Hank extended out over the end of the table. He had a plastic intubation tube in his mouth, and he was hooked up to wires and monitors.

"They tried every conceivable thing you could do," Dr. Hyslop said. "Mason went the whole nine yards. They even implanted a pacemaker in him. There was no response. He was gone."[10]

While he worked on Hank, Dr. Weiss instructed the ER staff to try to reach Dr. Hattori.

Dr. Hattori was watching television in the condo in Palm Springs. His friend, Dr. Ron Reichman, was dozing on a couch, while Dr. Michael Greenspun was in the shower. The images that filled the television screen were the shocking footage of Hank Gathers's collapse.

When he saw the footage of Hank being carried from the court, Dr. Hattori immediately dialed the hospital. He was put through to Dr. Weiss almost at once.

Weiss, Hattori recalled, "was clearly shaken up."

Dr. Weiss explained that Hank had been down for about an hour. He was flat-lined, and his pupils were fixed and dilated. Weiss went on to rapidly outline the frantic steps he had taken to revive Hank.

Hank's doctor interrupted.

"Mason, stop—he's dead."

Dr. Weiss and Dr. Hattori spoke for ten to fifteen minutes. Then Dr. Hattori hastily packed and headed back to Los Angeles. He sped along I-10 West with darkness chasing him from behind and a heavy blackness pressing in on him.[11]

After he spoke with Dr. Hattori, Dr. Mason Weiss left the emergency room.

"Mason and I went out together to tell Lucille that Hank was gone," Dr. Hyslop said. "It was an awful, awful thing. Then we allowed her to go in to see him."

Hank, still in his LMU uniform, jersey ripped raggedly open, was on the table. His dark muscular body seemed to glisten under the glaring lights in the cold white room.

"She was grief- stricken and sobbing. It was terrible," Dr. Hyslop said.

"Why, Hank? Why'd you do this to me?" Lucille demanded of her lifeless son in a rising voice.[12]

Had Hank been able to reply, he almost certainly would have said, "I did it for you, Momma. I did it for Aaron and for you. And because I loved to play basketball."

When Pete Priamos got to the hospital, he saw that Lucille and Bo were in the emergency room.

"I looked in and saw them there. I went in. I was very, very shook. I offered my condolences. Then I touched Hank and silently said good-bye to my friend and left," he said.[13]

Brian Quinn had arrived with Lane Bove, and they had been waiting outside.

"I was told to get someone to console the family," he said. "I got Father George Crain, an elderly priest who was there, to go with me. He was at all our games and always sat on the end of the bench. We went in, and the family was still with Hank.

"They were screaming and crying, and we tried to console them. There just wasn't anything we could do. Hank was there on the table on his back—still in his white uniform. He looked so strong. I will never be able to forget that picture," Quinn said.

Then Brian remembered he had left Maureen at the game.

"I tried to reach my wife. She and my other daughter were at church, and I couldn't reach her. Someone, though, from our neighborhood, saw Maureen and took her with them to dinner," he said. "They kept her with them until I returned home and then brought her over."

Maureen, 12 years old, insisted on sleeping with the lights on that night. She would do so for many nights to come.[14]

It fell to Brian Quinn to be the LMU spokesman who faced Chris Myers and the other reporters and photographers assembled outside the hospital's emergency room. His jaw muscles twitching with the strain, he delivered a short statement that Barry Zepel had helped him prepare. His voice as taut as his facial muscles, an obviously shaken Quinn said, "It's a tremendous loss for our university. He was an outstanding young man. We are all going to miss him, and we are truly grateful for the opportunity to be friends. How deeply we will miss him."

Then, speaking personally, Brian added, "We're all better people for having the opportunity to know him and be his friend. We will be praying. We hope you will, too."[15]

Chris Myers prevailed upon Dr. Weiss to do an interview. The startled-looking young physician peered over the large black glasses that were the most prominent feature on his owlish face and said that Hank had "been pronounced dead at 6:55 p.m." Weiss added that all that could have been done had been done, both at Gersten and at the hospital.[16]

Westhead left a prepared statement for Zepel to distribute to the growing crowd of reporters. Zepel personally relayed the coach's feelings: "Words are hard right now. This is the hardest thing I've ever experienced. To be so close to a player and see him fall and for it to be all over. I feel a deep hurt for his family."[17]

Lucille had left the treatment room and returned to the crowded waiting area with Derrick and Charles. Carole Livingston was outside on a pay phone calling Philadelphia. She had run out of the emergency room, yelling theatrically on her way, "He's died. He's died. What are we going to do?"

Livingston told whoever was at the other end of the line what had happened, then screamed again and collapsed to the floor.[18]

A young woman the press could not identify ran out of the building. She was crying as well. It was Vernell Ritchey.

"It can't be. He's just asleep," sobbed Hank's girlfriend, whom he had planned to marry.[19]

Either Derrick or Charles (witnesses' accounts vary) cried out in grief and anger and punched at the Sheetrock wall, putting a hole in it.

By now it was 6:58 p.m., P.S.T.

The players who had gone to the hospital—the group included Chris Knight, Marcus Slater, and Tony Walker—were outside. Dr. Hyslop summoned them in to say good-bye to their teammate.

"I was glad that I was there and able to do that for them. To give them a chance to say good-bye, privately, out of sight," Dr. Hyslop said. "It meant a lot to them. It was very emotional."[20]

Terrell Lowery was among those who saw Hank's body at the hospital. His relationship with Hank was more like that of a brother than a teammate. "I hugged Lucille and tried to comfort her," he said. "Then I said good-bye to my friend. It was hard. Very hard."[21]

Paul and Cassie Westhead also paid their respects to Hank at the hospital. "I will never forget the sight of that young man, still in his uniform and oversized sneakers, lying there. It was so, so tragic," she said.[22]

Later, they returned to Palos Verdes and delivered the news to their neighbors, the Conrads. "Paul [Westhead] took Hank's death hard—very hard. It affected him deeply," Kay Conrad said. Paul Conrad retreated to his studio where he began to express his grief in his own way.[23]

Outside Daniel Freeman, the players took out their frustrations, dismay, and fear on some flower urns. They turned them over, smashing the terra cotta and littering the ground with shards.

In a heap on the asphalt amid the rubble lay Chris Knight, wracked with sobs. Chris had served as Hank's back-up, and he was the player who had replaced Hank when he fainted in December. Like all back-up players, he wanted more playing time. Quite naturally, he was always silently praying for more. Now he felt that his selfish wishes were, in some way, responsible for Hank's death. The others attempted to assure him he was blameless. The young man, so slender that Hank called him "Blade," was inconsolable.[24]

His guilt didn't make sense to anyone else. But, then, none of what they had just witnessed, however, made any sense. Twenty-three-year-old athletes aren't supposed to die—especially not someone they all saw as the strongest man in the world. It was incomprehensible, and the players were overwhelmed by the enormity of what it meant: Their leader, Hank, the guy with the heart of a lion, wasn't coming back. No more jokes. No more laughter. No more arguments. No more slam dunks that rattled the rafters.

They would, in the next week, have to deal with that undeniable fact and work their way through it. They would not be permitted the luxury of doing so in private. The death of one of the country's top basketball players was news, and the dramatic and highly visible manner of his demise made it a major story.

Although the game was not televised, it was recorded, and ESPN made the video available to other networks. It quickly made its way to the nation's airwaves, allowing viewers to watch Hank's death throes from the comfort of their own living rooms. They watched as his scantily clad body jerked and twitched. They watched as his lifeless arm fell to his side as he took his last breaths on that stretcher. Hank Gathers died in public, and his death was the lead story from coast to coast that Sunday night. The tape of his last moments was replayed thousands of times.

In fact, ESPN debated what it should do before airing and releasing the footage that freelancer Carter Trigg had shot. Sportscaster Chris Berman described the internal debate and the ultimate decision by the cable sports network to air the graphic and disturbing tape. "A picture tells a lot, so you have to be careful what you show. You don't want to do a disservice to the family. Maybe, down the line, some high school or college kid might have a condition checked. That would be a plus," he said of the network's thinking.[25]

The ESPN 8:30 p.m. telecast of Sports Center that night found the usually bombastic Berman subdued and warning, as he introduced the footage, "If you're a little squeamish, you might not want to watch this."[26]

In Philadelphia, Marva Crump and her son, Aaron, were snuggled together in her bed.

"Hank had a picture of Aaron on his TV at home so that it was the first thing he saw when he woke up. Hank couldn't wait to get out of school to do more for him," Bo said.

It was nearly 10:30 p.m. in Philly and way past Aaron's normal bedtime, but he had wanted to see how Hank had done, and Marva had allowed him to stay up to watch the ESPN show. "Hank was Aaron's hero. He'd see him on TV and he'd just get so excited," she said.[27]

In growing horror, she and Aaron clung to each other as Berman played the tape of Hank's collapse and the violent seizures. Aaron "just cried all night," Marva said. "He just lay in my lap and cried. He didn't fall asleep until 4 a.m. He just kept asking, over and over, 'Why did God take my daddy from me?'

"What do you say to that?"[28]

David Spencer had also been at the hospital and had called Stan Morrison as soon as he got there. "I told him it didn't look good. I said I'd call back when I knew more," Spence said.[29]

"David called me at home and told me Hank was gone," Morrison said. "When David told me the circumstances—how Hank had collapsed after the slam dunk, I couldn't help but remember that, when Hank was with me at USC, I had told him, 'If you are going to go for the basket, go for it like it's the last thing you are ever going to do on this Earth.'"

Now, as those words, intended to motivate a freshman, came back to his former coach, Morrison paused to consider the irony. Then he pulled himself together, picked up the phone, and called Marva in Philadelphia.[30]

Darrell Gates was awakened by a jangling phone.

"It was my friend Walt calling. He was crying and carrying on about Hank. He was so upset I couldn't make much sense out of what he was saying," Heat said. "He kept saying, 'Hank is dead.' I thought I must be dreaming. I thought I was having a nightmare.

"I called Father Dave, right away. He told me to get dressed and come right over. "When I got there, Father Dave told me what had happened. I couldn't believe it," Heat said.

But this nightmare was real.

"The next day, we left by plane for California together," he said.[31]

Father Dave took Hank's death especially hard.

Derrick had called him at around 9:25, E.S.T., to say that Hank didn't have a pulse.

"He called me from the emergency room," Father Hagan told reporters. "I was very, very surprised. I could only hope that he was still alive. We all prayed."[32]

Hank's death, said Father McNamee, "took a heavy toll" on Father Hagan. "It was a heartbreak from which he never recovered."[33]

Yank had been at a Public League game and returned home to find his phone ringing.

The caller told him that Hank had collapsed and was gravely ill. "About 20 minutes later, the phone rang again, and I learned he had passed," Hank's high school coach said. "After that, the phone never stopped ringing. I took calls from all over the country seeking quotes and information on Hank.

"I didn't get any sleep, and the next day I went to school and entered my office above the gymnasium. I just broke down completely. It just overwhelmed me that Hank was gone. My principal stopped by and told me Sandra Beech would take over all my classes for me for the next two weeks. After that, all I did was take calls from 8:30 to 5 each day. The phone never stopped ringing."[34]

Tommy Lewis had been in the stands when Hank collapsed. His Pepperdine team was slated to play in the second game of the day.

"I usually spent time in the locker room, preparing with some meditation, but my mom had come to see me play, and I went out to sit with her," he said.

When Hank collapsed, Tom said, "it was one of the strangest things I'd ever experienced. The place went from thousands screaming and cheering and celebrating to complete silence. It was so quiet, you could hear your heart beating. I had a feeling of complete helplessness as I watched Hank go into convulsions. There was a horrifying feeling in that place. Everyone was just numb."

After the announcement that the tournament had been suspended, Tom and his mother walked outside. They didn't know then what had happened to Hank.

"It was a sparkling clear day. As we walked out of the gymnasium, there was one cloud in the sky. It was a rain cloud, as angry and dark as it could be, blocking the sun. It was very spooky. Like the fog rolling in is scary," he said. "We were numb. It represented something bad had happened. It was warm outside, but we both shivered."[35]

In Albany, snow still clung in patches to the ground outside the Knickerbocker Arena where La Salle was dispatching Siena with ease.

"A buzzing started in the arena," Doug Overton said. "We were up by about 20 points and you could hear the buzz from the court."

The news that Hank was gone had reached Albany and was passed down to the Explorers' bench.

"Lionel heard it on the bench and burst into tears. He buried his head in a towel and just cried. When I heard what had happened, I just ran off the court. I couldn't go on," Doug said. "People all around the arena were crying. It was just awful."[36]

It was early Sunday evening when Hank died on the West Coast. The Monday morning papers throughout the country devoted considerable space—with photos, usually of his prostrate form—to the story.

Heat and Father Dave, en route to California, had to make a connection at Chicago's O'Hare Airport. "I saw the papers all had a picture of Hank on the front page," Father Hagan said. Only then did the priest realize the breadth and scope of the story.

26

THE WORD GOES FORTH

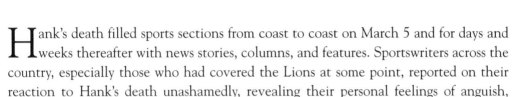

Hank's death filled sports sections from coast to coast on March 5 and for days and weeks thereafter with news stories, columns, and features. Sportswriters across the country, especially those who had covered the Lions at some point, reported on their reaction to Hank's death unashamedly, revealing their personal feelings of anguish, grief, and loss. At KTLA in Los Angeles, it fell to Ed Arnold to report the death of the station's former intern that Sunday.

"I was in the conference room at KTLA when the call came in that he had died," Ed said. "I just broke down." A consummate professional with a wide following in Los Angeles, Arnold tried to do his job during that evening's newscast. "I just couldn't get through it," he said. "I tried, but I couldn't do it."

In full view of his audience, under the glare of the lights, in front of the unblinking cameras, Ed Arnold broke into wracking sobs as he tried to tell viewers about the death of his intern and friend, Hank Gathers. "It was the only time that I ever broke down on the air," Arnold said. "It was tough. I loved Hank."[1]

Finally, mercifully, the camera cut away.

At his home home in Hermosa Beach, Nick Schneider, LMU's ball boy, learned of Hank's death while watching the Lakers' game on television.[2] "I cried for hours and hours," he recalled.

In the Los Angeles area the story was front-page news, as well as sports news.

One of the many photographs that filled the papers showed a distraught Kristin Ramage, hands to her face, eyes brimming with tears, as Hank was carried off the court. Her image, frozen in time, captures the feeling of fear and helplessness that nearly everyone in the gym had felt as they watched Hank leave the court at Gersten Pavilion for the last time.

The Los Angeles Times considered it "our story," according to John Cherwa, who was the associate sports editor at the time. He was determined to give readers the most complete coverage possible. The paper's daily circulation at the time was 1.1 million.

"On Sunday night, when the call came in around six, I called everyone in to work the story," recalled Cherwa. "For all intents and purposes, it was the first time that you got to see an athlete die on TV. It may have happened once or twice before in football, but they are all covered up in helmets and pads, and you can't really see anything of the person. When Hank went down on that court, it was a very public death in full view of everyone there. He was visible for all to see," Cherwa said.

Cherwa's team of reporters would explore every aspect and angle of the story. Like the rest of the *LA Times*, the sports section is a very serious section; because the area has so many pro teams and top college teams, it even had a team of investigative reporters.

"This," Cherwa said, "was a very serious story. . . a story cloaked in a mystery. In general, a sports section is not very good at matching up interests of people with what they want to read about. We felt we had a responsibility to write about things that people don't want to read about. This was an important story. If you took this plot, it could have been a mystery novel.

"You had this largely mythical Hank and Bo friendship stuff—which wasn't really true at all. The Rosen projects' life he'd had to overcome. There was Hank's heart problem and the foreshadowing of a possible doomsday ending. The commitment he'd made to his family to help them. It had all the elements of a major story. We decided we'd run with it and produce a story a day."

The sports reporters met the next day at Cherwa's house "and decided to work around the clock on it. It was our story, and I was determined we weren't going to be beaten on it," he said.[3]

Hank Gathers and LMU, which only a few short years before had merited one reporter and a few column inches grudgingly allotted to reporting by Alan Drooz, now became a major focus of one of the nation's leading daily newspapers. Hank Gathers's life, death, medical history, family history, and every aspect of his existence were to be scrutinized and examined under a microscope by the team of reporters, including investigative reporters, that Cherwa assembled. Al Drooz was now joined by Elliot Almond, an investigative sports reporter, who would cover the medical angle. Maryann Hudson, a feature writer in the sports department, would cover the family angle and then the legal ramifications of Hank's death. Danny Robbins, another investigative sports reporter, and Jim Hodges were among the reporters charged with ferreting out every bit of information about "the mystery." The stories they produced would be given prominent placement in the *Los Angeles Times* in the weeks after Hank's death.

The Daily Breeze, in Torrance, Calif., while considerably smaller in circulation, was the paper that considered Loyola Marymount University to be its turf. The paper gave the Gathers story wide coverage from the outset. The March 5 edition carried a front-page banner headline: "LMU Star Player Collapses, Dies." Accompanying the story was a large photo of Hank. Chris Long, who had covered LMU and Hank for the paper, provided extensive coverage, along with staff reporters Eric Stephens, Jennifer Lewis, and others. Columnist Mike Waldner devoted considerable space to the story, as well.

Waldner's column on March 5 ran alongside a photo by Bruce Hazelton that was shot as Hank was struggling to rise from the court. Dr. Ben Shaffer and trainer Chip Schaeffer are treating Hank. Westhead, concern on his face, is looking at Hank. Carole Livingston is bending over and reaching toward her nephew. Printed in color, it was prominently displayed on the sports front, which bore another banner headline: "Death Silences Lion's Roar."

Also on the page was a photo of Hank's last shot. The color picture, of a slam dunk by a vital, athletic player that rattled the backboard and brought the crowd to its feet, was juxtaposed with the larger one of a prostrate young man, confused, frightened, and struggling to rise with only seconds to live.

Waldner's column, which ran down the left-hand side of the page column, was entitled, "Memories of a Kind Lion," and it began:

"I want to remember Hank Gathers with the big smile on his face and the friendly "Hi, howyadoing?" greeting.

I want to remember Hank Gathers rattling the entire building with one of his monster slam dunks. . . .

I will never forget watching Gathers crumble to the court early Sunday evening at Loyola Marymount University during a meaningless game against the University of Portland.

I will never forget watching Gathers go into convulsions on the floor.

I will never forget watching the medical people trying to save his life on the cold concrete slab outside Gersten Pavilion."[4]

The Los Angeles Times'coverage began with a front-page color photo taken by Gary Friedman that covered nearly half the area above the fold. It shows Hank from a side view, his head cradled gently by Dr. Ben Shaffer while trainers Chip Schaefer and Tom Fregoso kneel alongside. It was snapped seconds after Hank fell. Carole Livingston is hovering above them.

Beneath it was the news story by Jim Hodges, "Gathers, Loyola Basketball Star, Collapses, Dies," with a list of other stories in the sports section. There, readers found another, larger photo of Hank on his back on the court, his eyes open and staring, as

Portland's Eric Mobley spontaneously grasps Hank's left hand to help him up. Hank's right arm is extended behind him. The caption describes him as semiconscious. It is a gripping image.

A smaller, poignant photo shows Lucille in near collapse, supported by an unidentified white male. His eyes are wide and his mouth agape as he comforts Hank's distraught mother. It is David Spencer, the man who first recruited Hank to sunny California.

Mike Downey's column in the *Los Angeles Times* on March 5 appeared just to the left of the photo of Spence and Lucille.

On this day, Downey, who had spoken at length with Hank in December, while he was still recovering from the first fainting episode, wrote with passion and from his heart. Hank Gathers, he recalled, "Was dying to play. Dying to play."

Downey wrote of Hank's aspirations to become a sportscaster and his willingness to learn the trade. How Hank, back on court, had returned almost to his old form. Then Downey graphically described what he had witnessed at Gersten the day before, how "a young man, a handsome and articulate young man, a gifted and engaging young man, an indecently unlucky young man, has passed away." After quoting Dr. Mason Weiss, Downey concluded: "Hank Gathers gone. Taken away by the unforgiving beeping of a monitor, by the uneven beating of a heart. I can still see him falling, falling, falling. Tell me he's going to be O.K. Tell me they can run more tests. Tell me anything at all, anything except the terrible thing you keep telling me."[5]

Alan Drooz had to write about Hank for the paper. It was his job and he would do it and do it well. But it would never, ever, be just a story for Alan. The scene at Gersten on March 4, 1990, would never leave his mind. Its gruesome image was burned into the talented writer's psyche. The man who had writhed in spasms on the hardwood was a player Drooz had come to know and to like. Hank was a player whom Alan covered for three years and more. He had interviewed Hank hundreds of times during those three Cinderella seasons.

On the night Hank died, Drooz filed the story of Hank's last game. It was written in the same crisp, accurate style that he had used for three seasons to cover LMU and Hank Gathers. He reported on the events and the aftermath professionally and objectively. Only in the last paragraph, in which he described the scene at Gersten as horrifying, did he reveal his feelings. Like so many others, Alan Drooz would miss Hank deeply.[6]

The extensive *Los Angeles Times* coverage included a long article by Maryann Hudson that featured quotes from Hank's former coaches: Stan Morrison, whom she had interviewed, along with Rich Yankowitz and Sonny Hill in Philadelphia.[7] Her coverage would continue until the young USC graduate began to complain that Hank "felt like he'd become my beat."[8] Accompanying her story was Gary Friedman's shot of Kristin Ramage.

Beneath the photo of Kristin ran a Jim Lindgren article, accompanied by a picture of Hank's final basket.[9] It catches him with his hands gripping the rim and bending it downward, his powerful biceps bulging. His action had prompted Kristin to cheer and bounce, pom-poms thrust in the air.

In Frank Deford's short-lived tabloid devoted exclusively to sports, *The National*, Steve Lowery found himself reliving the death of someone else 10 years earlier. The first death was so troubling to Lowery that he'd never discussed it, even with his wife. He had watched helplessly from the bank as a boy drowned in the icy waters of California's Merced River. Hank's death, which Lowery had seen on TV, forced him to face some hard questions. He did so in print, in a column read by hundreds of thousands of readers.

Lowery had been haunted by the drowning boy and whether he might have been able to save him.

"But weighing down just as heavily today," Lowery wrote, "is the knowledge that no one could have done anything for Hank Gathers. The knowledge that someone so strong, so capable, was so helpless frightens and outrages me."

He concluded his column with, "Maybe we're just durable creatures, or maybe we just have durable masks. I wore one for 10 years. That is, until Hank Gathers died and proved that life may be for the living, but that it hangs by the thinnest of threads."[10]

In the *Pasadena Star News*, a suburban Los Angeles paper, Jeff Parenti began his column with, "I watched a man die Sunday night." Describing the scene he'd witnessed at Gersten, he added, "I wish I hadn't gone."

Parenti wrote further, "I met Hank Gathers—interviewed him—a couple of times when I was a student at San Diego State. Great guy. Friendly. I've watched with awe as he clobbered college basketball defenses. Now I've watched him die."

A friend who attended the game with Parenti had cried that night, Parenti said, adding, "I haven't cried like my friend, but I haven't felt right. Maybe I won't feel right until I understand why. Maybe I will never feel right, not about this. No answer is good enough."[11]

Hank Gathers was mourned on the serene and subdued leafy campus in Westchester, Calif., and a continent away, in the mean and gritty streets of North Philly. In a place where dreams go to die, Hank's death was felt especially hard.

Temple coach John Chaney, whose Owls had just defeated Duquesne University in Pittsburg, Pa., and were fighting for an NCAA bid, was in the dressing room when he learned of Hank's death. The emotional coach wept openly as he spoke of Hank: "This basketball game meant nothing tonight. . . . The kid was a soldier for a lot of kids, and a champion for a lot of causes.

"How unfair. Somewhere, I know Hank Gathers has a smile on his face, because [playing basketball is] really where he wanted to be."

Clayton Adams, who had played with Hank at St. Elizabeth's, said that never before had he been told that a friend of his had died. "I didn't want to believe it," he said. "Hank was a big influence on me. He was always talking to me about keeping my head on straight, no matter what was happening around me, on the court and off. He was as terrific a person as you would ever want to meet. Always had time for people. A great attitude about life, a funny guy, the kind of person who you enjoyed being around, because he made you feel good about life. It's heartbreaking for the city of Philadelphia. I just wish the people who enjoyed watching Hank play, at Dobbins, on TV, at St. Joe's, or against La Salle, could have met him to know the person. Because he was even more enjoyable to know than he was to watch as a basketball player."[12]

In an unusual move the *Philadelphia Inquirer* devoted an editorial to Hank's passing, writing, "Nothing can alleviate the sense of tragedy. Growing up in the rough Raymond Rosen Public Housing Project in North Philadelphia, Mr. Gathers was filled with [the] dreams of all those who manage through athletics to escape the poverty that destroys some and stifles the hopes of so many. He was on the verge of signing with the pros and winning a measure of security for himself and his family."

Quoting Sonny Hill, the editorial continued, "'He never forgot from whence he came and always took time to reach back to the youngsters in his community to offer positive thoughts about life.'"

The editorial concluded, "You don't have to be poor or black to feel saddened. Just human."[13]

CHAPTER
27

THOSE LEFT BEHIND

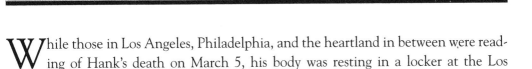

While those in Los Angeles, Philadelphia, and the heartland in between were reading of Hank's death on March 5, his body was resting in a locker at the Los Angeles County Medical Examiner-Coroner's Office, awaiting an autopsy.

Derrick and the other members of the Gathers family were closeted in their suite at the Hilton Hotel with friends and their palpable sorrow. Their grief was deep and real. Their anger, confusion, and dismay at the prospect of life without Hank would lead them to make a quick decision. Derrick, the more volatile son, would now become titular head of the family.

Derrick had accompanied his more athletically and academically talented brother to California and had enjoyed the ride. He'd relished the companionship of his brother's friends. He'd partied and played ball with the NBA stars Hank knew. Derrick had basked, too, in the reflected glory of the nation's leading scorer and rebounder, someone who was an All-American and would be a first-round draft pick. Hank had been generous with his brother.

"Whatever Hank had, Derrick had," Pete Priamos observed. "Hank made sure Derrick was taken care of."[1] Derrick had spent five years on the West Coast, close to his older brother. He had spent two years in junior colleges and was in his final year of eligibility at Cal State-Northridge. He had produced impressive stats on the court there. Yet after five years, he still lacked the academic credits he needed for a diploma.[2]

Hank's death presented a very real problem for Derrick: He had no college degree and lacked the talent to play professional basketball. Soon school would be over, and, lacking further eligibility, he would need a place to live. He had no job and no prospects in that regard.

Like Lucille and other members of the extended Gathers family, Derrick assumed his brother would land a fat NBA contract, and that would be the end of all their economic problems. They would share in his good fortune. He'd promised them that, and Hank was a man of his word. When he died on the stretcher as he was carried from the court at Gersten Pavilion, so did the dream of ending the family's poverty.

As the reality of the family's situation sank in, Derrick's grief competed for attention with another emotion, one that usually accompanies grief. He was angry, and the volatility that he had displayed with little provocation took command.

This was not the way it was supposed to end. This was not the way Hank had promised it would be. Derrick was now the head of the family. He would find a way. On the day after his brother's death, Derrick visited Los Angeles attorney Leonard Armato's offices. With him was Bo Kimble, who would be using David Spencer, now with Armato's firm, as his agent for negotiations after the NBA draft. Armato arranged for Derrick to meet with another attorney with offices in the building.

After the initial meeting that day, Derrick had second thoughts about using an attorney that Bo's representative had recommended. Derrick wanted someone whose loyalty to the Gathers family came first.[3] At Hank's condo later that evening, Derrick, Al Gersten, and Jim Hill, the sports anchor at CBS's Los Angeles affiliate, were discussing the options. Hill was emphatic that the Gathers family should proceed with a lawsuit. Derrick wasn't sure who the lawyer should be.[4]

"He wasn't comfortable using Bo's attorney," said Al Gersten. "So I said, 'I know a good attorney. Bruce Fagel.'"[5] Gersten quickly made the arrangements for Derrick to meet with the well-known Beverly Hills malpractice attorney on Wednesday.

Westhead and the team faced the press on Monday in a hastily arranged press conference. About 100 reporters, as well as sound and camera people, were at LMU's auxiliary gym when the 11 a.m. session began. Father Loughran, Westhead, Brian Quinn, and some players sat on a temporary podium as incredibly bright sunlight streamed in, but it did nothing to lighten the mood.

The scene was tense, as the players and officials tried to put into words what they were feeling and respond to reporters' questions. Quinn's eyes were red and moist throughout. Westhead was somber and direct as he spoke to the press from prepared notes: "Hank was an incredible life force. We went to him for everything—for rebounds, for points, for life. There was never anything dull about Hank Gathers. He especially attracted and was attracted to little kids. Little kids instinctively know the good from the bad."[6]

Asked by a reporter about blame in Hank's death, Westhead replied, "Blame? I only have grief and sorrow."

Most players wore dark glasses to conceal their red-rimmed eyes and the tears that wouldn't stop flowing—no matter how hard they tried to compose themselves. Bo broke down as he tried to speak. "We were like brothers, we were so close. We overcame so many obstacles. I know Hank would want us—his teammates—to be strong and go on," he said, gulping for air to compose himself.

Bo said he'd been nearby when Hank collapsed and had been one of the first to reach his side. "He was fighting it, whatever it was," he sobbed. "That was Hank, always fighting."[7]

When Bo spotted Ed Arnold among the reporters, he embraced the man who had taken him and Hank on as interns. They clung tightly together, oblivious of the crowd and cameras, as they tried to console one another.

Terrell Lowery, in a warm-up suit and baseball cap, dabbed at his eyes with a handkerchief as he told a reporter in subdued, almost incredulous, tones, "He was our guy. He was it for us. We thought he was invincible."[8]

Jeff Fryer never removed his dark glasses as he explained, through sniffles and sobs, that he "just couldn't understand how someone that strong could have died so suddenly."[9] And, Fryer recalled, "Before the game, in the locker room, Hank said, 'I feel as strong as ever.'"[10]

Bo Kimble fought stoically through the news conference. Red-eyed and straining to maintain his composure, he concluded by saying, "This is the hardest time I have ever had in my life. I lost a great friend. There will always be a piece of Hank with me."[11]

As the emotion-charged press conference wound mercifully down, a reporter asked Paul to characterize how the team was handling Hank's death. The coach reported that he'd met with the team before the press conference. "There was just a great deal of quietness that took place," he said. Adding, "Concerning Hank, there was no sharing of feelings, because as I said to them, we who were with him need not talk about him. We all shared that every day."[12]

University officials quickly arranged a memorial mass and service for Hank. It was scheduled for Tuesday, March 6, and was to be held at Gersten Pavilion. The campus chapel was far too small to accommodate the crowd that was expected.

On Tuesday, so many mourners formed a long, silent line—it stretched all the way back onto the 80th Street entrance to the campus, a distance of about 500 yards—that they taxed the capacity of Gersten Pavilion. An estimated 5,200 people gained admittance for the service. They received a small mass card with a smiling Hank on one side and an inspirational passage on the reverse. Under Hank's picture was printed simply, "In loving memory of Hank Gathers," followed by the dates that represented his short life span: "February 11, 1967-March 4, 1990."

A raised altar had been erected on the court where Hank had played his last game only a few days before. The closed silver casket containing Hank's body was in front of the altar, a spray of flowers on top. The shroud that Jamie Sanchez had described as hanging over the campus hung heavily over the crowd in Gersten.

The mournful pealing of low chimes drifted toward the gymnasium from the chapel's bell tower at the other end of Loyola Boulevard as the noon service began.

Hank's mother, brothers, and aunt, along with the team and the coaches, entered last and were seated just in front of the casket. Nearly everyone who attended was weeping.

Father Loughran performed the mass, and then the service began with a short eulogy by Father Thomas Higgins, who attempted to explain the inexplicable in a comforting way.

"I once told Hank, 'You're the only person I know who is funnier than me,'" Father Higgins said.

"Definitely, Father," had been Hank's reply.[13]

Higgins asked, "Why did Hank have to die? Our books don't have the answers. Why did Hank live? Your presence here answers that."[14]

Reworking a line from Shakespeare, Higgins said, "What a piece of work was Hank. . . . In action so like an angel. Except at the foul line." That drew some relieved chuckles.

In conclusion, Higgins said of Hank, "He spoke from the heart, with a twinkle in his eye, the leader of the team—with the heart of a lion. I loved how he loved himself. He died doing what he loved most. Maybe God needed a power forward in heaven."[15]

Hank's former roommate, Tom Peabody, read a prayer. As he approached the podium, he paused at Hank's coffin and, ever so gently, touched it.

Struggling with his emotions, Tom read the handwritten prayer. It included this sincere petition: "For the kids Hank touched, may they learn from his death. . . not to be afraid, to never give up." As they watched their tough-as-nails teammate struggle valiantly through his tears and emotions to honor their friend, the rest of the team wept openly and unashamedly.

Olivia La Bouff, who had tutored Hank during his time at LMU, was to share the reading of the prayer with Peabody. Sensing his distress, she stepped in to complete it herself when he was unable to continue.

Brian Quinn read a passage from the Book of Wisdom: "He that lived among us is taken."

After communion, Derrick and Charles placed a picture of Hank and his number 44 uniform jersey next to the casket.[16]

The music for the service included the heart-wrenching "On Eagles' Wings," and then "Amazing Grace" and "We Will Rise Again." The recessional gospel hymn was Andraé

Crouch's "Soon and Very Soon." Soloist Rodrick Hines concluded with the words "Hallelujah, Hallelujah, We're going to see the King."[17]

Few were able to get through any verse of any of the hymns without sobbing. Sorrow hung heavy in the stillness.

Chris Myers, the ESPN journalist, was among those so overcome that he "had to leave the room. I was just so emotionally overwhelmed by it all," he said, revealing the very human side of the press that was evident throughout the service.[18]

Paul Westhead approached the podium and faced the audience. His face and manner were serious as he surveyed the people assembled to honor Hank's memory. He stood quietly for several seconds as he composed himself. Then he spoke with a sad smile on his face. His first words were "Welcome to Hank's House."

Paul Westhead is an eloquent and accomplished speaker, and on this day, when asked to address a crowd about someone whom he genuinely loved and cared for, he did not fail. As difficult as the task was for him, he delivered an emotional and heartfelt address that moved everyone who heard it.

"The paint was his domain. Hank with the ball in the paint was money in the bank. He was 'Hank the Bank,'" said Paul, intoning his nickname for Hank one last time. Paul then reflected on the last acts Hank had performed on this earth. "The next to last thing he did was a thunderous slam dunk, in the paint. In the bank. The last thing he did was to acknowledge the pass, to slap a teammate's hand, an athlete's thank-you," he said.

Quoting Macbeth, he said, "Nothing he did became him like the leaving of him."[19]

Bo Kimble slowly made his way to the microphone.

Taking a deep breath, he began softly and eloquently: "It's so difficult being here, speaking of my beloved friend and brother. You never know how much they mean to you until they're gone. . . . We came from the streets of Philadelphia, and there were a lot of tough times. A lot of people doubted Hank would make it. Hey, he made it."

Bo then paused to look up at the vast throng that filled the gymnasium and made a spontaneous request.

"I asked them all for 'one last applause for Hank—here in his house,'" he said.[20]

Bo stepped back a few feet and began to clap his hands together. Taking its cue, the audience rose to its feet, uncertainly at first, and slowly joined him. The applause grew as everyone stood.

And cheered.

And cried.

In the very gymnasium where he had starred for three sensational seasons, on the very same court where his last thunderous dunk had shaken the rim only a few scant yards from where his shimmering casket now sat, 5,200 cheering, sobbing, applauding, foot-stomping people rose as one to pay a final tribute to Hank Gathers. They cheered and they cried. And they cried and cheered some more, rattling the rafters in homage to an athlete, as fans have done for centuries. As he'd done so many times before, Hank Gathers brought down the house. The applause continued unabated for two full, tension-relieving minutes.

Stan Morrison and Tommy Lewis were there. So was the entire Pepperdine University team, Pooh Richardson, and a number of college and professional players. All there to pay their respects to a warrior, the one with the heart of a lion.

Few in the crowd recognized Dr. Ben Shaffer, the man who had tried to breathe life into Hank as he struggled to save him.

After Bo's pressure-relieving moment, Father Dave Hagan rose to speak. He was not on the program that the university had distributed but had insisted on having a role in the service. Calling Hank by his given name, as he was wont to do, Father Dave said that Eric should "be awarded a degree by this university." Father Hagan also suggested that LMU establish a memorial fund for the family he left behind. "He broke his body for this university, and I hope the university will break its body for him," the priest said.

The Jesuit community, including Father Loughran, sat impassively as Father Dave turned his back to the audience and addressed the priests seated behind him, brashly preaching to them from the podium.

"I hope one day that this place will say up here, 'Hank's House,'" he said as he pointed to the far wall. Again the crowd broke into applause.

Finally, he said of his departed friend, "Coming out here was a miracle for Hank. God bless you, Hank."[21]

After the service, the players and family left the gymnasium and blinked as they emerged in the California sunshine. Lucille, a dazed look on her face, leaned heavily on Bo as she moved woodenly and slowly through the crowd to a waiting car from the Callanan Funeral Home.

As Derrick emerged, a reporter asked him why Hank didn't stop playing basketball if he knew he was in danger. In a rare, candid, and unguarded moment, as tears streamed in shiny rivulets down his dark cheeks, Derrick answered: "Only God could stop my brother from playing basketball."[22]

After the service, Dr. Ben Shaffer approached Lucille to "offer my condolences and to explain that we tried to save her son, [to say] how sorry I was for her loss," he said. "She looked at me and said, 'You guys killed my baby.'"[23]

Stung and hurt by the rebuke, he quickly backed away.

Dr. Shaffer wasn't the only physician to face the wrathful judgment of Hank's family and friends. Dr. Hattori and Dr. Mellman had both tried to reach the family. That night they called on the Gathers family in person at Hank's apartment. When Dr. Hattori identified himself as the doctor who had been treating Hank, "Derrick became very upset," recalled Bruce Woods, who was there.

It was Terrell Lowery, though, who began yelling and hollering at Dr. Hattori. "I thought he was going to beat the shit out of Hattori," Bruce recalled. Finally, Derrick and Bo restrained the angry and distraught Lowery and calmed him down. The doctors left without talking to the family.[24]

The following day, the *Los Angeles Times* carried an article that quoted an "unnamed cardiologist" as saying that Hank had been told not to play but insisted on doing so. The article also cited the anonymous source as saying that Hank had missed his testing appointments and may have ignored orders to take his medicine. The story and related articles discussing Hank's medical condition and the care he'd received raised more questions than they answered.[25]

The university announced that it had established a memorial fund to aid Hank's family, as Father Dave Hagan had suggested. Contributions began to pour in.

Derrick kept his appointment with attorney Bruce Fagel that morning. Fagel was a highly respected plaintiff's attorney and had won a number of large, well-publicized verdicts in a series of malpractice suits. He was considered a top litigator, known for his no-holds-barred style. He was also a licensed physician.

The vanity plate on his 1989 Lincoln read JUGULAR.

He was, Derrick decided, perfect.

On Thursday, Hank's body was loaded aboard a plane for the US Airways flight home to Philadelphia, arriving at 8:10 p.m. Waiting at the terminal were Yank and Ed Magliocci from Dobbins, who had sent Hank off only five years earlier. Hank's coffin was collected by the Keene and Carney Funeral Home, where it would remain until the viewing on Sunday.

On Friday, Dobbins Vo-Tech held a memorial service. The gymnasium, school officials announced, would be known for evermore as "Hank's Place," in his honor.

In Los Angeles the *Los Angeles Times* reported on Friday that Father Loughran was "comfortable with the way the University had handled things" with regard to Hank's care. Father Loughran pointed to the letter from Dr. Mellman clearing Hank to play and asked, "How can we possibly be liable?"[26]

When Fagel read what Father Loughran had said, the lawyer responded without even consulting his clients back in Philadelphia. He summoned reporters to his plush Beverly Hills office and said he had been retained to represent the Gathers family. He named

Lucille, Derrick, Charles, and Carole Livingston as his clients and said he would be bringing a lawsuit on their behalf.[27]

Many found the timing of the announcement shocking. Hank had not yet been buried, and the family was announcing a lawsuit. Even Father Dave was nonplussed. "I thought he was going to wait until Tuesday," he said of Fagel, then added, "I guess it was all the Hank bashing" in the *Los Angeles Times's* story.

Fagel, his designer suit freshly pressed and his salon-styled gray locks shining under the camera lights, said he had a number of targets in his sights. The most serious allegation was that someone in the athletic department had requested a reduction in Hank's medication because it was affecting his play. Fagel also questioned the treatment administered by the physicians attending Hank after he collapsed. He added that, as a former emergency room doctor himself, he was concerned about the care Hank had received. Further, Fagel claimed, the family members present that day had suffered emotional distress.[28]

Other lawyers following the case said later that they were dismayed that Fagel would say such things before he even filed his suit.

"That press conference was what transformed Lucille Gathers from an object of sympathy to a person who was seen to be an unfeeling, insensitive, money-hungry woman," Maryann Hudson said. "She had lost her son. Nothing will ever change that or the hurt she felt. But she lost public support when Fagel announced the lawsuit before the funeral had even been held. It wasn't fair to her and she didn't authorize it, but it colored the way she would be viewed from then on."[29]

In Los Angeles, contributions to the memorial fund at Security Pacific National Bank stopped abruptly. A number of donors asked that their checks be torn up.

Emmanuel Institutional Baptist Church was a few blocks from the Raymond Rosen Homes. It was where Lucille worshipped and where Hank's funeral would be held.

On Sunday, thousands of mourners, as many as 5,000, by one estimate, waited patiently in a slow-moving line for the viewing of Hank's body at the church. It was an unusually warm day for March, and the crowded church was sweltering. Every five minutes, from nine until noon, the ushers allowed in a new group of mourners to view Hank's body.

His funeral was finally held on Monday, eight days after his death.

The church is a castle-like structure with gray turrets looming above the gloomy neighborhood of row houses, most of which are boarded up. The streets are filled with litter and debris. Despair and destruction are everywhere you look, in the facades of the burned-out buildings and on the faces of the residents.

For this day, when media attention would be focused on the neighborhood, the city had dispatched sanitation trucks to clean it up. For Hank's funeral, the neighborhood would look its best. It was a valiant effort, but no amount of scrubbing could ever remove the gloom from that place.

While the crowd of mourners made its way into the church for the service, Hank's teammates waited aboard a bus for several hours on the street outside. Hank's relatives arrived in limousines provided by Al Gersten.[30]

Marva watched from across the street as Aaron walked with the Gathers family into the service. He was wearing a tuxedo. He had had little to say since Hank's death, according to Marva. She told Maryann Hudson that Aaron had been writing letters to his father and drawing pictures. The letters varied, usually addressed "To Hank" and a few of his friends. But the pictures were always the same. "Aaron's been drawing stick figures of himself, only he gives himself a heart," his mother said.

Hudson saw the drawings. "On the chest of each stick figure," she wrote, "Aaron had drawn a Valentine heart and next to it had written, 'This is me.'"

"I used to make just stick figures, skinny ones," he told Hudson. "But I love my dad and myself. I worry about both my heart and my dad's heart."

Aaron had been to the viewing the day before with Marva's mother, Phyllis Crump. As he stood in front of Hank's coffin and stared at his dad, one of his uncles picked him up and told him to kiss his father. Aaron stiffened in his arms. On the way home in the car, Phyllis said, Aaron had begun to cry. Phyllis asked him gently, "Where is your father now?"

"He's in my heart, Grandma, he's in my heart."[31]

As 130 members of the extended Gathers family filed into the church, moving toward the right front section where they were to sit, the demonstrative Carole Livingston swooned again, setting off a domino effect as she fell heavily back into the line.

Once the other relatives were settled in their seats, Lucille entered the church from a side entrance and sat with her sons. She had been under a physician's care and had briefly been hospitalized after returning home from California.

The service, under the direction of Reverend Joseph E. Daniels, would last almost three and one-half hours.[32]

Hank was attired in a charcoal-gray pin-striped suit. He wore a red and gray tie, the colors of Dobbins Vo-Tech. Atop the casket was a floral arrangement that spelled out "My Son" in light blue. To the left was another in red that spelled out "Hank MVP 44." And along the wall in red and purple was another that read simply, "Hank the Bank."

About 500 people managed to gain seats in the church, while 100 more stood. Outside, 500-600 more listened silently to the service, which was piped over a loudspeaker to 22nd Street. Numerous players from area high schools and colleges, as well as their coaches, attended.

People all across the nation sent testimonials. Among those read during the service were tributes sent by former president Ronald Reagan, and playground and NBA legend Earl "The Pearl" Monroe.

Both Father Dave Hagan and Paul Westhead participated in the service. Father Hagan offered his remembrances of his friend and read a letter that Hank had sent him in his best, light-hearted, Muhammad Ali style, describing his life at LMU. U.S. Representative Bill Gray, the Pennsylvania Democrat, told the crowd that "there's no better way to go than to go doing what you do best. There's no better way to go than doing what you love doing the best. . . . Hank gave us all his best."

Derrick spoke with great emotion about his brother. Choking back tears, he said, "He loved life. He loved himself. More than anything else, he loved his son and his family. He was the strongest man alive."[33]

Then, in words directed at Hank's LMU teammates, who were seated in the front rows of the church—the players who would have to shed their grief and soon begin playing in the NCAA Tournament without their leader—Derrick said, "It's dedication time. Go out and do it for Hank."

Westhead, choking with emotion, wiped away tears as he added his personal tribute to the player he called "Bank Man." Describing Hank as "the best player I ever had or ever will have," he ended by quoting Shakespeare again, this time Hamlet:

"Goodnight sweet Prince,
And flights of angels sing thee to thy rest."[34]

The program for the service included a message from Lucille on the back cover:
"From Mother to Son. . . .

Hank as much as I loved you, will you ever know? Yes, I hope so. That spark in your eyes was always special. So sleep on in peace and remember I'll always hold you in my heart, as my beautiful baby."
—Your Mother—

At the conclusion of the service, the Lions and their coaches paid their final respects to their teammate.

"As I walked up to the open casket, I reached down and touched Hank's hand," Bruce Woods said. "I took off my WCC Championship ring from the 1988-89 season and put it in Hank's hand. I said, 'This is yours. I wouldn't have had it without you. I want you to take it with you,' and I left it in his hand."[35]

As he left the church to walk outside, Bruce's knees buckled. He wasn't the only one overcome by the finality of the moment. Pooh Richardson made it down the stairs, only to collapse into the arms of a startled Sonny Hill.[36]

As they tried to comfort her, Lucille threw herself upon Hank's form and wept as she embraced her son for the last time.

Hymns, accented by hand clapping, accompanied the Lions as they carried Hank's casket from the church.

Finally, at 3:30 p.m., Hank's coffin was placed in the waiting hearse for the trip to the Mount Lawn Cemetery in Sharon Hill. Until sometime after World War II, black families were restricted to burying their dead outside the city limits, and Mount Lawn, in neighboring Delaware County, was the popular choice.

The cortege made its way slowly to the grave site with a police escort. "It was almost like the pope had died," Rich Yankowitz would say later. "The whole city seemed to be in mourning for Hank."[37]

At the grave, the team and coaches joined the family. The site is within earshot of a busy highway, and oil storage tanks loom in the background. It is not a particularly well kept or scenic final resting spot.

"It was a very emotional scene. It was a very distraught feeling that I will never forget," Bruce Woods said of those final moments.[38]

After eight long, emotionally draining days since his collapse, Hank was laid to rest. But Hank Gathers, the man with the heart of a lion, was buried without the very organ that defined him. In the Los Angeles County Medical Examiner-Coroner's Office, three thousand miles away, Hank's heart was suspended in a solution of formaldehyde, in a specimen jar. It would remain there for examination and dissection for more than a year as the family's lawsuit wound its way through the courts.

On the Loyola Marymount campus, a large concrete statue of a roaring lion proudly guards the university quadrangle. After Hank died, it was adorned with pink and purple flowers, and someone propped a poignant note against it that read "Hank: We will always remember you. . . with the heart of a lion."[39]

Within days, on the bluffs beneath the chapel, next to the three large, whitewashed LMU letters, a smaller white sign appeared, visible to the tens of thousands who drove by it each day.

It read simply, "44."[40]

THE SIXTH MAN

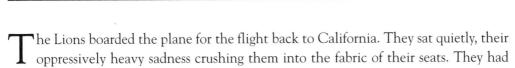

The Lions boarded the plane for the flight back to California. They sat quietly, their oppressively heavy sadness crushing them into the fabric of their seats. They had been through a grueling, emotionally draining week. Their leader was gone. They would have to accept that reality and move on.

After Hank died, the WCC had canceled its tournament and decided that LMU would be awarded the championship. Westhead had left it to the players to decide whether they wanted to continue to play, and the Lions had decided on March 7 that if the NCAA recognized their championship, they would go to the Dance.

"It is what Hank would have wanted us to do," Terrell Lowery said. "He would have kicked our butts if we hadn't."[1]

Somewhere over mid-America, as the team was flying east to Hank's funeral, the Lions had learned that the NCAA selection committee had decided to put them in the Western Regional at Long Beach. That they would stay on the West Coast was welcome news; that they were accorded no better than an 11 seed was not.

"There must be an awful lot of good teams out there," Westhead said, wryly, when he heard of the surprisingly low seed for his team.[2]

Paul had held his team together through the week since Hank's death. At the team meeting on March 7, he had addressed them with a very personal remembrance of Hank. Westhead's words, softly and eloquently delivered, had moved the players and coaches to tears, but somehow had lessened the sadness for them. "It was really very therapeutic for everyone," Jay Hillock said.[3]

"It is hard to say what makes you feel better. I just kind of told them a few things I felt personally about Hank," Westhead said.[4]

When he finished his remarks, Paul walked into his office, shut the door, and remained there alone for the remainder of the afternoon.[5]

His son, Paul Jr., told a reporter, "The first two or three days he spent in total grief. He couldn't talk about Hank on an emotional level. The only way he could deal with it was in a businesslike fashion."[6]

What most people saw was Westhead's calmly, coolly addressing the media, delivering the eulogy, and dealing with the team and the trauma the players were experiencing. It was all that Westhead would allow them to see. "I think that some people may see my dad as being cold or unemotional. That's not the case at all. That's just his way of handling it," Paul Jr. said.

The coach, himself, then 51 and a physical-fitness buff, revealed, "I've had a lot of dreams this past week. I wake up in the middle of the night with chest pains and feel my heart palpitating."[7] His mother, Jane, had died in 1988. "It's funny, but I remember Dad handled her death in much the same way," Paul Jr. said.[8]

Westhead had his moments, though, when even his stoic public facade was shaken. On Tuesday, the Lions had held their first informal practice since Hank's death. After it was over, the coach answered a few reporters' questions and walked out to his car. "I just felt awful," he said.

"It just hits you at different times," Westhead said of the loss that he felt far more deeply than he would allow anyone to see.[9]

The team's first practice back in Los Angeles, after the funeral, was a sight to behold.

All the pent-up emotion, frustration, and despair of the previous week was uncorked at once. Tempers and fist fights exploded. "We were awful," Bruce Woods said.[10]

"It was something. We were just battling each other so hard and taking out our frustrations on each other," Peabody recalled. What Woods remembered most was that "we spent the whole two hours separating people from each other."[11]

Bo helped to calm everyone down.

A few black eyes and bloody noses later, it was all over. The team, minus their leader, was back on the court where he had died.[12] They were together and they were united in a single goal: They would play in the NCAA tournament for Hank. He had carried the team for the two seasons that Bo had been injured. Hank had been their inspirational leader—as well as their floor leader. He had instilled in them his fiery competitiveness and never-say-no attitude. He may not have been out on the court with them now, but his lessons in leadership would be.

After the contentious practice ended, the players gathered near the spot where Hank had fallen. They huddled together and raised their arms toward the heavens, hands touching.

"On the count of three: 'Hank the Bank,'" instructed Terrell, with feeling.

"One-two-three. 'HANK THE BANK!'"[13]

Despair and mourning would be replaced by inspiration and dedication to Hank's memory. For the tournament, the crowds would see five Lions on the court, but in the hearts and minds of the team, there were six—and six against five would be tough to beat.

The Los Angeles County Medical Examiner-Coroner's Office released the autopsy report on Hank on Thursday, March 14, two days before the Lions resumed play. The office spokesman said that the coroner had not seen so much interest in a case since Natalie Wood had drowned off Santa Catalina Island, almost a decade earlier.[14] In Tinseltown, Hank was a star, and everyone was curious about his death. The dry medical findings assuaged no one's curiosity.

Here is the full text of the coroner's statement:

"Cause of death is idiopathic cardiomyopathy with residual interstitial myocarditis." No illegal drugs were found, and additional tests for the prescription drug Inderal were being conducted. Bob Dalembacher, the coroner's spokesman, said that the autopsy had revealed that Hank's heart muscle was diseased, inflamed, and scarred. The cause was unknown.[15]

In an article that would accompany Alan Drooz's NCAA recap of the first weekend's action in the Los Angeles Times, reporter Elliott Almond revealed that tests done by the coroner's office had found only 26 nanograms of Inderal in Hank's system. It was, said the coroner's spokesman, Bob Dalembacher, a "sub-therapeutic level."[16]

The report touched off a flurry of comments from various doctors who were eager to supply answers to the question of cause and to contest the findings. None of it mattered to the LMU Lions. Hank was gone, and they would play on in his memory. That was all that mattered to them now.

The NCAA may have figured that the loss of Hank Gathers had reduced a team that would have been seeded fouth or fifth to an 11th seed, but the Lions felt that with Hank's memory guiding them, they could take on the world.

"We just decided that we would do it for him," Tom Peabody said.[17] Hank's goal for the team that season had been to win two games in the NCAA tournament. He had repeated it constantly throughout the year. And, just as Hank had always believed in himself, the Lions believed that they would be able to do what the experts said they couldn't.

They would do it for Hank.

They would saddle and bridle the emotional hurricane that they had been riding since

March 4. They would use their emotions to honor Hank's memory with fearsome shots, courageous blocking, amazing reflexes. "When we lace the shoes up, there will be no holding us back. We're down now, but there's business to be taken care of and we're gonna get it taken care of for Hank," Terrell told a reporter.[18]

"The only way to go is up. We want to play right now," Bo said. "I see the look in our eyes, we're ready to play. We'll dedicate it to Hank. We're looking forward to playing and kicking some butt. We've gotta do it now. I'm sure he would want us to play in the tournament, and try to turn a negative into a positive thing."

As for Westhead, he said, "Time is on our side. Of course, if you asked Hank, he'd say, 'Play today.'"[19]

"There was no one better to manage that situation than Paul," Bruce Woods said. "He is a better person than a coach. And he is a great coach."[20]

A reporter asked Paul whether he thought Hank would have risked his life to realize his dream.

"I think he . . ." and his voice trailed off.

Then he paused for a moment and said, "Life's daily effort was a lifelong risk. His medication situation was just an added risk. He wanted to be the best. I think he felt he was O.K."[21]

Right after Hank's death, someone had asked Paul about Hank's universal appeal, and the coach had responded, "Hank represents the little kid in all of us, because to Hank Gathers, basketball was play. And we all want to play."[22]

It was mid-March and across the United States, on loading docks and in laboratories, in factories and offices, in stores and schools, an annual spring ritual began. Basketball fans were filling out their NCAA bracket picks for the millions of informal betting pools that form each year in March.

The Lions were unaware of it, but they were supported in their goal by Americans who saw their cause as a noble and worthy tribute. Millions who wanted desperately for the team to succeed said hopeful prayers and made good wishes. And so the Lions of Loyola Marymount University carried with them to Long Beach Arena the hopes and dreams of countless fans intrigued by their mission.

The players' decision to carry on in the name of their fallen leader resonated with fans as well as those who knew little about college basketball. Everyone could identify with the Lions and their quest to capture the crown for Hank. People were enthralled by the possibility that the Lions could somehow pull it off.

The odds were decidedly long. But Americans love the underdog, and in March 1990, Loyola Marymount University became America's team.

On the green chalkboard in the LMU locker room were three words scrawled in large letters set off in a box: "REMEMBER THE DREAM."[23]

As they prepared for their opening-round game on Saturday, March 16, against New Mexico State University (26-4), just 12 days after Hank's death, the Lions' normal practices of rigorous running and scrimmaging were curtailed. The sessions were now low-key shoot-arounds and strategy sessions. The coaches had decided that they would allow the Lions to feed off their emotion and hope that they could channel it into a winning performance on the court.[24]

Indeed, no one knew how the Lions would react when they took the court in Long Beach. Certainly, there was no precedent for their situation. They would be playing on adrenaline, and emotion, and feelings that sprang from an awful, and blessedly unique, event.

Bo had said after the funeral that every point he scored from then on, for the rest of his life, would be for Hank. Since Bo was the nation's leading scorer, that figured to be a lot of points, if LMU continued to win.

Bo made another decision, too, and he made a public announcement about it: he would shoot his first free throw in each game left-handed, in honor of Hank. It would have an impact that he could never have imagined.[25]

Before the New Mexico State game, the *Los Angeles Times'* Alan Drooz noted that Bo had been practicing his left-handed form. "It needs some work," Bo said. "But I'll get there."[26]

Ever mindful of how hungry sports fans are for statistics, Drooz noted that when Bo exceeded the 2,000-points mark earlier in the season, he had joined Hank and Tommy Lewis at that lofty level. It may have been, Drooz said, the first time that three players recruited together (by USC) had ever done so. Although Drooz was too kind to say so, the cellar-dwelling Trojans, minus those three former recruits, had not been invited to any postseason tournaments.[27]

The Lions made the 30-mile trip to Long Beach for their first game since March 4.

It was almost a home game for the Lions, so they would have support from their own fans in the stands. Athletic Director Brian Quinn had purchased 1,500 tickets for LMU at Long Beach Arena. The Lions were also the sentimental favorites of the other 10,700 basketball fans assembled there that day. "I think it's good for the team," Quinn said. "It will give them a chance to be home and have their friends and family there. I think it's important at this time, after all they have been through."[28]

The school had also bought gray Hank "hankies" with Hank and 44 emblazoned on them in crimson, for the LMU fans to wave. This was a clear violation of yet another inane NCAA rule, and, in a rare display of common sense, the NCAA ignored the infraction.

LMU had also had the team's jerseys altered. Each bore, on the upper left front, a black oval patch inscribed in white with 44. The cheerleaders wore the same patch.[29]

In the stands behind the Lions' bench, where the players couldn't miss seeing it, a hand-lettered sign appeared. Held aloft by a student who was wearing a Lion's Pride t-shirt, it read "HANK LIVES."

Another sign, farther up in the stands, announced in stenciled crimson, "HANK'S HERE."[30]

In a format in which a single loss means elimination, the Lions didn't need signs to tell them that Hank was with them. They felt—knew—that they were not alone on the court.

"I had been driving alone in my car a few days after we had returned to campus, and I felt, or sensed, something in the backseat," Bo said. "I turned around and sensed Hank's presence. I felt like I had a part of him within me. For the next two games, I jumped higher and ran faster than I ever had. I felt his spirit within me and felt that he was alive and well within me."[31]

Chris "Blade" Knight would replace Hank in the starting lineup. He had been particularly troubled by Hank's death. He had continued to feel in some way responsible for Hank's demise, believing that he had gotten his wish for more playing time at the cost of Hank's life. It was hard for the guilt-ridden player to get past that. He was having trouble sleeping. In the days after Hank's death, Blade had gotten only about five hours of sleep from Sunday until Thursday.

When he did go back on the court, it didn't get any better. "Our first shoot-around was the hardest," he recalled. "We were playing half-court, and I could hear him telling me stuff. They wanted to play full-court and I wouldn't. I just went up into the bleachers and was watching, and I kept seeing him there. I kept seeing him. I thought I saw him…."

Eventually, Chris started to come out of his fugue. By the time the game with New Mexico State was upon them, he said, "There is no way we're gonna lose. No way. I'd die before that happens. This is for Hank."

When told of his teammate's declaration, Jeff Fryer, the surfer dude, said, "Whoa. We want to win. I don't know if we want to die if we didn't."

Terrell Lowery and the others all shared Blade's sense of mission. It was pervasive. In practice, they were constantly aware of Hank's absence, and they took it upon themselves to remember him in small ways. Terrell stenciled Hank's number on his sneakers, and others traced Hank the Bank in Magic Marker on theirs. Reporters were constantly asking them about Hank, which meant they were never able to forget what had happened and what lay ahead.[32]

That they were united in their determination to honor Hank with their play was never in doubt. Whether they could pull it off in the crucible of a sudden-death national tournament was not so certain. As Bruce Woods said, "We didn't know what would happen. We had no benchmarks to go on. We were entering uncharted territory."

Westhead did all he could to keep the players focused, or as focused as possible, for a team riding a wave of emotion higher than anyone had ever seen. "Paul kept it very low-key. He was very matter of fact. There was no melodrama. There was no need for any," Woods said. "We all knew what the players were going through. We just hoped we could channel it in a positive direction on the court."

Though no one said it, "We knew the odds were against us," Woods said. "We had only had a couple of practices to get ready. Without Hank, we felt there was no way we were going to win."[33]

The Los Angeles Times' Alan Drooz asked Westhead if he was afraid that the Lions might try too hard. "That's something we need to be conscious of. It's easy to tell a team to relax. You can't do that in this circumstance. You have to allow the natural run of feelings . . . the (frantic) way we play, you can tend to forget yourself. I'm hoping that works to our advantage," he replied.

Tom Peabody said he wasn't sure what to expect. "We're ready. This is very hard. None of us have ever been through this before—dealing with it in our own way. We've got a lot of emotion going. Coach wants us to use the emotion the right way. If we come out and go crazy, foul all over the place, it will be a mess. We've gotta play within ourselves," Tom warned.[34]

"I've never felt so much pressure," Bo acknowledged.[35]

The national media was covering the Hank Gathers story intensely. *Time* and *Newsweek* ran feature stories on the tragedy, as did *Sports Illustrated*, in the week leading up to the opening-round game. The daily papers in every major city had provided detailed coverage of everything that had happened since March 4. The Lions' decision to play in Hank's memory was common knowledge and elicited a groundswell of emotional support.[36]

When Hank died, many sports reporters and columnists had openly—and appropriately—acknowledged how deeply Hank's death had affected them, although they had remained even-handed and probing in reporting on various issues arising from and about his death. But now, however, on the eve of the Lions' return to competition, Mike Downey led off his widely read *Los Angeles Times* column by acknowledging that he was far from ready to refrain from cheering them on:

"Never actually cheered for anybody like this before. Never actually sat down at a word processor and wrote, 'Good luck guys. Have a great game. We're with you.' Never homered so shamelessly. Never deliberately breached the canon of ethics, never lost sight of occupational objectivity, never put personal sentiment ahead of professional conduct. Not over one lousy game. Not until now.

This is a special occasion. . . .

Come on Loyola. Win one for the Gatherses—for Hank and his whole family. It is trite, it is corny, it is sentimental claptrap—and it couldn't be more real. Win one. Win as many as you can. Hank would have wanted it that way. We don't care how silly it sounds. Hank would have wanted it that way."[37]

Paul Westhead knew what was facing him and his team, and his approach was typical of his entire handling of events since March 4. "Everyone places a high value on this game," he said. "They feel a sense of commitment. They see it as a dedication to Hank. They know that a close friend of theirs had died, and the players want to show that they care. I just hope they do not relate winning and losing to their feelings. In a sense, this game doesn't really count at all."[38]

While the team may have lost the player that defined it, the Lions still had their anchor, their rock, their coach. He was there for them, as he had always been. Steady, calm, cool, and collected. When all about him swirled an emotional whirlwind, Paul Westhead provided his players with a safe haven of support and comfort. Whether anyone else could have handled the situation better, we will never know. That Paul Westhead handled it with aplomb and grace is undeniable.

When the team came out onto the court at Long Beach to warm up on March 16, the crowd echoed Downey's feelings. After the warm-up, the Lions headed back to their locker room for their final instructions from Westhead and the staff. The 12,000 people in the arena stood and cheered madly.

As Westhead calmly delivered his final, low-key instructions, the team couldn't miss the message on the blackboard: "THE DREAM IS ALIVE."

The players drew together in a huddle before they left the locker room. They raised their arms and their hands pointed aloft as they shouted in unison, "Bank Man!" and "Hank the Bank!" before heading out on to the court. No other words were necessary.

The LMU Lions' mascot led the team out onto the court, and the crowd greeted their appearance with a loud roar of sustained applause. Then the fans, prompted by the public address announcer, stood for "a moment of silence in memory of Hank Gathers."

Even the Aggies were wearing black ribbons on their uniforms, in honor of Hank. The partisan crowd ignored that, though, rudely greeting the Aggies with a chorus of boos as the announcer introduced each player. When the Lions' starters were announced, the applause was thunderous.[39]

CBS televised the game nationally as the final contest of the opening weekend. Jim Nantz and Mike Francesa, co-anchors in the CBS studio in New York, reviewed for viewers Hank's recent death and the task facing the Lions. "Bo Kimble, Gathers's childhood friend from Philadelphia, will be the key against a very good New Mexico State team," Francesa predicted.[40] Greg Gumbel and Quinn Buckner called the game for the network.

Despite the rust from not playing since March 4 and only limited practice time, the Lions did not disappoint the fans. Terrell Lowery, perhaps too intent on performing well for his best friend, was the exception. He was overanxious and, as a result, committed a number of turnovers and silly fouls. He suffered through a 3-10 shooting performance in 17 minutes before fouling out.

Nonetheless, buoyed by the support of the crowd, the Lions, led by Bo, sprinted to a 9-0 lead. But Bo, too, was being overly exuberant in his attempt to carry the team to victory. He soon found himself saddled with four fouls. One more and he would be gone, and the first half still had 4:45 to go. Losing Bo would have ended the Lions' quest then and there.

"Bo's going to have to come out now," said Buckner, who twice called his broadcast partner "Bryant." He was wrong about Bo, too.

Defying all coaching logic, Paul Westhead kept Bo in the game. He probably figured that after all his team had been through, there are worse things in the world than having a guy foul out.

"If he [Bo] would have picked up his fifth [foul], he probably would have talked his way back into the game," Westhead quipped later.[41]

Bo did take a short breather, but quickly went back in and was on the floor as the first half ended in a tie at 46.

The Lions regrouped during the intermission and jumped out to a 9-point lead, with Bo leading the charge. They strung together five straight baskets with no response from New Mexico State. The Aggies were clearly rattled by Loyola Marymount's suddenly clicking, up-tempo play. Jeff Fryer began to find his range, and Bo caught fire. He was virtually unstoppable, and the Aggies had no answer.[42]

Before long, the Aggies were looking at a 20-point deficit and gasping for air. LMU went on a 28-6 run, with Chris Knight contributing key rebounds and a put-back bucket, even though Hank's favorite Luther Vandross song ("If This World Was Mine") kept spinning through his brain.[43]

Each time he ran down the court, Tony Walker pushed the pace into a higher gear. All the Lions contributed to the run, including freshman Chris Scott, who added 6 points and 3 rebounds in five hectic minutes off the bench. But Bo was clearly finding his comfort level. He hit from all over the court, as the Lions outsprinted, outscored, and outplayed the Aggies. Never mind that these Aggies had shared their conference championship with Tark the Shark's UNLV, defeating the Rebels to gain a share of that crown. The Lions' torrid pace left the Aggies eating dust.

Chris Ello told *Pasadena Star-News* readers, "For the first 10 minutes of the second half, it seemed like Loyola Marymount jumpers were raining down from the heavens. Where else?"[44]

With the score at 64-50, Bo was fouled for the first time in the game. As CBS went to a time-out, viewers saw a short piece in which Bo explained that he was going to take his first foul shot left-handed. "In memory of Hank. This is for you, Hank," he said, staring straight into the camera.

When CBS returned from the commercial break, Bo was at the line and the LMU pep band was finishing a song. The cameras found a sign in the stands held high by a fan. "Hank Is Here," viewers read as the camera zoomed in.

Bo practiced his left-handed stroke once and then took the ball from the referee. The crowd, which knew from extensive press and television coverage what was coming, held its breath. The only sound in the building came from Bo's three purposeful dribbles. Then he lifted his head and looked at the basket. His eyes brimming with tears, he put up the left-handed shot.

Swish.

The crowd exploded with joy.[45]

The camera quickly found Paul Westhead, who was striding in front of his players, shaking his head in wonder. "I never wanted a damn shot to go in so bad in my life," he said years later.[46]

"I was only thinking of Hank," Bo told reporters who asked him later about his thoughts at the line. "I didn't really think about making it or not. I just thought about Hank."[47]

From then on, it was all anticlimactic and all Bo. He scored 33 points in the second half to lead the Lions' rout of the sixth-seeded team. His 45 points for the game was a new West Regional record. The final score was 111-92.

Neil McCarthy, the New Mexico State coach, could only observe that his Aggies were beaten by the System. "We had to play their game [in the second half], and you are not going to beat them playing their game," McCarthy said, stating the obvious.[48]

Bo was besieged by reporters after the game.

"Thoughts of Hank were with me all night. I knew he was watching everything I did," Bo told the press without embarrassment.[49]

If he was watching, Hank had to have been happy with what he saw. The team had come through with a convincing win against a formidable opponent under the most unusual and adverse circumstances imaginable. The Lions had, indeed, done it for him.

Mike Downey's column the next day included the observation that LMU had played so well, "you had to count the bodies to be sure it wasn't playing New Mexico State, six-against-five." He concluded: "They did everything they came to do. They came, they played, they proved that life is for the living. They made people smile. They made people's day. They raised their hands high above their heads, as though expecting somebody from high above to reach down and give them five. He would have if he could have."[50]

In the anchor booth at CBS, Jim Nantz, who had called LMU's performance "truly remarkable," asked Mike Francesa how the Lions would fare against their next foe on Sunday. Nantz was inquiring about their prospects against the defending national champion, the University of Michigan, which LMU would be meeting next.

"It will be a very tough game for LMU," Francesa offered.[51]

"We need to move on to the next act," Westhead said. "We'll see how we can react."[52]

Proving that he had paid attention in psychology class at St. Joseph's, Paul brought Terrell Lowery with him to the postgame press conference and said of him, despite his struggles against New Mexico State, "he is our sixth starter and very important to us. We wouldn't be where we are without Terrell."

Of Terrell's special relationship with Hank, Paul said, "He was more like Hank's son. He was his guy, like a father-son relationship. Of course, sometimes the son revolted." The feisty, street-smart Lowery, who hailed from Oakland, had been Hank's buddy, but never his patsy.

"I've been up and down," Terrell said. "It's hard to stay focused. On the court, I'm pretty focused on what I have to do. Away from the court, I have a hard time. It hits me—I can be in a classroom, alone in my apartment, watching TV. It happens a lot in the locker room. I'm so used to seeing Hank cracking jokes on everybody."

But, he said, "I'll play better. We'll all play better, because Hank is inside all of us."[53]

The ever-vigilant NCAA had enacted a random drug-testing program for players. After the game against New Mexico State, the testers selected Per Sturmer, Jeff Fryer, and Bo to pee in a bottle. Per and Jeff struggled to comply. Guzzling bottle after bottle of Evian water, the two dehydrated stars still hadn't peed nearly two hours later. Bo, who had been occupied with media interviews, arrived late. He quickly filled his beaker, to the amazement of his struggling teammates.

"He shoots faster than us. He scores quicker than us. He pees quicker than us," Per observed.[54]

The Lions had one day to get ready to meet the Michigan Wolverines in the second round on March 18. Michigan, the third seed, had trounced its first-round opponent, Illinois State.

For their dream to stay alive, the Lions would have to defeat the defending national champions. The winner would advance to the Sweet Sixteen in Oakland, California, the next weekend. The loser would go home.

Nobody had ever said it was going to be easy.

On Saturday night, Paul and Cassie shared a quiet dinner with two old friends, the Sandersons, at an out-of-the-way restaurant close to home. Paul and Wimp Sanderson, the Alabama coach, had been close friends since the 1970's and enjoyed each other's company, even though Paul, poking fun at Wimp's Ssouthern drawl, admitted, "I can't understand much of what he says."[55]

The NCAA tournament format leaves little time for preparation once play gets under way. The Lions were coming off an emotionally draining performance in their first game since March 4. They had played on adrenaline for much of that game, and no one knew how much the players had left to give.

Before they took the court against the reigning champions, Westhead assembled his Lions in front of him in the locker room. He told them that the strategy for the day was "same old, same old."

He calmly surveyed his players, who were seated on a bench. Then he said, "Per—bombs away!

"Jeff—bombs away!

"Tony—bombs away!

"Bo—bombs away!

"Terrell—bombs away!"

Looking at the next player in line, Tom Peabody, the less-than-accomplished shooter, Paul said, "Tom—no, not you, Tom," as the players broke into tension-relieving laughter.

"Oh, what the hell, let her fly," he added. "Tom—bombs away!"

The Lions had their game plan. It wasn't cerebral, but it was just what they needed to hear. Westhead wasn't going to allow them to be intimidated by the Wolverines. His instructions were simple. Play the way we have always played, and the System will take care of us. There would be no up-tight players in LMU crimson.

It was bombs away. It was going to be fun—and run and gun—just like any other game.

The Lions huddled in the privacy of their locker room and once again reached their arms and hands toward the ceiling, yelling in unison, "Hank the Bank!"

The message in the upper right-hand corner of the blackboard read, "THE DREAM IS ALIVE."

The Lions charged onto the court at Long Beach to a thunderous ovation. There was no doubt which side the crowd favored.[56]

.   The Michigan coach, Steve Fisher, had seen the Lions demolish New Mexico State. As he watched that game from the stands, he had turned to his wife and said, "I can't believe this."[57]

"I'm sure Loyola is on a mission," he told the *Daily Breeze*. "I said before the tournament that I'd hate to be New Mexico State. Loyola played with emotion, but controlled emotion. I was impressed with their poise on the court."

Asked how his Wolverines would stop Bo Kimble, Fisher replied, "We'll rotate a lot of people on him, but we won't stop him. He'll get his points no matter who he plays. We have to keep the others from getting record highs."[58]

In the Wolverines' starting lineup were three future NBA stars: Loy Vaught, Terry Mills, and Rumeal Robinson. They had lost Glen Rice to the NBA but were still a potent offensive force. And Fisher had a good plan. It just didn't work.

Westhead told Quinn Buckner of CBS what his plan was: "We're gonna run and press. Shoot the ball within four seconds. Run. Press. Create havoc and get Bo the ball."[59]

That is exactly what the Lions did. As the Wolverines tried to keep pace with the Lions, it must have dawned on them that Bo wasn't the only threat to their crown. The supporting cast of Lions was making its presence known. They pressed, ran, and created havoc, just as their coach had directed.

By the middle of the first half, Michigan was gasping for breath. The Lions had built a lead by scrambling for every loose ball, taking charges from Michigan, and playing at an up-tempo pace that the Wolverines couldn't sustain. The Lions also were draining 3-point shots from every conceivable angle on the court. Jeff Fryer and Per Sturmer hit from long range early, giving some indication of what the Wolverines might expect if they concentrated on Bo too much.

The Lions built a 9-point lead with about seven minutes to play in the half when Bo drove and scored on a layup. He was fouled for the first time and would go to the line. The CBS telecast provided a quick look back at his left-handed free throw against New Mexico State. Gumbel reiterated Bo's pledge to do so again, in memory of Hank.

Once again, the raucous arena grew strangely silent as Bo dribbled three times forcefully and launched his free throw left-handed.

Good!

The audience exploded. On the subsequent inbounds play by Michigan, Tom Peabody intercepted the pass and tossed a bullet to Terrell, who streaked in for a lay-up. The spectators, still on their feet, went nuts.

Fisher immediately called time-out.

The Lions returned to their bench amid a flurry of high fives and back slaps. The score was 42-30, with almost seven minutes to play in the first half, but the contrast in body language displayed by the two teams was unmistakable. The Lions were exuberant and ebullient. The Wolverines were dispirited. The defending champions didn't quit, but they were never again a threat as LMU grew increasingly confident and carefree.

Jeff Fryer, who had decided he had to step up in this game, did so. The southern California surfer dude became, for one unforgettable night, a mad bomber. He threw up threes from everywhere and seldom found anything but net. He was on fire and nothing Michigan tried could stop him.

As the intermission approached, Michigan clawed back into the game. But it was apparent that the Wolverines were winded and slowing down. The half ended with Michigan putting seven men on the court, before the referees removed the extra two, to defend against an inbounds pass with one second left.

At the break it was 65-58, and Jeff Fryer had scored 21 points.

While the Michigan band blared out the familiar "Hail!, Hail! to Michigan" fight song, it was clear the team doing the best fighting was dressed in crimson, not maize and blue.

At the half, Nantz and Francesa expressed their amazement at what was happening. "I really am surprised," said Francesa, who had picked Michigan to get to the Final Four. The difference, he pointed out, was in the threes. Michigan was 1-9 from beyond the arc, while LMU had made 9 of 19.

"Jeff wanted that game for Hank, very badly. It was very important to him," Tom Marumoto, his shooting coach, recalled.[60]

Fryer's tribute to Hank was as good as it could possibly be. Later he acknowledged that he had nearly broken into tears before taking the court. —"It hit me all of a sudden. It made me play hard," he said.[61]

Jeff saved the best performance of his career for the nationally televised game against the defending champions. He threw up 3-point shots as if he were back on the playground at Newport Beach with no one watching but Tom. Every lesson, every thought, just flowed naturally in the smooth, perfectly executed rainbows that he unleashed.

Bombs away, Westhead had said.

Bombs away was what he got.

The bombs dropped so fast and furiously that you could have called the game Thirty Seconds over Long Beach.

The second half was more of the same. The Lions literally ran the defending champs into the ground with a torrid fast break and unrelenting defensive pressure. Michigan went a full five minutes without a field goal. The Wolverines had hit a wall and had stopped dead.

That the Lions were getting uncharacteristic games from everybody on the team was a huge plus. Peabody—Peabody!—hit almost everything he threw up. Tom went 4 for 5 from the field and an even more incredible 6-6 from the line, where he had been a 53 percent shooter all season.

Of course, he gave up his body again. This time, he crashed hard to the court on his damaged and heavily taped wrist. He left the game briefly, and Chip applied ice to hold down the swelling. The Human Bruise was soon back on the court, diving for loose balls and scurrying for steals. He wasn't about to let severe ligament damage stop him. He was having too much fun.

The effort against Michigan was truly a team effort. Although Jeff's deadly air assault would be the highlight of the day, and win him the Chevrolet MVP award, his teammates' contributions can't be overlooked. Chris Scott took two hard-charging fouls at critical points in the game to kill Michigan rallies. Terrell Lowery and Tony Walker both played well at the point, and Per Sturmer showed his versatility. He battled the taller Michigan players for rebounds on both ends and stepped out to bury a 3-pointer when he was left unguarded.

The stats tell the story. Sturmer, 21 points; Fryer, 41; Lowery, 23; Peabody, 14 points, 5 assists, and 3 steals. Bo got his usual 37 before fouling out, but the others played the game of their lives. At the buzzer, little-used sub Marcus Lee sank a 3-pointer, his first ever. Magical stuff—but, then, this was LMU, and fans had learned to expect magical things from the Lions.

"We're doing it for Hank," Terrell told the press.[62]

The Lions shot a blazing 58 percent from the floor in the second half to run the Wolverines off the court and out of the national title picture.

"Hank is on my side at all times," Jeff told Mike Downey, "so that makes two of us out there." No doubt, he was echoing the suspicion of Michigan players, who had been unable to contain Fryer as he buried 11 of 15 3-pointers. "I wasn't about to have an off day with him watching me—and I won't have one the rest of the way. I just won't," Jeff said.[63]

Michigan coach Fisher said of LMU, "I honestly don't see anyone beating them if they keep shooting like that. They made NBA 3-point shots. They made them with people guarding them. They were truly sensational."[64] Indeed, Fisher had suffered his first NCAA tournament defeat at the hands of the Lions.

"Whatever they did to maintain the legacy-of-Hank-Gathers feeling on that team, they did it and it worked," Fisher said. "It wouldn't have mattered what we did to prepare— they would have beaten us. They were simply phenomenal."

Of LMU and Westhead, Fisher said, "He had a group of physically skilled and well-conditioned athletes. They made you play as they played. And they knew you couldn't keep up with them. Their success was a tribute to Westhead. He showed that with the right personnel, the System does work."[65]

It never worked any better or under more difficult circumstances than it did that day in Long Beach, when the Lions stunned the defending national champions and shocked the basketball world. The sentimental favorites of the tournament had, improbably, impossibly, won. The Lions of LMU, with an enrollment of fewer than 4,000, had turned back mighty Michigan. America's team was in the Sweet Sixteen.

In a moment of reflection about what had happened that weekend, Paul Westhead shook his head and said, "There's something more than basketball going on here."[66]

The win over Michigan was the top story in sports that Monday. With a break in tournament action until play resumed the following weekend, LMU was the talk of the sports world. The Arsenio Hall Show booked Jeff and Bo, and they appeared on Wednesday for an interview and an impromptu shooting demonstration. Hall, improbably, fared better at shooting than Jeff did in the studio.[67]

USA Today did a full-length feature on the Lions, pointing out the records established in the LMU-Michigan game. They included:

Most 3-pointers in a game (individual)—Fryer, 11

Most 3-point goals in a game (team)—LMU, 21

Most 3-point field-goal attempts in a game—LMU, 40

Most points in a game—LMU, 149

Most 3-point field goals by both teams in a game—LMU, UM, 25

Most 3-point field-goal attempts by both teams in a game—LMU, UM, 53

Most points in a game by both teams—LMU, UM, 264[68]

Sports Illustrated featured an action shot of Bo on the cover of its March 22 edition. The caption read, "For You, Hank." It had to have been the first time that a cover moved the magazine's largely male audience to tears. The feature inside reviewed events since Hank's death and the magical run that the Lions had begun in honor of their fallen leader.

Indeed, LMU was the main topic on sports pages and around water coolers everywhere. No matter which teams you were betting on to reach the Final Four in your $5 office pool, chances were that you and millions of other Americans were going to be rooting for LMU to keep the dream alive.

On the eve of the next game, *USA Today* featured LMU in yet another page-one story. It quoted CBS's resident basketball guru, Billy Packer, as saying: "Loyola Marymount's basketball talent has been underestimated. This is a Top 20 team. I think they have a legitimate shot at the Final Four. With Hank, they'd have an even better shot. They wouldn't have the crest of emotion going for them but they would have had another great player."

ESPN's Dick Vitale chimed in, predicting, "Emotion plus offense equals a W."

The *USA Today* story also quoted Jeff Fryer, who acknowledged, "We're on a mission now."

Father Dave Hagan went so far as to declare God a basketball fan—and an avid one at that: "It is a miracle in our theological parlance—a wonderful event of the sensible order attributable to God alone."

Father Dave Hagan told *USA Today* that Hank's mother had called him after the Michigan game. Lucille was calling from her hospital bed, where she had been confined since collapsing after the funeral. "She told me," Hagan said, 'My baby is there.'"

At the end of his long piece, *USA Today*'s Erik Brady raised the question of whether LMU could sustain its streak: "Impossible? No. Unlikely? Yes. But that's what makes the prospect so downright delightful. Like playing basketball in heaven."[69]

CHAPTER
29

THE LIONS SHARE

In an article that accompanied Alan Drooz's recap of the first weekend's action, *LA Times* reporter Elliott Almond revealed that tests done by the coroner's office had found only 26 nanograms of Inderal in Hank's system. It was, said the coroner's spokesman, Bob Dalembacher, a "sub-therapeutic level."

There was a reason for that, according to Pete Priamos's second-oldest son, Chris. As this book was going to press, he called me to tell me something he'd never told anyone before. Hank had called Chris, who was then in graduate school, in early February. "After swearing me to secrecy, he asked me about my experience with heart medication." Chris had been born with a congenital heart condition and underwent the first of many corrective surgeries when he was only five. He suffered the first of two heart attacks at twelve, and he had been on medication, including Inderal, for nearly two decades. Hank knew all that.

"Hank quizzed me on the medicine he was taking and then told me he had decided to take his medication every other day. 'I'm alternating the days. It's the only thing that works for me,'" he said. "He said on game days he wouldn't take any until after the game. On the off-days he would take it. He wanted my opinion on this course of action. I told him that the drug doesn't work that way. You need to take it continuously to have it build up in your system to be effective. I told him, 'You can't go off your meds.'" It was the last time Chris and Hank spoke. [1]

To sustain their streak the Lions would have to turn back the Crimson Tide of Alabama in the next game, and that assignment might require a full-blown miracle.

The Tide was ranked 22nd in the nation, and Alabama's trip to Oakland to play LMU would mark the sixth time in the last nine seasons that its colorful coach, Wimp Sanderson, had taken a team to the Sweet Sixteen. The Crimson Tide was seeded seventh for the tournament and had racked up a 30-12 record in the tough Southeastern Conference over the previous two seasons. Alabama had made it to the NCAA Tournament in 8 of Sanderson's 10 seasons there.

"They have momentum and some things on their side we don't have," Sanderson said, referring to the emotion that had carried the Lions this far.

Arizona coach Lute Olsen, whose Wildcats had fallen to Alabama, said, "I doubt that the Lakers could keep up with (Loyola)" and called LMU's shooting "almost eerie." Then, in a statement that reveals just how unlikely it was that LMU had beaten Michigan, Sanderson said, "I hadn't really thought much about them because I didn't think we'd be playing them."[2]

The national interest in LMU did not go unnoticed at CBS. The network made the game between LMU and Alabama its prime-time game and assigned its lead broadcast duo, Billy Packer and Brent Musburger, to handle the telecast.

Center stage at the NCAA Tournament belonged to the Lions. Their bus was escorted by a police motorcade from the hotel to the Oakland Coliseum.

But the pregame chalk talk was typical of Westhead. After diagramming the sets the Lions were likely to see from Alabama in its half-court style, Westhead simply looked at his team and said, "Same old. Same old. Let's go have some fun."

The chalkboard Paul had been using held a new message. In the upper right-hand corner in a box were the words, "FULFILL THE DREAM."

The players assembled in the same circle that they had formed before every game in the tournament. Raising their arms and hands high, they yelled in unison: "Hank the Bank!"[3]

Alabama was determined not to suffer the same fate as Michigan. Sanderson had used the time between games to drill into his team the need to milk the clock. This was a very good defensive team. The Crimson Tide had held Southeastern Conference opponent LSU to 55 points earlier in the year.

In a pregame piece aired by CBS, Westhead said, "Both teams want the game to be in the 50's. Alabama wants it to be 56-55, Alabama. We want it to be 156-155, LMU."[4]

The game was introduced by Jim Nantz and Mike Francesa from the CBS studio in New York. Viewers saw a shot of Hank in action before the camera cut to Nantz, who said that LMU was "one of the tournament's most emotional stories." Francesa said that he didn't think that Alabama would be able to "slam the door" on LMU. "I think LMU advances," he predicted. LMU, Nantz intoned, would be "playing for their spiritual leader and fallen teammate because that breathes passion into their dreams."

Musburger, who would call the game, began by describing it as the "amazing saga of

LMU." Billy Packer, the color analyst, confessed as the tip-off approached that "I don't have a clue as to which one of the teams will get the other to play their way."

He didn't have to wait long to find out.

Sanderson had schooled his Crimson Tide well. Alabama, not LMU, would dictate the game. The Tide would eschew the easy fast-break opportunities and instead milk the clock for every second it could. Whenever the Tide got the ball, Alabama players would run the shot clock down to five seconds before shooting.

LMU tried to goad Alabama players out of their plan when the Lions had the ball. Firing up shots every seven seconds or so, the Lions tried to tempt the Tide into a running game. No way. It wasn't going to happen. Soon it was apparent, despite the loud chorus of boos that greeted each Alabama stalling possession, that the Crimson Tide would not be lured into a race to the death with LMU. Alabama would stay the course and play the possession game.

The Lions, the highest-scoring team in the land, were forced to play Alabama's style. Alabama's slow pace throttled the Lions' offense. But their defense never failed them—their defense kept the Lions in the game.

The front line for Alabama was Robert Horry, 6-foot-9; Melvin Cheatum, 6-foot-8; and David Benoit, who was also 6-foot-8. Their size was formidable, and Per Sturmer and Chris Knight would have their hands full trying to keep them at bay.

The Alabama game plan, though, focused on getting the ball down inside when Tide players finally did take a shot. It was there that the Lions' defense stepped up. Per led the way as the Lions fought to deny the entrance passes. The strategy was largely successful. The game was not a foot race but a snail-paced affair. The turnovers mounted, as did the fouls, with the two teams locked into a defensive struggle in which each possession was magnified in importance as the game wore on.

The first half saw LMU jump out to a quick lead, only to see Alabama fight back. After only five minutes, the Lions held a 7-point lead at 9-2, before the Tide came back to score 4 straight points. The play of Tom Peabody and Tony Walker on the defensive end resulted in several steals; although LMU failed to convert them into points, the steals did disrupt Alabama's flow.

With Sanderson scowling and barking at the referees in a voice louder than his garish red plaid blazer, the Lions took an 18-14 lead with just over three minutes left in the first half. Then Bo was assessed for his third foul. He had struggled to get free of stifling defensive pressure all day. When Fryer had grown cold from the perimeter and missed several 3's, the pressure on Bo increased. He tried to do it all. Defensively and offensively, he began to press and paid the price. Westhead, of course, left him in the game.

Alabama drew within one point at 18-17 with 1:30 to play in the first half. LMU had gone 5:20 without a field goal, which pretty much sums up the way the game had gone. Very slowly.

Terrell Lowery finally hit a jumper to get LMU back on the board, and Jeff Fryer added a few free throws. LMU went up 22--21. With seven seconds left, Alabama took possession and missed its final attempt as time expired. The half ended with LMU leading Alabama, 22-21.

As he followed his team to the locker room, a jubilant Sanderson fired his fist into the air in triumph.

So far, so good.

Alabama had managed to control the tempo and contain the high-octane LMU offense throughout. The 22 points scored by high-scoring LMU was the lowest first-half total by any team in the 1990 tournament. The 13,000 fans in Oakland could scarcely believe that this was the same team that had averaged 125 points per game this season. Bo and Robert Horry had each tallied 8 points to lead their respective teams.

In the studio, Mike Francesa observed that "LMU needs to get their rhythm back. They were out of synch in the first half."

Alabama was indeed controlling the game. But while it had slowed and disrupted the LMU offense, the Tide had done nothing, though, to thwart the LMU defense. The Lions were fighting and clawing for every ball. They were forcing Alabama to make errors and altering the Tide's few shots. The Lions' defensive tenacity had kept them in the game.

"We knew we couldn't play worse than we had in the first half," Bo said. "We were confident."[5] Indeed, there was no sign of panic in the LMU locker room.

"At the half, I told them, 'O.K., guys, we only need 104 more points to get our average,'" Westhead said.[6] While it may not have been one of the most memorable pep talks in sports history, it nevertheless kept the Lions loose.

The second half began with an auspicious start for LMU as Jeff Fryer sank a 3-pointer. But Jeff was not left alone during the game and was largely ineffective when he did get the chance to fire. The Lions would need to get help from another source if they were going to survive.

The pace picked up a bit in the first part of the half before reverting to the slower tempo that Alabama preferred. Tony Walker took a nasty spill and hurt his back, requiring Chip to ice it. But Tony would return. Nothing would keep him out of this game for long. Terrell, playing in his hometown, filled in nicely and added some offense as well.

The lack of offensive production frustrated Bo. He was the victim of a hard block by Cheatum that drew no call, and then, on a driving attempt in the lane, he was obviously fouled hard—and again the referees ignored the foul. Bo was angry, and he quickly committed a hard retaliatory foul against Alabama that drew a technical foul call. "I lost my temper and I shouldn't have," he said.[7]

Blade went over to Bo, grabbed his jersey, and pointed at the black circle affixed there with the number 44 in white. "That was just his way of saying to me, 'Remember our overall purpose,'" Bo said. "I got the message."[8]

After the technical call, Alabama went on a 9-0 run that left LMU trailing, 49-41, with just over seven minutes to play.

Terrell managed to sink a 3-pointer from way outside, but Alabama countered and the pace slowed again. The score stood at 52-45 with 6:25 to play. Both Bo and Jeff took long 3-point shots. Both clanged harmlessly away.

"Kimble is getting rattled entirely," Packer said.

"Alabama," added Musburger, "is growing confident."[9]

The Lions needed help. And they needed it now.

And it arrived, thanks to a bandaged, banged-up, and bruised body wearing number 11. It was Tom Peabody, and he would supply an unexpected and most welcome offensive burst to the toothless Lions' attack.

"I heard them saying, 'Sag off that guy, he won't shoot,'" Tom said after the game.[10] The Tide underestimated him. First, he committed two consecutive fouls while diving and scrapping for the ball on Alabama's inbounds passes. The second foul was Tom's fourth. He had made a bad pass earlier and drew Westhead's wrath for carelessness in a game in which every possession was precious.

"The tempo really didn't bother me," Tom said. "I was used to that type of play from high school every game. I wasn't frustrated by it."

Tom was the last person that Alabama expected would take the ball inside where the Tide's giant sentinels were guarding the basket. But that is exactly what he did. "It was time," Tom said. "In the tournament, you've got to play your heart out."[11]

Westhead remarked afterward, "He's a '57 Chevy with bumps and bruises. You can't hurt him, though. He's got a cracked steering wheel but he is still going to make it to the beach."[12]

The driving, slashing Peabody caught Alabama completely off guard. The player they had ignored, because he never took a shot, flashed down the lane and converted two straight lay-ups. In between, he forced an Alabama turnover and, with Sturmer, controlled the boards.[13]

"Peabody turned the game around," Westhead said.

"Coach knows I'm going to gamble on some steals," Tom said. "He lets me loose to go crazy out there."[14]

What Tom did drove Sanderson and the Tide crazy. With 3:49 to play, his second lay-up had put LMU up 57-56, which gave the Lions their first lead in the half.

Sturmer and Chris Knight had battled valiantly and effectively against Alabama all night and had kept the Lions close with their defensive play, but it was Tom who provided the offensive spark when they needed it most, because Alabama was not going to go quietly.

With 2:30 remaining, Cheatum hit a jumper to put Alabama in front, 58-57. On LMU's next trip down court, Fryer lofted a 3-pointer that missed badly. Sturmer grabbed the rebound and quickly fired it back out to him.

Bingo!

Fryer's 3-pointer, the last of his 13 points, made it 60-57.[15]

"When we were down (in the second half), guys on the bench kept saying, 'Get it for Hank,'" Jeff related. "So we just jacked up the intensity some more. We were not going to lose."[16]

With the crowd wildly cheering LMU on, the Tide battled back to force a 60-60 tie with a Horry bucket at the 1:02 mark.

After Bo missed a jumper with forty-five seconds to play, Per made a seemingly impossible save, keeping the ball inbounds and the Lions' hopes alive.

The Coliseum's air was thick with tension.

Bo, attempting to drive, lost the ball in traffic, and it was miraculously deflected to Terrell Lowery at the left of the key. He drove hard for the basket as the shot clock ticked down toward zero. He lofted the lay-up—and it was good. Now LMU was leading 62-60 with 26 seconds to go.

Alabama quickly brought the ball down and got it to Horry, who found Cheatum beneath the basket and unguarded. Cheatum went up over Per, who reached for the shot. The ball fell away. Per grabbed the rebound and fired it out to Jeff, who was fouled.

Alabama was still not over the limit for fouls, and LMU got the ball out of bounds. Time was called as the two coaches drew up strategy for the final 3.6 seconds of play.

CBS's camera panned over the LMU huddle, showing the stenciled tributes to Hank and 44 on the LMU players' sneakers. In the stands, the camera found a fan holding a sign that said, "HANK LIVES." The two scenes prompted Musburger to say, "What an emotional roller coaster they have been on. It tugs at your heart."

The ball was put back into play at the LMU end of the court. The referee handed Per the ball, and he quickly asked for a time-out after surveying the Alabama defensive set. During the time-out, CBS showed viewers the chalkboard message in the LMU locker room: "FULFILL THE DREAM."

After the ball was placed in Per's hands again, he got it in to Terrell, who was immediately fouled. Terrell went to the free-throw line for a one-and-one opportunity to put the game away. Westhead pulled all the players off the line and back to guard the basket.

Terrell quickly put the shot up—and missed.

Sanderson, who had alerted officials that he wanted a time-out after the free throws, got one.

The two teams huddled one last time.

2.6 ticks remained.

Alabama's Cheatum, on the inbounds, passed the ball over a leaping Chris Knight, and it flew nearly the full length of the court. The pass hit Bo and then Horry's hands and bounced off. Horry regained control and, falling away, lofted a shot from beyond the top of the key on the left side of the court. The ball was in the air with 1.5 seconds to go.

Horry's high arcing shot took what seemed like an eternity to come down. It did, with 0.3 seconds showing. It hit the rim and—for a split second—hung there as if it might drop through—then fell away.

Peabody grabbed the rebound.

Horry collapsed to the floor in tears.[17]

The game was over. LMU had won. The dream was alive.

"I thought, as I watched that shot hang there for a split second—that seemed like forever—that Hank may have helped us there," Bruce Woods said.[18]

Now no one would argue with Westhead's assessment that "there's something more than basketball going on here."[19]

Tom Peabody, blood pouring from scrapes on both knees, his heavily bandaged wrist throbbing, grinned through it all and said, "Today we knew what was needed to keep Hank happy. Wherever he is, I'll bet he's wearing a big smile right now."

Per Sturmer received the MVP award from Chevrolet and Peabody the accolades from his coach. The Lions would play again. This time it would be for a trip to the Final Four.

"You have to give credit to Wimp and his team," Westhead said. "They played their game and we just had to go along for the ride.

"It was," he said with a grin, "a very slow ride."[20]

Sanderson told reporters that his team had executed his game plan to perfection: "We played the game in order to win the game. I told you we would be a well-prepared team. You may not like the way we played. You can put that crap in there about slowing down the game. We did what we had to do to win."[21]

Bruce Woods wasn't the only one thinking that the Lions might have gotten some extra help on the court. In her San Francisco Chronicle article, Pam King said of the improbable outcome that the Lions had "willed themselves to win."[22]

"It's like 'Star Wars,'" Per told Mike Downey. "It's like there's some force out there, looking out for us." Per had grabbed 12 rebounds, 6 on offense, and the last, in the final seconds, an absolute game saver that had allowed Fryer to convert. "We're getting to be a pretty fantastic story," Per said, prompting Downey to observe, "Hey, when the Force is with you, the Force is with you."[23]

Maybe it wasn't just magic, as C. W. Nevius explained in the *San Francisco Chronicle:* "Magic is a wonderful thing if the game is roulette. And if you're betting the long shot in the first race, you'd like to have destiny on your side. But, when you're down seven with six minutes to go you don't need luck. You need a belly-flop dive on a hardwood floor. You need to dig through a thicket of grasping arms to find a loose ball and you have to flip it in the basket. You need a Loyola Marymount."[24]

After describing the game as what the Indianapolis 500 might look like at 55 m.p.h., Chris Ello wrote, "Effectively downshifted, the LMU Lions didn't go on their usual scoring rampage. . . . But what happened was still unbelievable."[25]

As they left for their hotel, the players noticed that the blackboard in the LMU locker room had been altered by someone to read, "FULFILLING THE DREAM."[26]

To do so, the Lions would need the Force, light sabers, a healthy sprinkling of stardust, and everything else they could muster. Later that night, the University of Nevada-Las Vegas turned back a pesky Ball State University by 62-60, ruining David Letterman's day and setting up a rematch of LMU's season opener.

Everyone outside Clark County, Nev., would see the game as the Jedi warriors of LMU firing away at the dark side, or UNLV. The 11-seeded Lions would be taking on the rebellious Jerry Tarkanian's number one seed, aptly named the Runnin' Rebels, for a trip to Denver and the Final Four.

When they faced off on Sunday, March 25, only 5 of the 293 schools that had begun play in November were still competing for the national title. One of them—improbably, unbelievably, magically, mystically—was LMU.

As Mike Downey would wryly observe in his *Los Angeles Times* column, Loyola Marymount had a whole row of true believers on its bench who "honestly feel that this cuddly little cabbage-patch basketball team could win the national championship."

As he pointed out, "Loyola's got Judas (assistant coach Judas Prada) and the priest (Father George Crain, the cherubic-looking priest in a black fedora, who occupied a seat on the Lions' bench at every game). Loyola's got Bo Kimble, who averages 37 points on a bad day. Loyola's got Per Sturmer, one of those typical Swedish-street-ball stars out of Taljegymnasiet High. Loyola's got Terrell Lowery, who takes 17 shots coming off the bench. Loyola's got Terrorist Tom Peabody, who plays with all the calm and control of a Middle-East embassy riot.

"And Loyola's got Jeff Fryer. The beach boy. The surfer. The kid with sand in his sneakers. He's the drive-by-basketball shooter," Downey wrote.[27]

Reading Downey's column and his lighthearted assessment, it seems even more improbable than it was that the team he described would be playing UNLV. And that's not even considering that the Lions were coached by a man who thought 200 points was an attainable goal for his zany crew.

But that team and that coach would be facing the juggernaut known as UNLV.

The executives at CBS Sports were salivating. The match-up between LMU and UNLV was a dream come true. It promised a huge audience that would watch to see if the Lions' impossible dream would continue—if they really could win it for Hank. The game promised a television drama that was as much soap opera as sport.

The hype that accompanied the telecast was completely unnecessary. The entire country knew the story by then. No one who had even the slightest familiarity with college basketball was unaware of the emotionally charged quest of Westhead's Lions. LMU was America's team, and with each improbable win, the Lions drew more adherents to their cause.

The demand for tickets was so great that Jim Muldoon, the tournament manager, was all out when several Pac-10 athletic directors called him for seats. He could do nothing. LMU-UNLV was the hottest ticket in the land.

By the time the Lions took the court in the standing-room-only Oakland Coliseum to face Tark the Shark's team of future NBA stars, the Lions were underdogs everywhere but in the hearts of Americans from coast to coast. There the Lions were the clear favorites.

After Wednesday's practice, Westhead had assembled his players for a short talk. Tom Peabody said that the coach's last words to the team were, "Remember to play for Hank."[28]

Paul said he was preparing them for the grief they would surely feel the minute they no longer had a basketball game to worry about. "What I'm trying to convey to our players is that they not play to win for Hank, that they play for him, but not to win," Westhead explained. "Because in caring about him, their grief is deeper than winning or losing."[29]

On the LMU campus, the student body was thinking about nothing but basketball as the team left for Oakland in an airport van. A crowd of students had gathered to give the team a proper send-off, even perching in trees to glimpse the players.

"Our minds aren't on anything but basketball," said senior Diane Pleshe, who suggested, "They should cancel school."

"I feel awesome," said junior Leimomi Kekina, who brought leis for the players. "This is just the top of the world. Everyone is so happy."

Even the least- involved students were caught up in "the almost religious fervor" of the

Lions' attempt to honor Hank's memory, said English professor Lucy Wilson. "Almost a crusading spirit has invaded the campus. You can't not be touched by it," she said.

The university bookstore was deluged with phone and mail orders for "anything with an LMU logo on it," reported manager Sue Price. She said she had to add staff to keep up with the orders—about 50 a day from every state but Alaska. "I knew we'd be busy, but this is unbelievable," she said.[30]

One enterprising LMU alumnus had printed some T-shirts with "LMU Basketball Is Un 'BO' Lievable." He sold 300 in one hour outside the cafeteria.[31]

Two people combined to produce a cassette tape of a song they had written in tribute to Hank. It was entitled, "Hank's House," written and performed by P. R. Paul and Phil Booth, who lived near the campus. The song's chorus was: "Welcome to Hank's House, / Come on in and see the show. / It's the hottest ticket in town tonight, / Turn him loose, let him go. / As the applause rains down, like thunder from the Gods. / Making shots with three guys on his back, trying to beat the odds."[32]

It was advertised for sale in the *Los Angeles Loyolan* for $4.75, offered by what was said to be a nonprofit venture.

Sales were brisk.[33]

If basketball games were decided on sentimentality, if hopes and prayers played any role in the outcome, there is no question that the Lions would have prevailed in the last game of the Elite Eight on Sunday.

"I think it's the greatest thing to happen to basketball in a long time," said Pete Newell of the attention LMU's style and victories had focused on the tournament.[34]

But talent—not luck or hope or sentiment—is what determines the winners at this level. And UNLV had talent to spare.

"I really like my group of kids," Tark said with studied understatement.[35]

Indeed, Tarkanian's 1990 edition of the Runnin' Rebels made his droopy eyes light up with its awesome array of talent. It featured Larry Johnson, Stacey Augmon, Anderson Hunt, David Butler, and Greg Anthony. That lineup on the floor in the NBA would be as good as most. In the college ranks, they were formidable. On paper, they were simply unbeatable.

LMU, by contrast, had been a woeful 60-1 shot in Danny Sheridan's betting line before the tournament. Sheridan wasn't the only one to write them off. Most Las Vegas casinos had posted odds at least that long for LMU.

But here they were—still in it.

The Lions had lost to UNLV in their season opener with Hank Gathers playing. That was the team that had prompted Tark to proclaim, "I wouldn't want to face them again," after his bomb scare–aided win in November.

But now the Lions didn't have Hank Gathers, at least not in uniform. He was there only in their hearts, the Hank "hankies" that the crowd waved wildly, and the black patches sewn onto their uniforms. But patches don't rebound. Hankies don't score in the paint or slam dunk over Larry Johnson and David Butler.

The Lions could feel the fan support on the court at Oakland. They knew it and heard it and sensed it. The country was pulling with all its might for little LMU and its odd cast of players—but they didn't have Hank on the court as they prepared for their rematch with UNLV. Still, the Lions presented a brave face.

"We want to play UNLV," Jeff Fryer had said after the Alabama win. LMU wanted revenge, he said, for the early season loss.[36]

Tarkanian said all his assistants and "even my wife" had wanted the Rebels to play Alabama. But, Tark the Shark said, "I wanted to play LMU. They played the way we played. We practiced and played like them, and I felt we would have a much better chance with them than Alabama."[37]

So both sides got their wish.

On the day of the game, Mike Waldner summed up in his *Daily Breeze* column what had happened on the Westchester campus in the last three weeks: "A nation has discovered this basketball team. The death of Hank Gathers, merging with the David taking on Goliath plot whenever LMU plays in the NCAA Tournament, is a captivating story going far beyond zone defenses and the like."

"In basketball circles," Waldner suggested, "LMU is like an uninvited guest" in appearing in the Elite Eight. Defying the odds, "LMU has crashed the party," he said.[38]

The Alabama game should have silenced those who felt that Westhead just sat back and watched as his charges fired at will. The dogged defensive pressure and the refusal to panic and fold against Alabama, in a game in which the Lions did not dictate the tempo, was a tribute to Paul's coaching acumen. He had shown he could win in the 150's and in the 60's. He had demonstrated an ability to adjust and to win at a snail's pace as well as in a run-and-gun style. He would have preferred the latter, of course, but he had shown the world he was not an intractable devotee of the System. He was a damn good coach. That he liked to score was not in doubt. And the Alabama game had proved that he could win—even with a different strategy.

Next case.

UNLV was more than happy to play Westhead's game.

"We're not going to slow the game down," Tarkanian said. "We're not going to play like Alabama, but we don't want it to be a racehorse game either. We hope we won't play zone, but we will if it's dictated to us."

As usual, Westhead was candid in his assessment of the task ahead. "UNLV is a team that is capable of running with us," he told Chris Long of the *Daily Breeze*. "Oklahoma was able to function at that pace and Las Vegas is potentially in that category. We're not concerned that Larry Johnson might get his career high, but we can ill-afford to allow them to get second and third shots."[39]

He was right.

The two teams would meet again on the floor of the Oakland Coliseum at 1 p.m., P.S.T., on March 25, 1990. For one of them, it would be the last game of the season, which had begun with these two teams facing each other in Las Vegas. "That game has no significance now," Tarkanian said. "Both teams have changed a lot.

"Loyola is playing on great emotion now. I didn't think they'd beat New Mexico State," he confessed. "I knew they couldn't beat Michigan. I didn't think they'd beat Alabama."[40]

He may not have been a great prognosticator, but Tarkanian was a winner on the court. His UNLV team had been 25-2 since Butler joined the lineup after the first game of the year, and Tark was on an eight-game winning streak.

At Augmon's urging, the UNLV players wore black mourning bands on their uniforms in tribute to Hank.[41]

When LMU took the court, the Lions got a standing ovation from the capacity crowd. They were once again the sentimental favorites, oh so close to making the wishes and dreams of millions come true. But this was the real world. And in the real world, sometimes 23-year-old players die, glass slippers don't quite fit, and dreams don't always come true.

Three weeks after Hank died, UNLV, fielding one of the finest college teams of the era, ended LMU's magical run. It wasn't even close, and for the second time in four years, Tarkanian's team advanced to the Final Four.

The Rebels made it look easy. They dominated the boards offensively and defensively. Per Sturmer and Chris Knight looked like they were trapped in a pinball machine as they were bounced from side to side beneath the net by the aggressive UNLV front line.[42]

Hank's absence was most telling in the rebound numbers. UNLV grabbed 64 to LMU's 43. Those second and third shots that Westhead had dreaded were available and were often converted.

The Rebels shot 59 percent to LMU's 37 percent and played a smothering defense that forced 24 LMU turnovers. Jeff and Bo were hounded all night and found open shots few and far between. Jeff went ice cold, shooting only 4-16 from 3-point range. Stacey Augmon, considered one of the top defensive players in the country, shadowed Bo everywhere he went. Twenty-five of Augmon's 33 points came in the first half, while he held Bo to a 14-32 night from the floor. Stacey added 11 rebounds to take the West

Regional's MVP award. He deserved it.

The 14,298 on hand did their best to will LMU to victory, but the dominance of UNLV was apparent from the outset. The Runnin' Rebels jumped out quickly to a 16-4 lead and never looked back. LMU was forced to adopt a more risky, gambling defensive scheme that led to more UNLV scoring opportunities, and the game quickly became a rout. At one point, the Rebs were ahead by 38 points. The final score was UNLV, 131-LMU, 101.

Per Sturmer, who had battled the 6-foot-10 Butler, 6-foot-8 Augmon, and 6-foot-7 Johnson all night with little success, said, "I think tonight was one of those nights when you can really see that we missed our power center. Tonight was Hank's night. If he had been here. . . . This is one of those nights when Hank was at his best. He would have taken over, being the great athlete that he was."[43]

But he wasn't there, and Augmon, in particular, got easy attempts beneath the basket, and the Lions couldn't stop him. Of the Rebels' 51 field goals, 42 were virtual gimmes, which illustrates their total dominance of the paint.[44] Which was where Hank would have been.

LMU had rallied to make one run in the first half when, after falling behind by 18 points, the Lions had closed the gap to 42-39, inciting the crowd. The Rebels then went on a 13-0 run of their own, silencing the crowd and putting an end to the LMU dream.[45]

With the outcome long since decided and only a few minutes remaining, Westhead removed Bo and Jeff Fryer from the game. The crowd at the Coliseum rose to give a standing ovation to the two stars—and to one who was not there. Watching, you got the feeling that people all across the country were doing the same. Paul's daughter, Monica Luccenti, was in the stands and said that moment "made it clear that Hank was gone for good."[46]

30

WHEN THE CHEERING STOPPED

Paul Westhead was philosophical: "We were playing basketball on another level. It wasn't on the level of wins and losses, which, for better or worse, is what sports is all about. We weren't playing sports. We were playing something else."

Though they were outclassed and outplayed throughout, the Lions had continued to fight, scrap, dive for loose balls, and play with energy and enthusiasm until the end. On their final possession, hopelessly beaten, Marcus Lee again put up a 3-pointer and again made it. His bucket put LMU over 100 points. "It was for Hank," said Lee, whose only two 3-pointers all season came in NCAA Tournament games. "It's just a matter of going all-out, a devotion to that pride that Hank represented to the game."[1]

The team had taken that attitude and that pride and gone further than any LMU team had ever gone. It had been a goal of Hank's to win at least two games in the tournament. They had won three and had done so without him.[2]

But, as Westhead told Steve Carp of the *Las Vegas Sun*, the Lions had never been alone since Hank's death. "We've been together at the funeral and during the tournament. I think it's going to be tougher on us later on, now that basketball is removed from our lives. The country has rallied around our team, and that was nice. Now, it's time to reflect on this season, and know in our hearts, that there will never be another one like it in our lifetimes."[3]

Bo ended his college career with a 42-point performance that included another successful left-handed free throw. When he came off the floor after the standing ovation, he embraced each of his teammates in turn. "I don't want to be still," he said after he realized that he had no more tournament games to prepare for. Now he would have to face Hank's death.

"I know I'm going to have to face the situation," he told Tom Weir, "but the more busy

I am, the easier it is."[4]

Most of the Lions took the end of their dream hard, none harder than Tom Peabody. The battle-scarred, bruised, and battered Peabody had left every ounce of energy and effort on the court. As it hit him that the dream was over, he broke down in the locker room. The player who epitomized the courage with which the LMU team had carried on after Hank's death was finally caught up in the emotion of the moment.

Peabody had backed down from no one. Had sacrificed his body time and again in an effort to do whatever it took to win. But Tom could do no more. Now he could only face the reality that it was over.

"We were running scared," he said—not scared of losing, but of facing the awful finality that they now couldn't avoid.[5]

Somehow, Tom and the others all would face reality, and all would move on. Youth is resilient and time heals. But they would never, ever forget.

As they gathered their gear and left the Coliseum, on the blackboard in their locker room was a final message: "REMEMBER THE DREAM."[6]

Westhead admitted to having made a technical mistake by not allowing his team to view the film of LMU's first game with UNLV. Hank was in that film, of course, and he felt that he simply could not show it to the players. That may have been a coaching error, but his decision was a humane one that few would dare question.

The column in which Mike Downey summed up the season for *Los Angeles Times* readers began, "I typed this column left-handed. Just a little gesture for a little school down the lane. Bye, guys. Thanks for all the Loyola merriment. You lived, you died, you laughed, you cried. You got through the worst and gave it your best. Thanks, Paul, Bo, Jeff, Per, Tony, Terrell, Tom, Chris, everybody."[7]

Paul Westhead was pragmatic about events of the last three weeks. "Today was the way the last three (games) should have been, proof the last three were unexplainable," he said. "They were examples of the human spirit rising above the occasions. But we're not angels, and we can't always rise above."[8]

Bo closed out his college career as the nation's leading scorer, making LMU only the second school in history to have back-to-back scoring leaders. (Furman University was the other, in the 1950's, with Frank Selvy and Darrell Floyd.)

"I think we'll be remembered as a team that had heart and showed its love for Hank Gathers and basketball," said Bo, whose left-handed free throws had raised his profile higher than that of any other player in the tournament. He added, "Even though we're out of the tournament, I think we're still America's team."

Mike Downey agreed. "Loyola Marymount University," he wrote, "had lost the game but they won just about everything else there was to win. Won games. Won respect. Won friends. The whole team should put the season to rest with a peaceful, easy feeling. Let somebody else run scared for a while. Let the Lions sleep tonight."[9]

In his *L.A.Wave News* column, Dave Werstine told readers that LMU had something to be proud of. They had given their all. "Somewhere Hank Gathers has a smile on his face," he said. Addressing the Lions, Werstine continued, "You brought meaning back to what college basketball is supposed to be—an innocent game filled with emotion. You brought every viewer with you on a roller coaster ride to the top. We laughed with you, we cried with you, won with you and, finally, lost with you. You made Hank Gathers proud."[10]

As the Rebels prepared to move on to Denver and the Final Four, UNLV's Larry Johnson insisted that his team would carry on in the tournament in Hank's memory for LMU. "You don't have to be on their team to be stricken by the tragedy," he told the *Daily Breeze*. "We wear the patch, too. Hank Gathers' dream is still going on."[11]

The Rebels would join Duke, Arkansas, and Georgia Tech in Colorado and would go on to win it all in 1990.

For the Lions, the cheering had stopped, replaced by the aching pain of the loss of their friend and leader. No longer artificially buoyed by adrenaline, applause, and the outpouring of support from fans, the players returned to LMU to face the bleak realization that Hank wasn't there. They would do so on the campus of a school that, as Hank had boldly predicted years earlier, everyone now knew about.

BITTER SEASON

"If this world were mine, I would place at your feet
All that I own; you've been so good to me
If this world were mine . . .
I'd give you anything."

"If This World Were Mine," Hank's favorite song
—Marvin Gaye, covered by Luther Vandross

Although the entire country was captivated by the emotional saga of LMU's improbable run through the NCAA tournament, that was only half of the Hank Gathers story. In the *Los Angeles Times* and other area papers, the success of the Lions on the court dominated the sports pages, while investigative reporters continued to dig into Hank's death and others reported on the litigation threatened by his family.

The *Los Angeles Times's* investigative team mined the doctors, university officials, and others for information. The young, gifted reporters whom John Cherwa had assigned to the story left no lead unexamined in covering all aspects of Hank's death and the pending litigation. Hardly a day went by without a new story on these angles, and the reporting would run side by side with the accounts of LMU's tournament success.

Now, with the tournament over for the Lions, the only coverage focused on Hank's death and the medical treatment he had received. The exhaustive and professional reporting by Cherwa's team appeared as a four-page special insert in the sports section of the *Los Angeles Times* on April 1.[1] The paper ran off extra copies and shipped them to Denver, where the special section was distributed to the massive press corps and others attending the Final Four.

The section featured articles on every aspect of Hank's life and death. The stories were accompanied by numerous photos, provided a comprehensive review of Hank's life and death, and examined the issues that his demise had raised.

The other Los Angeles-area papers devoted hundreds of column inches to new developments, as well. *The Daily Breeze*, the *Los Angeles Daily News*, *The Orange County Register*, and others kept pace with the unfolding story of the lawsuit that the family was planning. The inspiring season that LMU had concluded in March soon became a bitter season of charges and allegations related to Hank's medical treatment and subsequent death.

With the arrival of spring and the flowering of the jacaranda trees that form regal purple canopies over suburban streets and avenues in Southern California came the end of the tumultuous school year.

At Loyola Marymount, Father Loughran announced on April 26 that there would be no commencement speaker at graduation because Katharine Hepburn had cancelled her appearance, and he had no plan to replace her. Students were outraged. The May 2 edition of the *Los Angeles Loyolan* carried an editorial with a banner headline that demanded: "We Want Westhead."

"At first the administration had a negative reaction," said Michelle Nadeau, the student body president. "Then they relented under pressure."[2] Father Loughran reluctantly acceded to the students' demand and asked Paul Westhead to speak at graduation.

Ten days later, Westhead stood before the graduates and their families in the scenic Sunken Gardens section of the campus. The man once characterized as "the nutty professor" and the "guru of go" would be providing words of wisdom and inspiration as the senior class prepared to enter the world. He chose to speak about life and living in the face of all that they had just been through collectively, a decision that reflects both his intelligence and his instinctive sense of what they needed to hear.

Westhead's uplifting message was poignant and marked the graduation ceremony for what it was—a beginning, not an ending. He told them that they could reflect on their years spent among an incredible life force known as Hank Gathers and that those memories were theirs to treasure as they moved beyond the campus gates. Hank's contribution to their renewed sense of pride in their school and in themselves was his gift to them. His genuine warmth toward children and self-effacing humor were lessons they could take with them. His respect and regard for his mother and family and his loyalty and affection for his teammates were traits they would do well to emulate. Hank's steadfast refusal to give up— no matter the odds—would be an example to follow when they faced their own challenges in the future. Westhead spoke only of the future and the lessons that could be learned from a life that had ended all too soon.

"Hank found his bliss here. We should all be that lucky. In *The Power of Myth*, Joseph

Campbell advises us to follow our bliss—if we want to be happy. Well, Hank found and followed his bliss," he said.

As he surveyed the class, which included three of his players and his wife, Cassie, Westhead concluded by saying,

"Now it is time to say farewell. Farewell to Number 44, and this Class of 1990. As a teacher of writing, I searched for the exact word to fit my meaning. Au revoir—too much like perfume. Caio—too quick. Arrivederci—it sounds like lunch.

"Sayonara—too sad, and Marlon Brando beat me to it. Good-bye—good-bye makes the journey harder still. And then I found it. My collegiate years of studying—or, should I say, struggling with—German provided me with the exact words: Auf Weidersehen; Auf Weidersehen; Auf Weidersehen! Till we meet again; till we meet again; till we meet again!

"And we will meet again."[3]

After his speech came the roll call of graduating seniors, and as his or her name was read, each approached the podium to receive a diploma. In the program's list of graduates, between the names of Kristin Lee Gardiner and Michelle A. Hannisee, was Eric W. Gathers.

Barbara Busse, associate academic vice president, announced, "Loyola Marymount University is proud to confer the degree of bachelor of arts on Eric Hank Gathers."

Lucille, supported by Derrick, Charles, and Bo, slowly made her way to the podium to accept the diploma. Sustained by loud waves of applause, she embraced Father Loughran. She returned unsteadily to her seat as her head bobbed and tears welled in her eyes.[4] The applause for the missing graduate was the loudest and longest of the day.

Soon after that warm spring day, Paul Westhead announced that he, too, was leaving LMU. He had been offered a chance to coach the Denver Nuggets of the NBA and had accepted the lucrative offer to return to the ranks of the pros.

Gregory Kevin "Bo" Kimble also received his diploma and was soon taping commercial endorsements arranged by his agents. His high-profile role in paying tribute to Hank in the NCAA Tournament had made him a highly sought-after commercial property at the Leonard Armato Agency. Bo profited from the direction and guidance of David Spencer and Armato. He accepted a starring role in a basketball film, *Heaven Is a Playground*, and he was awarded $100,000 for winning the Collegiate One-on-One Challenge competition in Atlantic City, N.J.

That June, he realized the dream that he and Hank had shared. Bo Kimble was selected in the first round of the 1990 NBA draft by the Los Angeles Clippers. His contract was for a reported $8 million.[5]

With Bo's success came a growing suspicion on the part of Lucille and Derrick that Bo was profiting from their misfortune. Although Bo had watched the NCAA Finals with Lucille in her home, the Gathers family's once-warm feelings toward him had chilled with each new success.[6] In the end, the two families were estranged. The final blow came as the trial neared in the Gathers family lawsuit and Bo received a six-figure advance against royalties for his book about his relationship with Hank. The book, *For You, Hank*, was released in 1992 by Delacourt Press as the case was going to trial. Bo, by then an affluent, if not wildly successful, NBA player, had shared his advance with Hank's son, Aaron.[7] Yet the rift between Bo and the Gathers family widened and remained a gaping chasm for years to come.

What replaced the storybook season of 1989-90 was a new and bitter season of legal wrangling and litigious finger pointing. The public, which had responded with an outpouring of support for Lucille after Hank's death, soon changed its mind as a result of the ill-timed press conference held by Bruce Fagel, the family's attorney. Coming as it did within days of Hank's death, the announcement of the family's intention to sue the university and Hank's doctors was seen as an avaricious move to capitalize on the tragedy.

Lucille "became the object of horrible, racist remarks about greedy blacks," former *Los Angeles Times* reporter Maryann Hudson Harvey recalled.[8]

The truth is that a grief-stricken woman, who had just witnessed her son's death, was not, for one of the few times in her life, in control of what was happening—events that would lead to her being cast as cold and unfeeling.[9] "What got lost in all the publicity over the lawsuit was the fact that a mother had lost her son and a child had lost his father," Hudson Harvey said. "Nothing was ever going to change that."[10]

Unfortunately, the perception created by Fagel's actions obscured those facts. Fagel had a reputation for winning large awards and using the press to his advantage. In the months after his announcement of the lawsuit, he became a ubiquitous presence in the papers and on local television.

With his salon-coiffed silver locks perfectly in place, expensive designer suits, and movie-star good looks, Fagel was milking the publicity for all it was worth. It didn't hurt that he was always accompanied by a stunningly attractive, dark-eyed brunette, whom he identified as his assistant. Her name was Trudy Miller, she was a paralegal, and she was married to Fagel. They were a legal team straight out of Central Casting.

Fagel said he called that first press conference "because we were getting swamped with phone calls from the media. LMU had also begun to place stories in the press that were designed to show that they were blameless in the death. We had to protect the jury pool at that point, and so the press conference was called to do that and to educate the sports community on some difficult medical questions that they knew very little about."

Fagel admitted years later that he "had no idea that the case would be so popular. I was used to trying medical malpractice cases in a very low-profile manner, with little or no press coverage. I was astounded at the intense coverage this case received. We were getting 20 phone calls an hour about it."[11]

Eventually, Fagel filed a 52-count suit naming almost everyone with any connection, no matter how remote, alleging that he or she contributed to or caused the death of Hank Gathers. The suit named seven doctors; three medical practices; and coach Paul Westhead, trainer Chip Schaefer, and athletic director Brian Quinn at LMU. At one point, the suit involved twenty-nine attorneys from ten law firms, an unwieldy conglomeration of interests and egos that often clashed.

The numerous defendants were vulnerable to speculation about their roles—simply because they had been named in the suit. They were subjected to intense questioning at depositions in which they were compelled to participate and that consumed hundreds of hours and produced a mountain of sworn testimony.

Fagel succeeded in earning substantial out-of-court settlements for his clients, Lucille, Derrick, and Charles Gathers, and Carole Livingston. Aaron was represented by Martin Krimsky of Philadelphia, who had been appointed to represent Hank's son by the Register of Wills of Philadelphia County, Pa. which also had appointed Krimsky to serve as an administrator of Hank's estate.

In 1991, Dr. Vernon Hattori's malpractice insurance carrier settled for the amount of his policy, $1 million, to be divided between Lucille and a trust in Aaron's name. The judge in the case awarded $650,000 to Aaron and the balance to Lucille.

In his deposition, Dr. Hattori had testified in great detail about his treatment of Hank. The cardiologist did so, even though he was the only person on Earth who knew what he and Hank had discussed in that last, fateful conversation the day before his death, the one in which Hank had browbeaten Hattori into agreeing to let him play without being tested and in which Hank had promised to take himself out of the game if he felt any symptoms whatsoever. Dr. Hattori also testified that he was well aware that Dr. Charles Swerdlow had disagreed with his approach and treatment.[12]

The university also settled with Lucille and Aaron, even though LMU's lawyer, Marty Blake, and Wayne Boehle, the lawyer for LMU's insurance carrier, were confidant "we would win any lawsuit that went to court," Boehle said. But he had also had to tell the Jesuits, though, that it would cost about $350,000 to try the case.

"The Jesuit hierarchy in San Francisco eventually decided that the adverse publicity that a lengthy and acrimonious court case would bring was not worth the risk," Boehle said.[13] In September 1992, LMU settled for $1.4 million, with $855,000 put in trust for Aaron and $545,000 going to Lucille.[14]

Those settlements left Fagel with a case against only the doctors who had treated Hank after he collapsed on March 4. The central claim was that negligence by the doctors had caused emotional distress to members of the Gathers family. Under California law, Fagel had to prove not only the central allegation but also that, when he died, Hank had been supporting his mother and that she was entitled to an award based on his future earnings.[15]

"It was a difficult case from the outset," Fagel said. "It was extremely difficult to get a jury seated. It was almost impossible to find jurors that didn't believe that Hank was responsible for his own actions and that the doctors were blameless. It was the most challenging case I have ever had. It also was a new area of case law. There had been no other high-profile wrongful death cases involving a collegiate athlete to date, and the case was attracting national attention."[16]

Proving that Hank had been supporting his mother promised to open "the door for a very dicey area for LMU," Fagel said. "We had sworn testimony from Derrick and others that Hank had been receiving money from supporters and was giving it to his mom. That would, of course, have to be revealed at the trial in an effort to make our case that he was supporting her."[17]

An inkling of what might come was revealed in a number of articles alluding to the deposition testimony by Derrick and others regarding assistance Hank had received. In *The Orange County Register*, Janis Carr reported in late December 1990 that Bob Minnix, assistant director for enforcement at the NCAA, was "interested in the accusations made by Gathers' mother that the former star had received financial support from a prominent Loyola Marymount booster." Carr's article alluded to the *Los Angeles Times* coverage of Lucille's having received gifts and money from Hank through Al Gersten. *The Los Angeles Times'* report, Carr said, included Gersten's denials and his response to the charges: "I didn't help Hank." Minnix told Carr that the NCAA was waiting to see how the case played out. "We will need to see everything. . .talk to everybody. We would need a broad base background and determine how it relates to NCAA rules before we would assign an investigator."[18]

The stories continued throughout 1991 as deposition testimony and settlement talks progressed.

By late summer 1992, when the trial finally got underway, Fagel had a problem: his clients were not that eager to proceed. "Lucille didn't want to come to California," he said. "She was back in Philadelphia and didn't want to come out to testify in the trial."[19] Also, the family was uneasy about testifying to Hank's having received large sums of money from boosters throughout his college career. But the Gatherses needed to do that to have any chance of winning damages. Lucille had also been upset with Fagel for announcing the lawsuit before Hank was even buried. Only Derrick's insistence kept her from changing lawyers.[20]

Thus, the plaintiffs were hoping that all remaining parties would succumb to the pressure to settle.[21] Those hopes were dashed when the attorneys for the Kerlan-Jobe Orthopedic Group in Inglewood, and Dr. Dan Hyslop, refused to do so. They would, instead, contest the charges and fight it out in court to clear their clients' names and professional reputations.

At one point, the Kerlan-Jobe clinic nearly did settle. "Dr. Kerlan said he would settle if the money went to the son," said Morris Silberberg, the lead attorney and senior partner in the firm representing the clinic's insurance carrier. Dr. Kerlan was so incensed that the suit had been announced— even before Hank was buried— that he said "he wouldn't pay a dime to the mother," Silberberg told the *Los Angeles Times*.[22]

And so the only parties who were eventually forced into a courtroom to defend their actions in relation to Hank's death were the very same men who had fought desperately to save his life. The public, which had been following the case through newspaper and television reports, found the situation to be unfair.[23] Fagel's pursuit of the case inflicted further damage to Lucille's already tarnished reputation. The large settlements she had received from Dr. Hattori and LMU were well known, and as the trial progressed—it was one of the first trials televised by Court TV—any remaining public support for Lucille evaporated.[24]

In making his case that Hank, a full-time college student who had reported no income to the IRS while he was at LMU, had in fact supported his family, Fagel had to rely on the sworn testimony of Derrick, Charles, and Lucille. Derrick had testified under oath in his deposition that Hank had received more than $50,000 from Al Gersten, who had been not just an overzealous booster but an LMU regent while Hank was a student.[25]

Gersten and LMU were not happy. Foremost among the concerns of LMU administrators as the trial approached had been the prospect of NCAA sanctions and a backlash of criticism from alumni, whose support the university needed for its ambitious fund-raising plans, according to a trustee who preferred to remain anonymous.

Gersten, who had recommended Fagel to Hank's family in the first place, was now about to be excoriated in open court by that very lawyer. Indeed, Gersten adamantly denies having been the source of the money that Hank had been forwarding to his family while he was at LMU. "I attended the trial every day. I wanted to testify," Gersten said. He was eager to defend himself from what he saw as spurious charges by Derrick.[26] LMU wasn't happy that Gersten was in court every day.[27]

In August 1992, more than two years after Hank died, the civil trial began before Superior Court Judge J. Gary Hastings in Torrance, California. The third-floor courtroom was crowded with reporters, camera crews, and observers.

"The trial was full of so much emotion. Whatever I wrote offended someone," Maryann Hudson Harvey recalled.[28]

A string of witnesses from the university took the stand to be grilled, in turn, by Fagel.

"I had to watch Hank die over and over again in slow motion [on the video of March 4]," LMU Athletic Director Brian Quinn said. Fagel had replayed the video in court, stopping it frame by frame to ask Brian questions. "I will never forgive that man for that."[29]

Dr. Ben Shaffer spent two days on the witness stand and walked away convinced the jury would see that he had acted properly.

Fagel, an accomplished litigator, used his trademark no-holds-barred style to question Dr. Dan Hyslop, who, along with Dr. Shaffer and LMU trainer Chip Schaeffer, had been one of the most active participants in the valiant effort to revive Hank outside Gersten. Dr. Hyslop knew in his heart that he had acted properly, and he refused all entreaties to settle the case out of court.

Throughout most of the questioning, Dr. Hyslop remained calm and coolly answered Fagel's questions with brief and direct responses. Only when Fagel attempted to insinuate that Dr. Hyslop had, in some way, been inept or in part responsible for Hank's demise, did the young physician react.

"I resent the fact that you would even ask me that," he responded with feeling.[30] The Court TV camera showed the jury nodding in silent agreement with the sincere-sounding Dr. Hyslop's indignation at Fagel's damning suggestion.

"I knew from the difficult time we had in empanelling a jury that the case was going to be a difficult one to win," Fagel said. "It was challenging, but I recognized that it was an uphill battle from the outset."[31]

The uphill battle became a mountain when the day came for Derrick to take the stand. Fagel believed the jury had been bombarded with enough medical testimony and had decided to move up the testimony of the Gathers family. With the Labor Day weekend looming, he sent plane tickets to Lucille and Charles. They would join Derrick in testifying on the Tuesday morning after the long weekend.

By that time, the proceedings were nearly three weeks along. Fagel told Maryann Hudson that it had cost him $75,000, thus far. Kerlan-Jobe estimated its outlay at $90,000. Although the average malpractice case requires about a dozen depositions, more than 60 had been taken in this case.[32]

When she got to California, Lucille told Fagel she didn't want to continue, he said. "She told me she was upset about the whole thing, Hank's death and everything that came after, and wanted to drop the suit."[33] Instead of having Derrick Gathers take the stand as scheduled that Tuesday, the disheartened Bruce Fagel had to tell Judge Hastings he was having trouble with his clients. "I've lost control and communication with my clients," he acknowledged.[34] Hastings gave him a day to change their minds.[35]

The next morning, no one from the Gathers family was in court when it was time for the trial to resume. Fagel stood before Hastings and explained that Lucille was tired of the case. She had thought she was through with the suit after the settlements by LMU and Dr. Hattori's insurance company and her recent decision to drop her action on behalf of Derrick; she didn't want to have to relive Hank's death while she was on the witness stand.

Later she would say, "I've already lost one son over this and I don't want to lose another over this lawsuit." Derrick was being treated for an irregular heartbeat at the time; many years later she said that was the main reason she chose not to pursue the lawsuit. She also referred to Fagel as "that fool" and expressed regret at the strain the lawsuit caused between her family and LMU.[36]

Since no one in the Gathers family would talk to him, Fagel lacked written permission to drop the suit. He was forced to ask Hastings to dismiss the case. Hastings, who said he had never had such a thing happen during a trial, dismissed the case, thanked the jury, and discharged the panel. Interviews with jurors later revealed that Fagel had been right: it would have taken a miracle for the jurors to find against the doctors who had fought to save Hank. After viewing the tape of his collapse and on-court treatment and hearing the testimony, one juror said to Maryann Hudson, "How could they [Chip and the doctors] be blamed?"[37]

The dramatic film of March 4, which Fagel had played repeatedly in court, had convinced jurors that they were witnessing two doctors trying to save a life. Another juror, Bethann Harrington, told Hudson, "You could see for yourself. It wasn't what somebody else saw or said they saw."

Eight of the twelve jurors told the reporter that when the case was dismissed, they were heavily in favor of the defendants, based on the testimony that they had heard.[38]

But Dr. Hyslop was bitter, even years later, that the jury never rendered a verdict. "I was left hanging," he said. "I never got the benefit of having been found innocent."[39]

Outside the courthouse, a teary-eyed Dr. Hyslop said, "I would say that, among many people, I miss Hank. There are no winners here. Let's get beyond this—winning, losing, hating, accusing."[40] Dr. Hyslop's lawyer asked him afterward if he wanted to sue the Gathers family for malicious prosecution. The case had already cost Dr. Hyslop $250,000 in legal fees, and he demurred.

One thing that continues to bother Dr. Hyslop today is that the trial obscured larger issues that the death of Hank Gathers should have brought to the fore. "We have to stop the downward spiral," he said. "If we could spend some of the millions we spent arguing over dead people on changing the conditions that cause a playground full of black kids to believe that they can get out of the mess they live in and definitely earn a living in the NBA, that might break the bitterness."[41]

Two years after the trial, Lucille turned up on the LMU campus unannounced and asked to be allowed to sit in the stands at Gersten for a while. She did so for about 45 minutes, staring silently at the court where her son was last seen alive. She left without saying a word.

Dr. Ben Shaffer was no happier than Dr. Hyslop that the case had been dismissed. "There was no closure," he said.

The lawsuit had prevented the man who had struggled to save Hank on the court and outside Gersten Pavilion on March 4, 1990, from discussing the case. "I wish I could have called the family and told them what happened that night on the court, but I couldn't because it would have been misconstrued as manipulating the legal system," he said. "So, basically, our legal system prevents the right thing from being done."[42]

Dr. Shaffer said he was relieved but angry when Dick Carroll, the lawyer for his insurance company, called to tell him it was over. "I wanted the jury to accept me and my actions as proper. I wanted to be vindicated," Dr. Shaffer said. "They told reporters and they told us that they were convinced we did the right things, but it was never announced as a verdict. I never felt exonerated."[43]

Shortly after the case was dismissed, Maryann Hudson met with Fagel at La Scala in Beverly Hills. Even in the forgiving lighting of the posh eatery, the attorney who had always looked like a GQ cover boy looked awful, she recalled.

"He looked worn out to me. He'd never looked tired before. In fact, each day when he'd appear in court, he looked so good, I thought he must have had a face-lift overnight," she said. At La Scala that day, "he was still trying to explain what had happened and was having a hard time understanding it himself."[44]

What is important to understand is that, despite what Lucille and Derrick may have said, or felt, their lawyer had won a considerable victory for them. Attorneys Dick Carroll and Marshall Silberberg, who jousted with Fagel often in court, agreed that Fagel "had done an outstanding job" for his clients. Even Hastings applauded Fagel's efforts for having taken the case as far as he did.[45]

Much of the bad blood between Fagel and his clients had to do with the unfortunate timing of the announcement of the suit. Fagel defends the decision as having been necessary in light of the self-serving information that LMU was putting out.[46] Additionally, Fagel had taken the case on a contingency basis. He would be paid and recover his expenses only if he won.

Those expenses were considerable. They included paying expert witnesses and the cost of maintaining Derrick in Hank's old apartment. Derrick had insisted that he needed a place to stay while he finished his degree at Cal State-Northridge. Fagel, of course, deducted the rent payments and other expenses from the gross awards that he secured for Lucille, subtracting $200,000 from her settlements. This only prompted more bad feelings.

"Usually we get thank-you notes from clients," Trudy Miller told Hudson, but "this time we didn't even get a good-bye."[47]

FINAL SCORE

The trial was over but its effects lingered.

"Lucille took the brunt of the blame for the unpopular lawsuit. "It all goes back to the press conference Fagel called, announcing the suit. It was a decision which she had no role in, yet it put her under a cloud from then on," Maryann Hudson Harvey said. "After that, she lost public support and was seen as just a greedy woman. Her love for Hank got lost. People forgot she was still a mom and had watched her son die before her eyes. Hank was a delight, maybe the only one, in her otherwise dismal life, and she lost him."[1]

Loyola Marymount University officials, who were as angry as anyone about the lawsuit, were delighted when it was dismissed. The testimony that Derrick, Charles, and Lucille were expected to provide, based on their depositions, would have been a serious blow to the school.

David Burst of the NCAA said that, while he had heard rumors and allegations regarding illegal payments, the NCAA was waiting for the sworn testimony before launching an investigation of LMU. "The person that would have been responsible for investigating any charges made in court would have been me. When the case was dismissed and the trial ended without producing any statements of wrongdoing, I felt no investigation was deemed necessary," he said.[2]

The NCAA ultimately chose to ignore Hank's residence in a $1,100-a-month condo and his driving a new Mercury Cougar, often to the racetrack, during his senior year. He was doing so while on a scholarship that provided an allowance of $600 a month for room and board.

Although there was no NCAA investigation, LMU was nonetheless tarnished by Derrick's charges that Hank had received $50,000 from an LMU booster. The allegation, which Derrick made during his deposition, before at least a dozen people, was subsequently leaked to the press and made public.

For several years thereafter, whenever the LMU Lions took the court in a WCC game, they would be rudely greeted with loud, raucous, profane chants about money and playing for payola by the opposing team's student rooting section. For the Jesuit school, which took great pride in its academic reputation, this was a continuing source of embarrassment. LMU administrators placed the blame for the situation squarely on Lucille and the other members of the Gathers family, according to sources.

Dr. Ben Shaffer and Dr. Dan Hyslop, the two physicians who had ministered to Hank in his last moments, fighting desperately to help him survive, managed to move on after their agonizing ordeal was ended.

Dr. Hyslop remains on the staff at LMU, where he continues to treat students as the school physician.

Dr. Shaffer moved on to Georgetown University, where he was team physician for John Thompson Jr.'s Hoyas, and he established a thriving orthopedic practice in Washington, D.C. He was named by *DC Magazine* as one of the area's top physicians in the late 1990's. He later served as team physician for the Washington Capitals of the National Hockey League. During his tenure, Dr. Shaffer served on an NHL executive committee of team doctors that, at his insistent urging, managed to get the league to require that an ambulance and portable defibrillator be present at rink level for every NHL game. When Jiri Fischer of the Detroit Red Wings suffered a cardiac event during a game in 2005, the portable defibrillator that Dr. Ben Shaffer had fought for was used to save Fischer's life.[3]

"Every March 4, I am reminded of what happened to Hank," Dr. Shaffer said. "I will never be able to forget it. I have gone over it a million times. I've examined what I might have done differently. I wish to God that I had saved Hank's life. I'd like to go back in my life to that moment and try all over again. Could I have put the paddles on him 10 seconds earlier, a minute earlier? But there is no answer. I have to be content with the knowledge that I know I did the very best I could under the circumstances. Time heals. That others are now benefiting from the safeguards and the heightened awareness and higher standards that his death produced is a positive by-product of a very tragic event."[4]

Brian Quinn eventually left LMU to become athletic director at Cal State-Fullerton. His office there, in Titan House on the campus, features a large display of Hank Gathers memorabilia and pictures.

"For years after Hank's death, I would wake up from a nightmare, sweating," Brian said.

"I was asking myself, 'Could I have done something [different] to save him?'

"I knew we had provided the best doctors, trainers, coach, and that there was nothing more that we could have done, but still it preyed on my mind," he said. "Finally, a priest I confided in told me, 'Brian, God never gives you more than you can handle. Now you can let go.' Only then did I let go of the guilt I had felt all those years."

Brian's daughter, Maureen, whom he had inadvertently abandoned on March 4 in his haste to get to the hospital, was similarly affected. "Her room became a shrine to Hank," Brian said. "She even kept some pressed flowers that had been on his coffin at the memorial service. She kept it just that way until she left home when she married."[5]

Chip Schaeffer, the young trainer who had attended to Hank in December and again in March, also was haunted by his death. He sought a meeting with Dr. Hattori a week or so after the tragedy and told the doctor he was troubled by what had happened. Dr. Hattori assured Chip he had done all he could. Schaeffer eventually left LMU and enjoyed a successful NBA career as trainer for the Chicago Bulls during the Michael Jordan era, and later with the Los Angeles Lakers, where he is still employed. On the team's visits to Philadelphia, he often leaves tickets at the will-call window for Derrick.[6]

Jay Hillock, assistant basketball coach at LMU under Paul Westhead, succeeded him in September 1990. After several disappointing seasons there, he moved on. Hillock is now Director of Pro-Personnel for the Chicago Bulls.[7]

Bruce Woods, Westhead's assistant coach who slipped his own conference championship ring off his finger to place it in Hank's coffin, is out of basketball. He serves as a sales representative for Jostens, the maker of the ring that he gave Hank. Bruce still has the ring from the 1990 Elite Eight performance. It is a heavy burnished gold with a large garnet-colored stone. Inscribed around the ring are the words "NCAA–Final Eight," a lion's head, and "Run the system." The stone contains three letters—LMU—and the number 44.

Bruce married the pretty strawberry blond who Hank loved to kid him about. Their firstborn son is named Hank.[8]

Dr. Lane Bove is still at LMU. In her office at the Malone Student Center is a picture of a younger Lane with her arms around Hank and Bo. Several magazine covers featuring the two athletes are framed and signed for her with affection.

"We never got to celebrate the great season we had in 1990. Instead we had to mourn a death of a student and then there was the threat of a lawsuit," she said. "It wasn't really until 2000, when the university decided to retire Hank and Bo's numbers, that we were able to enjoy all they had done that year."

Since 1990, her March 4 birthday has been a bittersweet day for her. Yet she consoles herself with memories of Hank. "He died with thunderous applause ringing in his ears. That last dunk—it was who Hank was. For him to have to restructure his life without basketball would have been very difficult for him," she said.[9]

Hank's high school coach shares Bove's opinion.

Rich Yankowitz retired in 2005 after amassing the most wins of any high school coach in Philadelphia public school history. He is still active and coaching a Penn State satellite campus team. He has a defibrillator implanted in his chest to regulate an irregular heart rate. His opinions about Hank are as candid as ever.

"If you had told Hank he couldn't play collegiate ball anymore, he would have played on the playground in pick-up games," Yank said. "Nothing would have stopped him. Basketball meant more to him than life itself."[10]

At Dobbins Vo-Tech, the gymnasium where Hank played has been named Hank's Place. The trophies his team won in the mid-1980's sit behind a glass case outside the gym. The photos of a young Hank, Bo, Heat, Derrick, and Doug—all full of youthful life and promise—are prominently displayed.

The school gives an annual Hank Gathers Award at graduation to the senior who best exemplifies the high ideals Hank represented. A scholarship goes with the award.

"Hank was determined to succeed," Yank said. "He wanted so much to help his mom, he would do anything he could for her. In the end, it took his life to reach the ideals he set for himself," Yank said.[11]

The opinionated, liberal priest who had been a surrogate father to Hank Gathers and many others never really recovered from his death. Father Dave Hagan remained saddened and burdened with guilt until his own death in May, 2005. His work in saving souls, and bodies, and minds against the enormous obstacles in the decaying inner city of North Philadelphia now is carried on by his friend, Father John McNamee.

At St. Malachy's Roman Catholic Church, on the fringe of the neighborhood where Hank grew up, Father McNamee toils on. His work with young people and the grim reality he faces each day have been documented in his 1993 book, *Diary of a City Priest*. He writes with eloquence and passion about his life and the struggles that inner-city inhabitants face every day, as well as his struggle to understand their plight in this land of plenty. The book was later made into a movie (premiering at the Sundance Film Festival in 2001) and is available on DVD. It is a chillingly depressing view of a world about which most of us are oblivious.[12]

LMU cheerleader Kristin Ramage Nelson graduated from Loyola Marymount University. She worked for a few years in the athletic department and later in customer relations for a pharmaceutical company. She has two children and helps her husband, TK Nelson, with his chiropractic medicine practice.

Every year, on March 4, a florist has delivered a dozen roses from an anonymous sender to Gersten Pavilion, where they are placed on a bench near the spot where Hank was laid on the concrete apron. They are from Kristin.[13]

Stan Morrison, who led Hank and Bo's team at USC, continued to coach basketball for a number of years. After his tenure at UC-Santa Barbara, he coached at San Jose State. Eventually, he arrived at UC-Riverside as athletic director. In the spring of 2005, he named a new basketball coach for the Highlanders. Morrison's choice was David Spencer, who immediately announced that his team would "run the System" that Hank and Bo had made so successful at LMU.[14] He lasted only two unsuccessful seasons before a freak accident sent him to the hospital with a fractured femur and left him on crutches for months. Spence resigned from UC-Riverside shortly thereafter. He and his wife remain in Riverside, where he is looking for work.

The Spencers have moved three times since the night in March 1990 when David noticed Hank's partially consumed bottle of cranberry juice in his cup holder and saved it for the next time he would see Hank. The bottle is still in their refrigerator.

In 2006, Paul Westhead was named head coach of the Phoenix Mercury of the WNBA. In his second season at the helm, his team captured the WNBA Championship, using the System to defeat the defending champ, the Detroit Shock. He is the first person to win both an NBA and WNBA championship.

One of his assistant coaches on the bench in September 2007 was Corey Gaines, who had triggered the System at LMU during Hank's first season there. With a commanding lead and time running down, Westhead, nearly 70, could be heard yelling to a player who was slowing the pace, "Shoot the ball!"

Westhead returned to the NBA in 2008 as an assistant to P. J. Carlesimo of the Seattle Supersonics. P.J. said he hired Paul because he believes Westhead deserves another chance to be a head coach in the NBA.[15] Carlesimo's vote of confidence notwithstanding, when the team, relocated to Oklahoma, struggled early in the season, both Carlesimo and Westhead were fired.

In the spring of 2009, Westhead was introduced at a press conference as the new head coach of the women's basketball team at the University of Oregon. "I love the game and want to feel the vibrations in the arena again," he said.

When a reporter asked what style of play fans could expect, Westhead smiled and replied, "We're going to shoot the ball every 5 seconds—hopefully less." Westhead, now 70, assured Eugene that the team would, at the very least, "create a lot of excitement."[16]

Bombs away!

Father James Loughran left LMU abruptly in 1991, just a year after the departure of the coach whose success on the court he never fully appreciated. The priest served at several other positions in education administration before arriving at St. Peter's University in Jersey City, New Jersey, in 1995.[17] He was president of the small Division I Jesuit school when he died on Christmas Eve 2006. Hypertensive cardiovascular disease was the suspected cause of the fall that resulted in his death at home.[18]

Bo Kimble, whose highly emotional tribute to his childhood friend in the 1990 NCAA tournament remains one of the most memorable moments in the history of college basketball, never fulfilled the promise that the Los Angeles Clippers saw in him.

An ominous omen of what was to come occurred in his first appearance at the foul line in a Clippers game. Bo took the free throw left-handed. It was a brick. He subsequently suffered nagging injuries and a lack of playing time and was sent off to the New York Knicks as an afterthought in a trade several seasons later. Soon he was in the minor leagues of the game, and then out entirely.[19]

Bo's relationship with Hank was a complex one. It was never quite what it seemed or what Bo's agents wanted it to appear to be. What it was, though, was real. The two gifted, competitive athletes from North Philly gave hope, through their example, to thousands of other kids who came after. Hank and Bo were like brothers. And like brothers, they fought, bickered, argued, and competed for attention throughout their lives. Like brothers, they formed a familial bond that was strong enough to withstand it all.

During the ceremony at Gersten Pavilion in 2000 that Lane Bove mentioned, Hank's number 44 and Bo's number 30 were retired by the university. The jerseys hang close together, just as the two players always did.

"There isn't a day that goes by that some stranger doesn't stop me and tell me that they remember the shot from the tournament," said Bo, who today is a successful executive of a firm that builds low-income housing in the United States and Africa. "If it keeps Hank's memory alive, that's all that matters. Hank will always be a part of me."[20]

Those weren't just empty words.

Bo's poignant, left-handed free throw in tribute to his friend in the NCAA Tournament in 1990 has bound the two players inextricably together. Both ESPN and CSTV have enshrined it as one of the most memorable moments in the history of college basketball. The 2008 book *Dick Vitale's Fabulous Fifty Players and Moments in*

College Basketball rates Bo's tribute and LMU's storybook run through the NCAA tourney at No. 13.

In 2007, Bo was present when a young man named Robert Smith collapsed on a basketball court in a YMCA league game in suburban New Jersey, It was cardiac arrest and he did not survive. "It was déjà vu for me. I looked at that guy and I saw Hank again. It was almost like Hank was there," he said.[21]

Shortly thereafter, Bo became certified in CPR and established a nonprofit foundation that is dedicated to educating people about the risks of heart disease, teaching CPR, and raising awareness about the need for defibrillators in all public arenas. He testified before a proceeding in Washington, D.C., to urge that **all public buildings in that city** have defibrillators on hand.

The logo for Bo's foundation, based in Silver Springs, Md., is a basketball encircled by a heart with a heart-rate tracing running through the ball. The slogan is: "Saving Lives… One Heartbeat At A Time."

The foundation is called Forty-Four For Life.

Lucille attended the LMU ceremony in 2000 that honored her son and his friend. It was her second visit to the LMU campus since Hank died there on March 4, 1990. She addressed the crowd with tears in her eyes. "This will always be a second home to me. I will be back," she said.

Bo attended, and the ceremony, in many ways, provided the closure that never occurred 10 years earlier, because of Fagel's lawsuit. It also allowed Bo and the Gathers family an opportunity to reconcile.

In 2005, Lucille and Bo attended the induction of the 1990 team into the LMU Hall of Fame. She has not returned since.

Lucille and her family used the money from the settlements to purchase a home in the Fairmount section of Philadelphia. She has married for the third time and lives there with her new husband.

Her health is not good and she remains "upset about Hank" to this day.[22]

Derrick Gathers works for a big-box home improvement store in suburban Philadelphia. Charles was a high school teacher in the Philadelphia school system for years and now is mentoring young people in the city. Chris Marable, Lucille's oldest son, remains incarcerated in Graterford prison, where he has been since Hank's death. He becomes eligible for parole in 2011.

Aaron Crump moved with his mother, Marva, and her mother, Phyllis, to a new home in Cheltenham, a leafy suburb of Philadelphia. Aaron played basketball at Cheltenham

High, where Paul Westhead began his coaching career, and today is a college student.

Hank's dream for those he loved came true. He got them out. He delivered on his promise.

Hank Gathers has been gone for 20 years. Anyone old enough to recall the 1990 NCAA tournament remembers him reflexively as, "Ooh, yeah—the guy who died on the court."

That Hank Gathers should be recalled by so many for his tragic and public death does a disservice to a man who led an inspiring and extraordinary life.

His legacy goes beyond the memories of his astonishing play, fearsome determination, up-from-poverty story, dead-on mimickry, and charming smile. Every high school and collegiate athlete who takes a physical examination today is indebted to Hank for the more stringent protocol used and questions that are posed. Many owe their lives to the more strenuous testing, which detects heart problems in young athletes that would never otherwise have come to anyone's attention.[23]

Red Wings hockey star Jiri Fischer is one person whose life was saved because a portable defibrillator was present. On March 6, 2006, eerily just two days after the anniversary of Hank's death on the basketball court, Vanderbilt's Davis Nwankwo was stricken during a practice— and was saved— because the portable defibrillator was at hand. No arena or large public facility in the United States is without one now. The publicity from Hank's death and the resulting litigation brought a heightened sense of awareness to the problems his death pointed out.

Once a cover boy for basketball magazines, Hank, since his death, has graced the cover of *Hampton Roads Orthopedics & Sports Medicine News* and has been the subject of countless articles in professional medical journals. The man who once was profiled in *Sports Illustrated* and other sports publications has been the subject of lengthy articles in the *New England Journal of Medicine* and other weighty tomes.

Hank's death served as a clarion call to the medical profession, especially sports medicine practitioners. It spawned dozens of conferences and seminars that explored the topic of sudden death in young athletes and the treatment and care of those athletes. It also gave rise to an equal number of forums that dealt with the questions first raised by Randy Harvey in the *Los Angeles Times* shortly after Hank died, about the responsibility of universities to their athletes.

Those symposiums grappled with the responsibility and ethical and moral questions facing doctors who treat blue-chip athletes. They debated the often inimical demands of "keep them playing" and the doctor's obligation to the patient, not to the doctor's employer. The concept of the patient's being ultimately responsible for his own care in following the physician's advice was brought home once more by the death of Reggie Lewis, the Boston Celtics star who collapsed while shooting baskets in July 1993. A series of doctors had advised him not to play basketball. Yet the former Dunbar High School standout continued to search for a doctor who would clear him. He eventually found one.

The tremendous publicity generated by Hank's death brought a new understanding to the real and present danger of sudden death in young athletes. No one in the medical community doubts that Hank's death was a strong contributing factor to the heightened awareness.[24]

Hank's example is followed by kids on the courts and playgrounds in Philadelphia and Los Angeles, and everywhere in between. From Hank Gathers, they learned:

No obstacle is too great to overcome.

No goal worth pursuing is ever too difficult to reach.

No dream worth dreaming should ever to be abandoned.

It is fair to say that most take those lessons and try to apply them to basketball, or another sport, in an effort to attain the athletic prowess that will bring them a professional contract with its attendant riches. It would also be fair to say that most of them fail to see and understand how Hank himself applied those lessons to everything he did, not just basketball.

In fact, his accomplishments off the court—seldom acknowledged and mostly ignored—are better examples than his basketball achievements for the preteens and teens who dream of being like Hank. For he achieved his greatest victory not in the gym, but in the classrooms of a prestigious academic institution.

In an era of abysmally poor graduation rates for college players and the farcical "rent-a-player" mentality that has major college teams scrambling for the player that can bring them a national title in a single season (Greg Oden and his move to the Portland Trail Blazers after playing one year at Ohio State and O. J. Mayo, now playing for the Memphis Grizzlies after one year at USC, come to mind), Hank's decision to remain at LMU after his record-breaking junior year reveals much about him.

As the all-time leading scorer in the WCC and only the second player in the history of the game to lead the country in both scoring and rebounding, he certainly deserves recognition and honor for his prowess on the court.

But he deserves even more honor and recognition, though, for his achievements in the classroom. The refrigeration and cooling major from Dobbins Vo-Tech did not coast through LMU. That was simply not possible. His transcript shows no electives in ballroom dancing, basket weaving wasn't part of the curriculum, and LMU didn't even offer such infamous courses as "rocks for jocks," as an especially easy geology class is often called.

From the moment he entered USC and came under the watchful eyes of Joanne Gallagher— as he tackled Russian, and as he later faced other tough courses in his years at LMU, Hank Gathers battled his poor academic preparation in order to survive in the classroom. At LMU, he had the assistance of Olivia La Bouff, English-language arts administrator, and Lane Bove, senior vice president of student affairs, as he chased his degree in communications. In addition to the study techniques in which they schooled him, Hank brought to the academic challenge the sponge-like concentration he used when he studied the X's and O's in a Paul Westhead chalkboard session. His battles to succeed academically were no less ferocious than his duels on the court with 7-footers. Hank fought just as hard to pass his history exams—and earn a better grade than Cassie Westhead did—as he did to wrestle a rebound from Shaquille O'Neal.

Despite some moments when the task before him seemed so insurmountable that he froze with fear, Hank survived the intellectual tests. He could easily have jumped to the NBA after his record-setting junior year. Given his circumstances, no one would have blamed him. Yet Hank stayed the course, not only to improve his chances for an especially fat contract but also to earn his degree.

Had he lived to accept it, that sheepskin would have been as proud a possession as any of the basketball honors, trophies, and awards he amassed.

Hank's dedication, diligence, and determination to succeed—to finish college and earn his degree—are an example that the young people who hope to be like Hank would do well to follow.

The young man who fell to the court on March 4, 1990, will be long recalled, perhaps forever, for his leaving. Yet it was his living that is noteworthy. Hank's work ethic, devotion to his family, loathing of street drugs, sense of humor, charm, intelligence, and genuine caring for others make him an especially worthy role model. Basketball gave Hank an opportunity that came to few others in the projects. Hank seized that opportunity and made the most of it. He enriched the lives of his teammates and coaches. He earned the respect of his opponents and the accolades of the sporting press. Hank Gathers was among us for less than a quarter century, yet his impact on countless others endures to this day.

His last coach once described Hank as a walking thunderbolt. The next time you see a late-night summer thunderstorm, notice how the lightning illuminates and brightens everything around it and think of Hank.

As Paul Westhead said in his commencement address in 1990: "Hank Gathers— what an achievement. A young boy from the streets of North Philadelphia who pulled himself up to earn his bachelor of arts degree in communications. Hank needed help from the faculty and staff to uncover his talents. He needed the loving suppport from his mother, Lucille, to stay with his studies; but most of all he needed the inner drive and courage to do the job.

"And," he added, "Hank found his bliss."[25] He followed his bliss to the end—not a bad example for any of us.

EPILOGUE
HANK'S HOUSE

Despite Father Dave Hagan's brash suggestion (and Al Gersten's approval) that Gersten Pavilion be renamed in Hank's honor, it never happened. The announcement of Lucille's lawsuit killed whatever chance the proposal may have had.

Shortly after Hank died, though, a banner was hung in the gymnasium in honor of Hank and the 1990 team. It was replaced a few years later by a new, larger one that hangs on the wall above the court where Hank played and died.

It is in the school's colors of crimson, gray, and blue and bears his number 44. It says, simply, "HANK'S HOUSE."

After Hank's death the Lions of LMU never again achieved the degree of success they had enjoyed while Hank and Bo were leading the way. LMU teams struggled, with little luck, to return to the form that had brought them conference titles and NCAA bids. Attendance sagged and interest waned.

In the late 1990s Coach Steve Aggers brought out of a dusty storage bin the trophies and mementos of the glory years, including Hank's NCAA Final Eight ring and various photos, and displayed them proudly in his office. Slowly, the spirit and enthusiasm returned.

Athletic Director Bill Husak helped heal the schism between the university and the Gathers family. His decision to honor Hank by retiring his number in 2000 was salve to the wounds both sides felt.

Today, when you attend an LMU home game, the student section is once more packed. Students proudly wear the crimson t-shirts that identify them as members of the Lion's Pride—shirts adorned with number 44 over their hearts—and before tipoff they greet opposing teams with a loud, raucous chant, roaring, "THIS IS. . .HANK'S HOUSE!!"

While I was researching this book, many people told me about strange things that had occurred at Gersten Pavilion since Hank's death. At first I ignored them or simply put them aside as interesting rumors and gossip.

Then I came across a 2004 column by Bill Plaschke in the *LA Times's* sports section. It was entitled "A Spirited Presence," and it explored in detail some of the tales people had been telling me.[1]

I decided to follow the leads and talk with as many people as I could find—I wanted to know about their experiences, observations, feelings, and sightings in the place called Hank's House.

More than a half-dozen people were willing to tell me what they experienced. I listened attentively, probed politely, and recorded their stories.

None of these people was in any way embarrassed or ashamed in sharing with a stranger what they had seen and heard at Gersten. None was interested in publicity or attention. I sought them out. Some, I found, were reluctant to speak on the record, while others—the majority—were perfectly willing to do so.

I listened to their stories and recorded them without judgment. All were honest, sincere, and open about what they experienced. I have no reason to doubt that they believe everything they told me.

The tall, thin young woman walked toward me with a slight limp. I greeted her and asked, "Bad knee?"

"No, it's sarcoma," twenty-two-year-old Pamela Ham informed me matter-of-factly.

As we made our way to the table in BJ's, a Burbank restaurant near her Pasadena apartment, male heads swiveled to admire the young raven-haired woman with dark almond eyes.

After she apologized for not turning off her cell phone—she was expecting a call from her doctor so she could report the pain that the growing tumor was inflicting on her—we began our talk.

She nibbled absentmindedly at her salad as she described her experiences at Gersten Pavilion while an LMU student.

"I knew about Hank from the references to him in the gym [the banners], and, from a girlfriend, I learned he had died there, but that was about all I knew," she said.

During her sophomore year, 1999, she became a cheerleader and was spending a lot of time in the gym for practice. "When I started cheering, there were about twenty or thirty students attending the games. It was terrible. The stands were empty. The team was terrible and no one supported them," she said. "Then, when they had the ceremony in 2000 to retire their jerseys [Hank's and Bo's], the place was packed. Even the student section was full. They knew about Hank. In fact, there was a feeling that the place and the team were cursed by Hank. We were so bad [that] people thought it had to be some reason like that.

"And then there were these strange things happening. We would hear toilets flushing by themselves in the men's locker room when we were there alone. It happened a number of times."

Other incidents occurred more often late at night, when the cheer and dance team was in the gym.

"We heard the distinctive sound of a ball being bounced as we were making our way out of the gym after practice. Yet there was no one in the gym. No one was out there that we could see. Yet the sound was unmistakable," she said. "It was a ball being dribbled."

At other times they'd hear a radio playing in Gersten. "The radio in the men's locker room would go on by itself. There was no one there to turn it on," she said. "It would just suddenly turn on. When we'd turn it off, it would go back on again. It happened often."

These strange goings-on startled Pam at first, but she said she never felt frightened or threatened.

"At first I thought, with the toilets, it must be some sort of a plumbing problem. Then, when the balls started being bounced and dribbled and no one was there to shoot them, I thought, OK, there is something else going on here," she said.

Eventually, Pam and the other cheerleaders came to accept them as part of the place. "We even started to say, 'Good night, Hank,' when we left the building," she related.

By her senior year, when she was one of the captains, she was spending a lot of time at night in Gersten. The incidents would occur when only a few people were left in the gym. Pam never felt any sense of danger. "When the radio would suddenly come on by itself, I'd go turn it off. Then, when it came back on again, I'd just say, 'OK, Hank, have fun,' she recalled.

"When I talked to Rudy [Ramirez, the long-time facilities manager at LMU] about what I had observed one time, he said, 'Don't worry about it, Pam. It's just Hank.' And I never was worried, never felt scared or that something was going to hurt us. Hank's spirit, or whatever it is, didn't appear to everyone," she said. She was never alone when these incidents occurred, and she gave me the names of people who had been with her. All confirmed what she told me.[2]

Tim Collins served as student manager of the basketball team at LMU before he graduated in 2005. He was in charge of preparing the game video footage for the coaches to review and helped out with practice drills and other tasks. He was always around the gym.

"I used to sneak into Gersten late at night to shoot some baskets. I would turn on just enough lights to be able to see and shoot. I was doing this one night when I suddenly felt a chill pass across my whole body, and it gave me goose bumps." he said. "It was warm and the doors were not open so I couldn't figure out what had caused it. It was strange. I went on shooting a while longer and then went to my office in back to do some work. While I was back there, I heard a basketball being bounced on the court. I went out and there was no one there. The ball I had been using was still there, right where I'd left it."

Tim described another incident that occurred while he was a freshman.

"We were playing Portland, and the game was a nip-and-tuck affair," he said. "Whenever Portland made a run, the scoreboard clock would suddenly malfunction. No matter what they did to try to fix it, it wouldn't work. The referees would have to stop the game, stopping Portland's momentum as well. It seemed to happen every time they had a scoring spurt. It worked fine when we were having a good run, and no one could figure out what was wrong. The clock operator couldn't explain it." Finally, the student seated next to Tim turned to him and said, "'Man, it's Hank. It's been thirteen years since he died playing against them—it's him.'"[3]

As the manager of athletic facilities at LMU, Rudy Ramirez was responsible for the gymnasium and spent a lot of his time in his office there. He had been at LMU when Hank was a student there and remained until a heart condition forced him to leave in 2005. While he was recovering from a recent hospital stay, he spoke with me.

"Over the years I saw and heard many things happen there that just can't be explained any other way," he said. "There would be the sound of the ball being dribbled, and then, when I looked, there was no one out there. I'd be back in my office working on paperwork, and I would hear it as clear as anything. It would be usually late at night, and I knew there was no one else in the place at that time. It has to be him. Nothing else makes any sense."

A recently hired employee who had been sweeping the gym out reported seeing a male figure in the darkness at the top of the stands. "He said he'd yelled at him to leave and the guy ignored him. He went up to the top, and when he got there, he was gone. He came into my office and told me what he'd seen. Then he pointed at me and said, 'It's you.'

"'No. It's not me. That was Hank,' I told him."[4]

Michelle Stabile was a student at LMU from 2000 to 2004. She too was a cheer-leader and eventually became a co-captain of the squad. When I spoke with her in 2005, she was on summer hiatus from her job as an elementary school teacher in the San Diego area. Her experiences while at LMU were similar to those described by her friend Pamela Ham. Michelle remembered seeing Hank's jersey suddenly begin moving as if a breeze were blowing. Yet the doors were shut and there was no wind. Nothing else was moving.

Another incident is especially memorable.

The only light in the gym was the faint reddish glow from the exit signs above the doors. The place that seemed so warm and alive during games now seemed cav-ernous and cold as she went through the familiar closing-up routine after cheerlead-ing practice.

As the captain, Michelle was responsible for ascertaining that all the doors were locked and the lights in the locker rooms were off. Her task nearly completed, the young blond student headed across the hardwood floor to the double glass doors that led outside.

As she neared the center of the floor, she glanced up toward the far end of the building, where the scoreboard clock was faintly visible in the gloom. There hung a familiar banner containing a white oval surrounding a black number 44. Darkness obscured the sign, but she knew well that its big bold letters read "HANK'S HOUSE."

She strode toward the exit, duffel bag slung over her shoulder, keys in her hand. Then she heard it.

"It was the unmistakable sound of water running. I had just been back in the locker room and knew that no one was there, yet the shower was running. I went on back and hollered in, 'Is there anyone here?'

"When no one answered, I went in cautiously and, sure enough, a shower in the men's locker room was going full blast," she said. "I knew it hadn't been on when I was in there just a few minutes earlier, and there was no one in the locker room. I turned it off and hit the lights again and went back out to leave.

"When I got about half way across the court, I heard the shower come on again. I went back in, and, without hollering this time, I went into the empty shower room and turned the water off. 'OK, Hank,' I said, 'turn it off when you're done. I don't want to get in any trouble.'"

A sad smile crossed her face as she approached the exit doors and heard the shower come on yet again. With a resigned shake of her head and a shrug of her shoulders, Michelle locked the double doors and left the gym. She walked purposefully in the cool California night as she crossed the still campus, bound for her dorm.

It was just past ten o'clock on January 12, 2004.

Hank had been dead for fourteen years.

More than a year later she told me, "I just knew it was him. I had no doubt about it at all. I still don't."[5]

The next morning, when the custodian opened up the gymnasium, the shower was off.

Whether you believe that Hank's spirit dwells in the place they call Hank's House is up to you.

What is important is that a spirit there continues to inspire all who play for LMU. As they enter the court from the locker room, each in turn taps a sign placed over the entrance to the court. It reads, *Play with Pride,* and is believed to bring good luck to all LMU athletes who pass beneath it.

The player whose death inspired one of college basketball's most memorable moments continues to inspire players and students to this day. Those who never saw him deliver a thundering dunk are inspired by his example nonetheless.

As Barry Zepel wrote in his moving tribute to Hank in the LMU alumni publication *Spirit,* "Hank Gathers left us with his dreams."[6]

And as Hank and his LMU teammates taught us, even if dreams don't always come true, we should never stop pursuing them.

Hank's legacy lives on and if his spirit lingers in the place where he breathed his last, it wouldn't surprise his friends.

"It's where we played late at night time after time. We were gym rats," Bo told me. "Hank loved basketball more than anything else, and he loved LMU. If there is any place that Hank would want to be, that is the place. His spirit is alive and well within everyone who knew him.

"He is there."[7]

On the evening that Hank died, the Pulitzer Prize–winning cartoonist Paul Conrad, saddened by the news, quietly retreated to his studio, where he produced a pen-and-ink tribute to Hank. It appeared in the *Los Angeles Times* on March 7, 1990, above a caption that reads, "Hank Gathers, 1967–1990."

The drawing depicts a basketball-like comet streaking toward the heavens against an inky black sky. Its long trail of cosmic dust separates it, for just that instant, from all the other celestial bodies. Burned into the sky is a line from the poet Stephen Spender: "Born of the sun, he traveled a short while toward the sun and left the vivid air signed with his honor."

NOTES

PREFACE

1 "Hero," Dictionary.com Unabridged (vol. 1.1), Random House, http://dictionary.reference.com/browse/hero. Although I use a somewhat different definition, I would like to acknowledge my debt to Jerry Izenberg, award-winning columnist for *The* (Newark, N.J,.) *Star-Ledger*. His 2003 tribute to the late Larry Doby, Izenberg's friend and the first African-American to play in the American League, inspired much of what I say about Hank Gathers as a hero. Izenberg is now semi-retired, which is our loss. His column appears only sporadically, but is always beautifully crafted.

2 Michael Schmidt, "30 Seconds with Paul Westhead," *The New York Times,* November 11, 2007.

REMEMBER

CHAPTER 1: BROTHERLY LOVE

1 Darrell Gates, interview by author, Philadelphia, June 21, 2006; Richard Yankowitz, interview by author, Philadelphia, June 9, 2005.

2 Yankowitz interview.

3 Roger Cohn, "High Rise Hell," *APF Reporter* 8, no. 1 (1985), www.aliciapatterson.org/APF0801/Cohn/Cohn.html.

4 Father David Hagan to Nevada Gov. Kenny Guinn, n.d., seeking clemency for Thomas Nevius, quoted in International Secretariat of Amnesty International, "Nevada's Planned Killing of Thomas Nevius," white paper on the death penalty in the United States, prepared as part of the organization's international campaign against capital punishment, AMR 51/001/2001, March 2001, p. 3.

5 Douglas Culbreth to Guinn, n.d., quoted in International Secretariat, "Nevada's Planned Killing," p. 3.

6 Declaration of Carol Pierce, January 11, 2001, quoted in International Secretariat, "Nevada's Planned Killing," p. 3.

7 Father John P. McNamee, interview by author, Philadelphia, March 23, 2006.

8 Dawn Staley, interview by author, telephone, March 9, 2006.

9 Gates interview.

10 Doug Overton, interview by author, Philadelphia, January 27, 2006.

11 Father McNamee interview.

12 Father McNamee interview.

13 Father McNamee interview.

14 Father McNamee interview.

15 Father McNamee interview.

16 Father McNamee interview; Shelley Smith, "A Bitter Legacy," *Sports Illustrated,* March 1992.

[17] Father McNamee interview; "Inner City House," undated brochure, www.student.nvcc.edu/home/CHMCKEON/ichouse/donations.html.

[18] Father McNamee interview.

[19] Father McNamee and Gates interviews; Bo Kimble, interview by author, North Wales, Pa, June 22, 2006.

[20] Gates interview; Cohn, "High Rise Hell."

[21] Gates interview.

[22] Maryann Hudson, "Hank Gathers and a Son He Left Behind," the *Los Angeles Times,* March 12, 1990, p. C1.

[23] Hudson, "Hank Gathers and a Son."

[24] Gates interview.

[25] Gates interview.

[26] Gates, Kimble, and Overton interviews.

[27] Gates interview.

[28] Ted Silary, *Philadelphia Daily News,* March 6, 1990.

CHAPTER 2: A FOOT IN THE DOOR

[1] Yankowitz interview.

[2] "CAT Results, 1981-82," *The Philadelphia Inquirer,* November 1983.

[3] Gates interview.

[4] Yankowitz interview.

[5] Yankowitz interview.

[6] Bo Kimble, interview by author, New Wales, Pa., June 22, 2006.

[7] Kimble interview.

[8] Kimble interview.

[9] Kimble interview.

[10] Kimble interview.

[11] Kimble interview; Bo Kimble, *For You, Hank* (New York: Delacorte, 1992), p. 14.

[12] Kimble, *For You, Hank,* p. 14.

[13] Gates interview.

[14] Yankowitz interview.

[15] Gates interview; Yankowitz interview.

[16] Yankowitz interview.

[17] Gates interview.

[18] Gates interview.

[19] Gates interview; Yankowitz interview.

[20] Kimble interview.

[21] Kimble and Yankowitz interviews.

[22] Gates interview.

[23] Yankowitz interview.

[24] Gates interview; Overton interview.

[25] Gates interview.

[26] Yankowitz interview.

[27] Yankowitz interview.

[28] Kimble interview.

[29] Yankowitz interview; Gates interview.

[30] Kimble, *For You, Hank,* p. 23.

[31] Kimble interview; see also *For You, Hank,* p. 26.

[32] Yankowitz interview.

[33] Hudson, "Hank Gathers and a Son."

[34] Hudson, "Hank Gathers and a Son"; Marva Crump, interview by author, telephone, June 2006.

CHAPTER 3: AMERICA'S MOST WANTED

[1] Gates interview.

[2] Ted Silary, "A Discard Still Gives Dobbins Two Aces," *Philadelphia Daily News,* January 6, 1984; Ray Parrillo, "Disciplined Mustangs Tie Up Gratz, 82-62, in Public Opener," *The Philadelphia Inquirer,* January 6, 1984.

[3] Ted Silary, "Trottie's Direction Has Dobbins Fired Up," *Philadelphia Daily News,* January 25, 1983.

[4] Ray Parrillo, "O'Hara 11-1 and Rated 7th, But Coach Is Unimpressed," *The Philadelphia Inquirer,* December 31, 1984.

[5] Silary, "A Discard."

[6] Silary, "A Discard."

[7] Silary, "A Discard."

[8] Silary, "A Discard"; Ray Parrillo, "Disciplined Mustangs Tie Up Gratz."

[9] Overton interview.

[10] Overton interview.

[11] Overton interview.

[12] Overton interview.

[13] Ray Parrillo, "No. 1 Franklin Turns Back Dobbins, 74-67," *The Philadelphia Inquirer,* February 8, 1984.

[14] Ray Parrillo, "No.1 Franklin Turns Back Dobbins."

[15] Kimble, *For You, Hank,* p. 39.

[16] Ted Silary, "Dobbins Goes on the Defensive, Makes Final," *Philadelphia Daily News,* March 9, 1984.

[17] Ray Parrillo, "A Last Look at the Highlights of the School Basketball Year," *The Philadelphia Inquirer,* April 3, 1984, p. C-5.

[18] Ted Silary, "Franklin Has the Will to Capture the Crown," *Philadelphia Daily News,* March 12, 1984.

[19] Gates interview.

[20] "Blake Leads All-City Team," *The Philadelphia Inquirer,* March 29, 1984, p. C-7; Ray Parrillo, "A Last Look at the Highlights."

[21] Yankowitz interview.

[22] Gates interview.

[23] Overton interview.

[24] Gates interview.

[25] Overton interview.

[26] Overton interview.

[27] Yankowitz interview.

[28] David Spencer, interview by author, Riverside, Calif., April 7, 2005.

[29] Yankowitz, Kimble, and Gates interviews.

[30] Kimble interview.

[31] Yankowitz interview.

[32] Gates interview.

CHAPTER 4: MAKING THE GRADE

[1] Yankowitz, Father McNamee, and Kimble interviews. See also Ted Silary, "Dobbins Players Conquer U. City, Books,"

Philadelphia Daily News, January 30, 1985, in which Hank discusses his academic struggles.

[2]Ted Silary, "Southern Cal Might Lure Gathers, Kimble," *Philadelphia Daily News,* April 17, 1985; Kimble, Yankowitz, and McNamee interviews.

[3] Yankowitz interviews.

[4] Ray Parrillo, "The 20 Basketball Players to Watch This Season," *The Philadelphia Inquirer,* December 2, 1984.

[5] Ray Parrillo, "Between Dobbins and Franklin It's Anybody's Guess," *The Philadelphia Inquirer,* November 25, 1984.

[6] Parrillo, "Between Dobbins and Franklin."

[7] Parrillo, "The 20 Basketball Players to Watch."

[8] Ray Parrillo, "Here Come Holidays, There Go Teams," *The Philadelphia Inquirer,* December 16, 1984, p. E15.

[9] Parrillo, "Here Come Holidays."

[10] Parrillo, "Here Come Holidays."

[11] Bruce W. Branch, "Who Will Be King?" *The Louisville* (Ky.) *Times,* December 13, 1984, p. E1.

[12] Mark Shallcross, "Kenny Payne Scores 38 in Losing Effort," *The Louisville* (Ky.) *Times,* December 20, 1984, p. C-2.

[13] Shallcross, " Kenny Payne Scores 38."

[14] Shallcross, "Kenny Payne Scores 38."

[15] Mark Shallcross, "Valley Explodes on Offense; Dobbins Tech Keeps Hot Hand," *The Louisville* (Ky.) *Times,* December 21, 1984, p. C-5.

[16] Shallcross, Valley Explodes on Offense."

[17] Rick Cushing, "Valley Outguns Logan; Dobbins Outworks St. Raymonds," *The Louisville* (Ky.) *Courier-Journal,* December 21, 1984, p. D-3.

[18] Bob White, "Philadelphia School Is No Cream Cheese, Meets Seneca in Final," *The* (Louisville Ky.) *Courier-Journal,* December 22, 1984, p. C-1.

[19] Bob White, "Kimbro's 38 Futile as Seneca Falls," *The* (Louisville,Ky.) *Courier-Journal,* December 23, 1984, C-8.

[20] Bob White, "Kimbro's 38 Futile.]

[21] Bob White, "Kimbro's 38 Futile,"

[22] White, "Kimbro's 38 Futile."

[23] White, "Kimbro's 38 Futile."

[24] Yankowitz interview.

[25] Sam Ross Jr., "Dobbins Tech Road Show Stops in Johnstown for CCWM Tourney," *Johnstown* (Pa.) *Tribune-Democrat,* December 27, 1984, p. 18.

[26] John P. James, "Dobbins Clobbers Coatesville," *Johnstown* (Pa.) *Tribune-Democrat,* December 29, 1984, p.13.

[27] James, "Dobbins Clobbers Coatesville."

[28] Rod Frisco, "Dobbins Thumps Trojans," *Johnstown* (Pa.) *Tribune-Democrat,* December 30, 1984. p. C-1. Frisco said of Dobbins, "They are more than good. The Mustangs have all the ingredients that, when merged, make for greatness."

[29] Rod Frisco, "Dobbins Thumps Trojans," *Johnstown* (Pa.) *Tribune-Democrat,* December 30, 1984.

[30] Ray Parrillo, "Court Poetry: A Coach and a Team Pull Tall Twins Back to the City Streets They Fled,' *The Philadelphia Inquirer,* December 26, 1984, p. F-1.

[31] Parillo, "Court Poetry:.

[32] Sam Carchidi, "Camden Takes a Loss, Keeps No. 1 Ranking," *The Philadelphia Inquirer,* December 31, 1984; Ted Silary, "High Stakes High School Hoops," *Philadelphia Daily News,* January 3,1985. Carchidi's story mentions Dunbar's national ranking and Dobbins' ranking.

[33] Ted Silary, "Victory Small Consolation for Dobbins," *Philadelphia Daily News,* January 7, 1985.

[34] Silary, "Victory Small Consolation."

[35]Gates interview.

[36] Ted Silary, "Dobbins Gathers in a Big Victory," *Philadelphia Daily News,* February 15, 1984. I am indebted to this story for the game account that follows and postgame interviews with the Dobbins players and coach.

[37] The games with the most rivalry were usually scheduled for the afternoon, in the hope that fans would not have been drinking for hours in anticipation.

[38] Ted Silary, "Dobbins Gathers in a Big Victory"; Yankowitz and Kimble interviews.

[39] Ted Silary, "Trojan Horses? Southern Cal Might Lure Gathers, Kimble," *Philadelphia Daily News,* April 17, 1985.

[40] Ted Silary, "Dobbins Players Conquer U. City, Books," *Philadelphia Daily News,* January 30,1985.

[41] Ted Silary, "Dobbins Players Conquer."

[42] Silary, "Southern Cal Might Lure Gathers, Kimble."

[43] Kimble, Yankowitz, and McNamee interviews.

CHAPTER 5: UNFINISHED BUSINESS

[1] Ted Silary, "Dobbins Rolls to Title as Kimble Flashes Major League Talent," *Philadelphia Daily News,* March 11, 1985.

[2] Yankowitz interview.

[3] Gates interview.

[4] Spencer interview.

[5] Stan Morrison, interview by author, Riverside, Calif., April 2005.

[6] Spencer interview.

[7] Kimble interview.

[8] Silary, "Dobbins Rolls to Title."

[9] Kimble interview.

[10] Yankowitz interview; Ted Silary, "Kimble, Gathers Have a Tie That Binds," *Philadelphia Daily News,* April 25,1985.

[11] The account of the press conference and all quotes are from Silary, "Kimble, Gathers Have a Tie That Binds."

[12] Silary, "Dobbins Rolls to Title."

[13] Father McNamee interview.

[14] Gates interview.

[15] Spencer interview; Kimble interview.

[16] Spencer interview.

[17] The account of the MOVE debacle is based on reporting in *The Philadelphia Inquirer,* including Rich Heidorn Jr., "What Led to the Confrontation at West Philadelphia Compound," May 13, 1985; Thomas J. Gibbons Jr., Russell Cooke, and Michael Coakley, "Move House Is Bombed," May 14, 1985; Janet McMillan, Vanessa Williams, and Steve Lopez, "Watching, But Scarcely Believing in West Phila.," May 14, 1985; William K. Marimow, "Talks Settlement Hopes Foundered on Issues of Future Arrests," May 14, 1985; Beth Gillin, "Sympathetic Ears, Smattering of Residents around City Don't Blame Goode for the Tragedy," May 15, 1985; Russell Cooke, "The Damage to Goode and the City," May 19, 1985; Mary Jane Fine, "A Day of Prayer for Fire Victims," May 20, 1985.

CHAPTER 6: PROMISED LAND

[1] Bo Kimble, *For You, Hank* (New York: Delacorte, 1992), p. 62.

[2] Kimble, *For You, Hank,* p. 62.

[3] Tom Lewis, interview by author, San Juan Capistrano, Calif., June 4, 2006.

[4] Bo Kimble, interview by author, North Wales, Pa., June 22, 2006.

[5] Mal Florence, "USC Goes a Bit Philly-Silly," the *Los Angeles Times,* February 6, 1986, Sports, p. 1.

[6] Kimble, *For You, Hank,* p. 62.

[7] Lewis interview.

[8] Lewis interview.

[9] Nielsen Sports, "NCAA Men's Basketball Championship Game, 1975-2007, Selected Audience Trends," spreadsheet provided to the author by e-mail attachment from Greg Weitkamp, NCAA, August 15, 2008.

[10] "A Call to Action: Reconnecting Sports and Higher Education," 2001 report of the Knight Foundation Commission

on Intercollegiate Athletics, in Scott Rosner and Kenneth L. Shropshire, eds., *The Business of Sport* (Sudbury, Mass.: Rosner and Shropshire, 2004), 684. In fact, the 2001 report is excerpted in Rosner and Shropshire. For the full report by William C. Friday and the Rev. Theodore Hesburgh, see www.knightcommission.org/images/uploads/KCfinal-06-2001.pdf. Copies of all the commission's reports, including the first in 1991, are available at its Web site, www.knight-commission.org.

11 "A Call to Action," 684.

12 Maguire is quoted in Tates Locke and Bob Ibach, *Caught in the Net* (West Point, N.Y.: Leisure Press, 1982), 170.

13 Alexander Woolf and Armand Keteyian, *Raw Recruits* (New York: Pocket Books, 1991), 61.

14 Ibid.

15 Ibid., 62-63.

16 Ibid., 60.

17 Pat Barrett continues to coach one of the top AAU basketball teams and has sent scores of players to major college programs. Kevin Love of UCLA is only the latest example. Barrett is a paradoxical figure whose efforts to aid young players is at odds with the unflattering recollections of his representation of Tom Lewis. When I reached Barrett to set up an interview, he agreed to speak with me, then became unavailable.

18 Stan Morrison, interview by author, Riverside, Calif., April 2005; Lewis interview.

Chapter 7: Helping Hands

1 For discussions of college recruiting practices of the era, see Wolff and Keteyian, *Raw Recruits*; Dan Wetzel and Don Yaeger, *Sole Influence: Basketball, Corporate Greed and the Corruption of America's Youth* (New York: Grand Central Publishing, 2000); John Valanti and Ron Neclairio, *Swee' Pea and other Playground Legends* (New York: Kesend, 1990); Allen Sack and Ellen Staurowsky, *College Athletes for Hire* (Westport, Conn.: Praeger, 1998), 104-105.

2 "A Call to Action," 685.

3 Ibid., 678.

4 Ibid.

5 They add, "Relatedly, we should be wary of assuming that morality is class-based and that affluence insulates against misconduct" (68). For their conclusions, see Francis T. Cullen and Edward J. Latessa, "The Extent and Sources of NCAA Rule Infractions: A National Self-Report Study of Student-Athletes, a Report to the National Collegiate Athletic Association," 1993, University of Cincinnati, http://www.uc.edu/criminaljustice/ProjectReports/NCAA_Rule_Infractions.pdf, 68-70.

6 Ibid., 39, 51, 59, 69.

7 Locke and Ibach, *Caught in the Net,* 44. Locke and Ibach provide an insider's view of recruiting collegiate players.

8 Locke and Ibach, *Caught in the Net,* 44.

9 Ibid., 169.

10 Ibid., 64.

11 According to a story that ran in *USA Today* on October 17, 2008 ("Knight Says He'd Consider Return," p. 8C), Knight made these comments during an appearance on *Mickey's Corner,* WFYI, Indianapolis, Ind., taped September 10, 2008, and aired on October 15, 2008. Ironically, it was Tates Locke who hired the young Bob Knight as his assistant at West Point. When Locke left, Knight became the head coach.

12 Alan Drooz, interview by author, San Diego, Calif., July 18, 2005.

13 Mal Florence, "College Basketball Coaches, Players, Teams, Trends to Watch in the 1985-86 Season," the *Los Angeles Times*, November 21, 1985, p. 1.

14 Lewis interview.

15 Lewis interview

16 Lewis interview.

17 Lewis interview.

18 Lewis, Kimble interviews.

19 Florence, "College Basketball Coaches, Players, Teams."

[20] Drooz interview.

[21] Scott Howard-Cooper, "Easy Opener Boomerangs on Trojans," the *Los Angeles Times*, November 20, 1985, p. 2.

[22] Howard-Cooper, "Easy Opener Boomerangs."

[23] Larry Stewart, "Dowell Hits Right Notes, and USC Scores a Win," the *Los Angeles Times*, November 23, 1985, p. 12.

[24] Stewart, "Dowell Hits Right Notes."

[25] Stewart, "Dowell Hits Right Notes."

[26] Stewart, "Dowell Hits Right Notes."

[27] Stewart, "Dowell Hits Right Notes."

[28] Scott Howard-Cooper, "Hokies Are No Joke to Trojans," the *Los Angeles Times*, November 26, 1985, p. 4.

[29] "Morrison Likes Efforts of Trojans," the *Los Angeles Times*, Sports, November 27, 1985, p. 5.

[30] Peter Priamos, interview by author, Sherman Oaks, Calif., July 11, 2005.

[31] The exemption may be found in *NCAA Manual*, By Laws, Sections 16.02.3 (Extra Benefits) and 16.11 (Benefits, Gifts and Services).

[32] Chris Priamos, interview by author, Las Vegas, July 16, 2009.

[33] "Morrison Likes Effort of Trojans."

[34] "USC Plays Syracuse Tonight," the *Los Angeles Times*, Sports, November 29, 1985, p. 8.

[35] Mal Florence, "Morrison Decides to Let Young Players Sit a Spell," the *Los Angeles Times*, December 5,1985, p. 9.

[36] Lewis interview.

[37] Richard Yankowitz, interview by author, Philadelphia, Pa., June 9, 2005.

[38] Chuck Newman, "Penn's Late Rally Upsets Southern Cal," *The Philadelphia Inquirer*, December 3,1985, p. C-1.

[39] Lewis interview.

[40] Florence, "Morrison Decides to Let Young Players Sit."

[41] David Spencer, interview by author, Riverside, Calif., April 7, 2005.

[42] Florence, "Morrison Decides to Let Young Players Sit."

[43] Lewis interview.

[44] Morrison interview.

[45] Lewis interview.

[46] Lewis interview.

[47] Derrick Dowell, interview by author, telephone, August 26, 2006.

[48] Lewis interview.

[49] Yankowitz and Spencer interviews.

[50] Deposition summaries of Lucille Gathers (August 1, 1990), Charles Gathers (August 30, 1991), and David Hagan (August 29, 1991), in *Gathers et al. v. Loyola Marymount University et al.,* No. C795027, Los Angeles Superior Court, filed April 20, 1990, from the files of Richard D. Carroll, one of the attorneys who represented Norcal Mutual Insurance Company, which had issued the malpractice insurance policy for three of the doctors named in the medical malpractice suit brought by Hank's family after his death.

[51] Yankowitz interview

[52] Lewis interview. Tom Peabody, a teammate of Hank's at Loyola Marymount, told a similar story (Tom Peabody, interview by author, Long Beach, Calif., June 22, 2005).

[53] Mal Florence, "Morrison, Longhorns Can't Cramp Lewis' Style," the *Los Angeles Times*, December 6, 1985, p.7.

[54] Spencer interview.

[55] Morrison interview..

[56] Morrison interview.

[57] Morrison interview.

[58] Drooz interview.

[59] Mal Florence, "Trojans Play Bah Humbug Opener," the *Los Angeles Times*, December 23, 1985, p. 12.

[60] Mal Florence, "Trojans Play Bah Humbug Opener."

[61] Mal Florence, "Bo Kimble's 22 Points Play a Big Role as USC Defeats Oregon, 75-60," the *Los Angeles Times*, January 6, 1986, Sports, p. 3.

[62] Mal Florence, "Bo Kimble's 22 Points."

[63] Mal Florence, "Bo Kimble's 22 Points."

[64] Mal Florence, "Bo Kimble's 22 Points."

[65] Tracy Dodds, "Washington Showing Cohesiveness, Beats USC Inside and Out," the *Los Angeles Times*, January 12, 1986, Sports, p. 5.

[66] Dodds, "Washington Showing Cohesiveness."

[67] Dodds, "Washington Showing Cohesiveness."

[68] Mal Florence, "To Morrison USC Trip Was a Joke," the *Los Angeles Times*, January 14, 1986, Sports, p. 5.

[69] Mal Florence, "USC Wins with No Time Left," the *Los Angeles Times*, January 17, 1986, Sports, p.1.

[70] Florence, "USC Wins."

[71] Florence, "USC Wins."

[72] Mal Florence, "Four Freshman Make Sweet Music in USC Victory," the *Los Angeles Times*, January 19, 1986, Sports, p.4.

[73] Florence, "Four Freshman Make Sweet Music."

[74] Spencer interview.

[75] Florence, "Four Freshman Make Sweet Music."

[76] Florence, "Four Freshman Make Sweet Music."

[77] Dan Flesser, "Cal Defeats USC," the *San Jose Mercury News*, January 23, 1986, Sports, p. 1D.

[78] Dan Flesser, "Cal Defeats USC."

Chapter 8: Trouble in Paradise

[1] Mal Florence, "Lewis Cites 'Turmoil' at USC, Then Recants;" the *Los Angeles Times*, January 29, 1986, Sports, p.1.

[2] Florence, "Lewis Cites 'Turmoil.' "

[3] Lewis interview.

[4] Florence, "Lewis Cites 'Turmoil.'"

[5] Lewis interview.

[6] Florence, "Lewis Cites 'Turmoil.' "

[7] John Gutekunst, interview by author, telephone, February 15, 2007.

[8] Mike McGee, interview by author, telephone, February 16, 2007.

[9] Ross Newhan, "USC, Shooting Only 36 Percent, Loses to Washington St. in Overtime," the *Los Angeles Times*, February 7, 1986, p. 6.

[10] Mal Florence, "USC Will Try to End Pac-10 Slump at Tempe Tonight," the *Los Angeles Times*, February 13, 1986, p. 4.

[11] Scott Howard-Cooper, "USC Goes Down Fighting in a 70-64 Loss to Huskies" the *Los Angeles Times*, February 9, 1986, p. 1.

[12] Phil Collin, "Washington May Have Given USC Pac-10 Knockout Punch," the *Daily Breeze*, February 9, 1986, Sports, p. C-1.

[13] Mal Florence, "USC Goes a Bit Philly Silly." *The Los Angeles Times*, February 6, 1986, p.c-1.

[14] Florence, "USC Goes a Bit Philly Silly."

[15] Lewis interview.

[16] Darrell Gates, interview by author, Philadelphia, Pa., June 21, 2006.

[17] Mal Florence, "USC Gets Win of the Month," the *Los Angeles Times*, February 23, 1986, Sports, p.1.

[18] Gary Jones, "USC Pulls an Inside Job on UCLA," the *Los Angeles Daily News,* February 23, 1986, Sports, p. 1.

[19] Jones, "USC Pulls an Inside Job."

[20] Florence, "USC Gets Win."

[21] Mal Florence, "Foul Shots with No Time Left Beat USC, 65-63," the*Los Angeles Timess,* February 25, 1986, p. 2.

[22] Gary Jones, "Dowell Is Suspended by Morrison," the *Los Angeles Daily News,* February 27, 1986, Sports, p. 1.

[23] Dowell interview.

[24] Dowell interview.

[25] Mal Florence, "Change Is Hinted in USC Basketball," the *Los Angeles Times*, March 11, 1986, Sports, p. 5.

[26] Morrison interview.

[27] McGee interview.

[28] Gary Jones, "From Top to Bottom, Then Out, Morrison Resigns as USC Coach," the *Los Angeles Daily News,* March 12, 1986, Sports, p. 1

[29] Spencer interview.

CHAPTER 9: A NEW DEAL

[1] Mal Florence, "Kimble and Gathers Express Disappointment at Resignation," the *Los Angeles Times*, March 12, 1986, Sports, p. 5.

[2] Lewis interview. Spencer, in a remarkable display of optimism, or a severe case of denial, was in San Francisco attempting to convince Chris Monk to sign with USC while the press conference was taking place. Monk eventually did come to USC and finished his career as their ninth leading rebounder. He later played in 11 games with the Utah Jazz of the NBA.

[3] Kimble interview.

[4] Lewis interview.

[5] Lewis interview.

[6] McGee interview.

[7] Aaron Brown, *"I Have a Dream"Remembered,* CNN, January 17, 2005.

[8] Bill Mulligan, interview by author, telephone, 2006.

[9] Mal Florence, "Harrick, Mulligan Express Interest in USC Job," the *Los Angeles Times*, March 13, 1986, Sports, p. 2.

[10] Mike Downey, "He Has Finally Found Right Place for Man with a Sense of Humor," the *Los Angeles Timess,* March 28, 1986, Sports, p. 1.

[11] Lewis interview.

[12] Kimble interview.

[13] Spencer interview.

[14] Lewis interview.

[15] Kimble interview.

[16] McGee interview.

[17] Gary Jones, "Dowell Drops Classes at USC," the *Los Angeles Daily News,* April 17, 1986, Sports, p. 1.

[18] John Cherwa, interview by author, telephone, October 19, 2005.

[19] George Raveling, interview by author, telephone, March 7, 2006.

[20] "Raveling, a Philly guy and a black, lost them all," Jerry Pimm, then the coach at UC-Santa Barbara, commented years later, reflecting on the irony of the events (Pimm, interview by author, telephone, February 6, 2006).

[21] Harrick would leave Pepperdine for UCLA after the 1987-88 season. At UCLA, he won the NCAA title in 1995 and was named Coach of the Year. A year later. he was fired for falsifying expense reports. He made stops at Rhode Island (1997-99) and at Georgia (1999-2003, where the president was Michael Adams, who had been Pepperdine's president while Harrick was there), always with success on the court and controversy and scandal off it. He resigned from Georgia after a scandal over grades. Connelly would star at Santa Clara and then for years in professional ball in South America, where he became a fan favorite.

22 Spencer interview.

23 Peter Priamos interview.

24 Jerry Tarkanian, interview by author, telephone, August 17, 2006.

25 Kimble interview.

26 Gary Jones, "USC Players Were Urged to Transfer," the *Los Angeles Daily News,* March 10, 1986, Sports, p. 2.

27 Father John McNamee, interview by author, Philadelphia, March 23, 2006.

28 Paul Westhead, interview by author, Hermosa Beach, Calif., June 22, 2005.

29 Westhead interview.

30 Cassie Westhead, interview by author, telephone, April 26, 2006.

31 Brian Quinn, interview by author, Fullerton, Calif., July 14, 2005; Father James Loughran, interview by author, Jersey City, N.J., August 2006.

32 Paul Westhead, Cassie Westhead, Quinn, and Loughran interviews.

33 Cassie Westhead interview.

CHAPTER 10: SETTLIN' IN

1 Pete Priamos, interview by author, Sherman Oaks, Calif. July 11, 2005.

2 Bo Kimble, interview by author, North Wales, Pa, June 25, 2006.

3 Paul Westhead, interview by author, Hermosa Beach, Calif., June 22, 2005.

4 Priamos interview.

5 Kimble interview.

6 Maryann Hudson Harvey, interview by author, Baltimore, Md.,October 6, 2005.

7 NCAA, "Men's Basketball Attendance, 1970-2006," www.ncaa.org/stats/m_basketball/attendance/index.html. LMU would be an exception. In the Westhead era, LMU's average attendance would soar from fewer than 1,000 to 4,037 in 1990. Of the 306 schools in Division I, LMU moved from no. 275 to no. 128 in attendance.

8 Mal Florence, "Scholarships Taken from Three USC Freshmen; Lewis, Gathers and Kimble Receive Word from Raveling," the *Los Angeles Times,* April 29, 1986, Sports, p. 1. See also Randy Harvey, "USC's Bo Kimble, Hank Gathers Are Given Releases," the *Los Angeles Times,* May 2, 1986, Sports, p. 6.

9 Scott Ostler, "USC's Four Freshmen Emerge as Campus Activists of the 80's," the *Los Angeles Times,* March 26, 1986, Sports, p. 1.

10 Alan Drooz, interview by author, San Diego, Calif., July18, 2005.

11 Alan Drooz, "Philadelphia Connection Is Key for Loyola," the *Los Angeles Times,* May 10, 1986, Sports, p. 10.

12 Randy Harvey, "Gathers and Kimble Are Set for Loyola," the *Los Angeles Times,* May 9, 1986, Sports, p. 1.

13 Randy Harvey, "Un-Raveling at USC: A Failure to Communicate," the *Los Angeles Times,* May 13, 1986, Sports, p. 1.

14 Doug Overton, interview by author, Philadelphia, Pa., January 27, 2006.

15 Darrell Gates, interview by author, Philadelphia, Pa., June 21, 2006.

16 Corey Gaines, interview by author, telephone, March 2, 2006.

CHAPTER 11: RARIN' TO GO

1 Bruce Woods, interview by author, Pittsburgh, Pa., January 24, 2006.

2 Gaines interview.

3 Gaines interview.

4 Gates interview.

5 Chris Priamos, interview by author, Las Vegas, Nev., July 16, 2009.

6 Brian Quinn, interview by author, Fullerton, Calif., July 14, 2005.

7 Alan Drooz, "Waves and Loyola Have Lost a Lot but Still Look Strong," the *Los Angeles Times,* November 27, 1986, Sports, p. 14.

[8] Alan Drooz, "Lions Want Something to Roar about; Redshirts May Hold Answer," the *Los Angeles Times,* March 12, 1907, Sports, p. 10.

[9] "History of LMU," www.lmu.edu; Barry Zepel, Loyola Marymount Basketball Media Guide, 1989 results; Barry Zepel, interview by author, Anaheim, Calif., July 15, 2005; Dr. Lane Bove, interview by author, Los Angeles, Calif., October 17, 2005; Quinn interview.

[10] Albert Gersten II, interview by author, Los Angeles, Calif., July 8, 2005.

[11] Waxman, of course, went on to a long and illustrious career in the House, to which he was first elected in 1975. Berman and Levine joined him there in 1983; Waxman and Berman continue to represent California, whereas Levine left Congress in 1992 and is a lawyer in private practice in Los Angeles, Calif.

[12] Gersten interview; Janice Dickinson, *No Lifeguard on Duty* (New York: HarperCollins, 2002).

[13] Gersten interview.

CHAPTER 12: RUNNIN' THE SYSTEM

[1] Jim Foster, interview by author, telephone, July 3, 2006.

[2] Enoch Simmons, interview by author, telephone, January 8, 2006.

[3] Brooks's jersey, along with that worn by Lionel Simmons, has been retired by the Explorers. Brooks was named the NBA's 1980 Player of the Year.

[4] Westhead interview.

[5] Foster interview.

[6] Alan Drooz, "WCAC Touched by the Pac-10," the *Los Angeles Times,* November 26, 1987, Sports, p. 1.

[7] Tom Peabody, interview by author, Long Beach, Calif., June 22, 2005.

[8] Ann Killion, "Moving Away Isn't Always the Right Move," *Los Angeles Times,* Orange County Edition, January 27, 1988, Sports, p. 10.

[9] Peabody interview.

CHAPTER 13: TAKIN' THE COURT

[1] Alan Drooz, "Loyola Marymount Puts Aussies Down Under," the *Los Angeles Times,* November 22, 1987, Sports, p. 26.

[2] Alan Drooz, "Biting the Big Apple," the *Los Angeles Times,* November 27, 1987, Sports, p. 24.

[3] Alan Drooz, "Reborn Gaines Leads Loyola to Easy Victory Against Tennessee Tech," the*Los Angeles Times,* November 29, 1987, Sports, p. 18.

[4] Alan Drooz, "Gaines, Gathers Help Lead Loyola Rout," the *Los Angeles Times,* November 29,1987, Sports, p. 8.

[5] Alan Drooz, "Loyola's Run at St. John's Streak Falls Just Shy," the *Los Angeles Times,* November 30, 1987, Sports, p. 5.

[6] Alan Drooz, "Loyola Gets a Workout before Putting Westmont Away, 100-84," the *Los Angeles Times,* December 3, 1987, Sports, p. 8.

[7] the *Los Angeles Loyolan,* December 3, 1987.

[8] Tom Marumoto, interview by author, telephone, March 24, 2006.

[9] The old mark, set by UNLV, was 117 points.

[10] Alan Drooz, "Pacific Can't Keep Up with Loyola, 130-110," the *Los Angeles Timess,* December 6, 1987, Sports, p. 8.

[11] Tim Hubbard, "LMU Runs over Pacific with 130-point Effort," the *Daily Breeze,* December 6, 1987, Sports, p. D-6.

[12] Bruce Woods, interview by author, Pittsburgh, Pa., January 24, 2006.

[13] Gaines interview.

[14] Woods interview.

[15] After the 1987-88 season, LMU produced, through its communications and film departments, a promotional film entitled, *Run the System.* It includes interviews with Westhead, Hank, and Bo as they explain the fundamentals of the System, accompanied by clips of LMU executing it. It has a throbbing musical score and was a slick and effective promotional vehicle.

[16] Kimble interview.

[17] Alan Drooz, "Loyola's Offense Is Slowed to a Crawl in an 84-69 Loss to Oregon State," the *Los Angeles Times*, December 10, 1987.

[18] Tim Tuttle, "49'ers Entertain Crowd, Coach," *The Orange County Register,* December 14, 1987, Sports, p. D-12.

[19] Dick Wagner, "Long Beach Comes Long Way Back to Win; 49ers, Down by 22, End Up Beating Loyola Marymount in Overtime,117-113," the *Los Angeles Times*, December 14, 1987.

[20] Alan Drooz, "Torrid Loyola Cagers Rank Third among Division 1 Teams," the *Los Angeles Times*, December 18, 1987.

CHAPTER 14: THE HANK AND BO SHOW

[1] Drooz, "Loyola, with Kimble."

[2] Alan Drooz, "Loyola Marymount . . . Lions Are Not Out to Grab National Spotlight," the *Los Angeles Times*, December 17, 1987, Sports, p. 17.

[3] Gersten interview.

[4] Drooz, "Loyola Marymount."

[5] Gersten interview.

[6] Drooz, "Loyola Marymount."

[7] Alan Drooz, "Kimble's Bo-dacious Debut: 28 Points in Easy Loyola Romp," the *Los Angeles Times,* December 20, 1987, Sports, p. 24.

[8] Alan Drooz, "Loyola Crushes Brooklyn in a 123-72 Record Setter," the *Los Angeles Times*, December 24, 1987, Sports, p. 4.

[9] Alan Drooz, "Loyola Marymount Tops Loyola of Chicago with a Deeper Bench," the *Los Angeles Times*, December 29, 1987, Sports, p. 3.

[10] Alan Drooz, "Loyola's Press Leads to impressive Win over Holy Cross, 127-104" the *Los Angeles Times,* December 31, 1987, Sports, p. 5.

[11] Alan Drooz, "College Notebook: Loyola Could Use a Traffic Controller," the *Los Angeles Times*, January 1, 1988, Sports, p. 1.

[12] Alan Drooz, "Loyola Marymount to Play Marquette," the *Los Angeles Times*, January 6, 1988, Sports, p. 7.

[13] Alan Drooz, "Loyola Struggles to Victory over Wisconsin-Green Bay," the *Los Angeles Times*, January 5, 1988, Sports, p. 4.

[14] Alan Drooz, "Marquette Is Beaten by Loyola," the *Los Angeles Times*, January 7, 1988, Sports, p. 3.

[15] Alan Drooz, "Loyola Marymount Wins Seventh Game in a Row, 113-89," the *Los Angeles Times,* January 10, 1988, Sports, p. 6.

[16] Chris Ello, "WCAC Preview: Flood of Transfers Could Cause Favorites, Also-rans to Flip," the *Los Angeles Times,* January 15, 1988, Sports, p. 2A.

[17] Don Norcross, "Don Norcross's WCAC Handicap and All-conference Picks," *The San Diego Union-Tribune,* January 16, 1988, Sports, p. C-1.

[18] Drooz , "Loyola Marymount Wins Seventh Game."

[19] Mark Ziegler, "Toreros Routed by Loyola in WCAC Open," January 16, 1988, Sports, p. D-10.

[20] Chris Long, "LMU Wins but Loses Bid for 100 Points," the *Daily Breeze,* January 17, 1988, Sports, p. C-3.

[21] Alan Drooz, "Loyola Pours It On," the *Los Angeles Times*, January 17, 1988, Sports, p. 9.

[22] "Loyola's Victory Is a Record Breaker, 134-106," the *Los Angeles Times,* January 22, 1988, Sports, p. 7.

[23] "LMU Needs Big Second Half," the *Daily Breeze,* January 24, 1988, Sports, p. C-3.

[24] Alan Drooz, "Today's Lion Cagers Revive Memories of Glory Season of 1960-61," the *Los Angeles Times*, January 29, 1988, Sports, p. 16.

[25] Alan Drooz, "Loyola Runs Away and Beats Gonzaga, 116-100," the *Los Angeles Times*, January 30, 1988, Sports, p. 10.

[26] Alan Drooz, "Loyola Wins, 122-109, Leads Nation in Scoring," the *Los Angeles Times*, January 31, 1988, Sports, p. 6.

Chapter 15: Wildfire Spreads

[1] Zepel interview.

[2] Alan Drooz, "Loyola Does a Number on USF, 128-111," the *Los Angeles Times*, February 6, 1988, Sports, p. 10.

[3] Alan Drooz, "Loyola Marymount Has Foes on Run," the *Los Angeles Times*, February 10, 1988; Zepel interview.

[4] "Pressure? Lion Mike Yoest Felt It but Beat It with Last-Second Shot," the *Los Angeles Times*, February 12, 1988, Sports, p. 14.

[5] Drooz, "Loyola Marymount Has Foes on Run."

[6] Alan Drooz, "Loyola Turns It on after Gaines Is Lost, 108-98," the *Los Angeles Times*, February 13, 1988, Sports, p. 1.

[7] Gersten and Quinn interviews.

[8] Drooz, "Loyola Turns It On."

[9] Alan Drooz, "Loyola Gets Seventeenth Straight, Twentieth Victory," the *Los Angeles Times*, February 14, 1988, Sports, p. 1.

[10] Matt Lait, "Westhead's Loyola Scores Like Lakers, Soars above USC, UCLA," *The Washington Post*, February 17, 1988, Sports, p. 4.

[11] Lait, "Westhead's Loyola Scores Like Lakers."

[12] "Sports People, Team on the Rise," *The New York Times*, February 17, 1988, p. A16.

[13] Ray Ripton, "Waves vs. Lions: A Worthy Centennial," the *Los Angeles Times*, February 17, 1988, Sports, p. 4.

[14] Alan Drooz, "It's a Cinch: Loyola Takes Title in Stride, Focuses on Staying Unbeaten in Conference," the *Los Angeles Times*, February 18, 1988, Sports, p. 10.

[15] Alan Drooz, "When It Comes to Basketball, Loyola's Lions Have the Horse," the *Los Angeles Times*, February 19, 1988, Sports, p. 16.

[16] Drooz, "When It Comes to Basketball."

[17] Alan Drooz, "Loyola Wins Nineteenth Straight, WCAC Title," the *Los Angeles Times*, February 21, 1988, Sports, p. 1.

[18] Keith Cormer, the *Los Angeles Loyolan*, February 17, 1988.

[19] Cormer, the *Los Angeles Loyolan*, February 17, 1988.

[20] Alan Drooz, "Yoest's Buzzer Shot Gives Loyola Twentieth Straight Win," the *Los Angeles Times*, February 26, 1988, Sports, p. 1.

[21] Alan Drooz, "Lion Cagers Find Recipe for Winning on Training Table," the *Los Angeles Times*, February 26, 1988, Sports, p. 16.

[22] Alan Drooz, "Loyola Perfect in WCAC after 141-126 Romp," the *Los Angeles Times*, February 28, 1988, Sports, p. 1.

[23] Alan Drooz, "Loyola Needs Tourney Win to Clinch NCAA Bid," the *Los Angeles Times*, March 4, 1988, Sports, p. 14.

[24] Alan Drooz, "Waves Make It Rough; Loyola Wins,109-106," the *Los Angeles Times*, March 7, 1988, Sports, p. 1; Alan Drooz, "Loyola Runs into Trouble but Slips Past Portland," the *Los Angeles Times*, March 6, 1988, Sports, p. 1.

[25] Alan Drooz, "Loyola Marymount Gains NCAA Berth with 104-96 Win," the *Los Angeles Times*, March 8, 1988.

[26] Mike Downey, "Mighty Lions—Changing an Attitude," the *Los Angeles Times*, March 9, 1988, Sports, p. 1.

[27] John Cherwa, interview by author, telephone, October 19, 2005.

[28] Alan Drooz, "Loyola, They Stand Bayou from L.A. to La.," the *Los Angeles Times*, March 11, 1988, Sports, p. 8. See also, Mindy Brodhouse Avarit, interview by author, telephone, August 14, 2009.

[29] Robyn Norwood, "Loyola Goes on the Road; Pac-10 Gets 2," the *Los Angeles Times*, March 14, 1988, Sports, p. 1.

[30] Gaines and Kimble interviews.

[31] Mal Florence, "Loyola Going Like in '61 in '88," the *Los Angeles Times*, March 16, 1988, Sports, p. 1.

[32] Richard Hoffer, "Feeding Frenzy: Top Teams in the Country Are Running Wild," the *Los Angeles Times*, March 16, 1988, Sports, p. 8.

[33] Robyn Norwood, "The NCAA Tournament: No Favorites, but Contenders All Over Place," the *Los Angeles Times*, March 17, 1988, Sports.

[34] Alan Drooz, "Loyola's Unsung Basketball Heroes," the *Los Angeles Times*, March 17, 1988, Sports, p. 16.

[35] Alan Drooz, "Free-Wheeling, New Lions Ready to Run Wyoming," the *Los Angeles Times*, March 17, 1988, Sports, p. 1.

[36] Bennie Dees, interview by author, telephone, April 20, 2006.

[37] Drooz, "Free-Wheeling, New Lions."

[38] Dees interview.

[39] the *Los Angeles Times*, March 23, 1988.

[40] William Rhoden, "NCAA Tournament: Tar Heels Stop Loyola, 123-97," *The New York Times*, March 20, 1988, Sports, p. A1.

[41] Keith Cameron, the *Los Angeles Loyolan*, March 23, 1988.

[42] Quinn interview.

CHAPTER 16: A HEAVY LOAD

[1] "Newswire," the *Los Angeles Times*, March 3, 1988, Sports, p. 8.

[2] "Newswire," the *Los Angeles Times*, May 6, 1988, Sports, p. 2.

[3] Scott Ostler, "The NBA Playoffs Ex-Laker Haywood Tells of Plan He Had to Kill Westhead," tje *Los Angeles Times*, June 5, 1988, Sports, p. 15.

[4] Dr. Lane Bove, interview by author, Los Angeles, Calif., October 17, 2005.

[5] Cassie Westhead, interview by author, telephone, April 26, 2006.

[6] Enoch Simmons, interview by author, telephone, January 8, 2006; see also Alan Drooz, "Diamond's Sparkle Lures Lion Cager," the *Los Angeles Times*, January 16, 1988.

[7] Bruce Woods, interview by author, January 24, 2006.

[8] Per Sturmer, interview by author, telephone, September 8, 2006.

[9] Darrell Gates, interview by author, Philadelphia, Pa., June 21, 2006.

[10] Woods and Gates interviews; Bo Kimble, *For You, Hank* (New York: Delacorte, 1992); Derrick Dowell, interview by author, telephone, August 26, 2006.

[11] Woods interview.

[12] Ed Arnold, interview by author, Tustin, Calif., July 2005.

[13] David Spencer, interview by author, Riverside, Calif., April 7, 2005.

[14] Barry Zepel, Loyola Marymount University Basketball Media Guide, 1988-89.

CHAPTER 17: A FEW STEPS BACK

[1] Bo Kimble, *For You, Hank* (New York: Delacorte, 1992), p. 131.

[2] Kimble, *For You, Hank*, p. 132.

[3] Kimble, *For You, Hank*, p. 133.

[4] Alan Drooz, "Loyola Cagers Tally 320 Points in Practice Game," *Los Angeles Times*, November 13, 1988, Sports, p. 18.

[5] Alan Drooz, "Lion Cagers Slip by Czechs Minus Three Top Scorers," the *Los Angeles Times*, November 25, 1988, Sports, p. 26.

[6] Alan Drooz, "Soviet Cage Stunner Could Sell Westhead's 3-Point Shot," the *Los Angeles Times*, September 30, 1988, Sports, p. 18.

[7] A game between Troy State and George Mason in 1994 set the high watermark for three-point attempts— a combined 108 attempts between the two schools, 44 of which were good. The George Mason coach was heard to ask after the game, "How could anyone take 40 more 3's than my guys?" His name was Paul Westhead.

[8] Dave Sell and Steve Berkowitz, "New Season Brings New, Stricter Rules," *The Washington Post*, Sports, December 5, 1988, Sports, p. 10. Rolling Hills High School in Palos Verdes, Calif., also adopted the System. Coach Cliff Warner's team went 25-8 and averaged 90 points per game in the 1980's.

[9] Alan Drooz, "Loyola Cagers Collide with the Dune, Mountain of Torture," the *Los Angeles Times*, October 7, 1988, Sports, p. 12.

[10] Drooz, "Loyola Cagers Collide"; Terrell Lowery, interview by author, Sacramento, Calif., August 14, 2005; Bo Kimble,

interview by author, North Wales, Pa, June 25, 2006; Tom Peabody, interview by author, Long Beach, Calif., June 22, 2005; Woods and Sturmer interviews.

[11] Alan Drooz, "College Basketball '88—'89, Loyola Marymount Hopes to Turn Its Sprint Up Another Notch," the *Los Angeles Times*, November 23, 1988, Sports, p. 8.

[12] Paul Westhead, interview by author, Hermosa Beach, Calif., June 22, 2005.

[13] Kristin Ramage, interview by author, Loma Linda, Calif., September 12, 2005.

[14] Ramage interview.

[15] Cassie Westhead interview.

[16] Alan Drooz, "Loyola, Pepperdine Announce TV Pacts," the *Los Angeles Times*, November 2, 1988, Sports, p. 9.

[17] Alan Drooz, "Loyola Opens with Record-Breaking Victory," the *Los Angeles Times*, November 29, 1988, Sports, p. 1. The all-time record, according to Drooz, was 306, set December 2, 1969, in a Division II game between Livingston and Mississippi College.

[18] Alan Drooz, "Loyola's Scoring Machine to Test Gauchos Tonight," the *Los Angeles Times*, December 1, 1988, Sports, p. 13.

[19] Alan Drooz, "Loyola Becomes a Late-Night Loser," the *Los Angeles Times*, December 2, 1988, Sports, p. 5.

[20] Alan Drooz, "Loyola Plays Host to Oregon State," the *Los Angeles Times*, December 7, 1988, Sports, p. 3.

[21] Alan Drooz, "Loyola Can't Keep Up with Oregon State," the *Los Angeles Times*, December 8, 1988, Sports, p. 6.

[22] Alan Drooz, "Lame Lion Cager Kimble Expects to Return Next week," the *Los Angeles Times*, December 9, 1988, Sports, p. 20.

[23] Alan Drooz, "Smiles Return as Loyola Beats AIA,146-137," the *Los Angeles Times*, December 11, 1988, Sports, p. 23.

[24] Alan Drooz, "Can Bo Show for Sooners?" the *Los Angeles Times*, December 16, 1988, Sports, p. 20.

[25] Chris Baker, "USC Violations Bring NCAA Reprimand," the *Los Angeles Times*, December 17, 1988, Sports, p. 2.

[26] Priamos interviews.

[27] Alan Drooz, "He's Fired Up and Firing Back Foes' Shots," the *Los Angeles Times*, December 17, 1988, Sports, p. 8.

[28] Drooz, "He's Fired Up."

[29] Andy Martino, the *Los Angeles Loyolan*, December 7, 1988.

[30] "Loyola Gunners Off-target against OU," the *Los Angeles Times*, December 18, 1988, Sports, p. 21.

[31] Alan Drooz, "Loyola Runs but Can't Hide in 136-103 Loss," the *Los Angeles Times*, December 18, 1988, Sports, p. 1.

[32] Alan Drooz, "Loyola Edges Austin Peay, Faces DePaul," the *Los Angeles Times*, December 23, 1988, Sports, p. 5.

[33] Alan Drooz, "Loyola Is Beaten by DePaul, 115-111," the *Los Angeles Times*, December 24, 1988, Sports, p. 10.

[34] Alan Drooz, "Lions Roar, Enough about Being Called 'Marymount' on TV," the *Los Angeles Times*, December 30, 1988, Sports, p. 12.

[35] Kimble interview; Bo also provides a detailed account of the injury and his decision about when to have the surgery in *For You, Hank*.

[36] Kimble, *For You, Hank*, p. 137.

[37] Kimble interview.

[38] Woods interview; Alan Drooz, "Loyola Runs Marist Ragged in Scoring 131-107 Victory," the *Los Angeles Times*, December 29, 1988, Sports, p. 4.

[39] Drooz, "Lions "Lions Roar."

[40] Woods interview; Alan Drooz, "Loyola Runs Marist."

CHAPTER 18: STRONGEST MAN ALIVE

[1] Alan Drooz, "Loyola Wins as Gathers Scores 49," the *Los Angeles Times*, December 31, 1988, Sports, p. 6.

[2] Westhead interview.

[3] Drooz, "Loyola Wins as Gathers Scores 49."

[4] Kimble interview.

[5] Kimble interview.

[6] Peabody, Lowery, and Sturmer interviews.

[7] Barry Zepel, Loyola Marymount Basketball Media Guide,1989 results.

[8] Alan Drooz, "Xavier More Than a Match for Loyola's Game, 118-113," the *Los Angeles Times*, January 5, 1989, Sports, p. 3.

[9] Pete Gillen, interview by author, telephone, March 29, 2006.

[10] Don Casey, interview by author, telephone, September 8, 2006.

[11] Alan Drooz, "Three Records Set as Loyola Wins, 162-144," the *Los Angeles Times*, January 8, 1989, Sports, p. 1.

[12] Alan Drooz, "Loyola Uses Defense to Defeat USF, 113-95," the *Los Angeles Times*, January 12, 1989, Sports, p. 6.

[13] Alan Drooz, "Loyola Starts Slowly but Beats Santa Clara," the *Los Angeles Times*, January 13, 1989, Sports, p. 8.

[14] Westhead, Woods, and Hillock interviews; film clips of games over several seasons from a variety of sources.

[15] Alan Drooz, "Brundy Helps Carry DePaul Past Loyola," the *Los Angeles Times*, January 15, 1989, Sports, p. 6.

[16] Alan Drooz, "Full Speed Ahead: Even without Kimble, Gathers Steps Up for Loyola," the *Los Angeles Times*, January 14, 1989, Sports, p. 1.

[17] Drooz, "Full Speed Ahead."

[18] Alan Drooz, "Fryer, Gathers Help Loyola Break Away," the *Los Angeles Times*, January 21, 1989, Sports, p. 7.

[19] the *Los Angeles Loyolan,* January 18, 1989.]

[20] Alan Drooz, "Gathers Helps Loyola Defeat Portland," the *Los Angeles Times*, January 22, 1989, Sports, p. 22.

[21] Ray Ripton, "Pepperdine Puts Stop to Loyola Run, 104-79," the *Los Angeles Times*, January 26, 1989, Sports, p. 1.

[22] Keith Cameron, the *Los Angeles Loyolan,* February 1, 1989.

[23] Steve Lowery, "Loyola's 'Human Bruise,' " the *Los Angeles Times,* February 16, 1989, Sports, p. 3.

[24] Dolores Peabody, interview by author, telephone, April 20, 2007.

[25] Peabody interview.

[26] Peabody interview.

[27] Dr. Ben Shaffer, interview by author, Washington, D.C., January 26, 2006.

[28] Alan Drooz, "Loyola Marymount Sets Records: It's 181-150," *The Washington Post*, February 1, 1989; Alan Drooz, "All Those Points, Loyola Marymount's Scoring Records Leave More Than Players Breathless," the*Los Angeles Times,* February 2, 1989, Sports, p. 10.

[29] Drooz, "Loyola Marymount Sets Records."

[30] Drooz, "Loyola Marymount Sets Records."

[31] Alan Drooz, "Loyola Is Outrun by St. Mary's Gaels,116-104," *The Los Angeles Times*, February 4, 1989, Sports, p. 1.

[32] Alan Drooz, "WCAC Roundup: Loyola Finds Touch, Beats San Diego, 139-104," the *Los Angeles Times*, February 5, 1989, Sports, p. 4.

[33] Keith Cameron, the *Los Angeles Loyolan*, February 8, 1989.

[34] Alan Drooz, "St. Mary's 95-81 Win over Loyola Leaves Gaels in Good Shape in WCAC," the *Los Angeles Times*, February 12, 1989, Sports, p. 1.

[35] Alan Drooz, "Kimble Returns, Scores 29 to Lead Loyola, 144-92," the *Los Angeles Times*, February 18, 1989, Sports, p. 11.

[36] Keith Cameron, *the* Los Angeles Loyolan, February 22, 1989.

[37] Keith Cameron, the *Los Angeles Loyolan*, February 22, 1989.

[38] Alan Drooz, "Kimble, Gathers Each Score 40 in Loyola's 147-136 Victory," the *Los Angeles Times*, February 19, 1989, Sports, p. 8.

[39] Alan Drooz, "Kimble, Gathers Each Score 40 in Loyola's 147-136 Victory," the *Los Angeles Times*, February 19, 1989, Sports, p. 8.

CHAPTER 19: HEART OF A LION

[1] Peabody, Paul Westhead, and Lowery interviews.

[2] Peabody interview.

[3] Peabody, Paul Westhead, and Lowery interviews.

[4] Alan Drooz, "Gathers and Fryer Lead Loyola Past Santa Clara," the *Los Angeles Times*, February 26, 1989, Sports, p. 7.

[5] Alan Drooz, "Mr. Outside: Corona del Mar's Jeff Fryer Finds That His Jump Shot Continues to Be a Hot Item at Loyola Marymount," the *Los Angeles Times*, February 20, 1989, Sports, p. 14.

[6] Alan Drooz, "USF Wins Again, This Time Beating Loyola," the *Los Angeles Times*, February 26, 1989, Sports, p. 7.

[7] Alan Drooz, "Lions Senior Center Answers Coach's Challenge," the *Los Angeles Times*, February 24, 1989, Sports, p. 12.

[8] Priamos interview.

[9] Alan Drooz, "Loyola Wins Title in Overtime," the *Los Angeles Times*, March 7,1 989, Sports, p. 1.

[10] Keith Cameron, the *Los Angeles Loyolan*, March 15, 1989.

[11] Alan Drooz, the *Los Angeles Times*, March 10, 1989, Sports, p. 14.

[12] Alan Drooz, "Loyola Opens against Arkansas; Lions, Razorbacks Ready to Run in Midwest Regional," the *Los Angeles Times*, March 16, 1989.

[13] Drooz, "Loyola Opens against Arkansas."

[14] Michael Hurd, "On His Way: Gathers Has Come Long Way from Philly Projects," *USA Today*, March 15, 1989, p. 12C.

[15] Hurd, "On His Way."

[16] Alan Drooz, "Loyola Just Can't Stop Arkansas in the Long Run," the *Los Angeles Times*, March 17, 1989, Sports, p. 1.

[17] Drooz, "Loyola Just Can't Stop Arkansas."

[18] Keith Cameron, the *Los Angeles Loyolan*, March 22, 1989.

[19] Darrell Gates, interview by author, Philadelphia, Pa., June 21, 2006.

[20] Priamos interview.

[21] Spencer interview.

[22] Alan Drooz, "Come Back, Hank, Loyola's Wish for '89 Is for Center to Resist NBA Lure," the *Los Angeles Times*, March 26, 1989, Sports, p. 16.

[23] Cassie Westhead interview.

[24] Father John McNamee, interview by author, Philadelphia, Pa., March 23, 2006.

[25] Spencer interview.

[26] Alan Drooz, "Gathers Stars as Toastmaster for Lion Cagers," the *Los Angeles Times*, April 14, 1989, Sports, p. 14.

[27] Zepel and Drooz interviews.

[28] Lowery and Peabody interviews.

[29] Alan Drooz, "Loyola Cheers as 'The Bank' Returns," the *Los Angeles Times*, April 28, 1989, Sports, p. 14.

CHAPTER 20: GETTING IN GEAR

[1] Summary of deposition of Charles Gathers (August 30, 1991), prepared by Richard D. Carroll for *Gathers et al. v. Loyola Marymount University et al.*, No. C795027, Los Angeles Superior Court, filed April 20, 1990, from the files of Carroll, a lawyer with the firm of Baker, Silberberg and Keener in Santa Monica, Calif. Carroll's firm represented Norcal Mutual Insurance Company, which had issued the malpractice insurance policy for three of the doctors named in the medical malpractice suit brought by Hank's family after his death. Carroll attended the depositions and prepared the summaries.

[2] Father John P. McNamee, interview by author, Philadelphia, Pa., March 23, 2006.

[3] Summary of Father David Hagan's deposition (August 29, 1991).

[4] Ted Silary, "The Positive Influence: Gathers Touched Those Around Him," the *Philadelphia Daily News*, March 6, 1990.

[5] Father Hagan deposition summary.

[6] Father Hagan deposition summary.

[7] Pennsylvania Department of Corrections Web site; Albert Gersten II, interview by author, Los Angeles, Calif., July 8, 2005; Richard Yankowitz, interview by author, Philadelphia, Pa., June 9, 2005; and Maryann Hudson Harvey, interview by author, Baltimore, Md., October 6, 2005. Chris's conviction and sentence are discussed in Shelley Smith, "A Bitter Legacy," *Sports Illustrated,* March 4, 1991.

[8] Richard Yankowitz, Bo Kimble, Derrick "Heat" Gates, and Doug Overton all spoke to me at length about Hank's relationship with his mother and his determination to get her, his brothers, and other members of his immediate family out of the projects once he landed a fat NBA contract. Much has also been published elsewhere about the driving force in Hank's life, which was to rescue his family from poverty.

[9] Many people spoke to me of the romance between Hank and Vernell, whom I was unable to locate. Those who were aware of Hank's determination to marry her after graduation included Pete Priamos, Al Gersten, Bo, and Heat. Lucille Gathers also spoke of Hank and Vernell's love in her deposition (see deposition summary of Lucille Gathers).

[10] Peter Priamos, interview by author, Sherman Oaks, Calif., July 11, 2005.

[11] Father Hagan deposition summary.

[12] David Burst, interview by author, telephone, March 8, 2006.

[13] Barry Zepel, interview by author, Anaheim, Calif., July 15, 2005; Brian Quinn, interview by author, Fullerton, Calif., July 14, 2005; Priamos and Gersten interviews; David Burst, interview by author, telephone, March 8, 2006.

[14] Tom Peabody, interview by author, Long Beach, Calif., June 22, 2005; Bo Kimble, interview by author, North Wales, Pa., June 22, 2006.

[15] Terrell Lowery, interview by author, Sacramento, Calif., August 14, 2005; Peabody interview.

[16] David Spencer, Riverside, Calif., April 7, 2005.

[17] Derrick Gathers led the team in scoring (averaging 17.6 points per game) and rebounding (7.1) in 1989-90. He was an honorable mention All-CCAA that season. He still ranks on five Cal-North Ridge all-time single-season lists and three all-time career lists. He twice scored 28 points in 1989-90 and 20 or more points 10 times, including a streak of five straight games (Ryan Finney, sports information director, Cal-North Ridge, e-mail, June 28, 2006).

[18] Bruce Woods, interview by author, Pittsburgh, Pa., January 24, 2006.

[19] Jay Hillock, interview by author, telephone, February 6, 2006.

[20] Woods interview.

[21] Ed Arnold, interview by author, Tustin, Calif., 2005.

[22] Mike Waldner, interview by author, Los Angeles, Ca., July 31, 2006.

[23] Arnold interview.

[24] Bill Glauber, "Stakes High in Colleges, and Coaches Feel Pressure," the *Los Angeles Times,* April 1, 1989.

[25] Dr. Elena Bove, interview by author, Los Angeles, Calif., October 17, 2005.

[26] Father James Loughran, personal communication, e-mail, May 1, 2006.

[27] Terry Lanni, interview by author, Las Vegas, Nev., December 14, 2006; Bove interview.

[28] Bove interview.

[29] Lanni interview.

[30] Kimble interview.

[31] Alan Drooz, "Could Cause Recruiting Problems: 'Westhead Leaving' Rumors Fly as Fast as Loyola's Attack," the *Los Angeles Times,* June 16, 1989, Sports, p. 16.

[32] Doug Overton, interview by author, Philadelphia, Pa., January 27, 2006.

[33] Alan Drooz, "Coach Paul Westhead Joins Kareem's Tour for an 'Exciting Finale,'" the *Los Angeles Times,* August 18, 1989.

[34] Woods interview.

CHAPTER 21: TAKING CENTER COURT

[1] Dr. Ben Shaffer, interview by author, Washington, D.C., January 26, 2006.

[2] "The Kerlan-Jobe Story," www.kerlanjob.com (March 6, 2007).

[3] Dr. Shaffer interview.

[4] Brian Berger, "Brian's Box Seat," the *Los Angeles Loyolan,* September 27, 1989.

[5] Alan Drooz, "Really Big: That's the Name of the Game for Loyola Basketball This Season," the *Los Angeles Times,* October 19, 1989, Sports, p. 16.

[6] Alan Drooz, "Powerful Lions Not Rated among Anybody's Top 40," the *Los Angeles Times,* November 3, 1989, Sports, p. 18.

[7] Alan Drooz, "Powerful Lions Not Rated."

[8] Woods interview.

[9] Priamos interview.

[10] Drooz, "Powerful Lions Not Rated."

[11] Alan Drooz, "Loyola Loses Player before Game, Then Falls to Australian team," the *Los Angeles Times,* November 5, 1989, Sports, p. 18.

[12] Alan Drooz, "Loyola, UNLV Will Be Off and Running in NIT," the *Los Angeles Times,* November 15, 1989, Sports, p. 7.

[13] Tarkanian enjoyed the highest winning percentage among all active coaches.

[14] Steve Carp, interview by author, telephone, July 20, 2006.

[15] LMU v. UNLV, ESPN, November 15, 1989.

[16] Carp interview.

[17] Brian Berger kindly put together for me, from a variety of sources, a DVD of film clips of the 1989-90 season, hereafter cited as "'89-'90 LMU basketball, assorted videos," the original sources of which I am largely unable to identify.

[18] Carp interview.

[19] Carp interview. Also see Paul Arnett, "No.1 Rebels Overcome Marymount," the *Las Vegas Sun,* November 16, 1989, and Joe Hawk, "Rebels Capture Opener," the *Las Vegas Sun,* November 16, 1989, for accounts of the bomb scare as well as the game.

[20] Paul Arnett, "No.1 Rebels Overcome Marymount," the *Las Vegas Sun,* November 16, 1989, Sports, C-1.

[21] Woods and Carp interviews.

[22] Carp interview.

[23] Lowery interview.

[24] Carp interview.

[25] Earl Schuman, the *Los Angeles Loyolan,* November 29, 1989.

[26] Carp interview.

[27] Alan Drooz, "Loyola Gets Rolling with Win over Reno," the *Los Angeles Times,* November 26, 1989, Sports, p. 12.

[28] Steve Berkowitz, "Notebook: Nevada- Las Vegas Still Best of the Big West," *The Washington Post,* December 28, 1989, Sports, p. 4.

[29] Alan Drooz, "Loyola Races to Easy Win over Stetson," the *Los Angeles Times,* December 2, 1989, Sports, p. 10.

[30] Drooz, "Loyola Races to Easy Win."

[31] Alan Drooz, "Loyola Marymount Wins on Late Rally," the *Los Angeles Times,* December 3,1989, Sports, p. 11.

[32] Alan Drooz, "Lions Win Game and also Fall 48 Points Short . . . in a Match Projected to Bring First 200-Point Performance," the *Los Angeles Times,* December 8, 1989, Sports, p. 6.

[33] Woods interview.

[34] Drooz, " Lions Win Game."

[35] Jerry Pimm, interview by author, telephone, February 6, 2006.

[36] Alan Drooz, "Loyola Will Face a Tough Test against Rested Santa Barbara," the *Los Angeles Times,* December 8, 1989.

[37] Kristin Ramage, interview by author, Loma Linda, Calif., September 12, 2005; Quinn and Bove interviews.

[38] Mike Downey, "He's Trying to Gather Enough Strength," the *Los Angeles Times,* December 17,1989, Sports, p. 2.

[39] Dr. Dan Hyslop, interview by author interview, Los Angeles, Calif., June 20, 2005.

[40] Dr. Nick Di Gioviane, interview by author, telephone, July 2006.

[41] Dr. Di Gioviane interview; Chip Schaefer, interview by author , Los Angeles, Calif., June 20, 2005.

[42] Dr. Hyslop, Dr. Di Gioviane, and Schaefer interviews.

[43] Dr. Di Gioviane interview.

[44] Dr. Hyslop interview.

[45] Priamos interview.

[46] Stan Morrison, interview by author, Riverside, Calif., April 2005.

[47] Summary of deposition of Dr. Michael Mellman (August 8, 1990).

[48] Dr. Mellman deposition summary.

[49] Dr. Hyslop interview.

[50] Dr. Mellman deposition summary.

[51] Spencer interview.

[52] Bove interview.

[53] Morrison interview.

[54] Summary of deposition of Dr. Elena Bove (October 16, 1990).

[55] Dr. Mellman deposition summary (August 8, 1990).

[56] Peabody, Lowery, and Kimble interviews. Also see Alan Drooz, "Loyola's Gathers Facing More Tests; Doctors Can't Find a Cause for Player's Fainting," the *Los Angeles Times,* December 13, 1989.

[57] Associated Press, *The New York Times,* December 12, 1989, p. B16.

[58] Drooz, "Loyola's Gathers Facing More Tests."

[59] Peabody interview.

CHAPTER 22: ROLLING THE DICE

[1] Summary of deposition of Dr. Vernon Hattori (December 17, 1990).

[2] Dr. Hattori deposition summary; hospital notes.

[3] Elliott Almond, Alan Drooz, Maryann Hudson, Danny Robbins, and John Cherwa, "Hank Gathers: The Death of a Dream," Special Report, the *Los Angeles Times*, April 1, 1990, p. C-13.

[4] Dr. Charles Swerdlow, interview by author, Los Angeles, October 13, 2006.

[5] Downey, "He's Trying to Gather Enough Strength."

[6] Downey, "He's Trying to Gather Enough Strength"; Lane Bove, telephone interview by author, February 26, 2009.

[7] Dr. Hattori deposition summary; Dr. Swerdlow deposition summary; notes dated March 12, 1990, that Dr. Swerdlow prepared for his attorney, Ken Mueller, and that the doctor made available to me (cited hereafter as "Dr. Swerdlow to Mueller").

[8] Dr. Hattori deposition summary; Dr. Swerdlow interview; Dr. Swerdlow deposition summary; Dr. Swerdlow to Mueller.

[9] Dr. Swerdlow deposition summary; Dr. Swerdlow to Mueller; hospital records; Dr. Swerdlow interview.

[10] Dr. Swerdlow interview.

[11] Dr. Swerdlow interview; Dr. Swerdlow deposition summary; Dr. Swerdlow to Mueller.

[12] Summary of deposition of Lucille Gathers.

[13] Priamos interview.

[14] Dr. Swerdlow interview; deposition summaries of Dr. Hattori and Dr. Mellman.

[15] Summary of medical records from Daniel Freeman Memorial Hospital, prepared by Richard D. Carroll for *Gathers v. Loyola Marymount*.

[16] Dr. Swerdlow deposition summary.

[17] Dr. Swerdlow to Mueller.

[18] Dr. Swerdlow to Mueller.

[19] Priamos interview.

[20] Dr. Swerdlow interview. According to Dr. Swerdlow, he at least hinted to Dr. Mellman his suspicions that Hank Gathers might never be able to play basketball again.

[21] Dr. Hattori deposition summary.

[22] Summary of deposition of Barry Zepel; Quinn interview.

[23] Dr. Hattori deposition summary.

[24] Dr. Vernon Hattori, deposition summary (October 17, 1990). Bove and Quinn also testified in their depositions about the date that the university received the letter.

[25] Alan Drooz, "Loyola's Gathers Will Return to Practice Next Week," the *Los Angeles Times*, December 22, 1989, Sports, p. 3.

[26] Alan Drooz, "Oregon State Falls,117-113, to Kimble's 53," the *Los Angeles Times*, December 20, 1989; Alan Drooz, "Kimble Scores 46, but Oklahoma Runs Past Cold Loyla,136-121," the *Los Angeles Times*, December 24, 1989.

[27] Dr. Hattori deposition summary.

[28] Ventricular tachycardia occurs when the heart races too rapidly to pump blood. If the condition continues, it causes a drop in blood pressure and loss of consciousness. If sustained, it will cause the heart to begin to quiver (fibrillation) and leads to death if the rhythm does not revert to normal on its own or through external shock. The information about Lance Armstrong's maximum heart rate comes from his Web site, www.lancearmstrong.com.

[29] Dr. Hattori deposition summary.

[30] Dr. Hattori deposition summary.

[31] Dr. Hattori deposition summary; Dr. Swerdlow deposition summary; Dr. Swerdlow to Mueller.

[32] Dr. Hattori deposition summary; Dr. Swerdlow deposition summary; Dr. Swerdlow noted that "Hattori consulted me informally about the Holter monitor" (Dr. Swerdlow to Mueller).

[33] Dr. Swerdlow to Mueller; Dr. Hattori deposition summary.

[34] Dr. Hattori deposition summary; Dr. Mellman deposition summary.

[35] Dr. Hattori deposition summary (October 17, 1990).

[36] Schaefer interview.

[37] Alan Drooz, "Lions Need Final 3 of Kimble's 54," the *Los Angeles Times*, January 5, 1990, Sports, p. 14.

[38] Dr. Mellman insisted he told everyone at that meeting that Hank's continuing to play "could be dangerous" (Dr. Mellman deposition summary, August 8, 1990).

[39] Dr. Swerdlow interview.

[40] Priamos interview. Also, Hank repeatedly made comments to reporters that reflected his impatience with the testing. See, for example, Mike Downey, "He's Trying to Gather Enough Strength," the *Los Angeles Times*, December 17, 1989.

[41] Dr. Hattori deposition summary.

[42] Dr. Shaffer interview.

[43] In his interview, Dr. Shaffer said that he and the other Kerlan-Jobe fellows were the only doctors in attendance on most occasions.

[44] Dr. Swerdlow to Mueller.

[45] Dr. Swerdlow deposition summary; Dr. Swerdlow to Mueller; Dr. Swerdlow interview.

[46] Dr. Swerdlow deposition summary.

[47] Dr. Swerdlow interview.

[48] Schaefer interview.

[49] Nearly everyone I interviewed told me how upset Hank was with the effect that Inderal was having on his performance on the basketball court. Dr. Hattori also referred to Hank's unhappiness in his depositions.

[50] Schaefer interview.

[51] Alan Drooz, interview by author, San Diego, Calif., July 18, 2005.

[52] Lowery, Kimble, Peabody, and Ramage all mentioned this when I interviewed them.

[53] Dr. Swerdlow deposition summary; Dr. Hattori deposition summary.

[54] Alan Drooz, "Lion's Hopes Go by the Boards against Xavier," the *Los Angeles Times,* January 3, 1989.

[55] Pete Gillen, interview by author, telephone, March 29, 2006.

[56] Westhead interview.

[57] Overton interview.

[58] Yankowitz interview.

[59] Yankowitz interview.

[60] Yankowitz interview; Father Hagan deposition summary.

[61] " '89-'90 LMU basketball," videotape; assorted videos.

[62] Yankowitz interview.

[63] Peabody interview.

[64] Gates interview.

[65] Kimble, Lowery, Peabody, and Schaefer interviews.

[66] Schaefer and Yankowitz interviews.

[67] Lowery interview.

[68] C. L. Smith-Muniz, "Lion's Share: Gathers Lives up to Name," *The Washington Post,* February 2, 1989, Sports, p. C-7.

[69] Lowery and Gates interviews.

[70] Gates and Schaefer interviews. In her article for *Sports Illustrated,* "A Bitter Legacy," Shelley Smith has Hank staying with Paul and Cassie Westhead that night. Neither Westhead recalls that that was the case.

[71] Father Hagan deposition summary.

[72] Father Hagan deposition summary.

[73] Dr. Hattori deposition summary (August 4, 1990).

[74] Westhead confirmed Dr. Hattori's recollection but stressed that he simply asked if "there were any alternative treatments available. I would never be presumptuous enough to suggest that the doctor do something medically. I am a coach, not a doctor" (Paul Westhead, interview by author, Hermosa Beach, Calif., June 22, 2005; Paul Westhead, deposition summary, July 26,1990).

[75] Dr. Hattori deposition summary.

[76] Dr. Hattori, deposition summary (August 4, 1990).

[77] Dr. Hattori deposition summary.

[78] Dr. Hattori deposition summary (August 4, 1990).

[79] Dr. Hattori deposition summary (August 4, 1990).

[80] Dr. Hattori deposition summary (August 4,1990).

[81] Dr. Swerdlow to Mueller.

[82] Maryann Hudson, "Hank Gathers and a Son He Left Behind," the *Los Angeles Times*, March 12, 1990, Sports, p. C1.

[83] Almond, Drooz, Hudson, Robbins, and Cherwa, "Hank Gathers: The Death of a Dream," p. C-13.

[84] Summaries of Marva Crump and Phyllis Crump depositions; see also Maryann Hudson, "Hank Gathers and the Son He Left Behind," the *Los Angeles Times,* March 12, 1990.

[85] For descriptions of Hank's final visit to Philadelphia, Pa., see Almond, Drooz, Hudson, Robbins, and Cherwa, "Hank Gathers: The Death of a Dream."

[86] Peabody interview.

[87] Yankowitz interview.

[88] " '89-'90 LMU basketball," videotape; assorted videos; Woods and Hillock interviews.

[89] Steve Berkowitz, "Loyola Marymount Runs, Guns, Wins," *The Washington Post,* January 5, 1990, Sports, p. 9.

[90] Alan Drooz, "Loyola Marymount Outruns La Salle College," the *Los Angeles Times,* January 7, 1990, Sports, p. 6.

[91] Kimble interview.

[92] Drooz, "Loyola Marymount Outruns La Salle."

[93] Father Hagan deposition summary.

CHAPTER 23: THE COMEBACK KID

[1] Dr. Hattori deposition summary (August 4, 1990).

[2] Dr. Hattori deposition summary.

[3] Alan Drooz, "Lions Quickly Serve Notice . . . Team Rolls over Santa Clara in WCC Opener," the *Los Angeles Times*, January 12, 1990, Sports, p. 4.

[4] Jim Lundgren, "Loyola Finds Pace to Its Liking," the *Los Angeles Times,* January 14, 1990, Sports, p. 11.

[5] Alan Drooz, "College Notes: What Happened to WCC?" the *Los Angeles Times*, January 19, 1990, Sports, p. 14.

[6] Drooz, "College Notes: What Happened to WCC?"

[7] Dr. Hattori deposition summary. In early January, when Dr. Hattori was contemplating a decrease to 160 mg, Dr. Swerdlow advised that such a dose "might be possible. If he [Dr. Hattori] did so, I advised him to give the patient an 80 mg. long-lasting dose in the morning and an 80 mg. short-acting dose in the late afternoon, prior to game time, so that he would have a high blood level of [Inderal] prior to basketball" (Dr. Swerdlow to Mueller).

[8] Alan Drooz, "Lions Roar Past Portland by 25," the *Los Angeles Times,* January 21, 1990, Sports, p. 11.

[9] Alan Drooz, "Lions' D Is Dynamite Defense?" the *Los Angeles Times,* January 21, 1990, Sports, p. 20.

[10] Drooz, "Lions' D Is Dynamite Defense?"

[11] Lowery interview.

[12] Summary of deposition of Paul Westhead (July 26, 1990).

[13] Westhead deposition summary; Westhead interview.

[14] Summary of Dr. Hattori deposition (August 4, 1990).

[15] Westhead deposition summary; Westhead interview.

[16] Lowery, Kimble, Schaefer, and Hillock interviews.

[17] Westhead interview.

[18] Alan Drooz, "College Notes: Gonzaga Knows How to Play Loyola but Isn't Physical Enough to Do It," the *Los Angeles Times,* January 26, 1990, Sports, p. 16.

[19] Dr. Hattori deposition summary (August 4, 1990).

[20] Dr. Hattori deposition summary.

[21] Dr. Swerdlow to Mueller.

[22] Don Casey, interview by author, telephone, September 8, 2006.

[23] Dr. Hattori deposition summary (August 4, 1990).

[24] Dr. Hattori deposition summary.

[25] Drooz, "College Notes: Gonzaga Knows How to Play Loyola."

[26] Alan Drooz, "Gonzaga Slows, Can't Stop Loyola Lions," the *Los Angeles Times*, January 28, 1990, Sports, p. C20.

[27] Alan Drooz, "Loyola Finds Gaels Defenseless,150-119," the *Los Angeles Times,* February 2, 1990, Sports, p. 6.

[28] Westhead, Lowery, Peabody, and Kimble interviews.

[29] Westhead interview.

[30] LSU vs. LMU, CBS Sports, February 3, 1990. Various people whom I interviewed gave me copies of their videotapes of the games. Unless otherwise noted, all quotes used in the description of this game come from the video of the CBS telecast, upon which I also based my descriptions of the play.

[31] CBS telecast, February 3, 1990.

[32] Dale Brown, interview by author, telephone, March 3, 2006.

[33] CBS telecast, February 3, 1990.

[34] Brown interview.

[35] CBS telecast, February 3, 1990.

[36] CBS telecast, February 3, 1990.

[37] Father Dave Hagan, interview for "Hank Gathers," ESPN.

[38] Brown interview.

[39] Alan Drooz, "Loyola Keeps Up the Pace," the *Los Angeles Times*, February 5, 1990, Sports, p. 2.

[40] Alan Drooz, "Loyola's Gathers Cries Foul over Foul," the *Los Angeles Times*, February 16, 1990.

[41] Alan Drooz, "Loyola Gets Its Usual Bursts, Its Usual Victory, 139-110 over St. Mary's," the *Los Angeles Times*, February 11,1990, Sports, p. 11.

[42] Alan Drooz, "Loyola Hotshots Clinch Tie for Title," the *Los Angeles Times*, February 15, 1990, Sports, p. 1.

[43] Ray Ripton, "Pepperdine Gets Even with Loyola," the *Los Angeles Times*, February 18, 1990, Sports, p. 1.

[44] the *Los Angeles Loyolan*, February 21, 1990.

[45] Bernie Wilson, "Kimble Sounds Like NBA Star in Making," the *Chicago Sun-Times*, February 18, 1990, Sports, p. 16.

[46] Todd Phipers, "Catch 'Em If You Can: Lions Play It Fast and Loose," *The Denver Post*, February 18, 1990, Sports.

[47] Woods, Lowery, and Kimble interviews.

[48] Dr. Hattori deposition summary.

[49] Alan Drooz, "Loyola Clinches Conference Title," the *Los Angeles Times*, February 24, 1990, Sports, p. 1.

[50] " '89-'90 LMU basketball," videotape; assorted videos.

[51] Steve Grimley, "Loyola Springs Trap in Victory," *The Orange County Register*, February 25, 1990, p. 9.

[52] Grimley, "Loyola Springs Trap."

[53] Alan Drooz, "Lions Use Power of the Press, 117-81," the *Los Angeles Times*, February 25, 1990, Sports, p. 10.

[54] Dr. Hattori deposition summary (August 4, 1990).

[55] Dr. Swerdlow interview.

[56] Dr. Hattori deposition summary.

[57] Dr. Hattori deposition summary.

[58] Dr. Hattori deposition summary (August 4,1990).

[59] Dr. Hattori deposition summary.

[60] Dr. Hattori deposition summary.

[61] Dr. Hattori deposition summary (August 4,1990).

[62] Dr. Hattori deposition summary (August 4, 1990).

[63] Dr. Hattori deposition summary.

CHAPTER 24: TIME RUNS OUT

[1] Larry Steele, interview by author, telephone, January 20, 2006.

[2] Alan Drooz, "WCC Tournament Trouble? Not for Loyola," the *Los Angeles Times*, March 4, 1990, Sports, p. 1.

[3] Eric Johnston, "University Mourns Loss of Hank Gathers," the *Los Angeles Loyolan*, March 7, 1990.

[4] Ed Arnold, interview by author, Tustin, Calif., 2005.

[5] Paul Westhead, interview by author, Hermosa Beach, Calif., June 22, 2005.

[6] Dr. Charles Swerdlow, interview by author, Los Angeles, Calif., October 13, 2006.

[7] Mike Gilleran, interview by author, San Francisco, Calif., August 15, 2006.

[8] Kristin Ramage, interview by author, Yorba Linda, Calif, September 25, 2005.

[9] An AP story that ran in the *Pasadena Star-News*, March 6, 1990, quotes Fryer as saying that Hank ran before the game and had told Terrell Lowery and him that he was going to do so.)

[10] Notes dated March 12, 1990, that Dr. Swerdlow prepared for his attorney, Ken Mueller, and that the doctor made available to me (cited hereafter as "Dr. Swerdlow to Mueller").

[11] Summary of deposition of Dr. Vernon Hattori prepared by Richard D. Carroll for *Gathers et al. v. Loyola Marymount University et al.*, No. C795027, Los Angeles Superior Court, filed April 20, 1990, from the files of Carroll, a lawyer with the firm of Baker, Silberberg and Keener in Santa Monica, Calif. Carroll's firm represented Norcal Mutual Insurance Company, which had issued the malpractice insurance policy for three of the doctors named in the medical malpractice suit brought by Hank's family after his death. Carroll attended the depositions and prepared the summaries.

[12] Steele interview.

[13] Steele interview

[14] Gilleran interview.

[15] Per Sturmer, interview by author, telephone, September 8, 2006.

[16] David Spencer, interview by author, Riverside, Calif, April 7, 2005.

[17] Brian Quinn, interview by author, Fullerton, Calif., July 14, 2005.

[18] Lane Bove, interview by author, Los Angeles, Calif., October 17, 2005.

[19] Albert Gersten II, interview by author, Los Angeles, Calif., July 8, 2005.

[20] Kay Conrad, interview by author, telephone, November 3, 2006.

[21] Barry Zepel, interview by author, Anaheim, Calif., July 15, 2005.

[22] Dr. Dan Hyslop, interview by author, Los Angeles, Calif., June 20, 2005.

[23] Dr. Ben Shaffer, interview by author, Washington, D.C., January 26, 2006.

[24] Peter Priamos, interview by author, Burbank, Calif., July 11, 2005.

[25] Alan Drooz, "Investing Memories in Hank the Bank," *The San Diego Union-Tribune,* March 1, 2005.

[26] Various people testified in their depositions about where these people were sitting when Hank collapsed.

[27] Spencer interview.

[28] Darrell Gates, interview by author, Philadelphia, Pa., June 21, 2006.

[29] Brian Patterson, "Aaron Saw His Daddy Collapse," the *Daily Breeze*, March 7, 1990.

[30] Brian Berger, interview by author, Portland, Ore., October 18, 2005.

[31] Quinn interview.

[32] Tape recording of KXLU-FM broadcast of March 4, 1990, courtesy of Brian Berger and Keith Forman. Verbatim transcription from tape.

[33] My description of what happened on the court comes from videotape of that day shot by LMU's camera; Carter Trigg, the free-lance cameraman for ESPN; and an unnamed spectator, all tapes graciously provided to me by Dr. Ben Shaffer.

[34] Terrell Lowery, interview by author, Sacramento, Calif., August 14, 2005; Nick Schneider, e-mail to author, February 27 and March 2, 2009.

[35] Sturmer interview.

[36] Brian Berger and Keith Forman, interview by author, Portland, Ore., October 18, 2005.

[37] Ramage interview.

[38] Dr. Shaffer interview.

[39] Dr. Shaffer interview.

[40] Dr. Shaffer interview; summary of interview of Tom Fregoso, conducted by Richard Carroll, September 27, 1990, in preparation for Fregoso's deposition in *Gathers v. Loyola Marymount University*. Carroll prepared the summary of the interview.

[41] Summary of deposition of Dr. Ben Shaffer (February 28, 1991).

[42] Chip Schaefer, interview by author, Los Angeles, Ca., June 20, 2005.

[43] Quinn interview.

[44] Bove interview.

[45] Dr. Shaffer interview.

[46] Dr. Shaffer interview.

[47] Dr. Hyslop interview

[48] Dr. Shaffer deposition (February 28, 1991).

[49] All quotes and descriptions of the actions of the doctors and others during Hank's final crisis come from a tape recording made by the LifePak 200 defibrillator, March 4, 1990, tape courtesy of Dr. Ben Shaffer.

CHAPTER 25: THE REST IS SILENCE

[1] Gilleran interview; Jim Lindgren, "Eerie Moment at Gersten Pavilion," the *Los Angeles Times*, March 5, 1990.

[2] Jamie Sanchez, interview by author, Los Angeles, Calif., June 21, 2005.

[3] Fregoso deposition summary.

[4] Tom Peabody, interview by author, Long Beach, Calif., June 22, 2005.

[5] Sanchez interview.

[6] Ramage interview.

[7] Joe Resnick, interview by author, telephone, November 27, 2006.

[8] Chris Myers, interview by author, telephone, November 13, 2006.

[9] Summary of deposition of Fred Ruiz, EMT (July 6, 1990).

[10] Dr. Hyslop interview.

[11] Dr. Hattori deposition summary (August 4, 1990).

[12] Dr. Hyslop interview.

[13] Priamos interview.

[14] Quinn interview.

[15] Michael Hurd, "Gathers Dies after Collapse," *USA Today*, March 5, 1990.

[16] Carter Trigg video, ESPN, March 4, 1990.

[17] Eric Stephens and Chris Long, "LMU Left Stunned by Death," the *Daily Breeze*, March 5, 1990, p. D-6.

[18] Tom Friend, "Family Was There but Felt Helpless," *The National*, March 5, 1990.

[19] Lowery interview.

[20] Dr. Hyslop interview

[21] Lowery interview.

[22] Cassie Westhead, interview by author, telephone, April 26, 2006.

[23] Conrad interview.

[24] Lowery and Dr. Hyslop interviews.

[25] "Hank Gathers," ESPN.

[26] Carter Trigg video, ESPN, March 4, 1990.

[27] Maryann Hudson, "Hank Gathers and a Son He Left Behind," the *Los Angeles Times*, March 12, 1990

[28] Brian Patterson, "Aaron Saw His Daddy Collapse," the *Daily Breeze*, March 9, 1990, p. D-4. The *Los Angeles Times* related a different version of how Aaron learned of his father's death: His maternal grandmother, Phyllis Crump, awakened the boy and told him that his father had died (Hudson, "Hank Gathers and a Son He Left Behind").

[29] Spencer interview.

[30] Stan Morrison, interview by author, Riverside, Calif., April 2005.

[31] Gates interview.

[32] Eric Stephens and Chris Long, "LMU Star Player Collapses, Dies," the *Daily Breeze*, March 5, 1990, p. D-1.

[33] Father John McNamee, interview by author, Philadelphia, Pa.,March 23, 2006.

[34] Richard Yankowitz, interview by author, Philadelphia, Pa., June 9, 2005.

[35] Tom Lewis, interview by author, San Juan Capistrano, Calif., June 4, 2006.

[36] Doug Overton, interview by author, Philadelphia, Pa., January 27, 2006.

CHAPTER 26: THE WORD GOES FORTH

[1] Arnold interview.

[2] Schneider to author and Schneider interview.

[3] John Cherwa, interview by author, telephone, October 19, 2005.

[4] Mike Waldner, "Memories of a Kind Lion," the *Daily Breeze*, March 5, 1990.

[5] Mike Downey, "Gathers Had It All, Everything Except Luck," the *Los Angeles Times*, March 5, 1990.

[6] Alan Drooz, "Loyola Star, 23, Taken off Court during Game," the *Los Angeles Times*, March 5, 1990.

[7] Maryann Hudson, "Gathers Dies with a Slam of Appreciation," the *Los Angeles Times*, March 5,1990.

[8] Maryann Hudson Harvey, interview by author, Baltimore, Md., October 6, 2005.

[9] Jim Lindgren, "Eerie Moment at Gersten Pavilion," the *Los Angeles Times*, March 5, 1990.

[10] Steve Lowery, "Death of Gathers Is Remindful of Helpless and Guilty Feelings," *The National*, March 7, 1990.

[11] Jeff Parenti, "This Is a Memory That Simply Isn't Going to Go Away," the *Pasadena Star-News*, March 6, 1990.

[12] Kevin Mulligan, "Gathers Death Hits Home: 'A Soldier for a Lot of Kids, A Champion of a Lot of Causes,'" the *Philadelphia Daily News*, March 5, 1990, Sports, p. 83.

[13] "Eric Hank Gathers," editorial, *The Philadelphia Inquirer*, March 6, 1990, p. A12.

CHAPTER 27: THOSE LEFT BEHIND

[1] Priamos interview.

[2] Bruce Fagel, interview by author, telephone, January 12, 2007.

[3] Bo Kimble, interview by author, North Wales, Pa., June 22, 2006; Spencer interview.

[4] Gersten interview.

[5] Gersten interview.

[6] Alan Drooz, "The Grieving Is Deepened by Questions," the *Los Angeles Times*, March 6, 1990, Sports, p. 1.

[7] Mark Kram, "A Lion Is Lost," *The Philadelphia Inquirer*, March 6, 1990, p. 76.

[8] Mark Heisler, "Mood Casts Long Shadow across the Campus as Loyola Mourns," the *Los Angeles Times*,March 6, 1990, Sports, p. 1.

[9] Mike Waldner, "Gathers' Buddies Feel Loss of Strength," the *Daily Breeze*, March 6, 1990, Sports, p. D-1.

[10] Kram, "A Lion Is Lost."

[11] Alan Drooz, "The Grieving Is Deepened by Questions," the *Los Angeles Times*, March 6, 1990, Sports, p. C-1.

[12] Kram, "A Lion Is Lost."

[13] Alan Drooz, "As He Did in Life, Gathers Brings the Crowd to Its Feet," the *LLos Angeles Times*, March 7, 1990, Sports, p. C-1.

[14] Timothy Dwyer, "A Call for Loyola to Remember Gathers," *The Philadelphia Inquirer*, March 7, 1990, Sports, p. D-1.

[15] Terry Johnson, "Five Thousand Give Gathers a Final Cheer," the *Daily Breeze*, March 7, 1990.
The service was a major media event, covered extensively by the *Los Angeles Times*, the *Los Angeles Daily News*, and the *Daily Breeze*, as well as the AP and other area papers. All the television networks and local Los Angeles stations sent reporters and camera crews, as did ESPN.

[16] Drooz, "As He Did in Life"; Johnson, "Five Thousand Give Gathers a Final Cheer."

[17] Program for memorial service for Hank Gathers.

[18] Myers interview.

[19] Drooz, "As He Did in Life."

[20] Kimble interview.

[21] Timothy Dwyer, "A Call for Loyola to Remember Gathers," *The Philadelphia Inquirer*, March 7, 1990, Sports, p. D-1.

[22] Maryann Hudson Harvey, "The Hank Gathers Death, 10 Years Later: The Pain Remains; Many Involved Will Gather Saturday at Loyola," the *Los Angeles Times*, February 18, 2000, Sports, p. D-1.

[23] Dr. Shaffer interview.

[24] Bruce Woods, interview by author, Pittsburgh, Pa., January 24, 2006.

[25] Maryann Hudson and Elliot Almond, "Doctors Advised Gathers to Quit Playing," the *Los Angeles Times*, March 7, 1990; Kenneth J. Garcia, "The Extent of Doctor's Role Becomes Point of Contention," the *Los Angeles Times*, March 8, 1990.

[26] Bill Dwyre, "Loyola President Satisfied with Reaction," the *Los Angeles Times*, March 9, 1990, Sports. p. 1.

[27] Brian Patterson, "LMU Liable in Gathers' Case," *Outlook*, March 9, 1990, p. A3.

[28] Brian Patterson, "Attorney Says LMU Liable in Gathers Case," the *Daily Breeze*, March 9, 1990.

[29] Hudson Harvey interview.

[30] Gwen Knapp and Jay Searcy, "Day of Sorrow and Rembrance: Thousands Drawn to Service for Hank Gathers," *The Philadelphia Inquirer*, March 13, 1990, Sports, C-1.

[31] Hudson, "Hank Gathers and a Son He Left Behind."

[32] Ted Silary, "Loved Ones Mourn a Fallen Hero," the *Philadelphia Daily News*, March 13, 1990.

[33] Knapp and Searcy, "Day of Sorrow and Remembrance"; Silary, "Loved Ones Mourn"; AP, "Hank Gathers Is Laid to Rest," the *Pasadena Star-News*, March 13, 1990.

[34] Westhead interview.

[35] Woods interview.

[36] Silary, "Loved Ones Mourn."

[37] Yankowitz interview.

[38] Woods, Kimble, Peabody, and Gates interviews.

[39] the *Los Angeles Loyolan*, March 21, 1990.

[40] Nancy Reed, "Gathers May Receive Posthumous Degree," *Outlook*, photo of bluff by Richard Hartog, staff photographer, undated photocopy. The *Daily Breeze* was the small daily that covered the coastal communities south of Los Angeles. It put out more local editions under different names, including the *Outlook* and the *Wave*.

CHAPTER 28: THE SIXTH MAN

[1] Terrell Lowery, interview by author, Sacramento, Calif., August, 14, 2006.

[2] Alan Drooz, "Loyola Will Stay at Home," the *Los Angeles Times*, March 12, 1990, Sports, p. C-1. LMU had been ranked in the top 20 for most of the year. They had a top 15 Sagarin Power rating and should have received a fourth or fifth seed based on their record. The committee may have felt that without Hank Gathers, LMU was not worthy of that seeding, and dropped the Lions to 11th. Westhead would observe later that, if that was the case, it was a great tribute to Hank. "That's a compliment to him, not a slap to us," he said. As an 11th seed, the Lions' road to the Final Four would be a difficult one. Teams seeded that low are accorded little or no chance of making it.

[3] Jay Hillock, interview by author, telephone, February 6, 2006.

[4] Karen Crouse, "Death Haunts Coach: Loyola Marymount's Westhead Grieves for Gathers in Private Way," *The Orange County Register*, March 15, 1990, Sports, p. D-1.

[5] Bruce Woods, interview by author, Pittsburgh, Pa., January 24, 2006; Hillock interview.

[6] Crouse, "Death Haunts Coach."

[7] Crouse, "Death Haunts Coach."

[8] Crouse, "Death Haunts Coach."

[9] Crouse, "Death Haunts Coach."

[10] Woods interview.

[11] Tom Peabody, interview by author, Long Beach, Calif., June 22, 2005; Woods interview.

[12] Woods interview.

[13] Woods, Kimble, Peabody, and Lowery interviews.

[14] Ronald Soble and Elliott Almond, "Sources Give Partial Autopsy Results," the *Los Angeles Times*, March 15, 1990.

[15] AP, "Autopsy: No Drugs Found in Gathers," March 15, 1990.

[16] Elliott Almond, "Gathers Had Low Level of Medication," the *Los Angeles Times*, March 21, 1990.

[17] Peabody interview.

[18] Brian Patterson, "LMU Decides to Play," *Outlook*, March 8, 1990.

[19] This quote, and the earlier quote from Bo, come from an article by Alan Drooz in the *Los Angeles Times* to which Maryann Hudson contributed. I found a clipping of the story in a scrapbook kept by Tom Peabody's mother, but its date is unknown and the headline was cut off.

[20] Woods interview.

[21] Patterson, "LMU Decides to Play."

[22] Mark Whicker, "Player's Death Makes No Sense to Teammates," column, *The Orange County Register,* March 6, 1990, Sports, p. 1.

[23] " '89-'90 LMU Basketball," videotape.

[24] Woods interview.

[25] Bo Kimble, interview by author, North Wales, Pa., June 22, 2006.

[26] Alan Drooz, "When Top-Shot Kimble Scores, Ball Has Gathers' Name on It," the *Los Angeles Times*, March 16, 1990, Sports, p. 13.

[27] Alan Drooz, March 16, 1990, p.13.

[28] Kristin Ramage, interview by author, 2005; Brian Quinn, interview by author, Fullerton, Calif., July 14, 2005; Lane Bove, interview by author, Los Angeles, Calif., October 17, 2005.

[29] "'89-'90 LMU Basketball," videotape.

[30] Kimble interview.

[31] Lowery and Peabody interviews.

[32] Woods interview.

[33] Alan Drooz, "Lions Will Try to Keep Heads in This Game," the *Los Angeles Times*, March 16, 1990.

[34] Mike Downey, "He'll Be the One Rooting, Writing," the *Los Angeles Times,* March 16, 1990.

[35] Phillip Elmer Dewitt, "Death on the Basketball Court," *Time*, March 19, 1990; Charles Leerhsen, with Jean Gordon and Regina Elam, "Basketball Was His Life," *Newsweek*, March 19, 1990; Shelley Smith, "Death on the Court," *Sports Illustrated*, March 12, 1990.

[36] Downey, "He'll Be the One."

[37] Alan Drooz, "The Grieving Is Deepened by Questions," the *Los Angeles Times,* March 6, 1990, Sports, p. C-1.

[38] " '89-'90 LMU Basketball," videotape.

[39] LMU v. New Mexico State University, CBS Sports, March 16, 1990. Various people whom I interviewed gave me copies of their videotapes of the games. Unless otherwise noted, all quotes used in the description of this game come from the video of the CBS telecast, upon which I also based my descriptions of the play.

[40] "Kimble Symbol of Courage," the *Pasadena Star-News*, March 17, 1990.

[41] CBS telecast, March 16, 1990.

[42] Mike Waldner, "The Mind Game Has New Meaning," the *Daily Breeze*, March 17, 1990.

[43] Chris Ello, the *Pasadena Star-News.*

[44] CBS telecast, March 16, 1990.

[45] Paul Westhead, interview by author, Hermosa Beach, Calif., June 22, 2005.

[46] Chris Long, "Emotional Hurricane Swirling," the *Daily Breeze*, March 18, 1990.

[47] Chris Long, "LMU Gives Hank a Huge Victory," the *Daily Breeze*, March 17, 1990.

[48] "Kimble Symbol of Courage," the *Pasadena Star-News*, March 17, 1990.

[49] Mike Downey, "The Lions Played to Their Strength," the *Los Angeles Times,* March 17, 1990.

[50] CBS telecast, March 16, 1990.

[51] Mike Waldner, "LMU Players Move on to Next Act," *Outlook,* March 17, 1990.

[52] Alan Drooz, "These Two Teams Have Guards Up," the *Los Angeles Times*, March 21, 1990.

53 Chris Long, "Loyola's Relaxation Delayed with Lengthy Drug Testing," the *Daily Breeze*, March 18, 1990.

54 Alan Drooz, "Asbury Has Answer for Beating Loyola," the *Los Angeles Times,* March 19, 1990, Sports, p. C-1.

55 "'89-'90 LMU Basketball," videotape.

56 Steve Fisher, interview by author, telephone, June 5, 2006.

57 Long, "Emotional Hurricane Swirling."

58 LMU v. University of Michigan, CBS Sports, videotape, March 18, 1990. Unless otherwise noted, all quotes used in the description of this game come from the video of the CBS telecast, upon which I also based my descriptions of the play.

59 Tom Manumoto, interview by author, telephone, March 24, 2006.

60 Alan Drooz, "These Wipeouts Fine with Loyola's Fryer," the *Los Angeles Times,* March 20, 1990.

61 Chuck Abair, "Loyola Posts Record-Setting Victory," *The Orange County Register,* March 19, 1990.

62 Mike Downey, "Sixth Man Gives Lions the Edge," the *Los Angeles Times,* March 19, 1990.

63 Abair, "Loyola Posts Record-Setting Victory."

64 Fisher interview.

65 Mike Waldner, "More Than Basketball Going on at LMU," the *Daily Breeze*, March 19, 1990.

66 Patrick Kinahan, "Aches, Pains Won't Hurt LMU's Plans," the *Daily Breeze,* March 22, 1990.

67 "Lions Roar to Points Records," *USA Today,* March 19, 1990, p. 4-C, the sidebar to Michael Hurd, "Loyola Makes Fast Work of Michigan, 149-115," *USA Today,* March 15, 1990, p. 1.

68 Eric Brady, "Loyola Marymount: On a Mission," *USA Today,* March 22, 1990, p. 1.

CHAPTER 29: THE LIONS' SHARE

1 Chris Priamos, interview by author, Las Vegas, NV, July 2009.

2 Chuck Abair, "Emotions on Lions' Side," *The Orange County Register*, March 19, 1990.

3 " '89-'90 LMU Basketball," videotape.

4 LMU v. University of Alabama, CBS Sports, videotape, March 23, 1990. Unless otherwise noted, all quotes used in the description of this game come from the video of the CBS telecast, upon which I also based my descriptions of the play.

5 Kimble interview.

6 Westhead interview.

7 Kimble interview.

8 "Loyola Survives a Work Slowdown," *The Orange County Register,* March 24, 1990.

9 CBS telecast, March 23, 1990.

10 Elliott Almond, "He Went from Nobody to Peabody," the *Los Angeles Times,* March 24, 1990.

11 Peabody interview.

12 Almond, "He Went from Nobody to Peabody."

13 CBS telecast, March 23, 1990.

14 Almond, "He Went from Nobody to Peabody."

15 CBS telecast, March 23, 1990.

16 Frank Burlison, "Loyola Is Slowed But Not Stopped," the (Long Beach, Calif.) *Press-Telegram*, March 24, 1990.

17 CBS telecast, March 23, 1990.

18 Woods interview.

19 Waldner, "More Than Basketball Going on at LMU."

20 Bruce Jenkins, "Lowery Backs Up His Tough Talk," the *San Francisco Chronicle*, March 24, 1990.

21 Alan Drooz, "Loyola Beats Alabama at Own Game," the *Los Angeles Times*, March 24, 1990, Sports, p. C-1.

22 Pam King, "Loyola Keeps Dream Alive," the *San Francisco Chronicle*, March 24, 1990.

[23] Mike Downey, "Lions Refuse to Let Ship Be Grounded," the *Los Angeles Times*, March 24, 1990.

[24] C. M. Nevius, "Just Plain Desire Fuels Loyola Magic," the *San Francisco Chronicle,* March 24,1990.

[25] Chris Ello, "Slow Tide Can't Sink Loyola," the *Pasadena Star-News,* March 24, 1990.

[26] "'89-90 LMU Basketball," videotape

[27] Downey, "Sixth Man Gives Lions the Edge."

[28] Peabody interview

[29] Kinahan, "Aches, Pains Won't Hurt LMU's Plans."

[30] Nancy Reed, "LMU Joins Team's Crusading Spirit," *Outlook,* March 23, 1990.

[31] *Outlook,* March 23, 1990.

[32] Hank's House, copyright, P. R. Paul and Phil Booth, lyrics printed in the *Los Angeles Loyolan*, April 18, 1990. (P. R. Paul [Paul Rubenstein] was an actor who later appeared on the television show *Fame*.) Copies of the cassette tape are no longer available through LMU.

[33] the *Los Angeles Loyolan,* April 18, 1990.

[34] AP, "Westhead Wields Slings and Arrows," March 22, 1990.

[35] Chris Long, "Is This LMU's Final Act?" the *Daily Breeze*, March 25, 1990, Sports, p. C-6.

[36] Drooz, "Loyola Beats Alabama at Its Own Game."

[37] Jerry Tarkanian, interview by author, telephone, August 17, 2005.

[38] Mike Waldner, "Lions Have Crashed This Party," the *Daily Breeze*, March 25, 1990.

[39] Long, "Is This LMU's Final Act?"

[40] Long, "Is This LMU's Final Act?"

[41] Tarkanian interview.

[42] LMU v. UNLV, CBS Sports, videotape, March 25, 1990. Unless otherwise noted, all quotes used in the description of this game come from the video of the CBS telecast, upon which I also based my descriptions of the play.

[43] Michael Hurd, "Runnin' Rebels Roll," *USA Today*, March26, 1990.

[44] Joe Hawk, "Rebels Roar Past Lions," the *Las Vegas Review Journal,* March 26, 1990.

[45] CBS telecast, March 25, 1990.

[46] Steve Carp, "Rebels End Loyola Run," the *Las Vegas Sun,* March 26, 1990.

CHAPTER 30: WHEN THE CHEERING STOPPED

[1] Tom Weir, "Loyola's Effort Something Else," *USA Today*, March 26, 1990, p. 3-C.

[2] In a 2004 special commemorating its 25th anniversary, ESPN included Hank's death and LMU's run to the Elite Eight on its list of the Top 100 stories in the years since it went on the air. CSTV also ranks the story as one of the most memorable events in sports. Each March, during coverage of the NCAA Tournament, viewers are treated to repeats of Bo's left-handed free-throw attempts in CBS highlights of past tournament action.

[3] Carp, "Rebels End Loyola Run."

[4] Weir, "Loyola's Effort Something Else."

[5] Peabody interview.

[6] " '89-'90 LMU Basketball," videotape.

[7] Mike Downey, "They Leave Champions of the Spirit," the *Los Angeles Times*, March 26, 1990.

[8] Alan Drooz, "Loyola Gets Rude Awakening," the *Los Angeles Times*, Sports, March 2, 1990, p. C-1.

[9] Downey, "They Leave Champions."

[10] Dave Werstine, "Lions Have Brought a Smile to Gathers' Face," the *Los Angeles Wave*, March 26, 1990.

[11] Chris Long and Mike Waldner, "LMU's Fryer Can't Get Heated Up in Time," the *Daily Breeze,* March 26, 1990.

CHAPTER 31: BITTER SEASON

[1] Elliott Almond, Alan Drooz, Maryann Hudson, Danny Robbins, and John Cherwa, "Hank Gathers: The Death of a

Dream," Special Report, the *Los Angeles Times,* April 1, 1990.

[2] The *Los Angeles Loyolan*, May 2, 1990, p. 1.

[3] Paul W. Westhead, 1990 commencement address, Archives and Special Collections Department, Von der Ahe Library, Loyola Marymount University.

[4] Robert Reinhold, "Diploma for Hank Gathers," www.nytimes.com, May 13, 1990.

[5] David Spencer, interview by author, Riverside, Calif., April 7, 2005. The first player chosen in the draft was Derrick Coleman of Syracuse. The New Jersey Nets paid him in excess of $14 million, according to former Nets president Bob Casciola. Thus Hank, had he lived, might have garnered $8 million to $14 million in the draft.

[6] According to Bo, he and Lucille "laughed and had a good time" while watching the finals together. He added at the time, "I will always feel like a part of that family."

[7] Spencer interview. Bo also appeared in *Final Shot: The Hank Gathers Story* (1992), which was produced by Tribune Entertainment, a division of the company that owned the Los Angeles television station where Hank and Bo had worked as interns under Ed Arnold. The film was a made-for-television drama that featured Ed Arnold as himself. Nell Carter played Lucille, and George Kennedy played Father Dave. It is available in DVD format and from time to time can still be seen in late-night reruns.

[8] Maryann Hudson Harvey, interview by author, Baltimore, Md., October 6, 2005.

[9] Later Lucille would say she should never have permitted the suit to go forward. "I was not in my right mind," she said of the decision (Dick Heller, "Hank Gathers Death Stunned Nation's Fans in '90," *The Washington Post*, March 5, 2005).

[10] Hudson Harvey interview.

[11] Bruce Fagel, interview by author, telephone, January 12, 2007.

[12] When I contacted Dr. Hattori about sitting for an interview for this book, he responded that his lawyer advised him not to talk to me unless Lucille Gathers would formally release him from the doctor-patient confidentiality of his relationship with Hank. Her subsequent refusal to cooperate in this project in any way forced me to rely on the sworn depositions provided by Dr. Hattori and others in the case. Had Dr. Hattori not settled out of court, he personally would have been responsible for any monetary award over the policy limit, if a verdict had gone against him.

[13] Wayne Boehle, interview by author, Los Angeles, Calif., May 23, 2005.

[14] Boehle interview; Maryann Hudson, "A Legacy on Court in Court;" the *Los Angeles Times,* October 6, 1992, p. 1.

[15] The Medical Injury Compensation Recovery Act of 1975 limits recovery of damages to $250,000. Anything over that limit is considered to be economic damages, which must be proved and awarded by a jury. Fagel had to prove that Hank had been supporting his mother and that his death deprived his heirs of future income.

[16] Fagel interview.

[17] Fagel interview.

[18] Janis Carr, "NCAA Decision on Hold; Gathers Allegations Could Prompt Inquiry," *The Orange County Register,* December 28, 1990.

[19] Fagel interview.

[20] Hudson, "A Legacy on Court in Court."

[21] Richard Carroll, interview by author, Long Beach, Calif., May 20, 2005; Fagel interview; Boehle interview.

[22] Hudson, "A Legacy on Court in Court."

[23] See letters to the editor in papers throughout the Los Angeles area.

[24] Maryann Hudson, "Loyola Settles Lawsuit by Gathers' Mother," the *Los Angeles Times,* March 31, 1992; Hudson Harvey interview; Spencer interview.

[25] Richard Carroll, interview by author, Long Beach, Calif., May 20, 2005; deposition summary of Derrick Gathers, prepared by Richard D. Carroll for *Gathers et al. v. Loyola Marymount University et al.,* No. C795027, Los Angeles Superior Court, filed April 20, 1990, from the files of Carroll, a lawyer who represented Norcal Mutual Insurance Company, which had issued the malpractice insurance policy for three of the doctors named in the medical malpractice suit brought by Hank's family after his death.

[26] Albert Gersten II, interview by author, Los Angeles, Calif., July 8, 2005.

[27] Carroll, Boehle, and unnamed trustee interviews.

28 Hudson Harvey interview.

29 Brian Quinn, interview by author, Fullerton, Calif., July 14, 2005.

30 Court TV videotape of *Gathers v. Loyola Marymount University.*

31 Fagel interview.

32 Hudson, "A Legacy on Court in Court."

33 Fagel interview; Hudson, "Legacy on Court in Court."

34 Court TV tape; Fagel interview.

35 Hudson Harvey interview.

36 Maryann Hudson, "Gathers Lawsuit Is Dismissed," the *Los Angeles Times,* September 10, 1992. According to Fagel, Lucille claimed that Derrick, too, suffered from an irregular heart rate, and she feared that the stress of testifying would endanger his health.

37 Hudson, "Gathers Lawsuit Is Dismissed."

38 Hudson, "Gathers Lawsuit Is Dismissed."

39 Dr. Dan Hyslop, interview by author, Los Angeles, Calif., June 20, 2005.

40 Dr. Hyslop interview.

41 Dr. Hyslop interview.

42 Dr. Ben Shaffer, interview by author, Washington, D.C., January 26, 2006.

43 Dr. Shaffer interview.

44 Hudson Harvey interview. See also Hudson, "A Legacy on Court in Court."

45 Carroll and Boehle interviews.

46 Fagel interview.

47 Hudson, "A Legacy on Court in Court."

CHAPTER 32: FINAL SCORE

1 Hudson Harvey interview.

2 David Burst, interview by author, telephone, March 8, 2006.

3 Dr. Shaffer interview; AP, "Wings Player Suffers Seizure," *The (Newark, N.J.) Star-Ledger,* November 22, 2005, Sports, p. 55.

4 Dr. Shaffer interview.

5 Quinn interview.

6 Chip Schaefer, interview by author Los Angeles, Calif., June 20, 2005.

7 Hillock interview.

8 Bruce Woods, interview by author, Pittsburgh, Pa., January 24, 2006.

9 Dr. Elena Bove, interview by author, Los Angeles, Calif., October 17, 2005.

10 Richard Yankowitz, interview by author, Philadelphia, Pa., June 8, 2005.

11 Yankowitz interview.

12 David Morse, perhaps best known for his role as Dr. Jack Morrison on *St. Elsewhere,* played Father McNamee in the 2001 film, directed by Eugene Martin and produced by Martin, Ed Givnish, and Lisa Rosenstein. The book was published by Ward and Sheed of Kansas City, Mo., in 1993. The next time you feel the urge to make a small difference in the life of a child, send a contribution to Father McNamee at St. Malachy's, 1429 North 11th Street, Philadelphia, Pa 19122.

13 Kristin Ramage, interview by author, 2005.

14 Stan Morrison, interview by author, Riverside, Calif., April 2005.

15 David Friedman, "Paul Westhead: Never Slowing Down," www.hoopshype.com, January 15, 2008.

16 "NBA and WNBA Championship Head Coach Paul Westhead to Take Reins of Women's Basketball Program," University of Oregon press release, March 26, 2009. See also Video coverage of Westhead Press Conference, 3-26-09.

www.GoDucks.com

[17] Father Loughran, who grew up in Brooklyn as a die-hard Dodgers fan, served as interim president of Brooklyn College in 1992, a rare instance of a publicly supported college being led by a priest. He remained a life-long critic of big-time sports and its effect on academic integrity, calling for "an end to the use of tuition payers' bankrolling a vast entertainment industry that distracts from the educational mission and squanders millions." At his direction, the monies earned by Westhead-era teams in the NCAA Tournament went into the general fund at LMU, not the athletic department.

[18] Obituary, the *(Newark, N.J.) Star-Ledger,* December 27, 2006; Sid Dorfman, "Mourning a Man of Perspective," column, the *Star-Ledger,* January 30, 2007.

[19] Bo Kimble, interview by author, North Wales, Pa., June 22, 2006.

[20] Kimble interview.

[21] Bo Kimble, telephone interview by author, September 2008.

[22] Chris Marable, interview by author, Graterford Prison; Darrell Gates, interview by author, Philadelphia, June 21, 2006.

[23] Interviews with Dr. Shaffer, Dr. Hyslop, and several college coaches.

[24] Virtually all the doctors and basketball coaches whom I interviewed agreed that Hank's death was the single largest factor in the implementation of more stringent physical exams and medical histories.

[25] Westhead, 1990 commencement address.

EPILOGUE

[1] Bill Plaschke, "A Spirited Presence," the *Los Angeles Times,* December 25, 2004, Sports, D-1.

[2] Pamela Ham, interview by author, Burbank, Calif., August 26, 2005. Pam lost her battle with cancer in April 2006. She was 25.

[3] Tim Collins, interview by author, August 26, 2005, Fullerton, Calif.

[4] Rudy Ramirez, telephone interview by author, September 17, 2005.

[5] Michelle Stabile, interview by author, San Diego, Calif. August 23, 2005.

[6] Barry Zepel, "A Tribute," *Spirit* magazine, Summer 1990.

[7] Bo Kimble, interview by author, June 22, 2006, North Wales, Pa.

[8] Paul Conrad, the *Los Angeles Times,* March 7, 1990. Used with permission of Paul Conrad per Kay Conrad, November 3, 2006.

CHAPTER

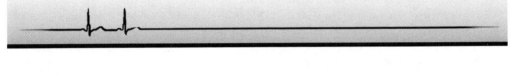

18

ACKNOWLEDGEMENTS

I am deeply indebted to the many writers that covered Hank Gathers from his days at Dobbins Vo-Tech, USC and Loyola Marymount. Their coverage made it possible for me to see, from a contemporaneous point of view, his development as a player and as a person. In their words Hank came alive again for me and I will always be grateful to them. In particular, for the high school years, I want to thank Ray Parrillo, of the *Philadelphia Inquirer* and *The Philadelphia Daily News*', Ted Silary, who remains the most authoritative source on Philadelphia high school sports and Dick Weiss, of *The Daily News*.

For the Dobbins years I want to thank Coach Richard Yankowitz, who was a prime source of information on Hank's development as a player and teammates, Doug Overton and Darrell Gates who shared their recollections of the young Hank Gathers.

Bo Kimble deserves special mention. He was generous with his time and was an enthusiastic supporter from the beginning, candidly recalling their years together in numerous conversations. He was also kind enough to provide the Foreword. Bo, who will always be recalled for his tribute to his late friend and teammate in the NCAA Tournament- one of the most memorable moments in college basketball- continues to honor his late friend to this day.

Father David Hagan passed away soon after our only, brief conversation, but I am grateful for the assistance provided by Father John McNamee, who agreed to provide the help I needed to begin to understand his friend and colleague who helped Hank in so many ways.

For the USC coverage the principal source was the late Mal Florence of the Los Angeles Times. Coverage by Larry Stewart, Julie Cart, Scott Howard-Cooper,

Robyn Norwood, Ray Nipton of that paper, along with Randy Harvey, now Sports Editor there, and Gary Jones of the *Los Angeles Daily News* was also helpful.

For the LMU years, Alan Drooz, then of *The Los Angeles Times*, who covered Hank, and agreed to talk at length about the rise from scant mention to a position of national focus by LMU and whose memories of those days remain bittersweet, was a primary source for me. John Cherwa, assistant Sports Editor at the *Times* during those years, was another who generously shared with me memories of the transfer from USC to LMU and the rise in coverage of LMU by his paper that resulted as well as the national impact of Hank's death and the subsequent events.

Daily Breeze columnist Mike Waldner, who also sat for hours with me outside Gersten Pavilion to share his recollections was another prime source as was Chris Long of that paper. Other writers who spoke with me at length include Chris Ello, Jeff Parenti and Steve Carp, then of the *Las Vegas Sun* and now at *The Review-Journal* who provided information on the LMU-UNLV games. Chris Myers, then with ESPN and now a sports anchor at Fox Sports was a valued source on coverage of the events of March 4, 1990 as was Joe Resnick of the Associated Press.

I also am indebted to the many reporters and columnists of national stature, whose names appear in the book, who covered the meteoric rise of LMU to national prominence.

To all those who covered Hank throughout his career I owe a debt I can never repay. I have identified them in the text and their own words serve to acknowledge their professionalism. I thank them all for their contributions.

David Spencer, who recruited Hank and Bo and served as assistant coach during their single season at USC, along with head coach Stan Morrison were gracious enough to spend time with me regarding the season that neither is particularly happy to relive and their experiences with Hank and his family.

Tommy Lewis and Derrick Dowell both agreed to interviews and added much to my understanding of the circumstances that led to the transfer from USC after Raveling's arrival. The late Peter Priamos was invaluable to me in understanding the USC year and the subsequent events that led to Hank's arrival at LMU. He shared his many recollections of important events with me in a long interview session. Both George Raveling and USC athletic director Mike McGee consented to interviews and John Gutekunst provided helpful background information.

Jim Foster and Don Casey both helped me to understand the coaching philosophy of Paul Westhead from the perspective of successful coaches.

I could not have been better served than to have had the full cooperation of former LMU Sports Information Director, Barry Zepel. Barry was a prime source of information on the LMU years and his insight along with his first class Media Guides of those years were invaluable.

Likewise, Brian Quinn, former Athletic Director was kind enough to share his memories of his tenure at LMU and his personal experiences during a period of time that was for him both the best and worst of times. He is a man who found himself thrust into a position few would envy and rose to the occasion.

Paul Westhead was patient and eloquent in his comments about his career, Hank's years at LMU and the aftermath. His wife, Cassie Westhead was also a principal source of information on Hank at LMU and background information and generously shared her memories pleasant and otherwise with me.

Other LMU coaches, Bruce Woods and Jay Hillock, both agreed to interviews and were more than helpful. Corey Gaines, Tom Peabody, Enoch Simmons, Per Sturmer and Terrell Lowery all consented to speak with me about their time at LMU for which I will always be grateful.

Dr. Lane Bove, now Sr. Vice-President for Student Affairs, was kind enough to provide background information on LMU and the Jesuit education system as well as her first hand knowledge of Hank and Bo as their principal aide in the Learning Resource Center. She also shared with me valuable insights into the effect of the basketball program's success on the school during those years. I am grateful for all her help.

Albert Gersten, and Terrance J. Lanni, both agreed to interviews that were essential in understanding the impact that Westhead's success had on the University.

Ed Arnold provided insight into the LMU road to a major LA media story as well as personal recollections of his experience with a budding sports broadcaster whom he mentored.

The many coaches who took the time to speak with me about their experiences in trying to cope with The System were more than cooperative and I especially want to thank them for doing so. They include Larry Steele, Jerry Tarkanian, Jerry Pimm, Benny Dees, Steve Fisher, Pete Gillen, Dale Brown, Bill Mulligan and Rolland Todd among others.

Both Brian Berger and Keith Foreman spoke with me at length about the coverage of March 4th, 1990, while they were student broadcasters at LMU and supplied numerous audio and video tapes for my use in re-creating the scene at Gersten.

For any layman to understand the medical condition that plagued Hank and his subsequent diagnosis and treatment is not easy. I was assisted in the task by many

Doctors who participated in Hank's treatment or were involved with him in some way as well as others I consulted for background information. I want to thank especially Dr. Charles Swerdlow, Dr. Dan Hyslop, Dr. Ben Shaffer, Dr. Nick Di Gioviane all of whom consented to be interviewed and were willing to take the time to translate medical terminology into a language I could understand. I was also assisted by Dr. Paul Maxwell, Dr. Paul Madonia and pharmacist Michael Wolf for valuable background data. Dr. Shaffer made available his files from the litigation as well as the deposition summaries in the case. Dr. Swerdlow kindly provided medical records related to Hank's treatment.

LMU trainer during Hank's years there, Chip Schaefer, was kind enough to spend time explaining the events of March 4th as he saw them as were Kristin Ramage Nelson and the players present.

Attorneys Wayne Boehle and Richard Carroll both supplied information on the lawsuit from the defendants side and Dr. Bruce Fagel explained the position of the plaintiff's in the case.

I am also indebted to Maryann Hudson Harvey, who spoke with me about the litigation and her coverage of the trial for the *Los Angeles Times*. She also shared valuable insights into the post March 4th events as the lawsuits wound their way through the courts and Hank remained in the public eye. Her follow-up articles on Hank and his family in the aftermath of March 4th, represent extraordinary examples of media coverage that is both informative and sensitive.

To those who agreed to talk with me about their experiences at Gersten Pavilion in the years since Hank's death I am especially thankful. They kindly and courageously detailed the events for me, as they had experienced them, without hesitation.

In addition I want to thank my editor, Polly Kummel, who, as always, has performed her magic on my work and remains the best in the business. My agent, Lawrence Jordan of the Lawrence Jordan Literary Agency, again represented me and has been a supporter of the project from the outset. Gilbert Fletcher did an outstanding job of designing the book.

To the many Sports Information Directors from Ursinus to UNLV and everywhere in between, who answered my questions and responded with information that was essential, I am especially thankful. They are invaluable to a writer and are always eager to assist.

The many research librarians I pestered for information and articles were always professional and cheerful. Those at the Flemington Free Public Library, The Las Vegas Public Library and The Henderson, Nevada, Library deserve special mention.

Also, I am indebted to Neal Bethke at the Von der Ahe Library Special Collections section at LMU who provided guidance and access to The Loyolan issues of the late eighties. The tapes and interviews associated with this book will be deposited there for future researchers.

I would like to acknowledge Ed McManimon and John Frangelli, both of whom read the book in manuscript form and provided helpful insights and suggestions.

Kara Polhemus provided research and copy editing services and emergency repairs to my computer whenever I managed to mangle it.

I am grateful to Fran and Norman Mannino for their years of friendship, warm hospitality and for the laughs we shared. Keep on fighting Nunzio.

My attorney and friend Alexander F. Keating, Jr. has been a good and loyal supporter for more years than either of us care to recount. He's a better person than an attorney and he is a great attorney. Hang in there Whiplash.

Also helpful, as always, in so many ways, was my loyal support team of more than 30 years, led by the incomparable Bill Faherty and including Bob Casciola and Bill Raftery. They are the best friends a man can have.

The home team was again there for me at all times. Barbara and Ky are the pillars of support on which I depend so much. The company of the four legged Pope was always welcome at my feet.

Finally, I want to say a special thank you to all those I interviewed during the course of my research who knew Hank. It was, I know, very difficult for them to have to trust to a complete stranger their innermost thoughts about a person they all cared deeply about. In agreeing to do so, they made this story possible. Without their help it could have never been told. I am deeply grateful for their willingness to go back in time to share memories- both happy and sad ones- with me.

The most common response I got when contacting people for an interview about Hank Gathers was some variation of, "You are asking about my favorite person."

Hank Gathers touched all their lives in a special way and I hope that after reading this book he will have touched yours as well.

Kyle R. Keiderling
Flemington, New Jersey

BIBLIOGRAPHY

J., S.J. *Jesuit Saturdays: Sharing the Ignatian Spirit with Lay Colleagues and Friends.* Chicago: Loyola Press, 2000.

Dickinson, Janice. *No Lifeguard on Duty: The Accidental Life of the World's First Supermodel.* New York: HarperEntertainment, 2002.

Fitzpatrick, Frank. *And the Walls Came Tumbling Down: Kentucky, Texas Western, and the Game That Changed American Sports.* Lincoln, Neb.: Bison Books, 2000.

Frey, Darcy. *The Last Shot: City Streets, Basketball Dreams.* New York: Mariner Books, 2004.

Kimble, Bo. *For You, Hank: The Story of Hank Gathers and Bo Kimble.* New York: Delacorte, 1992.

Lane, Jeffrey. *Under the Boards: The Cultural Revolution in Basketball.* Lincoln, Neb.: Bison Books, 2007.

Locke, Tates, with Bob Ibach. *Caught in the Net.* West Point, N.Y.: Leisure Press, 1982.

McNamee, John P., S.J. *Diary of a City Priest.* Franklin, Wisc.: Sheed and Ward, 1993.

O'Connor, Ian, *The Jump: Sebastian Telfair and the High Stakes Business of High School Ball.* Emmaus, Pa.: Rodale, 2005.

Rooney, John F. *The Recruiting Game: Toward a New System of Intercollegiate Sports.* Lincoln: University of Nebraska Press, 1980.

Sack, Allen L. *Counterfeit Amateurs: An Athlete's Journey through the Sixties to the Age of Academic Capitalism.* University Park: Pennsylvania State University Press, 2008.

Sack, Allen L., and Ellen J. Staurowsky. *College Athletes for Hire; The Evolution and Legacy of the NCAA's Amateur Myth.* Westport, Conn.: Praeger, 1998.

Valenti, John, and Ron Neclairio. *Swee' Pea and other Playground Legends: Tales of Drugs, Violence, and Basketball.* New York: Kesend, 1990.

Wetzel, Dan, and Don Yaeger. *Sole Influence: Basketball, Corporate Greed, and the Corruption of America's Youth.* New York: Grand Central Publishing, 2000.

Wolff, Alexander, and Armen Keteyian. *Raw Recruits.* New York: Pocket Books, 1991.

APPENDIX

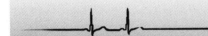

k1989–90 Loyola Marymount University Lions

No.	NAME	POS.	Hgt.	Wgt.	Yr.	Exp.	Hometown
00	Marcellus Lee	C	6-10	230	Sr.	2V	Pomona, Calif.
3	Greg Walker	G	5-11	163	Fr.	–	San Jose, Calif.
4	Per Stumer	F	6-7	210	Jr.	–	Sondentalje, Sweden
11	Tom Peabody	G	6-3	180	Jr.	1V	Santa Ana, Calif.
12	Tony Walker	G	6-1	170	Jr.	JC	Riverside, Calif.
14	John O'Connell	F	6-6	205	So.	1V	Glenside, Pa.
20	Terrell Lowery	G	6-2	160	So.	1V	Oakland, Calif.
21	Jeff Fryer	G	6-2	180	Sr.	3V	Newport Beach, Calif.
23	Jeff Roscoe	F	6-9	210	Sr.	3V	Puyallup, Wash.
30	Bo Kimble	G	6-5	190	Sr.	2V	Philadelphia
31	Chris Scott	C-F	6-8	205	Fr.	–	Union City, Calif.
34	Chris Knight	F	6-9	180	So.	1V	Los Angeles
44	Hank Gathers	F-C	6-7	215	Sr.	2V	Philadelphia
50	Marcus Slater	F	6-8	190	Jr.	2V	Carson, Calif.
	(transfer, in-eligible):						
	Brian McCloskey	F	6-7	190	So.	–	Buena Park, Calif.

HEAD COACH: Paul Westhead
ASSISTANT COACHES: Jay Hillock
       Judas Prada
       Bruce Woods
       Paul Westhead, Jr.

Bo Kimble's Foundation: Forty-four for Life Foundation
                          45 E. City Avenue
                          Bala Cynwyd, PA 19004
                          http://44forlife.org